Gods at War

Gods at War

Shotgun Takeovers, Government by Deal, and the Private Equity Implosion

Steven M. Davidoff

John Wiley & Sons, Inc.

Published by John Wiley & Sons, Inc., Hoboken, New Jersey.

Published simultaneously in Canada.

For general information on our other products and services or for technical support, please contact our Customer Care Department within the United States at (800) 762-2974, outside the United States at (317) 572-3993 or fax (317) 572-4002.

Wiley also publishes its books in a variety of electronic formats. Some content that appears in print may not be available in electronic books. For more information about Wiley products, visit our web site at www.wiley.com.

Davidoff, Steven M., 1970-
    Gods at war : shotgun takeovers, government by deal, and the private equity implosion / Steven M. Davidoff.
        p.   cm.
    Includes bibliographical references and index.
    ISBN 978-0-470-43129-0 (cloth)
        1.   Consolidation and merger of corporations—United States.   2. Private equity—United States.   3. Financial crises—United States.   I. Title.
HG4028.M4D38 2009
338.8'30973—dc22

                                                            2009016546

Printed in the United States of America

10 9 8 7 6 5 4 3 2 1

For Idit

Contents

Preface

I wrote this book for two reasons. First, readers of my *New York Times* DealBook column often ask me if there is a book explaining the mechanics of the deal and takeover markets. Prior to this time, there was nothing that quite fit. I hope this book fills this gap and provides even the most inexperienced reader and student an inside look into the intricacies, legal and otherwise, of deals and deal-making.

Second, recent catastrophic events in our capital markets have left many baffled, unable to understand what occurred and what it means for the future. This book is an attempt to order and make sense of the events leading up to and through the financial crisis. *Gods at War* is therefore the story of deal-making in the sixth takeover wave and through this crisis. It is about the private equity boom and its implosion, the return of the strategic transaction and hostile takeover, the failure of the investment banking model, the government's deal-making during the financial crisis, and the changes occurring in the capital markets during this time.

This book is ordered chronologically. I begin in Chapter 1 with a brief history of takeovers and a discussion of the key elements driving deals in today's capital markets. In Chapter 2, I trace the origins of private equity through a history of its creator, Kohlberg Kravis & Roberts Co. This detour is necessary because private equity is a key force driving the changes in today's deal market.

In Chapters 3 and 4, I move to fall 2007 and spring 2008. In these two chapters, I discuss the multiple implosions of private equity and other transactions and what it means for the future of deal-making, as well as private equity itself. I do so by first discussing in Chapter 3 the initial material adverse change disputes in the fall of 2007 and the key battles during this time, particularly that of Accredited Home Lenders, the mortgage originator, versus Lone Star Funds, the private equity firm. In Chapter 4, I discuss the second wave of deal disputes, which began in November 2007 with Cerberus's successful attempt to terminate its acquisition of United Rentals, the equipment rental company. This second wave of disputes would be driven by private equity's repeated attempts to terminate deals agreed to prior to the financial crisis and would be shaped by the material adverse change disputes earlier in the fall.

In Chapter 5, I discuss the sovereign wealth fund phenomenon. I use Temasek Holding's investment in Merrill Lynch as a launching board to discuss the nature of these investments during the initial phase of the financial crisis. Sovereign wealth funds may have had a brief heyday, but these investments tell us much about the regulation and importance of foreign capital. In Chapter 6, I move to the next phase of the book, discussing the fall of Bear Stearns. Much has already been written on this event, but my focus is new. In this chapter, I principally examine the innovative deal structures created and the deal's significance for later deal-making and government action.

In Chapters 7, 8, and 9, I turn to the time after Bear Stearns's fall. In Chapter 7, I discuss the rise of the hedge fund activist investor and its potential for transforming change in the deal market. I do so by detailing two significant shareholder activist battles in the spring of 2008: Jana Partners' targeting of CNET Networks, Inc., the Internet media company, and Children's Investment Fund's and 3G Capital Partner's targeting of CSX Corp., the railroad operator.

In Chapter 8, I discuss the increasing role of hostile takeovers in deal-making through the lens of Microsoft Co.'s hostile bid for Yahoo! Inc. and InBev NV/SA's hostile bid for the Anheuser-Busch

Companies Inc. I connect the rise in shareholder activism detailed in Chapter 7 with the increased rate of hostile activity in recent years.

Chapter 9 discusses the changing nature of strategic transactions through and beyond the financial crisis. I examine the innovation that has recently occurred in the strategic deal market, in particular the deal structures used in the acquisitions of Wm. Wrigley Jr. Co. by Mars Inc. and Wyeth by Pfizer Inc. Both transactions borrowed heavily from the private equity model and were engineered to address the issues raised by the serial implosion of private equity deals in 2007 and 2008, discussed in earlier chapters.

I conclude with Chapters 10, 11, and 12. Chapter 10 discusses the government as dealmaker in the serial bailouts of AIG, Bank of America, Citigroup, and others and the implications of "government by deal" for our economy and for deal-making specifically. The last two chapters look to the future. In Chapter 11, I discuss potential reform of the nation's takeover law. In the final chapter, Chapter 12, I draw on the conclusions of the prior 11 chapters to sketch the future of deal-making in a crisis age and beyond. In this final chapter, I also discuss whether deals and deal-making add value to our economy and examine the related question of the role of deals and deal-making in precipitating the global financial crisis.

We live in a time where many corporate veterans wonder whether a long 50-year cycle of deal-making that began with the go-go 1960s has come to an end, an end driven by a massive deleveraging of the financial system. But I am more hopeful believing that deals and deal-making will continue to be an integral, substantial, and necessary part of our capital markets. Either way, the events covered in this book are likely to set the course for deals and deal-making for the foreseeable future.

Ultimately, *Gods at War* is about the factors that drive and sustain deal-making. It is a legal-oriented history of the recent events that will alter and strongly influence the future of deal-making. It is also the story of the deal machine, the organizations built up to foster deal-making as well as the increasingly important role of shareholders themselves. In the midst of these forces sit the corporate executives and their advisers who decide whether to deal or not. Their own individual personalities and ego-driven decisions further shape and drive deal-making. It is here where I draw the title for this book. These individuals, like gods, can determine the future of companies and our economy.

Author's Note

Portions of this book cover topics first written about in the *New York Times* "DealBook" and the M&A Law Prof Blog. In addition, parts of this book were taken or based on my following prior writings: "Regulation by Deal: The Government's Response to the Financial Crisis" *Administrative Law Review* (forthcoming) (with David Zaring); "The Failure of Private Equity," 82 *Southern California Law Review* 481 (2009); "Black Market Capital," 2008 *Columbia Business Law Review* 172; "The SEC and the Failure of Federal Takeover Regulation," 34 *Florida State University Law Review* 211 (2007); and "*Accredited Home Lenders v. Lone Star Funds:* A MAC Case Study" (February 11, 2008) (with Kristen Baiardi).

Prologue

The social caste of New York is still set by money and the power to control it. Money provides an entrée into New York society, but the power quotient—your position in the financial industry—ranks you among your peers. It was thus no coincidence that the New York social event of 2007 was the 60th birthday party of Stephen Schwarzman, chief executive officer (CEO) and co-founder of the private equity firm the Blackstone Group.

The $3 million Valentine's Day–themed gala was held on February 13 at the Seventh Regiment Armory on Park Avenue. Amid the bomb-sniffing dogs and paparazzi, a who's who of finance, government, and media attended. These included John Thain, now the embattled former CEO of Merrill Lynch & Co., Inc.; Sir Howard Stringer, chairman of Sony Corp. of America; Leonard A. Lauder, chairman of the board of Estée Lauder Inc.; former Secretary of State Colin L. Powell; and Maria Bartiromo, the proclaimed money honey of CNBC. Rod Stewart and Patti LaBelle serenaded the guests, and the party ended at a punctual midnight, sufficiently early to allow everyone to return to work the next day.[1]

The media publicity and attendance were not just because it was an expensive birthday party thrown for a billionaire. Rather, this was the unofficial coronation of Schwarzman as the new king of private equity. Henry Kravis, along with Jerome Kohlberg Jr. and George R. Roberts, founded the private equity industry back in the 1970s and 1980s. Their firm, Kohlberg Kravis Roberts & Co., known as KKR, had dominated the field until the 1990s. Schwarzman's Blackstone had recently surpassed KKR as the largest of the private equity shops with assets under management of $78.7 billion.[2] This was Schwarzman's coming out party. Henry Kravis, still co-CEO of KKR, did not attend, and would not even publicly state whether he was invited.

And so what if the press coverage in the *New York Times*, the *Wall Street Journal*, and elsewhere was less than favorable, describing Schwarzman as "controlling" and nouveau riche, a man who would complain about his staff's squeaky sneakers and who regularly feasted on $400 apiece stone crabs.[3] Schwarzman, Blackstone, and the entire private equity industry were on top of the capital markets. In 2006, private equity would be responsible for 25.4 percent of all announced takeovers in the United States.[4] The year 2007 was shaping up to be even better. In the prior year, private equity had globally raised $229 billion in new funds to invest.[5] Given the availability of easy credit, these funds provided private equity with the ability to make more than a trillion dollars in new acquisitions. No company seemed immune from takeover.

Blackstone had proved this only a few days before. On February 9, Blackstone had completed the $39 billion leveraged buy-out of real estate company Equity Office Properties Trust. The buy-out was the largest private equity acquisition ever, even bigger than KKR's historic RJR/Nabisco acquisition. Blackstone had beaten out Steven Roth's Vornado Realty Trust in an epic takeover battle begun by an e-mail sent to Roth by Equity Office's founder, the cantankerous Samuel Zell. The e-mail had simply stated: "Roses are red, violets are blue; I hear a rumor, is it true?" Roth's reply: "Roses are red, violets are blue. I love you Sam, our bid is 52."[6] Schwartzman's Blackstone had trumped Vornado's love offer with a bid of $55 a share.

Schwartzman's party was thus not just for him, but for private equity. In a few short years, Schwarzman and his cohorts had revolutionized the takeover market. It was not just Schwarzman and private equity. The period from 2004 through 2008, a time of extraordinary growth and near financial calamity, transformed the U.S. capital markets. The financial revolution, globalization, and the financial crisis permanently changed deal-making, creating perils and opportunities for dealmakers and regulators. It is a pace of change and innovation so fast that regulators have yet to account for the new takeover scene and its systemic risks, a failure ably on display in recent years.

But Schwarzman's party not only marked this new paradigm but also was symbolic in the way of prior lavish Wall Street social events such as the Roman Empire–themed party Tyco International Ltd. CEO L. Dennis Kozlowski threw for his wife on the island of Sardinia or Saul Steinberg's 1988 party for his daughter's wedding in the Temple of Dendur at the Metropolitan Museum of Art. These parties not only heralded a new king but also ominously foreshadowed the perils of hubris and coming market disruption.[7]

In the years after Schwarzman's celebration, the federal government would implement the largest capital markets bailout in history; Blackstone would trade as low as a fifth of its initial public offering price; the stock market would viciously decline; the private equity market would evaporate; distressed acquisitions would overshadow a chastened and diminished takeover market; Bear, Stearns & Co., Inc. and Lehman Brothers Holdings, Inc. would implode; the credit markets would dry up; sovereign wealth funds would invest billions in ailing U.S. financial institutions; and both Anheuser-Busch Companies, Inc. and Yahoo! Inc. would be the subject of historic hostile offers. But all of this would be the future. Instead, on that night, February 13, 2007, Schwarzman was the symbol of private equity's wealth and dominance and the enduring nature of money in the city of New York. He was the epitome of the revolution occurring in the capital markets.

Chapter 1

The Modern Deal

I begin with a short deal story.

In 1868, Cornelius Vanderbilt, the railroad baron, went to war against the Erie Gang—Jay Gould, Daniel Drew, and James Fisk. The dispute's genesis was the rather reprehensible conduct of the Erie Gang with respect to the hapless New York & Erie Railroad. The three men had acquired a majority interest in the company, treating it as their personal piggy bank. Not content with the millions in profit reaped through outright theft, the gang further took advantage of Erie's public shareholders by manipulating Erie's stock to their benefit. The gang's machinations so financially weakened the Erie that it defaulted on its debt payments.

Meanwhile, Vanderbilt coveted the Erie railroad for its railroad line out of New York and to Lake Erie. The combination of the line with his routes would provide Vanderbilt with a stranglehold over much of the railroad traffic out of New York. Vanderbilt began to build a position in Erie by purchasing the stock sold by the Erie Gang. When the Erie Gang discovered this activity, they quickly acted to their own advantage. The gang arranged for Erie to issue out bonds convertible into Erie stock to sell to Vanderbilt, thereby diluting Vanderbilt's position.

Vanderbilt soon became aware of the stock issuance and arranged for his lawyers to obtain a court injunction halting them. This was easy for Vanderbilt's counsel as the judge issuing the injunction was on Vanderbilt's retainer. The Erie Gang responded by arranging to have their own kept judge issue a competing injunction restraining Vanderbilt's conduct. Meanwhile, Vanderbilt kept buying, and the Erie Gang circumvented the injunction by arranging for third parties to sell stock to the unknowing Vanderbilt. Fisk purportedly said at the time that "if this printing press don't break down, I'll be damned if I don't give the old hog all he wants of Erie."[1]

Vanderbilt then upped the ante and arranged for an arrest warrant to be issued for all three of the Erie Gang, who promptly fled from New York to New Jersey. They smartly, but illegally, took over $7 million of Erie's funds and yet more unissued Erie stock. The fight then became physical as Vanderbilt sent armed goons to attack the Erie Gang. Vanderbilt's henchmen were repelled by the gang's own hired men, and Fisk even went so far as to have 12-pound cannons mounted on the docks outside Erie's New Jersey refugee headquarters. Ultimately, the war was resolved when the Erie Gang succeeded in bribing the New York legislature to enact legislation validating the trio's actions. Vanderbilt was forced to cut his losses and settle, leaving the Erie Gang in control of the Erie Railroad, now forever known as the Scarlet Woman of Wall Street, and Vanderbilt was out an amount alleged to be over $1 million.[2]

A modern-day observer of corporate America may dismiss this well-known story as an interesting and well-cited relic of long-ago battles from a wilder age. The rule of law has grown stronger since the Gilded Age, and machinations like those of the Erie Gang and Vanderbilt are no longer a part of battles for corporate control. But before you agree, compare the war over Erie with a thoroughly modern dispute.

In August 2004, eBay Inc. acquired 28.5 percent of craigslist. The facts surrounding eBay's acquisition are a bit hazy, but it appears to have occurred due to a break among the prior owners of craigslist, Craig Newmark, James Buckmaster, and Phillip Knowlton. But for whatever reason, and no doubt in pursuit of money, Knowlton arranged to sell his interest to eBay for a rumored $16 million.[3] The sale placed Newmark and Buckmaster in an awkward position. Adamantly proclaimed anticorporatists, the two assert craigslist to be a community service and have publicly rejected the idea of selling any part of craigslist to the public or a third party. Nonetheless, perhaps because Newmark and Buckmaster had no choice, they acquiesced in eBay's purchase. At the time, the reason cited by the two for accepting the sale was that they believed that eBay would not interfere in the core mission of craigslist. "They have no interest in asking us to change that in anyway," Buckmaster stated. "They're happy with us having our full autonomy. They recognize us as experts at what we do."[4]

The parties' honeymoon was short. A dispute among them soon arose over eBay's decision to launch its own free classifieds service, Kijiji. Apparently, eBay didn't think the craigslist people were as expert as they thought. The business competed with craigslist and therefore triggered certain provisions in the shareholders agreement among eBay and the other two craigslist shareholders. Specifically, eBay lost its right of first refusal to purchase equity securities sold or issued by craigslist or to purchase Newmark's or Buckmaster's shares, should either attempt to sell them.

Newmark apparently thought this prenegotiated penalty was insufficient. He e-mailed Meg Whitman, eBay's CEO at the time, and stated that he no longer desired eBay as a craigslist shareholder. Whitman responded with a polite no, instead expressing eBay's own interest in buying craigslist. Clearly there was a communication gap among the parties. Newmark and Buckmaster, both directors of craigslist, responded by adopting (1) a share issuance plan under which any craigslist shareholder who granted craigslist a right of first refusal on their shares received a share issuance and (2) a poison pill preventing any current shareholder from transferring their shares other than to family members or heirs.

The poison pill effectively prevented eBay from transferring its shares, except in discrete blocks below a 15 percent threshold, to any single person. Moreover, Newmark and Buckmaster agreed to the right of first refusal and received the authorized share issuance; eBay did not, probably because it wanted to reserve the right to freely sell its position.

The result was to dilute eBay's ownership of craigslist to 24.85 percent. This action was important, because under the parties' shareholder agreement if eBay falls below the 25 percent ownership threshold, craigslist's charter can be amended to eliminate cumulative voting.

Cumulative voting provides minority shareholders the ability to concentrate their votes by allowing them to cast all of their board-of-director votes for a single candidate rather than one vote per candidate. So if, for example, there are three directors up for election, eBay would have three votes and could cast all of them for one candidate. In the case of craigslist, this right had enabled eBay to elect one director to the three-member craigslist board. But Newmark and Buckmaster now acted to amend craigslist's charter to eliminate this right, and eBay thus lost its board seat. Moreover, the poison pill effectively prevented eBay from selling its shares. Who would want to buy a minority position in a company where the other shareholders did not want you and you were effectively without any control rights? The amendment and the poison pill thus combined to lock eBay into a voiceless minority position.

So eBay sued craigslist, Newmark, and Buckmaster in Delaware, the place of craigslist's incorporation, for breach of fiduciary duty and to have their actions nullified. Meanwhile, craigslist countersued eBay in California State Court for false advertising and unfair and unlawful competition. The parties remain in litigation at the time of this writing, with the two craigslist directors still firmly in control of the company.[5] Given the tremendous dollar amounts at stake, whether the craigslist founders will succeed or desire to keep their grip remains to be seen.

Approximately 140 years separate these two events, but the story of craigslist and eBay shows that in deals, companies and the people running them are still not above fighting to the figurative death, employing every available tactic. The big difference is that these fights largely play out in the courts, the regulatory agencies, or the plains of shareholder and public opinion rather than as brawls in the street or bribery. Microsoft Corporation and Google Inc. will battle over relevant acquisitions in the halls of their antitrust regulator, the Federal Trade Commission, or in the marketplace. The CEO of Google Inc., Eric Schmidt, is hopefully not about to attempt to send armed men to assault

Steve Ballmer, Microsoft Corp.'s current CEO. They both will work within the rules, perhaps even stretching them, to fulfill their goals.

The strengthening of the rule of law and the immense economic and social changes of the past century and a half have placed lawyers in a primary role. The structure and manner of takeovers has not remained static over the years. Nonetheless, as illustrated in these two stories, central tenets of deal-making have emerged and remained. Deals are still in large part about money, earning a return on invested capital commensurate with the risk, but like so many things in life, it is not all about the money. Other factors come into play and skew the process. These include:

- The personality element—individuals often determine the outcome of deals, sometimes by acting outside their company's and share-holders' economic interests. In doing so, these individuals act in their own self-interest and with their own psychological biases to affect deals, sometimes acting to overtly enrich themselves or more subtly aggrandize themselves and build empires.
- The political and regulatory element—Congress, state legislatures, and other political bodies can take direct and indirect action to determine the course of deals, particularly takeovers. Meanwhile, deals have steadily become more regulated and impacted by regula-tion, whether by the federal securities laws or antitrust or national security regulation.
- The public element—popular opinion and the constituencies that are affected by deals increasingly matter.
- The adviser element—deals have become an institutionalized industry; advisers and the implementation of their strategic, legal, and other advice now affect the course of transactions.
- The game theory element—tactics and strategy continue to mat-ter in deals and deal-making, as these disputes show. As I discuss in Chapters 8 and 9, structuring deals within (and sometimes) outside the law and the tactics and strategy used to implement that plan can define the success or failure of a deal outside of economic drivers.

But of these five noneconomic factors I would argue that personality, the psychological biases and foundation of individuals, has historically been the most underestimated deal-making force.

The Import of Personality

The Erie story was as much about culture as it was about economics. Vanderbilt was self-made but also established money. He represented the period's dominant economic interests. The Erie group, and particularly Jay Gould, could best be characterized as new money, taking advantage of the emergent U.S. capital market to extract their own benefits. The intensity and length of the parties' dispute was no doubt enhanced by this cultural gap, which made each party want to win despite the benefits of compromise. Vanderbilt contemplated settling with these hooligans only when the New York legislature acted and he was left with no choice. The eBay-craigslist story is similarly one of stubborn will and cultural difference. The craigslist controlling shareholders have proclaimed that their opposition to eBay is moral. It is a desire to maintain an environment free from corporate influence in contrast to ex-eBay CEO Meg Whitman's seeming disbelief in Newmark and Buckmaster's expressed intentions and her and her successor's wish to exploit a very exploitable economic asset.

The cultural aspect to these disputes is not unique. Like many facets of our society, deals and takeovers in particular are often driven by culture, as well as other extrinsic factors such as morality, class, ideology, cognitive bias, and historical background. These affect not only whether deals succeed after they are completed but also whether they even occur. The epic battle for Revlon Inc. in the 1980s was likely as contentious as it was because of then Revlon Inc. CEO Michel Bergerac's deep hatred for Ronald O. Perelman, the hostile raider who controlled Pantry Pride Inc., the company that made a hostile bid for Revlon in competition against Teddy Fortsmann's Forstmann Little & Co. Perelman was described as an upstart Jew from Philadelphia, a corporate raider with a penchant for gruff manners and cigars. He was the antithesis of Bergerac's world; Bergerac could not see his prized company going to such a man and often referred to Perelman's bidding company as "Panty Pride."[6] Bergerac's hostile reaction lost him not only his company but also the $100 million pay package Perelman had initially offered Bergerac to induce him to support the takeover.

Similarly, the battle over Paramount Pictures Corp. between Viacom Inc. and QVC, Inc. in the 1990s was as much about Barry Diller, the CEO of QVC, needing to prove that he had escaped the grasp of

Martin Davis, CEO of Paramount, as much as it was about building an integrated media empire. Davis had previously been Diller's boss when Diller had been the head of Paramount. Diller had left the company after repeatedly clashing with Davis. The takeover of Paramount was his payback.[7]

The reason for this bias is in part that takeovers are a decision-driven process helmed by men (and they have been almost uniformly men) who make these choices about when and what to pay or otherwise sell for assets. It was, after all, J. P. Morgan who singlehandedly decided to purchase U.S. Steel and consolidate the steel industry in order to rein in price competition. As such, these are people driven by their own psychological considerations and backgrounds. It's not just about business. These biases can distort the deal process, most prominently injecting uneconomic or economically self-interested factors into takeover decisions. This has tended to be exacerbated by the increasing tendency of the media to personify corporations through the personality of their CEO: Microsoft becomes Bill Gates and then Steve Ballmer, Viacom becomes Sumner Redstone, JPMorgan Chase & Co. becomes Jamie Dimon, and so on.

The result has not been just a centrality in CEO decision making but the encouragement of CEO and individual hubris. In the 1960s, deal-making was about conglomerates—the idea was that management was a deployable resource and a company in diverse industries could resist a downturn in any single sector. But again it was about the individual who could ultimately control these empires. People like Charles Bluhdorn at Gulf + Western Inc., nicknamed Engulf and Devour for its acquisition practices, and James Joseph Ling at Ling-Temco-Vought were headline-making actors and stars of the business media. In the wake of the conglomerates, acquisition activity sharply rose from 1,361 acquisitions in 1963 to 6,107 in 1969.[8] It created an atmosphere ripe for investment in these conglomerates, but it also set up spectacular failures, as many of these companies were built on the idea of an individual CEO's capability without sound financial underpinning.

Conglomerates have largely been buried by Wall Street, but hubris often masked by labels such as "vision" still persist: Perhaps the most spectacular failure and example of the later age is the merger of America Online, Inc. (AOL) and Time Warner Inc. orchestrated by

Time Warner CEO Jerry Levin and AOL co-founder Stephen Case. The deal is cited as one of the worst bargains in history and has resulted in the destruction of up to $220 billion in value for Time Warner shareholders.[9] Moreover, in the deal-making arena, the market constantly proclaims winners and losers based on the outcome of takeover and other contests, rather than on pure economics. Whether it is the clash of wills in Yahoo! and Microsoft—will Steve Ballmer prove his mettle as the newly anointed CEO of Microsoft—or another Stephen, Stephen Schwarzman of Blackstone, out to crown himself the king of private equity, the need for perceived success and the psychology of the actors drive deals.

This latter phenomenon has a name in economics: the winner's curse. Auction theory predicts that winning bidders in any auction will tend to overpay because of a psychological bias toward winning. In takeovers, this has a documented effect that has caused many to overpay for assets, caught up in the dynamics of a given takeover contest.[10] A notorious example again comes from the 1980s, when KKR entered into a bidding war for RJR Nabisco, Inc. against CEO F. Ross Johnson's management-led buy-out team. In frenzied bidding, KKR ultimately won RJR but was forced in the 1990s into a refinancing of the company and an ultimate loss of $958 million.[11] In that time, this philosophy was personified by Bruce Wasserstein, the legendary investment banker sometimes labeled "bid 'em up Bruce." Wasserstein was allegedly notorious for his dare-to-be-great speeches, which egged on his clients to pay higher prices to win a deal. Some of these deals worked out perfectly fine, but others, such as the RJR Nabisco deal on which he advised KKR, didn't fare as well. Wasserstein, by the way, has also authored a book on takeovers, entitled *Big Deals*.[12] Notably, private equity is now suffering the same hangover during this downturn as it struggles with portfolio companies for which in hindsight it overpaid during the headier time of 2004–2007. The recent bankruptcies of such notable private equity acquisitions as Chrylser, LLC, Linens 'n Things and Mervyn's are examples.

This CEO hubris has been reinforced by the institutionalization of deal-making. The deal-making industry is now vast. It involves the investment banks who provide financial advice and debt financing, the law firms who structure and document these deals, the consultants who work on strategic issues, and the media that cover it all. The deal machine provides its own force toward deal-making and completion. In many circumstances, the vast proportion of the fees of these ancillary actors are based on the success of the transaction. If a deal is not completed, they are paid little. But if a deal does succeed, the deal machine reaps tens of millions, too often with little accountability for the future of the combined company. The result is that the voice heard by corporate executives is too often one that pushes their own biases toward completing and winning takeovers.[13]

If deal-making is an industry of individuals, noticeably absent from much of its history has been the board of directors, the entity with primary responsibility for running the corporation. Until the 1980s, deals and particularly takeovers were almost wholly an individual's decision, typically the CEO's. That changed in the 1980s, as a series of decisions in the Delaware courts starting with *Smith v. Van Gorkom* in 1985 placed seemingly heightened strictures on boards to exercise due care and oversight of the takeover process.[14] Since this time, the Delaware courts have tended to place the board as the ultimate decision maker in the sale of the company. This is perhaps the greatest lasting impact of the controversial *Van Gorkom* decision. And although the CEO maintains his or her ability to negotiate and influence the process, the Delaware courts have not hesitated to overrule sale decisions where the CEO has overcontrolled or overtly skewed the process.[15] The result is that today's board is significantly more involved in the sale decision, though boards still too often rubber-stamp CEO wishes.

The regulation of the takeover decision has also largely focused on the sell side. In the past 20 years, Delaware has erected an elaborate skein to govern the standard by which board decisions to sell—or not to sell—are measured. This is a framework we explore further and in more detail later in this book. But the Delaware courts have placed significantly fewer strictures on the buy side, and absent a conflict of interest, the Delaware courts review these decisions under the lower business judgment standard. Courts reviewing a decision under the business judgment rule will not second-guess the acquisition decision unless it is grossly negligent or irrational—a test almost impossible to fail. The result is that the CEO of a company still has fair leeway to negotiate a takeover and to initiate strategy. Take, for example, Bank of

America Corporation's 2008 acquisitions of Countrywide Financial Corporation and Merrill Lynch & Co, Inc. There a headstrong CEO, Kenneth D. Lewis, appeared to drive two quite risky and hasty acquisitions. These decisions ultimately bit the company hard when it was forced to seek a multibillion-dollar government bail-out in light of a $15.3 billion quarterly loss at Merrill Lynch.[16] Though but one example, the "deal from hell" phenomenon—buyer acquisitions that have gone stunningly bad as a result of individualized, bad decisions—has been a feature of deal-making throughout its history.

The result has been that the personality-driven model of deal-making has persisted, driven by the individuals who make the decision to buy rather than sell. In the first year of the financial crisis, this was on display as Treasury Secretary Henry J. Paulson Jr. turned into the market arbiter. During this time, it was Paulson who apparently decided which companies died and which lived and were acquired or bailed out. His choices dictated that Bear, Stearns & Co. should live but left Lehman Brothers to fall into bankruptcy. In the process, Paulson demanded, at least initially, that government-facilitated takeovers be structured in a manner that punished shareholders but did not specifically target officers or directors. Secretary Paulson, a veteran deal-maker and ex-CEO of the Goldman Sachs Group Inc., may have been bowing to political and legal reality in his decision-making. But his approach aligned with his deal-making experience: The bail-out can be viewed as a series of deals where the shareholders bore the costs over management.

The role of personality will be seen in the deals examined in this book and is the reason for its title: Failing to ignore the personality element in deals and deal-making is to ignore one of its central determinants. But if deal-making is to truly succeed, this personal element must be restrained. As will be seen, modern deal-making is often a fight to restrain this element for more rational, economic decision making.

The Evolution of the Takeover

While themes emerged and stayed through the past century and a half, change does come to deals and takeovers. The takeover market is a cyclical one. It has evolved over the past century principally through six boom-bust waves. Each of these cycles has had its own unique character and engendered its own differing and sometimes world-redefining change. This change has typically brought a new regulatory response as each wave alters the playing field for takeovers. The result has been that regulation of takeovers has largely been responsive to the prior or current wave. It has failed to anticipate or account for future possible change, instead regulating backward and shaping the course of the next waves. The regulation of deal-making through history has thus been one of catch-up and circumstance, leaving us with the piecemeal system that we have today, where takeovers are a matter of joint supervision by the Delaware courts and the Securities and Exchange Commission (SEC). Moreover, the regulatory response over the years has revealed another increasingly prominent noneconomic force on the deal market, government, and regulation.

The first true wave and movement for regulation of takeovers occurred during the period of 1890 through 1907 and in the wake of the American Industrial Revolution. This was the time of the trusts—large corporate entities combining diverse enterprises in a single industry with the purpose to control production and, more important, pricing. John Moody, the founder of Moody's Investor Service, calculated that during this first wave, approximately 5,300 industrial sites were consolidated into just 318 industrial trusts.[17] The wave marked the emergence of the modern industrial corporation as much as it was about the creation of monopoly. During this period, Standard Oil of New Jersey, the United Fruit Company, and the first billion-dollar corporation, U.S. Steel, were all created.[18]

The first wave also spurred the first real regulation of corporate combinations, regulation focused on stemming the monopoly power of these new corporate behemoths. Between 1881 and 1901, Congress introduced 45 different antitrust legislative acts intended to regulate the trusts.[19] Antitrust regulation did indeed come in the form of the Sherman Antitrust Act, the Clayton Antitrust Act, the creation of the Federal Trade Commission, and increased regulation of railroads through the Interstate Commerce Act, among other regulatory acts.[20] Moreover, the first corporate regulators were formed by Congress during this time. In 1898, the U.S. Industrial Commission was formed to investigate these new large businesses, and in 1903, the United States Bureau of Corporations was formed to further investigate antitrust violations.[21] But this regulation was focused on the perceived menace of the times—the anticompetitive effects of the trusts—rather than on corporations or takeovers themselves. There were scattered attempts in Congress to adopt a federal incorporation act and to implement a scheme of securities regulation. These attempts failed, and the takeover process was still largely unregulated at the end of this first wave.

The first takeover wave collapsed in the panic of 1907, but a second wave of merger activity occurred from 1916 to 1929. The trigger for this wave was World War I and a new industrial boom within the United States. This second wave was shaped by the regulation adopted in the prior age and the heightened antitrust enforcement of the time, which provided the government the ability to stall anticompetitive, horizontal takeovers. This second wave avoided horizontal mergers, or mergers of competitors, instead producing oligopolies consisting of vertically integrated industrials.[22] But like the prior wave, this takeover cycle did not produce regulation aimed at the takeover process. Rather, the regulatory response to this wave was shaped by the subsequent Great Depression and the general controversy over the collapse of the securities market and the perceived stock-trading abuses of the 1920s. The SEC was formed, and the Exchange Act and Securities Act were enacted to regulate the offering and trading of securities. Although specific regulation of takeovers was forgone, like the first wave of regulation, Congress' actions would shape the next wave of takeover regulation by providing an apparatus to add on future legislation and rules.

This third wave of U.S. merger activity transpired during the period 1960–1971 and was largely caused by that generation's bubble, the conglomerate acquisition craze.[23] At the wave's height, from 1967 to 1969, more than 10,000 companies were acquired, with approximately 25,000 acquisition transactions throughout the entire period.[24] It was in response to this flurry of activity and the consequent emergence of the cash tender offer that modern-day federal takeover regulation originated. In the post–World War II era, takeovers had been staid events conducted primarily through proxy solicitations regulated by both state and federal proxy law. These contests required that the target company approve the transaction and that the target's shareholders vote to approve or disapprove it. In the mid-1960s, however, at the crest of this third wave, there was a sharp comparative rise in unsolicited or hostile takeover attempts. These unsolicited bidders typically preferred to evade the federal and state regulatory apparatus applicable to proxy contests and, instead, often made their takeover attempts via cash tender offer, a vehicle that allowed them to purchase target shares directly without the approval of the target.[25]

These early tender offers were largely unregulated affairs, and bidder conduct was often egregious. The "Saturday night special" was a favorite. In one form, a bidder would embark on a preoffer buying raid to establish a substantial beachhead of ownership at a reduced price. This would be followed by a short period of a first-come, first-serve public tender offer. Stockholders would rush to tender, afraid that they would be left in a minority position in the company or that their shares would otherwise be purchased subsequently for less money. In the wake of these new and unfamiliar tactics, stockholders and target corporations were relatively helpless. Takeover defenses at the time were virtually nonexistent. Indeed, surveying takeover manuals published during this time period, one marvels at the breadth of subsequent developments.[26]

In light of the states' failure to respond, the SEC, the agency created at the end of the second wave, became the principal governmental actor in the drive to regulate cash tender offers. In 1968, Congress passed the tender offer regulation bill introduced by Senator Harrison A. Williams.[27] The Williams Act was almost entirely in the form recommended by the SEC. The act both substantively and procedurally regulated tender offers, and its terms were keyed specifically to respond to the perceived abuses of the time. It enacted a scheme of regulation of tender offers that included disclosure requirements as well as substantive requirements regulating how tender offers were made and prosecuted.

The third wave of merger activity subsided in the early 1970s with the popping of the conglomerate stock bubble and repeated U.S. economic recession. These two events combined to birth the next major issue of takeover regulation: the abusive going-private. These were largely take 'em public high, then buy 'em out low affairs: Majority owners of corporations who had only recently engaged in initial public offerings when stock market prices were substantially higher offered to buy out their own minority publicly held stock at markedly lower prices. Because there was an inherently coercive element in these transactions—the vote was a foregone conclusion since the parent had a controlling interest and the opportune timing was at the parent's discretion—these purchases engendered cries of fraud and unjust enrichment.[28]

In 1975, the SEC launched a fact-finding investigation and simultaneously proposed rules to govern going-private transactions. One form of the proposed rule would have required that a price paid in such a transaction be no lower than "that recommended jointly by two qualified independent persons."[29] Adoption of this rule was delayed, largely because of allegations that the SEC lacked rule-making authority under the Williams Act. Then, in 1977, the Supreme Court in *Green v. Sante Fe Industries, Inc.* overruled the Second Circuit's holding that the antifraud provisions of the Exchange Act embodied in Rule 10b-5 constituted a basis to challenge a going-private decision on substantive grounds.[30] This decision, as well as continued dissatisfaction with state regulation of going-privates, led the SEC to repropose rules. These rules were finally adopted by the SEC in 1979 and, although not as far-reaching as originally proposed, established a new disclosure-based regime for going-privates. The rules now obligate corporations in going-private transactions to express an opinion as to the fairness of the transaction to unaffiliated stockholders.[31] Most notably, the SEC action here marked the first significant regulation not in a takeover wave; takeover regulation had become a full-time affair.

The fourth wave of takeover activity commenced in the late 1970s and early 1980s and ended in 1989 in the wake of the collapse of the high-yield bond market and the S&L scandal. The heightened activity was again quantitatively marked: The annual value of domestic acquisition transactions rose from $43.5 billion in 1979 to a peak of $246.9 billion in 1988 before bottoming out at $71 billion in 1991.[32] Unsolicited takeover activity, mainly cash tender offers, also sharply and fiercely increased from 12 contested tender offers in 1980 to 46 such offers in 1988; the increase was juiced by cheap financing in the form of high-yield or junk bonds.[33] This was the time of the corporate raiders, men of brash personalities like T. Boone Pickens, who would launch hostile bids with a goal to break up or restructure the corporate target. Pickens, in fact, was labeled by *Fortune* magazine as "the most hated man in corporate America" because of his hostile offers for Gulf Oil, Phillips Petroleum, and Unocal Corp., among others.[34]

The fourth wave was different in one significant respect: This time, targets were equipped for defense. The fourth wave was notable for the widespread use of takeover defenses, including poison pills, shark repellents, Pac-Mans, golden parachutes, greenmail, and other defenses discussed more thoroughly in Chapter 8.[35] The renewed vigor of targets, as well as revised bidder tactics, spurred a revolution in takeover methods, resulted in more extended public takeover battles, and led state courts and legislatures, Congress, and the federal courts, as well as the SEC, to confront this phenomenon.

In this cauldron, much of the legal doctrine of takeovers was forged, as well as the structure of today's modern takeover. But to the extent this structure and mode was law-driven, the primary regulator of this period was no longer the SEC and the federal government, but the courts of the state of Delaware. During this time, the Delaware courts promulgated new rules governing the sale or change of control of a company, the appropriate defensive measures a company could use, the applicable standard of review for a going-private transaction, and the validity of the poison pill. The last act was perhaps the most controversial of the court and was opposed by the SEC, which battled and lost in the 1980s to limit takeover defenses. When the takeover market came to a screeching halt in 1989 with the collapse of the high-yield market, deal-making was a much more regulated affair. The Delaware courts had not only trumped the SEC as the primary regulator of these affairs but also erected a set process for takeovers interlaid with the federal one. It was a regulatory scheme that allowed companies to defend the corporate bastion against hostile raiders and activist shareholders with an array of takeover defenses, the most important and prominent of which was the poison pill.

The fifth and sixth waves of takeovers are recent history. The fifth coincided with the tech bubble and was marked by strategic transactions using inflated equity securities and breathtaking valuations. Who could forget the $4.66 billion paid by Yahoo in January 1999 for GeoCities, a company with only $18 million in revenues? Yahoo made the acquisition only months after the Disney–Infoseek, AOL–Netscape, @Home–Excite and USA Networks–Lycos deals—and thereby set off the Internet deal-making craze.[36] During this period, debt was less commonplace as a financing tool, and longer term business considerations dominated acquisition decisions. This wave was less beset by new takeover regulation, largely because any excesses were written off as merely a heady response to the tech bubble. The collapse of Enron Corporation and Worldcom Inc. also directed the typical postbubble regulatory impulses toward corporate governance rather than deal-making.

The downturn was short, and takeovers quickly entered into a sixth wave—the era of private equity and cross-border and global transactions.

This wave was boosted by its own bubble, an unprecedented wave of liquidity and cheap credit brought on by inordinately low interest rates and savings imbalances across the world. The twilight of the sixth wave and the financial crisis is the subject of this book. It covers the changing nature of deals and deal-making in these times and the consequences of the economic crisis we are still witnessing. And while we are currently in a postwave period, the truth is that these waves are coming faster and turning deal-making into a constant affair. Even in the terrible down year of 2008, takeovers globally still accounted for $2.9 trillion in value, and in 2009 takeovers are still likely to exceed $2 trillion in value.[37] Deals are continuing and, as we emerge from this current down cycle, will enter into new and uncharted territory, territory that will be marked by the response to recent events (see Figure 1.1).

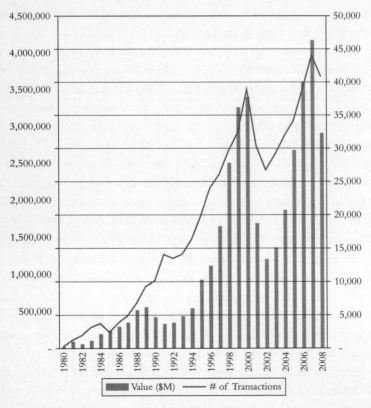

Figure 1.1 Global Takeover Volume 1980–2008
SOURCE: Thomson Reuters

The Takeover Revolution

Deal-making has evolved and moved past the day when Vanderbilt sent armed goons to assault the Erie Gang. Even then the law remained an important guidepost in deciding takeover battles. This was true despite the corrupt malleability of the judges and legislatures enacting these rules. It was, after all, the tainted law enacted by the New York legislature that finally brought the parties to settlement. Since that time, the role of law in deciding and regulating deals, particularly takeovers, has grown increasingly important.

The real shift in takeovers began in the 1960s. Prior to that time, the thuggery and bribery of Vanderbilt's era had gradually faded away into a stronger rule of law. But up until the 1960s, there was little law regulating what companies could and could not do in response to and in making takeovers. The change began only when a more active takeover market began to arise in the 1960s. The skein of law imposed created varying takeover standards. The result is that takeovers are now a regulated industry subject to and shaped by the rule of law. This made the industry the playground of lawyers. It also created a more organized, systematic approach to deal-making.

This latter aspect is reflected in the deal machine. Takeovers today are about party planning—putting together legal, financial, strategic, investor relations, and publicity considerations into one mix. And each of these elements has its own group of key advisers that one retains. So, for example, you see a handful of public relations firms on almost every large deal. Each has its own personality, depending upon the founder. Brunswick Group LLP, spearheaded in the United States by ex-*Wall Street Journal* reporter Stephen Lipin, is more staid and corporate; Joele Frank, Wilkinson Brimmer Katcher, led by the energetic Joele Frank, is perhaps more aggressive. The deal machine has become vast and organized.

In this regard, while central themes have emerged over the years, takeover tactics and strategy have shifted in light of these developments and with each wave. Moreover, as deal-making has evolved, each wave has brought its own mini-revolution, whereby new tactics and strategy bring further regulation in response. The first wave brought antitrust regulation; the third and fourth brought substantive regulation of the takeover process. The fifth wave was the first not to produce significant revolutionary tactics but also the first to fail to produce substantive regulatory change. Yet, this regulation has largely been adopted piece-meal without any holistic view. The result is that the regulation of takeovers today is a hodgepodge of state and federal regulation that both underregulates and overregulates.

The public and political elements of deal-making have become increasingly important over the years. The public here includes not just legislators but the executive bodies of the states and federal govern-ment; regulators on a broad-based level including the SEC, the Federal Trade Commission, and the Federal Reserve, as well as those with a particular industry focus; unions and employment bodies; media; lob-bying groups; and the public generally. Many of the deals described in this book such as InBev N.V./S.A.'s hostile takeover of Anheuser-Busch, Dubai Ports World's failed acquisition of a number of U.S. ports, and a private equity consortium's successful acquisition of Texas utility TXU, Inc. were more public successes than anything else.

Thus, going into the sixth wave, deals had become a complex affair—mixing economics, politics and interest groups, regulation, public relations, and personality. But the sixth wave brought about its own revolution, which threatens to upset this mix. The events of the past few years have changed deal-making as the quickening pace of financial innovation and extraordinary growth in the global capital markets have changed the way takeovers are structured and implemented. During the sixth wave, from 2004 to 2008:

- Deal-making became a truly global business.
- Sovereign wealth funds first appeared.
- Private equity dominated takeovers and then simply disappeared.
- Hedge funds became ubiquitous, driving shareholder activism and takeovers.
- Derivatives became increasingly complex and a controversial, frequent tool of activist hedge funds.
- The structure of strategic transactions changed in light of the credit bubble, the ensuing crisis, and the drying up of cash financing.
- Private markets became an increasingly important source of capital.
- The public became an increasingly important element of transactions.
- A series of strategic hostile takeovers transformed the playing field for these unfriendly bids.

In particular, shareholders led by activist hedge funds have become more active than ever before. Together with the good corporate governance movement led by the corporate governance proxy advisory services, they are driving a more disciplined approach to deal-making and corporate conduct. These are new actors and new weapons that are unlike anything ever before seen.

The changes fostered by these developments have been skewed by the financial crisis and the massive market panic that occurred beginning in September 2008. The crisis has been a crucible through which the recent changes in deal-making have crystallized and become self-apparent. The stresses brought upon the market created their own magnifying lens, exposing the flaws in the deal system but also shaping its future. It has exploded the old investment banking model and caused actors to reassess the role of financing, particularly debt, in deal-making.

The result is a transformed marketplace but also a regulatory system and an approach to deal-making that is a step behind. The deals that follow are about the past years of frantic change and crisis, the future of deals and deal-making, and the appropriate response of dealmakers and regulators. It is about the glory and failures of deal-making and the role of dealmakers. It is about the transformative transactions in the new millennium and a history of deal-making in a soaring and perilous time. It is about how deals will be done, and perhaps regulated, in the future.

But to understand deal-making today, it is first necessary to take a step back and explore its driving transformational force in the sixth wave—private equity.

Chapter 2

KKR, SunGard, and the Private Equity Phenomenon

The phenomenon of the sixth takeover wave, private equity, is a key force behind the current crisis-driven change in the takeover market.[1] Private equity dominated the sixth wave, accounting for $1.02 trillion in U.S. acquisitions or 20 percent of all domestic takeovers from 2004 through 2007.[2] At the time private equity was not only ubiquitous but also seemingly unstoppable. From the 2007 acquisition of Chrysler LLC by Cerberus Capital Management LP to the $44 billion acquisition of the power company TXU, the largest U.S. private equity deal ever, it appeared that private equity would not only be the preeminent force in takeovers but also transform the way companies operated and raised capital. As with previous booms, the words *paradigm shift* were murmured a lot, and many even spoke of private equity ending the primary role of the public markets for equity capital.[3]

Of course, we all know what happened. The credit market collapsed, the economy and housing and stock markets went into decline, and private equity entered into its own tumultuous period as these firms repeatedly attempted to terminate or otherwise escape their obligations to complete acquisitions agreed to in far better times. The failure of so many private equity deals left many seeking to assign blame for the collapse, pointing fingers at attorneys, investment bankers, banks, and private equity firms themselves. The private equity market came to a standstill, as credit dried up and targets became skittish about the ability of private equity firms to complete acquisitions. But the failure of private equity, the reasons for its collapse, and the implications for the future of deal-making are the subject of Chapter 4.

This chapter is about the seeds of this late failure. It is about the origins and history of private equity, a story that set the foundation and tension points for private equity's downfall, as well as for the general transformation it wrought in the takeover market. This story is not all about failure. This chapter is also about how private equity came to be such a game-changing force. Here, we actually have a deal that crystallizes this transformation: the $11.3 billion buy-out of SunGard Data Systems, Inc. by a who's who private equity consortium of Silver Lake Partners, Bain Capital LLC, Blackstone, Goldman Sachs Capital Partners, KKR, Providence Equity Partners LLC, and Texas Pacific Group (TPG). In order to understand SunGard and the origins of private equity's downfall, though, we need to go further back in time to KKR and its foundational role in private equity.

KKR and the Origins of Private Equity

The beginning of private equity is probably best traced to a 1976 proposal Jerome Kohlberg and first cousins Henry Kravis and George Roberts presented to their employer, the now-defunct investment bank Bear Stearns. The trio had spent the last decade building a niche investment banking practice. The entrepreneurs who had built post–World War II family businesses were beginning to retire. At the time these businessmen had limited choices for exiting the businesses they had built and nurtured. Extraordinarily high federal inheritance taxes made simply willing these businesses to the next generation an unattractive prospect. In many cases, the inheritance tax would force a sale of the company and eat up an inordinate share of any gains on the disposition. The only two other choices were thought to be to sell the business, either on the public markets or to a more sizable and willing corporation. In both cases, many of these companies were either unsuited to go public or unable to find a corporate buyer. The owner would also lose control of the company he had built from scratch, a horrifying prospect.[4]

Jerome Kohlberg had an idea to provide another option. In 1965, he put this idea in practice by orchestrating the buy-out of Stern Metals, a dental supplies company, for $9.5 million. A group of investors bought a majority position in the business for $500,000. This was the equity financing. The remainder of the capital for the purchase came from borrowed funds, so-called debt financing. The selling family, led by their 72-year-old patriarch, did not entirely exit the business. The family still retained an ownership stake, as well as operational control of the business. The deal turned out to be very profitable, and four years later, the family sold their remaining stake in a public offering. The family earned $4 million on their four-year reinvestment.[5]

In the Stern Metals deal, the ad hoc group of new investors intended to cash out at a future date but leave the family owners in place. The result would permit the family owners to continue to run their firm but monetize a significant portion of their ownership. The family owners of Stern decided to sell early and take their profits, but Kohlberg's goal was to provide an avenue for families to stay and maintain control. Kohlberg would later cite this as his key innovation.[6] Retention of the family as owners in the posttransaction structure strongly incentivized these managers to succeed and earn an outsize return for their new investors. Kohlberg took the cousins Henry Kravis and George Roberts under his wing and mentored them in the structure and completion of these family deals. The three quickly developed a thriving practice within the corporate finance department at Bear Stearns.

In the early 1970s, Kohlberg, Kravis, and Roberts added a second type of deal to their repertoire. The conglomerate takeover wave of the 1960s had faltered. These big companies almost uniformly underperformed the market, while the managers of the individual companies chafed under the supervision of often less experienced senior executives and the byzantine management organizations governing these conglomerates. Meanwhile, institutional investors preferred to diversify through separate investments suitable to their preferences rather than through a conglomerate that often owned weak-performing assets hidden within its jumble of companies. Wall Street, ever quick to change its tune, began to agitate for the disassembling of these empires. The conglomerates themselves responded by disposing of the companies they had only recently bought. By 1977, fully 53 percent of all U.S. takeovers were conglomerate divestitures.[7]

Kohlberg began to structure buy-outs of these companies based on the structure he had first tested with family businesses. Kohlberg would strike up a relationship with the management of these subsidiaries. He would then arrange a group of investors to buy the subsidiary from the conglomerate. Debt was used for the bulk of the financing, and management would be included as posttransaction owners of the now independent entity.

By 1976, things were going swimmingly. The trio had built a sizable and profitable business within their department at Bear Stearns. Moreover, the structure of these deals had been tested and found successful. Kohlberg and his lieutenants no longer had to spend hours explaining the workings of these transactions to unfamiliar management. You can just hear the conversation: "A leveraged buy-out, now what the hell is that?"

Kohlberg felt it was time to establish a bigger platform to support their work. The three submitted their proposal to do so within Bear Stearns. A new department would be created within the investment bank, with Kohlberg as the head and Kravis and Roberts as his lieutenants. This would provide them the latitude they needed to organize and possibly fund these deals internally. In what was in hindsight a particularly bad decision for the investment bank (not its last), senior management at Bear Stearns declined the proposal. The three promptly departed to set up their own firm. Kohlberg invested $100,000; Kravis and Roberts $10,000 each.[8] The firm was originally to be named "Kohlberg Roberts Kravis," according to their seniority at Bear Stearns. But public relations advisers nixed the idea because KRK didn't have the right ring to it; thus KKR was born.[9]

KKR had a slow start. In 1977, KKR completed three buy-outs, and in 1978 none.[10] These buy-outs were structured like the old deals. KKR did not initially have a source of committed capital. Wealthy investors were instead brought in for each deal to provide the needed equity investment. This limited KKR's ability to make significant acquisitions. Each time KKR wanted to complete a buy-out, it needed to spend laborious hours putting together a new investing consortium, the elements of which would substantially affect the structure of their deals. But the trio was working to change this, putting in place another key element for an active private equity buy-out market.

In 1978, KKR raised the first ever private equity buy-out fund. It was a meager $32 million in size but included as investors such notables as AllState, the insurance company; Teachers Insurance, the pension fund; and Citicorp, the commercial bank. Considering the economic conditions of the time—the prime rate would climb to 11.75 percent by year-end, and corporate lending would become increasingly scarce—it was a remarkable achievement. The fund also had a slightly different purpose. It was to invest in underperforming public companies, an area KKR had pegged as one where they could realize the greatest value.[11] The fund had the common features seen in the mega buy-out funds of today: a 1.5 percent management fee (these days rising to 2 percent) and a 20 percent cut of the profits above a hurdle rate were paid to the fund's general partners, Kohlberg, Kravis, and Roberts. The fund also contemplated administration fees that KKR would reap on each deal, including a fee of 1 percent of the transaction value for each deal paid as an investment banking fee and a fee of $20,000 per associate to serve on the board of the newly acquired company. These administration and deal-making fees would later become an important source of revenue for private equity.[12]

KKR now had dedicated funds to finance the equity portion of its buy-outs. It would not have to go through the laborious process of raising equity capital on a case-by-case basis. KKR quickly put this money to work. In the next year, KKR partners completed its fifth buy-out, the $380 million buy-out of New York Stock Exchange–listed Houdaille Industries. This was the largest leveraged buy-out to date and extraordinary for the time. It was the first buy-out of a midsize, publicly traded company.[13] Again, the structure of future private buy-outs lay in the framework of this landmark deal. The equity financing came from the KKR fund and friendly co-investors. Management also retained an interest in the now-private company, an incentive for them to achieve excess returns for their new investors.

The acquisition was highly leveraged, with 87 percent of the financing for the deal coming from debt financing. Previously, KKR had been
hampered in completing larger buy-outs because of the lack of willing
debt financiers. For example, KKR's first transaction, the 1977 leveraged
buy-out of A.J. Industries, had a total market value of $26 million.[14]
KKR was unable to raise any subordinated debt financing for this
acquisition. Instead, KKR was limited to financing 66 percent of the
deal with senior bank debt.[15] In the Houdaille buy-out, KKR succeeded
in implementing a capital structure that supported an approximately 85
percent debt-to-equity ratio but also inovatively allocated this debt to
a variety of different financing instruments. But it had taken almost a
year for KKR to raise these funds. Henry Kravis would later reminisce:
"Literally we had to add up the potential capital sources at that time,
which consisted of several banks and insurance companies, and one-by-
one go out and raise the money, and then create a capital structure based
on availability of funds."[16]

To make buy-outs of greater size, KKR needed more debt and equity
financing. This would become the lifeblood and driver of private
equity. The investors in KKR's first two funds in 1978 and 1980 were
mostly wealthy individual investors. Their assets would not be sufficient
to fund the increasingly larger buy-outs KKR was targeting. Again,
KKR innovated turning to a new source of untapped wealth, pension
funds, and an older, more traditional one, commercial banks. In KKR's
next four funds, raised in 1982, 1984, 1986, and 1987, commercial
banks invested approximately 30 percent of the total amount.[17]

Pension funds would provide an even more bountiful source
of wealth. In 1974, Congress had enacted the Employee Retirement
Income Security Act to promote the formation of private and public
pensions and encourage private individuals to save for retirement. Since
that time, public pension funds had accumulated hundreds of billions
in assets under management. However, state laws at the time severely
restricted the ability of these public pension funds to invest and typically
prohibited equity investments as too risky. Oregon State Treasurer Bob
Straub successfully lobbied his state legislature to lift these restrictions
in order to gain the chance to earn higher returns.[18]

This was a boon to both Oregon and KKR. The Oregon Council,
headed by Roger Meier, became KKR's first big investor, putting $178
million in KKR's 1981 leveraged buy-out of the Oregon-headquartered

Fred Meyer Inc. The total value of Fred Meyer was only $420 million. The council's investment paid off, returning more than 53 percent on its investment.[19] Other state pension funds rapidly took notice of Oregon's leap, the earnings potential in buy-outs, and KKR's early returns and also convinced their legislatures to permit investment in these funds. Pension funds quickly became KKR's biggest investors. In KKR's $1.6 billion 1986 fund, state public pension funds accounted for a significant portion of the funds committed, including a single $55 million investment by the New York State pension fund, which later upped its investment in KKR's 1987 fund to $370 million.[20]

The performance of private equity in the 1980s, as well as the increasing prominence of their transactions, established private equity's bona fides. Though the returns were not fully known at the time, the first five KKR funds earned an average return of almost 37 percent.[21] Meanwhile, other leveraged buy-outs were succeeding. In 1982, the management of Gibson Greetings Inc., a subsidiary of the conglomerate RCA Corp., arranged a leveraged buy-out of their own company for $80 million. The overwhelming portion of this was financed by debt, $79 million.[22] Only a year later, the company went public, selling 30 percent of itself with a price that valued the company at more than $330 million.[23] In the wake of KKR's Houdaille acquisition and the home run in Gibson Greetings, a host of other buy-out shops began to achieve public prominence. These included Forstmann Little, which acquired the Dr. Pepper Company in 1984 for $512 million.

Forstmann Little was headed up by the flamboyant Teddy Forstmann, who publicly juxtaposed himself against KKR and Henry Kravis as a more benign buy-out king, less interested in leverage and the restructurings that had arguably stigmatized private equity. Forstmann himself consorted with celebrities and politicians, enjoying the fruits of his wealth, yet he gave generously to philanthropic causes. He was also never afraid to speak his mind and made a point to do so, publicly criticizing the highly leveraged transactions KKR was under-taking and later decrying the use of high-yield financing. The fact that Kravis married dress designer Carolyne Roehm, whom Forstmann had previously dated, no doubt, added fuel to the fire.[24]

Money was to be made in leveraged buy-outs. But how was private equity able to earn money where independent corporate managers had not? People attributed the success to a number of reasons.

- *The Benefits of Increased Debt.* The debt placed on these companies worked to discipline management. No longer could profits be spent on corporate outings or jets, but rather money was required to pay financing costs. Management was forced to strictly budget and account for their expenses in order to meet financing costs and to pay down debt. During the 1980s, KKR would typically attempt to finance transactions with 80 percent to 90 percent debt, with the remainder in equity. Debt also had a tax advantage. The interest was tax deductible, allowing a company to increase its excess free cash by utilizing debt financing.[25]

- *Increased Incentives for Management.* The inclusion of management as equity investors strongly incentivized them to succeed. The money made on the Gibson Greetings transaction was an example all had seen and a large carrot. Before, corporate officers had a smaller stake in the success of their enterprise; their salaries were largely paid so long as they didn't entirely fail. Now managers could profit handsomely, together with their investors. They had more skin in the game and so were willing to take more risk and had more incentives to perform.[26]

- *Greater Alignment of Ownership and Control.* Private equity management itself was intimately involved in the operation of their acquisitions and constantly monitoring them for performance. KKR's partners served on the boards of the companies they bought, where they scrutinized their company's performance and constantly inquired and questioned management business decisions. This contrasted with the more laissez-faire approach in the public markets at the time when boards were largely passive, the members were often friends and colleagues of the CEO, and dispersed public shareholders lacked the capacity for concerted action.[27]

- *Diminished Regulation and Longer Term Operational Focus.* Private equity allowed firms to operate outside the glare of the public markets. While the benefits to the public markets existed in increased access to financing, liquidity, and analyst and other disclosure coverage, they also subjected the public corporation to litigation exposure, disclosure costs, and other costs associated with regulatory supervision. A private corporation eliminated a measure of these costs.[28] It also allowed the company to adopt a longer term focus over and above the next quarterly earnings report, which is too often the primary focus of public companies.

- *Longer Term Investing Horizon.* Finally, private equity firms adopted long-term investing horizons. During the 1980s, the average length of time KKR held a stake in an acquired company was 7.6 years.[29] This provided both management and their investors time to work with and influence the company. This long-term investment outlook permitted the companies in a private equity firm's portfolio to focus on long-term investments and make decisions that, while painful in the short term, would result in greater long-term profits.

KKR had succeeded in finding the equity for its deals. But an even greater portion of debt was needed to finance these ever larger transactions. Previously, KKR had relied on commercial banks and insurance companies for debt financing. The loans these entities were willing to provide were often only on a secured basis and at a senior level, meaning that they were paid first before any other debt. This limited the amount KKR could borrow to finance an acquisition. The acquired company needed to maintain a cushion of security to support this debt. Moreover, putting together this debt on a case-by-case basis made it harder to complete deals on a rapid time line, a necessity in the public markets.

If KKR was going to obtain the leverage it desired, it was going to have to find a source for large amounts of unsecured or junior debt that could be quickly raised in tandem with secured debt. This is where the brilliant and infamous Michael R. Milken and Drexel Burnham Lambert Inc. came in. Throughout the 1970s and 1980s, the perpetually working Michael Milken had been creating a larger market for high-yield debt, often known as junk bonds because this debt was either unrated or rated below investment grade. Historically, high-yield debt was shunned by investors and confined to small issuers who had no other financing choice. Milken had studied this market and found that investors in this debt could earn outsize returns. He popularized this notion and soon convinced many institutional and other investors to purchase the high-yield debt issuances he organized. To feed this clientele, Milken needed an even larger source of issuers for these securities.

The stars of Milken and private equity aligned. Not only could Milken provide a ready and rapid source of financing but also, by making this market in less secure, subordinated debt, he provided a means for private equity firms to raise more debt and increase leverage. Greater leverage on their acquisitions permitted private equity firms to make more frequent and larger buy-outs and enhanced opportunities to earn outsize returns. In 1983, the leverage buy-out firm Clayton & Dubilier (now Clayton, Dubilier & Rice) became one of the first private equity firm to use Milken's services for C&D's leveraged buy-out of the graphics division of Harris Corp. The other private equity firms followed, and by the mid-1980s, with few exceptions they began to uniformly resort to Milken and his junk debt to finance their acquisitions; Milken's annual high-yield debt conference became known as the predator's ball in honor of their consumption. In doing so, Milken and private equity created a debt market that would support the quick sale and securitization of debt.[30]

Again, KKR was the market leader, forming a tight partnership with Milken and Drexel Burnham Lambert. The partnership and its potential were revealed in 1985, when KKR announced the take-over of the conglomerate Beatrice Foods Co. Beatrice had started in the dairy business but rapidly expanded in the 1970s and 1980s into a mishmash of other businesses, including La Choy Chinese foods and Playtex underwear. KKR's unsolicited offer was made without the foreknowledge of Beatrice, then the 26th largest company on the Fortune 500 list. Before this offer, KKR had never completed a deal without management buy-in. It now joined league with the corporate raiders of the time, although Beatrice's management was known widely for its incompetence, which made KKR's leap easier. Beatrice rapidly capitulated, and the buy-out was completed at the record price of $6.2 billion. To finance this transaction, KKR resorted largely to Michael Milken and his junk debt machine and paid $248 million in banker and other fees associated with the deal.[31] For the remainder of the 1980s, KKR would find easy financing for its buy-outs. What bank wouldn't want to make the hundreds of millions of dollars in fees KKR offered up in any deal? In the wake of Beatrice, KKR raised its largest fund to date: a $5.6 billion 1987 fund. Eleven pension funds ponied up 53 percent of this amount.[32]

The private equity boom continued, and KKR remained at the epicenter of this activity. From 1985 to 1989, it completed only 28 buy-outs of the more than 1,625 private equity buy-outs that occurred. Yet, KKR's buy-outs numbered 8 of the 25 largest buy-outs of the period and comprised nearly a quarter of all buy-out activity as measured by value during this time.[33]

The buy-out frenzy of the 1980s appropriately crested in KKR's record $31.1 billion 1989 deal for RJR/Nabisco, documented so well in the book *Barbarians at the Gate*. KKR won RJR only after an extended bidding war against a management buy-out group led by RJR CEO and ex-salesman Ross Johnson. It was a battle of wills in which Henry Kravis became determined to beat Johnson. Wall Street was in awe at the stratospheric price KKR paid and generally attributed it to Kravis's need to show that he could not be beaten. The deal generated more than $1 billion in fees for the deal machine, including KKR and its armada of bankers and lawyers.

In the wake of the RJR deal, the buy-out market cratered. The reasons were varied. The credit markets tightened, the United States entered a recession, and regulations surrounding the issuance of high-yield debt financing tightened. In addition, the S&L crisis eliminated many buyers for this debt, while the RJR deal itself was so large that it absorbed a substantial amount of future investment capacity. Many also cited a bubble in credit and private equity, which simply popped. Whatever the cause, the easy credit of the 1980s dried up almost over-night in 1989. The event was publicly marked in the travails of First Boston Corp. caught in its "burning bed." When the market suddenly collapsed, First Boston was left unable to refinance the hundreds of millions it had lent to Ohio Mattress Company, the producer of Sealy mattresses, for a leveraged buy-out. First Boston escaped bankruptcy only via a bailout by Credit Suisse Group AG.[34]

If there was any doubt that the go-go days of easy credit were over, at least temporarily, the very public imprisonment of Michael Milken on insider trading charges and the early 1990s implosion of Drexel Burnham Lambert cemented its demise. Nonetheless, KKR and Milken had succeeded in creating a machine for quick and sometimes cheap financing for buy-outs. This would be the same machine that would engender the overleveraging of companies during 2004–2007 and savagely malfunction in the financial crisis of 2008.

The failure of the debt markets was mirrored by a decline in equity funding for buy-outs. New commitments to private equity fell from $11.9 billion in 1989 to $4.8 billion in 1990, and to $5.6 billion in 1991.[35] Without an active source of financing, private equity firms struggled to make acquisitions. The value of private equity buy-out activity plummeted from $75.8 billion in 1989 to $8 billion in 1992.[36] Private equity firms also encountered operational difficulties as they attempted to turn companies purchased at premium prices into profitable investments. KKR was not immune. KKR's investors lost $958 million on the RJR deal, and in 1991, KKR was forced to invest an additional $1.7 billion into RJR/Nabisco to refinance $7 billion worth of pay-in-kind securities. The press widely covered this event, proclaiming that Kravis and KKR were reaping its "punishment" for hubris in overpaying for RJR, a result of its need to be seen as the deal community's overlord.[37]

There were lessons to be learned. The lifeblood of private equity was clearly debt and equity—the financing for these acquisitions. The drying up of these sources led to a quiet period for the industry. Moreover, the cyclicality of these financing sources, and thus private equity, was ably revealed. After the collapse of the high-yield market in 1989, it was quite clear that private equity activity was now dependent on the debt markets for survival. Moreover, the credit crash of 1989 showed that the credit cycle and private equity would eventually peak, as with all other cycles. The travails of First Boston ably showed what would happen when the game of musical chairs stopped and the debt market entered a downturn: Someone would be left holding the debt at a substantial, perhaps perilous loss. This was yet another soon forgotten lesson to be repeated in 2007 and 2008.

In the wake of these excesses, private equity entered a quiet period. The 1990s were times of rebuilding. Deals continued to be had, but they were smaller, with a lower profile. Blackstone, Apollo Management L.P., the Carlyle Group, TPG, Thomas H. Lee, and Silver Lake all appeared as prominent players on the buy-out scene. KKR, though, continued to dominate the field. In 1996, it raised its biggest fund to date, $6 billion. KKR struggled to complete this fund, as investors still smarted from KKR's late-1980s investments and competitors began to shadow the firm. The prospective investors bargained hard with KKR over the terms of this fund, citing the competition and the poor performance of RJR's late-1990s investments. KKR was forced to reduce its management fee from 1.5 percent to 1.1 percent and cut in half its monitoring and transaction fees. The negotiation became so contentious that George Roberts reportedly told the giant California state pension fund CalPERS that they would not be welcome as investors because of their strident negotiating positions.[38]

The credit floodgates opened after September 11, 2001, as the Federal Reserve aggressively—in hindsight, perhaps too aggressively—lowered interest rates. Debt financing became both cheap and freely accessible. This would trigger private equity's renewed ascent. In 2001, private equity accounted for $17.6 billion in U.S. takeovers, but by 2006 private equity accounted for more than $389.5 billion in takeovers and more than 25.4 percent of all U.S. takeover activity.[39] It was growth spurred not just by the availability of inexpensive debt. Private equity's return was also aided by the continued rise of pension funds, endowments, and insurance funds and the equity financing they could provide. As of 2007, U.S. pension funds alone held $14 trillion in total assets and endowments $411 billion.[40] These funds were voracious investors, scouring the markets for investments and excess returns. Once again, these funds eagerly invested in private equity firms who were looking to leverage the loose credit markets to increase the number and size of their acquisitions. In 2006, private equity funds raised $229 billion in commitments, compared with only $38 billion in 2002.[41] In that year, Blackstone raised the largest private equity fund to that date, a $15.6 billion fund dwarfing KKR's record $10 billion fund, also completed in 2006. KKR had been publicly dethroned (see Figure 2.1).[42]

Despite its missteps, private equity could rely on its stellar historical track record dating from the 1980s to draw this investment. In its first 30 years, KKR had an annual average return of 20.2 percent net of fees on its first 10 private equity funds.[43] Similarly, the emergent Blackstone earned an annual return of 30.8 percent on its investments gross of fees since the firm began in 1987.[44] Although data were scarce and general studies were few and far between about the broader ability of the private equity industry, those available supported the conclusion that private equity was an industry of the large. The established, more sizable firms achieved excess returns consistently, with the bulk of smaller firms and

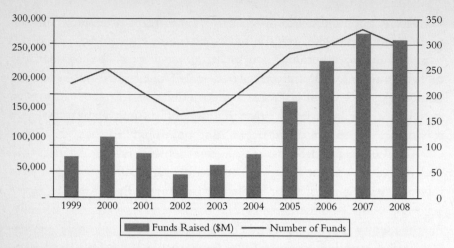

Figure 2.1   Funds Raised by Private Equity Firms (Globally) 1999–2008
SOURCE: Thomson Reuters (includes global buyout, mezzanine, recap, and turnaround funds)

the industry itself achieving earnings at best on par with the S&P 500 with adjustments for leverage.[45] As in the 1980s, a few extremely prof-itable public transactions in the new millennium highlighted to the world the extraordinary potential of private equity investing. In 2005, Blackstone took public the Celanese Corporation, a German chemical company. Blackstone quintupled its $650 million investment in only 12 months.[46] Not to be outdone, KKR, together with the Carlyle Group and Providence Equity, performed a similar investing feat in that year by selling PanAmSat Corp. less than 12 months after it was acquired to the tune of over $1.8 billion in profits.[47]

These investment funds were also drawn to private equity due to their focus on *alpha*. *Alpha* refers to the ability of an investment man-ager to earn excess returns over those predicted for an investment based on its prior response to market movements, or *beta*. Eliminating *beta* permits the manager's performance to be evaluated on the quality of their investment selections and not on market movements. Private equity funds were found to historically provide superior risk-adjusted performance, or positive alpha, higher than that of matching leveraged investments in the S&P 500 Index.[48] This was further evidence of the success of private equity in operating their businesses, and another key to again drawing in professional institutional investors.

The frenzy of the 1980s began to repeat itself in the new millennium. As in the 1980s, private equity began its rise quietly, but as the boom continued, it became an increasingly larger force. In 2004, the largest private equity deal of the year was the $4.8 billion buy-out of Metro-Goldwyn-Mayer by TPG, CSFB Private Equity, and Providence Equity, in conjunction with Sony Corporation.[49] However, the largest U.S. private equity deal of all time was announced on February 26, 2007, when TPG, Goldman Sachs Capital Partners, and KKR agreed to the $4.3 billion buy-out of TXU.[50] In 2006 and 2007, 9 of the 10 largest private equity buy-outs of all time would be announced (see Table 2.1).

Private equity once again ventured into new territory as the buy-out market simmered and then boiled. In the 1980s, these private equity buy-outs were often affected by shell subsidiaries set up specifically for this purpose by the private equity firm. The shells had no assets of their own. Instead, the acquisitions agreements required that

Table 2.1   Ten Largest Private Equity Buy-outs of All Time

Acquirer	Target	Total Value ($mm)	Date Announced	Date Closed
KKR/TPG/ Goldman Sachs	TXU	44,372	2/26/2007	10/10/2007
Blackstone Group	Equity Office	37,711	11/19/2006	2/9/2007
KKR/Bain Capital/ Merrill Lynch	HCA	33,000	7/24/2006	11/17/2006
KKR	RJR/Nabisco	31,100	12/01/1988	04/29/1989
TPG/Apollo/ Citigroup	Harrah's	27,800	10/02/2006	1/28/2008
KKR	FirstData	29,000	04/02/2007	9/24/2007
Thomas H Lee Partners/Bain Capital	Clear Channel	24,000	11/16/2006	7/30/2008
Goldman Sachs/TPG	Alltel	27,500	05/02/2007	11/16/2007
Blackstone Group	Hilton Hotels	26,702	07/03/2007	10/24/2007
KKR	Alliance Boots	22,179	05/09/2007	6/28/2007

Source: Thomson Reuters (completed buy-outs)

the shell use its reasonable best efforts to complete the buy-out. The shell could also often terminate the deal if financing was unavailable. This was accomplished by placing a financing condition in the acquisition agreement, conditioning the shell's obligation to acquire the target on the shell having obtained sufficient funds to do so. But since the shell had no assets of its own, targets demanded assurances that the financing would indeed be available. So these arrangements were also accompanied by a debt financing commitment letter from an investment or commercial bank. These commitments were often less than complete, though, to be finished with documented credit agreements at the time of deal completion. These debt commitment letters were also optional and contained a market out clause permitting the banks to terminate their financing obligations if market conditions deteriorated or otherwise impeded placement of the debt.

Because of the high leverage put on these transactions, banks were often unwilling to even provide this commitment. In such circumstances, a bank would issue a highly confident letter. These letters were first widely used by Michael Milken in deals where the success of the debt issuance was too uncertain to provide any firm written commitments. The financing bank would instead opine that it was "highly" confident that the debt could be raised in the markets but provide no contractual agreement to do so. In either case, though, the private equity fund itself was not liable if the transaction failed to complete. This effectively enabled the private equity firms to walk from the buy-out anytime before consummation of the acquisition if market or other circumstances dictated. Targets generally relied upon the reputation of the firms and on private equity firms' desire to complete the transaction to ensure their cooperation.

In the 1990s, targets began to contractually bind private equity firms to acquisitions by demanding and receiving equity commitment letters from the private equity firms. These letters obligated the firms to supply the shell with the necessary equity to complete the transaction. Previously, the target had relied on the good will of the private equity firm to provide the equity component. The gap in financing these transactions was filled by this change, ensuring that the shell subsidiary had access to both debt and equity to complete the transaction. During this time period, debt commitment letters commonly included terms for bridge financing. Bridge financing is interim financing between the completion of the transaction and the placement of any high-yield, permanent financing. Adding this facility provided greater comfort to the target that the transaction would be completed if the issuance of any of the permanent high-yield debt was delayed.[51]

SunGard and the Transformation of Private Equity

Then came SunGard. SunGard was the largest private equity deal since KKR's acquisition of RJR/Nabisco, more than a decade and a half before. It was also a club deal involving multiple private equity buyers, and it was something novel for private equity, a technology deal.[52] SunGard was an IT services and software company. In short, SunGard was a unique and historical private equity deal. Because of this, SunGard's lawyers at Shearman & Sterling LLP were worried about the financing risk. To address this issue, Shearman & Sterling negotiated the removal of the financing condition. The result was a tighter deal, ostensibly more favorable to the target. The equity portion of the transaction was agreed through an equity commitment letter executed by the seven private equity firms. The debt portion of the transaction was agreed through a commitment letter that included a bridge financing facility.

In exchange for agreeing to the removal of the financing condition, SunGard provided the private equity buyers the ability to terminate the agreement and walk on the deal if they paid a reverse termination fee of $300 million. If the shell was unable to complete the buy-out for financing or simply refused to do so—that is, the deal was terminated—the consortium would pay a fee of $300 million to SunGard as compensation.[53] The fee was called a reverse termination fee because it was patterned on the termination fees that targets typically agreed to pay buyers if they subsequently accepted a higher offer from another bidder. Since the shell was still that, an empty corporation without funds, the private equity buyers issued a guarantee for this payment.[54] (See Figure 2.2.)

This type of structure had previously been utilized in real estate deals. However, the SunGard "structure" was the first significantly sized private equity transaction to employ such architecture. It quickly took hold in private equity transactions for two reasons. First, private equity

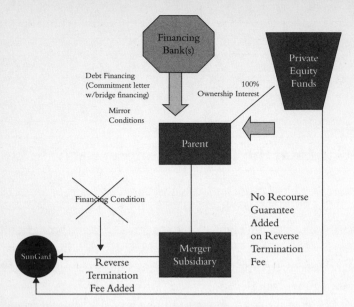

Figure 2.2   Structure of SunGard Data Systems, Inc Buy-out
SOURCE: SunGard Data Sys. Inc., Definitive Proxy Statement (Schedule 14A) (June 27, 2005)

firms preferred the structure because it eliminated an argument of veil piercing. Veil piercing allowed a target to pierce the limited liability of corporate acquisition shells and obtain a judgment against the fund itself. In exchange for agreeing to the reverse termination fees, the private equity firms provided a no-recourse guarantee, under which the targets waived any veil-piercing claim. Thus, the private equity firm capped its aggregate liability at the reverse termination fee. Second, targets preferred the structure because it ensured a measure of compensation if the financing on the transaction failed. The SunGard reverse termination fee structure thus represented an improvement on the old structure.

Figure 2.3 sets forth my own calculations as to the percentage of private equity deals utilizing a reverse termination fee structure from 2004 through 2008. The figure shows a rapid shift in practice as the use of financing conditions dropped in inverse proportion to utilization of the reverse termination fee structure.

The structure sometimes varied in important ways. For example, in the 2005 buy-out of Neiman Marcus Inc., the private equity buyers agreed to a two-tiered termination fee. A lower fee would be paid if the

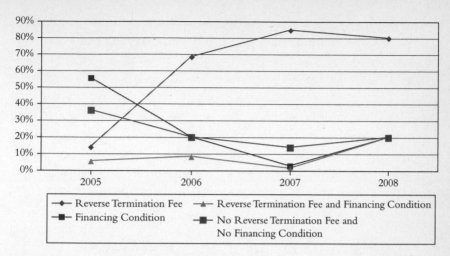

Figure 2.3   Adoption of Reverse Termination Fee by Private Equity Firms
(% of Total Acquisitions 2004–2008/Value Greater $100M)
Source: Factset MergerMetrics

deal collapsed on account of a failure of financing, a higher one if the buyer simply decided to walk on the transaction without reason. A third variation of this arrangement arose in other buy-outs where the target could supposedly force the private equity shell to enforce—in legal terms, specifically perform—the debt and equity commitment letters to complete the transaction, but if the shell was unable to do so and the financing failed, only the reverse termination fee was payable.

In its first two variations, this arrangement provided a flat-out option to the private equity firm to exit a transaction simply by paying the reverse termination fee. This was a high level of explicit optionality for private equity buyers. The reverse termination fee typically amounted to approximately 3 percent of the deal fee. Accordingly, before completing an acquisition, private equity firms could simply gauge whether the deal was worth completing or if it would be more economical to walk on the deal and pay the reverse termination fee. Lawyers at the time appeared well aware of this potential but often advised their clients that a private equity firm's need to preserve its reputation for making good on its deals would prevent this economic calculus.

Moreover, despite outliers, the fee largely stayed at 3 percent and was not varied for individual transaction or regulatory risk. Parties kept to this number because of the symmetry of the reverse termination fee with the regular termination fee. But this symmetry was false. The termination fee was regulated by Delaware law and was designed to compensate a buyer in case of a winning competing bid while the reverse termination fee was designed to compensate the target for a failed deal and deter a buyer from walking. The reverse termination fee structure was an improvement on the old structure since it provided compensation to the target if financing could not be arranged. However, in hindsight, the reverse termination fee was set too low, and the failure to appropriately set it would come to haunt targets during the financial crisis.

Private Equity in the Sixth Wave

Private equity was also learning from its prior missteps. The RJR-KKR transaction had taught the industry the dangers of single-handedly attempting to bag the elephant. Private equity firms began to increasingly work together on sizable transactions, sharing transaction expenses and risk. The SunGard transaction was the first significant one of these, but many more were to follow. Of the top 10 private equity deals from 2004 through 2007, six involved more than one private equity firm.[55] Gone were the days when Teddy Forstmann and Henry Kravis were mortal enemies, never to speak, let alone work together. Now private equity firms often collaborated, avoiding competition for transactions and another RJR-type bidding war. Again, the SunGard transaction was significant for being one of the first of these deals. Targets complained that this resulted in bid rigging and lower premiums paid to their shareholders, and the Department of Justice investigated private equity for anticompetitive behavior, but the practice continued unabated.[56]

Private Equity and Its Critics

As private equity again rose in prominence, it once again stirred public controversy. Private equity was criticized for cutting jobs, closing offices and factories, and underspending on capital investment in order to service their acquired companies' high debt. This was a criticism that harked back to the 1980s. One prominent study found that companies acquired by a private equity firm on average suffered a 7 percent decline in employees after a buy-out, though the fall was partly offset by new jobs generated at new facilities due to the "creative destruction" process private equity engendered.[57] The verdict on capital expenditures, though needing further research, generally found that private equity acquisitions resulted in increased capital spending.[58] Furthermore, other studies found that private equity acquisitions spurred innovation in the patenting process, though it remains to be seen whether private equity merely spurred patenting or actually fostered creativity.[59]

The new poster boy for private equity, Stephen Schwarzman, CEO of Blackstone, did not help its image. Labeled "Wall Street's Man of the Moment," he put a very public face on private equity when the writer Kurt Andersen described him in *New York* magazine as "a perfect poster boy for this age of greed, shark like, perpetually grinning, a tiny Gordon Gekko without the hair product."[60] A *Wall Street Journal* profile chronicled Schwarzman as regularly eating crab costing $400 a claw, obsessively haranguing his house staff, and generally behaving like a spoiled child. His $3 million 60th birthday party cemented his reputation as the not-so-nice public face of private equity.[61] Henry Kravis reportedly fumed at Schwarzman's bad publicity, but many termed his fury jealousy over Blackstone's usurpation of KKR as the largest of the buy-out firms in competition with the Carlyle Group. No matter, this publicity did not help the public perceptions of private equity as a greedy cast bent only on acquiring and rendering corporations. To counter growing negative perceptions, private equity even went so far as to create a new industry group, the Private Equity Council, to put a more human face on the business and coordinate lobbying among the firms with Congress and other governmental organizations.[62]

Private Equity's Bubble?

Then, there was talk of a bubble. By the beginning of 2007, private equity was paying ever higher prices and borrowing ever increasing amounts as the credit market continued to percolate. Not only were banks allowing greater leverage at low prices to private equity acquisitions but also they began to significantly liberalize the terms they demanded. The Neiman Marcus transaction, which followed shortly after SunGard, was notable for completely eliminating the market-out in debt commitment letters, a change to the structure that would persist in all of its variations. Private equity firms began to negotiate covenant "lite" high-yield debt, which provided their companies significantly more latitude to act and avoid a default. Financing also began to include payment in kind, or PIK, toggles as a standard feature—PIK toggles allowed a private equity acquisition to repay debt in kind with more debt rather than cash if the company's cash flows became insufficient to service the existing debt. These toggles and the lack of debt covenants would substantially benefit private equity in the workouts of the financial crisis. In 2008, private equity firms with respect to Clear Channel Communications Inc., Harrahs Entertainment Inc., Realogy Corp., and other troubled portfolio companies repeatedly exercised these toggles.[63]

Market watchers increasingly pointed to this conduct and vocally proclaimed both a credit and private equity bubble that would eventually burst. The $4.75 billion that Blackstone and its owners, including Schwarzman, reaped selling part of their interest in Blackstone in its June 2007 initial public offering was also cited as a sign of impending doom. Schwarzman himself received $684 million from the sale. He was not only capitalizing on the market but also needed to do something to allow buy-in for his more junior partners who could not afford to repurchase his stake upon his retirement. Still, if the smart money was selling, and selling at such lofty prices, it didn't bode well.[64]

The public gobbled up the Blackstone initial public offering, and others such as KKR attempted to follow. Here, the public was fulfilling its own desire to reap private equity riches. These alternative asset adviser IPOs were poor substitutes. The advisers still needed to pay and incentivize management, and their cash flows were much more volatile than the funds themselves and increasingly dependent on management fees. Nonetheless, the SEC continued to ban the public listing of private equity funds while permitting the listing of these advisers. The AFL–CIO accurately protested this dichotomy in a letter to the SEC, apparently preferring to keep both from the public markets.[65] They were ignored.

There were other problems on the horizon. As these private equity firms increased in size, they increasingly resembled the defunct conglomerates of the 1970s. KKR and Blackstone were now two of the largest

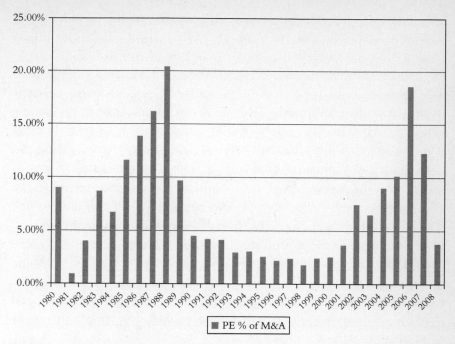

Figure 2.4   Private Equity Global Announced Takeovers (Percent of Total Global Announced Takeovers) 1980–2008
SOURCE: Thomson Reuters (includes all leveraged buy-outs)

private corporations in the world. KKR and Blackstone, in particular, began to expand into new areas by providing bank financing to other corporations, operating hedge funds, and providing investment banking services. Large private equity firms began to be called financial supermarkets because of their size and scope. Given their size, diverging business interests, and the growing number of private equity firms competing for business, it appeared uncertain whether private equity could reap the same profits as in previous years.

Nonetheless, into 2007 the private equity juggernaut continued (see Figure 2.4). In that year alone, private equity would raise more than $276 billion in new commitments, an amount that would sustain more than $1 trillion in new acquisitions.[66] As of March 2007, KKR alone had more than $53 billion in assets under management, and Blackstone had $78.7 billion.[67] All were prowling for acquisitions. In the first six months of 2007, private equity announced fully 50.6 percent of all U.S. acquisitions and more than $313.8 billion worth of

U.S. public acquisitions, including buy-outs of AllTel Corp., Bausch & Lomb Inc., ServiceMaster Co., and First Data Corp.[68] The media labeled private equity's managers the new titans (see Figure 2.5).

Meanwhile, private equity spearheaded the financial revolution. The firms increasingly put more sophisticated capital structures on their targets, including intricately layered senior, subordinated, unsecured, and preferred financing. The portfolio companies began to frequently dividend out cash from their acquisitions midstream, recapitalizing the companies and capturing value in real time. The result was to pry as much value as possible from the company through finance, slice the risk involved in the acquisition as discretely as possible, and allow for the minimum amount of equity to be placed on the acquired company. In doing so, private equity utilized the modern tools of financial engineering and the growing securitization market to price and sell these securities. Their techniques spilled over and began to be utilized in the more general takeover market. But their extreme resort to financial alchemy also engendered cries that their profits were simply the result of this magic rather than hard work.

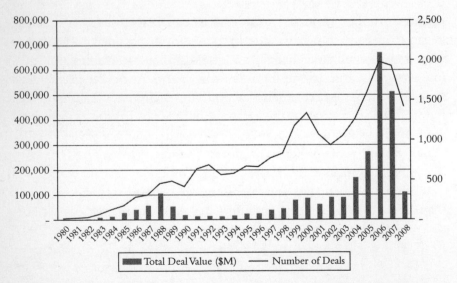

Figure 2.5   Private Equity Global Announced Takeovers (Value and Number) 1980–2008
SOURCE: Thomson Reuters (Includes all leveraged buy-outs)

Academics postulated that private equity's financing activities would spell the end of public markets as companies increasingly were acquired by private equity firms. The overregulation of Sarbanes–Oxley was particularly cited as a cause for the private equity boom. Companies were going private to avoid this regulation. Others cited the revolution in finance, which permitted more stable management of capital flows and allowed a company to avoid equity and the public markets as the cheapest cost bearer for risk.[69] Those who took this hypothesis and forecast the end of public markets were engaging in deliberate hyperbole. Private equity needed the public markets to exit their investments. Moreover, many private equity firms registered the debt of their newly acquired firms with the SEC, subjecting them to substantially the same regulatory requirements as when they were public.[70] The regulatory story thus also seemed overstated. Nonetheless, the talk spoke to private equity's lofty prominence.

Defying the criticism, private equity was again flying. The firms entered the summer of 2007 as the rulers of the capital markets egged on by the deal machine and the billions of fees private equity deals created. But many had forgotten a lesson from the 1980s; credit and private equity, like the economy, is cyclical. The up side of the cycle would not last. The seeds of private equity's downfall would lie in the SunGard transaction and private equity's life-need for debt financing. In 2007, private equity had paid the banks $15.6 billion in fees, and the banks jumped to do the firms' bidding.[71] In the midst of this, private equity had forgotten who was pet and who was master. It was the banks, and they would bite back savagely in the coming financial crisis.

Chapter 3

Accredited Home Lenders and the Attack of the MAC

The first hint of trouble came abruptly on February 27, 2007. On that day, the Dow Jones Industrial Average precipitously dropped 546 points, closing the day down by 3.29 percent, a fall mimicked in the other major indexes. The drop came unexpectedly and after a year of unusually low volatility in the stock markets. The source of the drop was hard to pinpoint; reports speculated that it was due to worry over a decline in the bubbling Chinese stock market, a possibly weakening U.S. economy, or remarks earlier that day by former chairman of the Federal Reserve Alan Greenspan.[1] Whatever the cause, at first it appeared to be a short-term blip. The markets would quickly bounce back, and investors would continue blithely along.

The drop would turn out to be a missed sign. A maelstrom was coming. Soon the implosion of the housing market and accompanying subprime mortgage crisis would initiate a parade of catastrophic events, including a steep decline in the stock market, credit and financial crises, a near market meltdown, and a sharp economic downturn. These events would buffet the capital markets and expose the faults and parameters of acquisition agreements and deals generally. In later stages of the crisis, deals would be stretched and stressed at every seam, as buyers struggled to escape contractual commitments and targets sought to hold buyers to their word. But in the beginning of this period, these disputes would focus on a clause embedded in acquisition agreements to address just such unexpected events: the material adverse change clause, or MAC. The financial crises' first echoes would produce a series of MAC claims, disputes that would markedly affect the course of later ill-fated takeover deals in 2008.

A MAC clause is a standard provision in acquisition agreements. It provides a buyer with the ability to terminate a deal when unexpected, bad events occur between the signing of the deal and its completion. They are thus the first option a buyer looks to in order to exit a deal. Their invocation beginning in August 2007, the start of the financial crisis, heralded a long period of disruption in takeovers, particularly private equity transactions.

The exact meaning of these clauses and the scope of their application has always been uncertain, though; their importance hidden from public view. The market turbulence caused by the subprime implosion and foreshadowed by the February market plummet would highlight the role of these clauses and their shortcomings. They would also bring a renewed focus on these clauses and their limitations.

One takeover, that of Accredited Home Lenders Holding Co. by the private equity firm Lone Star Funds, ably illustrates the issues surrounding MAC clause invocations in these early days of modern, distressed deal-making. This chapter is about the case of Accredited Home Lenders but also the MAC disputes that followed it. These later disputes are important because, together with the Accredited Home litigation, they showed how little latitude private equity firms had to escape their transactions through MAC claims. This would define the course and scope of the next wave of private equity failures to be discussed in Chapter 4.

The Fall of Accredited Home Lenders

The problems with the financial system began to come to light in the second quarter of 2007. It was in early April that New Century Financial

Corp., a leading subprime lender, filed for bankruptcy protection. Increased competition in the preceding years and dubious selling standards had led home lenders to lower their standards for creditworthy loans. Mortgage originators had simultaneously extended loans to increasingly riskier borrowers while accepting reduced profit margins. The model was inherently defective in that these borrowers often could not afford to service the loan in the long term. This rather large defect had been covered over by ever-rising house prices, which prevented borrowers from defaulting. Instead, these borrowers could simply refinance their mortgages or otherwise sell their houses to pay off their loans. The slowing housing market began to bring down this Ponzi scheme.

New Century was the first public victim, but as the market began to become aware of these problems, loan originators like Accredited Home Lenders found it increasingly difficult to sell the loans they had extended. Typically, loan originators sold these loans to investment banks or the government-sponsored entities Fannie Mae or Freddie Mac. The bought loans would then be grouped together and securitized, further sold as mortgage-backed securities. This would permit the loan originators to move the debt off their balance sheets, lock in their profits, and gain the capacity to extend new loans. It also enabled the mortgage originators to sell off these inherently risky and unstable mortgages, transferring the risk of default to third parties.

As the market deteriorated, mortgage buyers became skittish, offering lower prices or otherwise withdrawing from the market, further reducing the profit margin on the loans for originators such as Accredited Home Lenders. Also, as borrowers began to increasingly default, the supply of distressed loans on the market increased, further reducing loan prices and spurring still more defaults and lower prices. The downward spiral was both self-perpetuating and continuing. Consequently, loan originators became stuck with significantly devalued mortgages that had yet to be sold for securitization, resulting in margin calls from capital lenders. Accredited Home Lenders, a leading mortgage originator, was no exception, and it was hit by numerous margin calls beginning in early 2007. The entirety of the mortgage-brokering industry was beginning to feel the great pressure of the deflating housing bubble. It was payback for years of lax lending standards and a failure, or maybe prescience, to recognize market risks.[2]

Accredited was a leading subprime mortgage lender founded in 1990. It was still led by James A. Konrath who co-founded the company and served as its chairman and CEO. In February 2007, one analyst had described Accredited as the "best underwriter in the business . . . [and] the most efficient loan originator . . . [with a] more attractive corporate structure than many of its competitors [and] conservative [accounting and] plenty of liquidity."[3] The statement proved to be short-lived. In March 2007, Accredited disclosed just such liquidity problems and announced that it was "pursuing strategic options" to raise additional capital.[4] This type of language is code typically used by companies to inform the world that the board and management have decided to pursue a sale. At the time of the announcement, it was assumed in the market that Accredited was simply experiencing limited cash-flow difficulties. The analysts' view that Accredited was still one of the best positioned and run mortgage originators remained firm. In actuality, things were particularly bad for Accredited. The turmoil in the market had resulted in sustained losses for the company. Without additional capital, Accredited would have to file for bankruptcy.

Accredited's announcement started up the deal machine. Accredited's investment banker, the now-defunct Bear Stearns, began making the rounds to attempt to find a buyer by running an auction of the company. Bear Stearns was Accredited's historical banker, probably picked because of its strong background in structuring and trading mortgage securities, a connection that would come back to viciously haunt Bear Stearns, but then was viewed as a benefit for a quick sale.

The procedures for a company auction are fairly well set and a common way for public and private companies to sell themselves. First, a hired investment bank contacts interested parties, primarily strategic buyers and private equity firms. If the potential buyer expresses a desire to proceed, it signs a confidentiality agreement and receives an offering memorandum describing the for-sale company. The prospective buyers are then invited to submit preliminary indications of interest, including the range of prices they are willing to pay. From these indications, the seller decides whether to proceed and with whom. The field is narrowed to those buyers who provide acceptable indications. The remaining potential buyers then conduct due diligence, a technical term for an inspection of the company. During this time, an acquisition agreement is circulated, and sometimes another round of bids is requested and submitted. The remaining bidders then submit final bids with a marked-up agreement showing the terms they are willing to agree to in order to make the acquisition. The final negotiations then occur, and provided there is a winning bid, one acceptable to the seller's board, a buyer is picked and a deal announced.

The auction of Accredited largely followed this well-worn process. Between March 24 and April 9, 2007, 20 potentially interested parties entered into confidentiality agreements with Accredited and were provided access to company information. Meanwhile, in late 2006, Lone Star Funds had begun investigating acquiring or investing in a subprime lender. Lone Star, founded in 1995 and headed by John Grayken, is a private equity fund specializing in distressed acquisitions. Lone Star has invested in assets as diverse as golf courses in Japan, the Korea Exchange Bank, and Bi-Lo LLC, a chain of supermarkets headquartered in South Carolina.[5] Most famously, Lone Star's Korean Unit has been accused by the Korean government of illegally manipulating the stock price of Korea Exchange Bank to acquire it on the cheap, a claim that Lone Star has vigorously fought by claiming that the prosecution was politically motivated due to Lone Star's foreign status.

Lone Star entered the Accredited auction and submitted a second-round bid on June 1, 2007, along with four other bidders. This led to price negotiations between Lone Star and Accredited. Late on June 2, Accredited's special committee communicated that it would go forward with another bidder if Lone Star did not raise its bid, and Lone Star responded by making a final bid of $15.10 per share. On June 4, Accredited executed a definitive agreement with two affiliates of Lone Star. Lone Star had agreed to pay $15.10 a share in a deal valued at approximately $400 million. Lone Star had won its target. The heated competition showed that many informed people still thought that Accredited's and the industry's difficulties would be short-term and Accredited's capital troubles a passing phenomenon. They were, of course, completely, utterly wrong.[6]

Unaware of coming events, the parties now turned to completing the deal. Lone Star commenced its tender offer on June 19, 2007. Throughout July and into August, Lone Star extended the expiration dates for the tender offer a number of times. The extension was contemplated and necessary for Lone Star and Accredited to obtain approval for the transaction from lending regulators. The tender offer was conditioned on the receipt of regulatory approval from regulators in states representing 95 percent of Accredited's 2006 loan production volume. Lone Star was not required to close the tender offer until this condition was met.[7]

Accredited, though, continued to further deteriorate. On August 2, Accredited finally filed its overdue annual report with the SEC. In the report, Accredited's independent auditors qualified their 2006 audit opinion with the statement that Accredited may not "continue to operate as a going concern" and that its "financial and operational viability is uncertain."[8] This was auditor code for a possible bankruptcy.

The markets continued their own parallel decline. In June and July, two hedge funds run by Bear Stearns that invested in subprime mortgage securities, the High-Grade Structured Credit Enhanced Leveraged Fund and the High-Grade Structured Credit Fund, very publicly imploded, losing billions in capital.[9] A director of an agency rating service was quoted at the time as stating: "This is a watershed. . . . A leading player, which has honed a reputation as a sage investor in mortgage securities, has faltered. It begs the question of how other market participants have fared."[10] The implosion of these two funds and rapid decline of the housing market began to seep into the general market. Volatility increased almost exponentially, and the credit markets began to freeze up. Only a few months after Accredited's agreement to sell, the subprime crisis was becoming a general one, and Accredited's prospects were clearly diminished. Lone Star was now overpaying for its hard-won prize.

On August 10, 2007, Accredited announced that the required regulatory clearances had been received, satisfying the regulatory approval condition and clearing the way for Lone Star's tender offer to close. Later that day, Lone Star notified Accredited that it believed that Accredited would fail to satisfy the necessary conditions to close the tender offer. Lone Star was mum on what conditions were not met. However, it was widely speculated that Lone Star was asserting another condition to the tender offer had failed to be satisfied: namely, the condition requiring no MAC.

On August 11, Accredited responded to Lone Star's assertion by suing in Delaware Chancery Court. The suit was filed in Delaware because this was required by the forum selection clause in the acquisition agreement. That clause selected Delaware as the site of all litigation disputes between the parties. Lone Star responded to the suit on August 20, asserting that Accredited had indeed suffered a MAC.

Lone Star alleged a laundry list of adverse events in its answer to support its claim. It pointed to Accredited's recent disclosure in its annual report that it may not continue to operate as a going concern. In addition, Accredited's independent auditors had qualified their opinion. Management's projection of Accredited's losses for the third quarter had also increased from $64 million to $230 million in only a two-month period from May 28, 2007, to July 26, 2007.[11]

The day after Lone Star filed its answer, First Magnus Financial Corp., another large U.S. mortgage lender, filed for Chapter 11 bankruptcy protection.

Material Adverse Change Clauses

To fully understand the claims made by Lone Star, it is first necessary to understand the purpose and role a MAC clause plays in an acquisition agreement.

THE PARAMETERS OF AN ACQUISITION AGREEMENT

Acquisition agreements typically follow a standard format and structure. These agreements are necessary to govern payment of the consideration for the acquisition, as well as to privately order the parties' conduct between the time of the signing of the agreement and the completion of the acquisition. The following sets forth some typical terms in an acquisition agreement. For convenience, I have set out these items in their standard order of inclusion:

Section 1 (Form of Acquisition). Sets forth the form of the acquisition and whether it will be a merger, tender offer, asset sale, or other form of transaction. I further discuss the differences between these

(Continued)

forms of acquisition and the considerations informing this choice in Chapter 11.

Section 2 (Consideration). Sets forth the consideration to be received by the target and the mechanics of the consideration payment and calculation.

Section 3 (Target Representations and Warranties). Sets forth the representations and warranties of the target to the buyer. Representations and warranties are statements of fact about the target and provide the acquirer assurances as to the state of the target. A typical representation and warranty is that no MAC as defined in the agreement has occurred to the target since the date of the target's last full accounting period.

Section 4 (Buyer Representation and Warranties). Sets forth the representations and warranties of the buyer to the target. Typically, these are fewer than those made by the target, as the target is primarily concerned with the ability of the buyer to pay the consideration. If the buyer is paying stock consideration, the representations and warranties are usually more fulsome because the target's shareholders are effectively investing in the buyer.

Section 5 (Ordinary Course Covenant). Sets forth the agreements of the target to mandatorily operate the business in the ordinary course during the period between signing and closing.

Section 6 (Other Agreements). These include the obligations of the target and acquirer to prepare the necessary federal filings and hold the required shareholder meetings to complete the transaction, use some level of efforts to obtain regulatory clearances and other approvals, and, if applicable, obtain necessary financing. This section also sets forth the procedures a target must follow when considering or receiving a subsequent, higher bid by a third party.

Section 7 (Closing Conditions). These are the conditions to closing that must be satisfied for the parties to be required to complete the transaction. The failure of a condition allows a party to refuse to complete an acquisition. Typical conditions include obtaining regulatory clearances and shareholder approvals. Importantly, a standard condition is that the representations and warranties of the target be true and correct except as would have a MAC. Representations and warranties already qualified by MAC (such as the no MAC representation) are required to be true and correct in all respects. Thus, the MAC standard determines if the buyer is required to complete the transaction. This was the prime area of dispute during the MAC wars of 2007—buyers claimed that the no MAC representation was no longer true and therefore the related closing condition was not satisfied.

Section 8 (Termination and Expenses). Sets forth the termination rights of the parties. Typically, there is a drop-dead date, a date after which if the deal is still pending, it can be terminated by either party to the agreement. In addition, the termination and reverse termination fees are set forth here since they are triggered by a termination of the agreement. The reverse termination fee is often phrased as an aggregate cap on liability for the buyer.

Section 9 (Miscellaneous). These provisions contain the parties' choice of law and forum for disputes and other miscellaneous provisions. This section also typically contains a clause addressing the availability of specific performance in the transaction. It would be this last clause and its interaction with the liability cap often set forth in Section 8 (Termination and Expenses) that would spur the Cerberus–URI litigation discussed in Chapter 4.

The Purpose of a MAC Clause

A MAC clause is a device to allocate risk between a buyer and a seller. When a company like Accredited agrees to be acquired, there will typically be a period between the execution of the original acquisition agreement and completion of the transaction. During this period, necessary regulatory and shareholder consents required to complete the sale will be obtained. In particular, if the deal is in an amount greater than $260.7 million, adjusted each year for inflation, a mandatory waiting period for government antitrust review will need to elapse.[12] A MAC clause is a means for the parties to contractually allocate who will bear the risk of adverse events during this time between signing and closing.

The MAC clause is thus one of the most important provisions of the agreement. It is the catchall provision that provides the buyer the ability to walk, and it is a primary condition to deal completion. In deals without significant regulatory issues, it can be said that the entire agreement is really just one big MAC clause. Today, it is a particular focus of any takeover negotiation.[13]

An actual MAC clause is a defined term in the acquisition agreement. The seller will attempt to negotiate as narrow a definition as possible in order to place as much closing risk as possible on the acquiring entity. Conversely, the buyer will attempt to negotiate as broad a definition as feasible, one that will provide leeway to terminate the agreement in the event of postsigning adverse events. If you want to see the real beast, read the page-long MAC clause in Accredited's agreement with Lone Star.

MAC CLAUSE IN ACCREDITED'S AGREEMENT WITH LONE STAR

Section 1.01(A) (MAC Definition)

"Material Adverse Effect" means, with respect to [Accredited Home Lenders], an effect, event, development or change that is materially adverse to the business, results of operations or financial condition of [Accredited Home Lenders] and [Accredited Home Lenders'] Subsidiaries, taken as a whole; provided, however, that in no event shall any of the following, alone or in combination, be deemed to constitute, nor shall any of the following be taken into account in determining whether there has been, a Material Adverse Effect: (a) a decrease in the market price or trading volume of Company Common Shares (but not any effect, event, development or change underlying such decrease to the extent that such effect, event, development or change would otherwise constitute a Material Adverse Effect); (b) (i) changes in conditions in the U.S. or global economy or capital or financial markets generally, including changes in interest or exchange rates; (ii) changes in applicable Law or general legal, tax, regulatory or political conditions of a type and scope that, as of the date of this Agreement, could reasonably be expected to occur, based on information that is generally available to the public or has been Previously Disclosed; or (iii) changes generally affecting the industry in which [Accredited Home Lenders] and [Accredited Home Lenders'] Subsidiaries operate; provided, in the case of clause (i), (ii) or (iii), that such changes do not disproportionately affect [Accredited Home Lenders] and [Accredited Home Lenders'] Subsidiaries as compared to other companies operating in the industry in which [Accredited Home Lenders] and [Accredited Home Lenders'] Subsidiaries operate; (c) changes in GAAP; (d) the negotiation, execution, announcement or pendency of this Agreement or the transactions contemplated hereby or the consummation of the transactions contemplated by this Agreement, including the impact thereof on relationships, contractual or otherwise, with customers, suppliers, vendors, lenders, mortgage brokers, investors, venture partners or employees; (e) earthquakes, hurricanes, floods, or other natural disasters; (f) any affirmative action knowingly taken by [Accredited Home Lenders] or Purchaser that could reasonably be expected to give rise to a Material Adverse Effect (without giving effect to this clause (f) in the definition thereof); (g) any action taken by [Accredited Home Lenders] at the request or with the express consent of any of the Buyer Parties; (h) failure by [Accredited Home Lenders] or [Accredited Home Lenders'] Subsidiaries to meet any projections, estimates or budgets for any period prior to, on or after the dates of this Agreement (but not any effect, event, development or change underlying such failure to the extent such effect, event, development or change would otherwise constitute a Material Adverse Effect); (i) any deterioration in the business, results of operations, financial condition, liquidity, stockholders' equity and/or prospects of [Accredited Home Lenders] and/or [Accredited Home Lenders'] Subsidiaries substantially resulting from circumstances or conditions existing as of the date of this Agreement that were generally publicly known as of the date of this Agreement or that were Previously Disclosed; (j) any litigation or regulatory proceeding set forth in Section 5.09 of [Accredited Home Lenders'] Disclosure Schedule (but only to the extent of the specific claims and allegations comprising such litigation or regulatory proceeding existing as of the date of this Agreement; and (k) any action,

(Continued)

claim, audit, arbitration, mediation, investigation, proceeding or other legal proceeding (in each case whether threatened, pending or otherwise), or any penalties, sanctions, fines, injunctive relief, remediation or any other civil or criminal sanction solely resulting from, relating to or arising out of the failure by either [Accredited Home Lenders] or the Reporting Subsidiary to file in a timely manner its Annual Report on Form 10-K for the fiscal year ended December 31, 2006, its Quarterly Report on Form 10-Q for the quarter ended March 31, 2007, and/or the Quarterly Report on Form 10-Q for the second and third quarters of 2007.

The exact wording of a MAC clause traces back to bond indentures negotiated in nineteenth-century Britain. The substance of the wording has largely remained the same for this past century, but the actual wording varies from transaction to transaction and can be quite nuanced. For example, the Accredited MAC clause defined a MAC as "an effect, event, development or change that is materially adverse to the business, results of operations or financial condition of the Company and the Company's Subsidiaries, taken as a whole."[14] Translating this language, it means that a MAC for Accredited was whenever a single event or group of events, viewed collectively, negatively and materially impacted the entire business being sold.

Historically, this would be the entire clause. However, in the past two decades, practitioners have begun to negotiate carve-outs to this definition. These carve-outs define events that while materially adverse are excluded from the definition of a MAC clause. It is these exclusions that have become the focus of attorneys and are now the principal place in a MAC clause where buyers and sellers allocate closing risk.

The parties can agree to any carve-out they wish, but generally parties negotiate carve-outs that allocate market and systemic risk to the buyer and allocate closing risk to the seller for adverse events that particularly and disproportionately affect it. The reason for this is that the buyer is buying into an industry and an economy. The seller should not have to bear general risk that it cannot control and that the buyer would probably be subject to, no matter what its investment. Rather, the seller should only be responsible for the risks it can affect.

Two prominent academics have also speculated that MAC clauses generally incentivize a seller to maintain appropriate investment levels during signing and closing by allocating individualized risk to them.[15] The carve-outs are presumably merely an extension of this theory through their allocation of general risk to the buyer. However, the majority of takeovers are completed in one to three months, and therefore, these clauses appear unnecessary for ensuring investment. Moreover, other clauses in the agreement make certain that the company is operated in the ordinary course during this time period. Nonetheless, a MAC does place responsibility on the seller to ensure to the best it can that no adverse events occur. Another theory for the existence of MACs is that they are a symmetrical device. Target shareholders have a right to vote down the transaction or otherwise refuse to support it if the deal is no longer economical. A MAC provides a similar option to a buyer.[16] This latter explanation, though, does not fully explain the reason for MAC exclusions.

Whatever the reason for their inclusion, these carve-outs are privately negotiated and therefore can cover any exclusion the parties specify. Typically, these exclusions cover such acts as weather, terrorism, or war. But the two most significant carve-outs are the ones that exclude from a MAC any adverse events generally affecting the economy and the industry in which the company operates. Both of these exclusions provide broad ground for a seller to claim that a material adverse event has not occurred because it is something happening to other companies in its industry or the economy. Carve-outs particular to the seller are also often included. Common exclusions are for a failure of the seller to meet earnings projections and changes in the price of the securities of the issuer. In each such case, the actual adverse events causing such fluctuations are typically excluded from the carve-out but can still be exempted from being a MAC by another carve-out. Table 3.1 sets forth a study by the law firm of Nixon Peabody of the most common MAC exclusions utilized in acquisitions agreements during the period from June 1, 2007 through May 31, 2008.

Here, the Accredited MAC clause was unique for the strength of its exclusions. Accredited's MAC clause contained 13 carve-outs and

Table 3.1 Common MAC Exclusions

89%	"change in the economy or business in general"
70%	"changes in general conditions of the specific industry"
63%	"changes in laws or regulations"
60%	"changes due to acts of terrorism in the United States or abroad"
60%	"acts of war or major hostilities"
45%	"changes in the securities markets"
27%	"changes in interpretation of laws by courts or government entities"
25%	"changes caused by acts of God"
16%	"changes in interest rates"
12%	"natural calamities"

SOURCE: Nixon Peabody 2008 MAC Survey
www.nixonpeabody.com/publications_detail3.asp?ID=2474

excluded from the MAC definition (1) changes in conditions in the United States or global economy or capital or financial markets generally, (2) changes generally affecting the industry in which Accredited operated, and (3) any deterioration in the business of Accredited substantially resulting from circumstances or conditions known or previously disclosed to Lone Star. The auction for Accredited had been a hot one, and Accredited's lawyers had leveraged that demand to negotiate what they thought was a very tight MAC clause.

Like many remorseful buyers in this initial period, Lone Star thus had an uphill battle to prove a MAC. It was not only going to have to show a material adverse event but also have to prove that the decline in Accredited was unanticipated and that Accredited was uniquely impacted by these events in disproportion to the economy and Accredited's industry. Given the state of the subprime industry by September 2007, it was questionable whether even bankruptcy was a disproportionate event under Accredited's MAC clause.

The Law Governing MACs

Lone Star's case, though tough to establish, still had a chance at success. The facts as understood to Lone Star may indeed have established a MAC, or at least a colorable claim of one. This was not unique. A buyer invoking a MAC clause in an agreement is almost always uncertain of the ultimate validity of its claim. This is due to two reasons. First, MAC clauses are typically defined in qualitative terms and speak of adverse events. MAC clauses do not typically set forth quantitative thresholds, such as any event resulting in a loss of x dollars. Second, there is an unusual lack of case law setting forth what exactly is and is not a MAC.

The lack of case law interpreting MAC clauses is indicative of the pressures on parties to settle out of court. Most MAC disputes are settled before an opinion of a court is provided as to whether a MAC occurred. Nonetheless, parties still largely leave MAC clauses in an acquisition agreement undefined, referring to "material adverse effect" rather than a dollar amount to specifically define what *material* means. There is much speculation about why this practice continues, but a likely reason is that parties want to maintain the incentives and bargaining power an undefined MAC clause provides. When a MAC is undefined, there is uncertainty; this creates incentives on both sides to renegotiate the transaction, thereby saving it. Historically, these incentives were self-reinforcing because of the continued use of vague MAC clauses and the prior lack of significant and clear case law on the subject.

These uncertainties create a unique situation when an adverse event occurs. Because MACs are defined by reference to an adverse qualitative standard, a buyer may claim that a MAC has occurred for strategic reasons, perhaps because of buyer's remorse. In other words, a buyer like Lone Star may decide after the negotiation of a transaction that it no longer wishes to complete the acquisition. A buyer may invoke the MAC clause as an excuse to exit the transaction and as a way to limit its liability to the target. In this paradigm, the buyer will find an ostensible reason to claim a MAC to justify this position, but the validity of its ultimate claim in any litigation will be uncertain. This was the case of Accredited and Lone Star. Despite Lone Star's seemingly poor position, Lone Star no doubt invoked this MAC as a bargaining tool designed to leverage a renegotiation or exit from the deal. Lone Star's assessment of the validity of the MAC claim was a nonissue. It had enough evidence to invoke a MAC and thereby commence the rebargaining process.[17]

Lone Star may have still even wished to acquire Accredited, albeit at a lower price than first negotiated. Here, both parties were incentivized to renegotiate toward this lower price. Accredited would not want to risk the uncertainty of litigation and an adverse decision leaving its shareholders with no acquisition and premium for their shares. Conversely, Lone Star would not want to risk having to pay the full price for the seller if it was required to specifically perform under the agreement and complete the acquisition. These opposing forces worked toward a settlement.

This MAC strategy, the common one, allows a buyer to drive the price of an acquisition down by taking advantage of either changed market conditions or adverse events affecting the company to be purchased. Conversely, even though the buyer may utilize a MAC clause in this manner, a seller may also prefer a qualitative MAC clause in order to provide it with leeway to argue that an adverse event does not constitute a MAC. In both instances, the ambiguous wording of the MAC drives the parties toward settlement of their dispute, albeit at a lower, negotiated price. Contrast this with a MAC where an adverse event is defined in dollar terms. The bargaining incentives just described are absent, as the determination of a MAC can be ascertained numerically. The foregoing reasons are probably why MACs remain drafted in qualitative rather than quantitative terms.

This is not to say that there is no case law. Perhaps the most important decision prior to the financial crisis on the law of MACs was the 63-page opinion issued in 2001 by Vice Chancellor Leo E. Strine, Jr. of the Delaware Chancery Court in *In re IBP, Inc. Shareholders Litigation*.[18] This litigation arose over the agreed acquisition of IBP Inc., the largest U.S. meat producer and second largest pork producer, by Tyson Foods Inc., the poultry company. Tyson Foods had beaten back a competing bid by Smithfield Foods Co., the largest U.S. pork processor, and a management-led leveraged buy-out proposal to obtain a January 1, 2001, agreement to acquire IBP for approximately $4.7 billion.[19]

The Tyson Food win was short-lived. Soon thereafter, IBP announced its first quarter earnings; the figures were well below analysts' and Tyson Foods' estimates. Tyson Foods didn't take the failure well. It subsequently refused to close the acquisition and claimed that the earnings failure was a MAC to IBP, releasing Tyson Foods from its obligation to complete the deal. IBP responded by suing Tyson Foods in Delaware Chancery Court. This was one of the rare MAC cases not to settle before going to trial. The likely reason: Tyson's founder and controlling stockholder, Don Tyson, had decided that he no longer wanted to acquire IBP. He had ordered his son, Tyson's CEO John Tyson, to find a legal way to exit Tyson Foods' obligations. The MAC claim had followed.[20]

In his posttrial decision, Vice Chancellor Strine sided with IBP, agreeing that this was a case of buyer's remorse. In his opinion, Strine waxed eloquently about the role and meaning of MAC clauses, to conclude that:

> A buyer ought to have to make a strong showing to invoke a Material Adverse Effect exception to its obligation to close. Merger contracts are heavily negotiated and cover a large number of specific risks explicitly. As a result, even where a Material Adverse Effect condition is as broadly written as the one in the Acquisition agreement, that provision is best read as a backstop protecting the buyer from the occurrence of unknown events that substantially threaten the overall earnings potential of the target in a durationally-significant manner. A short-term hiccup in earnings should not suffice; rather the Material Adverse Effect should be material when viewed from the longer-term perspective of a reasonable buyer.[21]

In other words, a MAC was a safety valve, and a buyer would have to meet a high hurdle to establish one. The MAC had to be a significant, adverse event that was long term and durational in nature. Here, IBP's one quarter of earnings failure was a mere "hiccup," a "short-term" speed bump.[22] A specific failure to meet earnings projections without more was probably not a MAC. Vice Chancellor Strine further reinforced the high hurdle to invoke a MAC by finding that Tyson Foods should not be ordered to pay the usual remedy of monetary damages for breaching the contract by inappropriately claiming a MAC. Rather, Tyson Foods would be forced to specifically perform, that is, complete the acquisition. This was despite the fact that the acquisition agreement contained no clause providing for this remedy.[23]

Vice Chancellor Strine's decision finding no MAC was not a terrible surprise. His words largely reflected what practitioners thought was the law on MACs. By setting a relatively high threshold to establish a MAC, Strine allowed for the MAC test to be met only when the buyer was purchasing what it did not expect. If a buyer wanted a looser standard, it was welcome to negotiate one. In the wake of *IBP*, some speculated that MACs would be drafted in terms of dollar figures to ensure buyer certainty. This did not occur. The preference for qualitative MACs remained unchanged, and the only real shift was that sellers began to negotiate specific exclusions in MAC clauses for a failure to meet earnings projections.

The *IBP* decision was decided under New York law, the law selected by the parties in the acquisition agreement. Four years later, in *Frontier Oil Corp. v. Holly*,[24] the Delaware Chancery Court adopted *IBP*'s holding as Delaware law. Vice Chancellor Noble, the judge in *Frontier*, echoed the common notions of MAC jurisprudence when he stated: "The notion of an MAE is imprecise and varies both with the context of the transaction and its parties and with the words chosen by the parties."[25] Vice Chancellor Noble then adopted the holding of *IBP* as the law of Delaware. In doing so, he reiterated the requirement that the burden of proof rests on the party seeking to rely on the MAC clause. In the case of *Frontier*, it meant that "substantial" litigation costs and the potential of a "catastrophic" judgment of "hundreds of millions of dollars" did not constitute a MAC.[26] The reason was alarmingly simple. The substantial defense costs could be borne by the buyer without a MAC, and the buyer had not borne its burden to prove that the speculative nature of the potential damages in this case actually resulted in an adverse effect under the MAC definition. A MAC needed to be concrete in measure.

Taken together, *IBP*, as interpreted by *Frontier*, placed a substantial burden on a remorseful buyer attempting to prove a MAC. But the opinions left open a number of questions:

How bad did the adverse event have to be? Vice Chancellor Strine implied in his opinion that adverse equated with quite bad, and *Frontier* appeared to set an even higher watermark by failing to find a MAC because of a potential catastrophic loss. Though the cases left this open, the general practitioner thinking in light of both *IBP* and *Frontier* was that an adverse event resulting in a 10 percent or more decline in income would be sufficient to sustain a MAC claim. Here, some practitioners argued that before *IBP* the measure of materiality for a

MAC was analogous to the measure under U.S. Generally Accepted Accounting Principles (GAAP) rules, or a 5 percent drop in earnings. This difference of opinion again reflected the insufficient case law on MACs and their qualitative nature.[27]

When could specific performance be ordered? Vice Chancellor Strine stunned the takeover community by ordering specific performance of Tyson's merger obligations. This was the first time that a judge had ordered specific performance in a MAC case. But historically under the common law, specific performance was a remedy to be awarded only when monetary damages were inadequate. If a deal involved cash, presumably specific performance was not warranted unless the parties preagreed to such a remedy. Vice Chancellor Strine's opinion instead relied on Tyson's failure to argue the issue and the complications of determining a monetary remedy to justify an order of specific performance. Still, the *IBP* opinion left open the issue of when specific performance could be awarded in a MAC case or in an acquisition agreement involving cash consideration generally. Moreover, the *IBP* case also provided an additional incentive for a buyer to assert a MAC. The worst case scenario for a buyer asserting a MAC appeared to be that it had to complete the buy-out it had already agreed to.[28]

There was also the role and effect of exclusions on a MAC. Prior to the Accredited dispute, no courts had interpreted or looked at the effect of the MAC exclusions on a MAC claim. This was not surprising. The development of MAC exclusions was a recent phenomenon, and even the MAC clause in the Tyson's deal did not contain any. In the past decade, though, carve-outs had multiplied and become standard. One study found that by 2005, the average MAC clause had 6.5 carve-outs.[29] This was a drastic change when compared with MACs in the early 1990s, when only 20 percent of those had even contained a carve-out.[30] These carve-outs came in all types. In its 2007 MAC survey, the law firm Nixon Peabody listed 32 different types of carve-outs.[31]

The stunning growth in carve-outs and the reasons for their rise pose a puzzle. The carve-outs favored the seller but, in some respects, largely replicated the consensus MAC interpretation. The buyer was assuming the general risk while a MAC was meant to pick up significantly adverse events affecting only the seller. An exclusion for changes to the industry or the economy to a large extent duplicated what was already embedded in the commonly understood MAC definition.

But attorneys could use negotiated carve-outs to show value to clients. The more or fewer carve-outs negotiated, the better the job the lawyer could show to the client. The number reflected the bargaining power of the parties. Hence, it was no surprise that one study found that the more MAC carve-outs, the more likely the deal was to close.[32] Not only did carve-outs limit the outs of a buyer but also the number reflected a buyer's willingness to buy. The result was carve-out creep. New exclusions were being negotiated yearly, and the standard MAC was running 10 to 20 lines of text. Yet the scope and interpretation of these carve-outs had yet to be judicially addressed.

When Lone Star made its MAC claim, it thus had the guidance of *IBP* and *Frontier* but no answers to these open questions. The parties' arguments in this dispute unfolded around these uncertainties. Accredited's defense avoided the question of whether a material adverse change had occurred. It almost certainly had. Accredited was about to go bankrupt without this acquisition. Rather, Accredited argued that one of the 13 exclusions applied or, conversely, the events Lone Star now claimed to be a MAC were known at the time.

This left a number of areas for both Lone Star and Accredited to litigate. For example, under this standard MAC exclusion, was Accredited's performance really worse than others in the industry? Since early 2007, a significant number of mortgage brokers or originators had filed for bankruptcy. *Materially disproportionate* in this circumstance was almost undefinable. What was disproportionate anyway? Was it a dollar worse than everyone else, or did it have to be significant or constitute a material adverse effect in and of itself? There was literally no law on this.

The MAC Wars of Fall 2007

The Accredited MAC quarrel was one of the first of a number to emerge in the fall of 2007. These MAC disputes largely followed the same pattern as the Accredited litigation. The parties largely focused their arguments on the exclusions to the MAC clause and whether and how they were implicated.

Almost at the same time as Accredited's misfortunes, Radian Group Inc., a company in the subprime mortgage lending business, suffered a similar MAC claim. Radian had agreed to a merger of equals with rival Mortgage Guaranty Insurance Corporation (MGIC) in a deal valued at almost $4.9 billion when announced. On August 7, 2007, MGIC publicly disclosed that it believed a material adverse change had occurred with respect to Radian. MGIC claimed a MAC based on a $1 billion loss suffered by C-Bass LLC, a subprime loan subsidiary jointly owned by MGIC and Radian.[33] The MGIC-Radian MAC dispute raised a similar issue as the Accredited one, namely, the question of whether the adverse event to Radian was disproportionate under the industry exclusion in their agreement's MAC clause.

On August 21, 2007, MGIC sued Radian in federal district court in Milwaukee to obtain information from Radian to definitively determine whether a MAC had occurred. This tactic was not uncommon in the MAC wars of 2007. The buyer would make a claim that a MAC might have arisen but not actually claim one, instead suing to force the target to provide more information for such a determination. This maneuver allowed the buyer to stall for time and attempt to settle the claim while preserving its option to complete the transaction. MGIC's suit in Milwaukee also highlighted the importance of forum selection clauses in these disputes. The MGIC-Radian acquisition agreement stipulated that the parties accepted jurisdiction for any suit in the courts of New York. However, this was not a mandatory requirement. MGIC was therefore able to sue in a Milwaukee court, its headquarters, establishing home court advantage for any subsequent MAC litigation.[34]

Two weeks later on September 5, the parties suddenly and jointly announced the termination of their transaction. This was the first deal during the emerging financial crisis to be terminated on MAC grounds. It was also a clean break, and neither party paid any funds to the other. This was a bit surprising. Based on the publicly available facts, Radian appeared to have reasonable grounds to deny that a MAC had occurred. C-Bass, the affected subsidiary, was jointly owned by the parties, and the MAC industry exclusion in their agreement provided a firm defense that Radian's troubles were borne equally by the entire industry. Nonetheless, Radian chose to drop its claims. Presumably, Radian was much more aware of the facts of their case. Radian's shareholders were to receive stock in the combined entity, and so Radian may no longer have viewed MGIC as a particularly good investment. The settlement also highlighted why there is so little case law on MACs. The parties typically resolve these cases by terminating the deal or renegotiating the price, rather than going to trial. As was also typical in these disputes, neither Radian nor MGIC disclosed any significant information about the merits of each party's case or the reasons for settlement.

The largest MAC dispute to arise during this period was the October 2007 litigation surrounding the $25.3 billion buy-out of SLM Corp., otherwise known as Sallie Mae, by a consortium led by the J.C. Flowers Group. In that dispute, the J.C. Flowers Group, and its partners Bank of America Co. and JPMorgan Chase & Co., alleged that Congress's new student education bill, the College Cost Reduction and Access Act of 2007, had resulted in a MAC to SLM.[35] SLM countered that this legislation was not a MAC because the MAC clause in their agreement specifically excluded:

> changes in Applicable Law provided that, for purposes of this definition, "changes in Applicable Law" shall not include any changes in Applicable Law relating specifically to the education finance industry that are in the aggregate more adverse to [SLM] than the legislative and budget proposals described under the heading "Recent Developments" in the Company 10-K. . . . [36]

This double-negative clause excluded changes from applicable law out of the MAC definition. The Congressional bill was surely that. However, the clause then put back into the MAC clause any changes engendered by legislation that were collectively more adverse than disclosed in SLM's annual report filed with the SEC on Form 10-K. The parties seemed to agree that the Congressional bill was a material adverse effect on SLM causing a significant long-term decline in its earnings. However, the parties disputed whether the change was more adverse than what was in the SEC filings. The Flowers consortium argued that disproportional needed to be only $1 more, while SLM argued disproportional was something materially adverse.[37]

The contract language favored Flowers. The parties had bargained for this legislative change, and the risk appeared to have been allocated to Flowers only up to what had been disclosed in SLM's 10-K. But the chairman of SLM, Albert L. Lord, took the whole thing personally, attending the hearings in Delaware and arguing that this was not the case. At first, he refused to settle for anything less than the initial price the Flowers consortium had agreed to pay. Lord rejected a renegotiation offer by the consortium to reduce the consideration from approximately $60 a share in cash to $50 a share in cash and $7 to $10 a share in warrants.[38] Market observers called Lord's stance foolish, one based on his ego-driven view of SLM and the transaction. Lord too late came to agree with these observers, after the Flowers group withdrew their offer. By December 2007, Lord was reduced to arguing for a deal at any price, stating: "The [original] objective was to do a transaction at $60 [per share]. The ongoing objective is to do a transaction at a price that shareholders would accept."[39]

In the SLM and Accredited cases, we were left with no judicial answer as to whether a MAC actually existed. The better argument in the Accredited case appeared to be that the MAC was excused because Accredited's failings were no worse than what had happened in the general industry. Lone Star also knowingly bought into Accredited's problems. Conversely, SLM seemed to be hit harder than expected and more disproportionately than others in its industry, an event that put them outside the safe harbor of their specifically bargained-for MAC exclusion.

The uncertainties over the scope and meaning of these clauses played out as they typically do in MAC disputes—toward settlement. On September 19, 2007, Accredited announced that it had settled its dispute with Lone Star and agreed to be bought out for $11.75 a share. The fact that the price was relatively close to the original one of $15.10 per share reflected the parties' assessment of the risks of litigation. Accredited's troubles were being experienced throughout the mortgage industry and were driven by the general decline in the economy and the housing market. These supported a strong argument against Lone Star's MAC claim.

SLM, after a management upheaval, settled in exchange for a new financing package from Bank of America and JPMorgan Chase & Co. The deal was canceled, but this was probably due to the existence of a private equity acquisition structure that capped the liability of the SLM buyers to a maximum of $700 million. The settlement amount was hard to calculate but appeared to be far less than the $700 million cap. Again, the settlement reflected the relative merits of the parties' claims and appeared to show that SLM lost badly.

Accredited and these other early MAC cases set an example. Going into the financial crisis, any MAC claim was likely to face a high hurdle and would probably depend on the applicability of the MAC exclusions. Still, even a colorable MAC claim could work to advantage a buyer and force a settlement. Here, as J.C. Flowers found to its benefit in the SLM dispute, the wording of the MAC could make the difference in the scope and amount of the settlement. This would lead to more creative deal-escape strategies as the financial crisis progressed into 2008 and it became increasingly difficult to prove a MAC in light of the general downturn.

The MAC Clause in Flux

The two major MAC cases to go to trial during this time highlighted the difficulty of establishing a MAC claim in court. The first of these was the litigation between the shoe retailers Genesco Inc., and The Finish Line Inc. The Genesco–Finish Line dispute was perhaps the most unfortunate of the fall 2007 period. In an auction before the financial crisis, Finish Line had outbid Foot Locker, Inc. to acquire Genesco. Finish Line was the minnow swallowing the whale. Finish Line was a third the size of Genesco; to pay for the deal, it was going to borrow almost the entire $1.5 billion purchase price from its investment banker, UBS AG.[40] After the announcement of the deal, the market jeered at this extreme leverage, and Finish Line's stock slumped.

In August 2007, Genesco announced disappointing quarterly earnings. Finish Line's banker and investment adviser UBS promptly abandoned Finish Line. UBS claimed that the combined entity would be insolvent and that it was no longer obligated to finance the acquisition.

Unfortunately for Finish Line, its lawyers had negotiated an agreement that did not contain a financing condition and provided for specific performance of the agreement. Finish Line was left obligated to consummate an acquisition that it couldn't pay for and its shareholders did not want. Instead, it did the only thing it could do; it asked the court to declare that a MAC to Genesco had occurred.[41]

This case was different. The acquisition agreement was governed by Tennessee law and selected Tennessee as the forum for all disputes. This was not a Delaware case, with experienced judges and courts versed in business disputes and the governing precedent. Rather, the judge, though quite intelligent, was a local judge in Nashville, and this appeared to be her first significant national business dispute.

It was also the first MAC case to be litigated in Tennessee under the laws of that state. The opinion in the dispute reflected this.[42] The judge in the case found that there was no MAC because the MAC exclusion for general economic conditions applied. The court relied on Genesco's expert testimony that high gas, heating, oil, and food prices; housing and mortgage issues; and increased consumer debt loads were generally responsible for Genesco's condition. She also found that Genesco's decline was not disproportionate to others in the industry and, therefore, no MAC had occurred. The opinion did not provide any guidance beyond the unique situation of the parties or on what exactly *disproportionate* means. Because of this, it is likely to have little precedential effect on future MAC cases. Like most other MAC cases, the Genesco–Finish Line dispute was ultimately settled before appeal. It was a smart move for Finish Line. If it had lost, Finish Line would have probably faced bankruptcy. UBS, which had turned on Finish Line, its own client, escaped with a small payment to Genesco of $136 million,[43] small penance for its misdeeds and betrayal.

The second MAC opinion issued during the financial crisis came later in September 2008. It was issued by Vice Chancellor Stephen P. Lamb in the litigation between the chemical makers Huntsman Corp. and Hexion Specialty Chemicals, Inc. Hexion, a portfolio company of the private equity firm the Apollo Group, had agreed to acquire Huntsman back in the heady days of July 2007, beating out a competing bid by the Dutch chemical company Basell AF. The deal had remained outstanding into 2008, as the parties waited for regulatory clearances and Hexion developed a case of buyer's remorse. When these regulatory approvals appeared imminent, Hexion finally could delay no longer and sued Huntsman in Delaware Chancery Court, claiming that it was no longer obligated to complete the acquisition because the combined entity would be insolvent and, in any event, Huntsman had experienced a MAC.[44] At the time of the suit, Peter R. Huntsman, the founder of Huntsman, denied the claims and issued a statement:

> Apollo's recent action in filing this suit represents one of the most unethical contract breaches I have observed in fifty years of business. Leon Black and Josh Harris [the heads of Apollo] should be disgraced. Our company will fight Apollo vigorously on all fronts.[45]

Vice Chancellor Lamb agreed with Huntsman as to the validity of Hexion's MAC claim. Lamb relied heavily on *IBP* to describe a MAC as being a "significantly durational" adverse event "expected to persist in the future."[46] In Huntsman's case, there was no MAC to its business, since Huntsman's 2007 EBITDA, or earnings before interest, taxes, depreciation, and amortization, was only 3 percent below its 2006 EBITDA. In addition, its 2008 EBITDA would be only 7 percent below its 2007 EBITDA. Lamb found that since EBITDA is independent of capital structure, it is a better measure of the operational results of a business for determining a MAC. Here, he held that the burden is on the buyer to prove a MAC, unless otherwise agreed by the parties.

Moreover, to determine a MAC, Vice Chancellor Lamb refused to consider projections of Huntsman's future performance, instead preferring to ascertain a MAC by reviewing a year-to-year comparison of results. He did not rely on projections because of standard disclaimers about reliance on projections in the parties' acquisition agreement. He also implied that he would have done so even without this disclaimer language, as actual year-to-year earnings are a better measure of a MAC. This was a significant finding and largely eliminated any forward-looking element to the typical MAC. In this case, it made a difference. According to forecasts from Huntsman management, Huntsman's EBITDA projections for 2008 have gone from $1.289 billion as of June 2007 to $863 million at the time of trial, a significant decline. This probably put Huntsman in the range of a MAC claim before the exclusions were accounted for.

Vice Chancellor Lamb finally ruled that the carve-outs to the MAC come into play only if there is indeed first a MAC. He rejected Hexion's argument that "the relevant standard to apply in judging whether an MAE has occurred is to compare Huntsman's performance since the signing of the acquisition agreement and its expected future performance to the rest of the chemical industry."[47] Hexion made this argument based on an exclusion in the MAC clause for changes in the chemical industry generally. Instead, Lamb first looked to whether a material adverse change had occurred to the Huntsman business before even turning to the exclusions. Since he found that no such material adverse change had occurred, he never looked to see if the exclusions applied.

The Future of the MAC

The great MAC wars of 2007 and the coda with Huntsman in 2008 confirmed the high bar a court would set before it would find a MAC. It also left open continuing questions about the scope of a MAC. In the period from August 2007 through August 2008, MAC claims were publicly made in approximately 5 to 10 transactions, with only 2 going to trial; the remainder settled before a judicial opinion could be issued. In both trials, the judge found that a MAC had not occurred. In fact, no Delaware court has found a MAC . . . ever. The consequence is that in future disputes, targets are likely to resist these claims in greater measure. Furthermore, the role and nature of the MAC exclusions appear to be increasingly important. Yet, the uncertainties as to the appropriate role and interpretation of these exclusions remain, even after the wreckage of these disputes had cleared.[48]

A MAC creates option value for a buyer. It provides the buyer an ability to abandon the acquisition in certain adverse circumstances. Conversely, the target has its own option to put the company to the buyer at a set or renegotiated price. This is value that should be reflected in the deal price and the negotiation. But in practice, deal pricing generally occurs before the negotiation of the MAC. The details are worked out after price is agreed. The price and the bargaining power it implies drive the negotiation. This is arguably reflected in the number of exclusions.

The events of 2007 and 2008 confirm the most important reason for a MAC clause. A MAC provision is a prenegotiated bargaining tool to preserve value for the target and buyer. It allows the parties to ensure that if there is a significant deterioration of the target, both parties preserve value. The target does not lose entirely in such an instance, as it can still leverage the dynamics of a MAC to renegotiate the price, albeit for a lower amount. Similarly, the buyer can utilize the same dynamics to forgo paying the prior full price, paying a reduced amount. In both circumstances, the buyer is still purchasing the business for a reduced value that it finds acceptable taking into account litigation risk. This is a situation a target similarly finds itself in a MAC renegotiation. In light of the recent market events, a MAC is therefore best seen as a bonding device to ensure a renegotiation and loss sharing in the event of an adverse event. In other words, it is a form of insurance for both sides.[49]

It would thus appear that the point of a MAC clause as the fulcrum of the agreement has been lost. In England and other jurisdictions, agreements are simplified with a bare MAC. Lawyers no doubt find that they can show value to clients by negotiating 20 pages of representations and warranties that must be true as of closing if the buyer is going to be required to complete the acquisition. In the end, these are qualified by MAC and so in essence really just a form of MAC themselves. Moreover, the number of exclusions has grown, but in the repeated negotiation of these carve-outs has occurred a failure to recognize that the meaning and effect of these exclusions is unknown.

Only a few exclusions actually ever came into play in these disputes. The remainder appear to be gravy and boilerplate exclusions included on a pro forma basis with little meaning. How and why did we get here? It is time to rethink the wording and scope of MAC clauses. Unfortunately, change, if it comes, though, is likely to go in the opposite direction, making MAC clauses more complex rather than clearer and simpler. The reason is the role of lawyers. Attorneys want to show value, and simplifying would be out of line with prior precedent. We are therefore probably stuck with a burgeoning world of MAC clauses, with sparse case law to guide us through this morass. This is why the Accredited case was important. The settlement provided guidance to others in the financial crisis as to how parties should assess the validity of a MAC.

In the few cases the Delaware courts have considered a MAC, the courts appear to have set a high burden of proof for buyers. The Delaware courts are on solid ground to set a sizable threshold for finding a MAC. Economically, a buyer can compensate for the specific risk of its target by negotiating an agreement and due diligence, that is, preacquisition investigation of the target. When unexpected events occur, the risk of loss is now just a zero sum game. Will it be allocated to the target's shareholders or the buyer? By erecting a hard rule in prior and future cases, the Delaware courts ensure that parties who really want to avoid this problem will draft around it. Moreover, this will ensure that the MAC clause is not triggered by systemic risk, risk that cannot be avoided.

By keeping the wording vague, MAC clauses encourage parties to renegotiate and allocate this loss. However, by setting the bar too high, Delaware courts risk upsetting this renegotiation game and the insurance purpose of a MAC by creating too much certainty in a MAC renegotiation. After all, it is the uncertainty of a MAC that creates these options for target and buyer and bonds the parties further in any renegotiation. In further interpreting *IBP*, *Frontier*, and *Huntsman*, the Delaware courts would do well to preserve the opening for a MAC assertion to leave room for renegotiation. Thus, the true impact of these cases will come in later disputes as the standards they set are fleshed out.

Attorneys would do well to simplify MACs, but it will be in the courts where the MAC is actually further defined. Once again, there has been practitioner talk of converting MACs to dollar amounts in light of the *Huntsman* case. Given the MAC's traditional role of ensuring a renegotiation, a numerical MAC is not likely to gain widespread adoption. Thus, while lawyers may indeed go against their penchant for complexity, and exclusions may be cut back or vary in language, it will be the courts that continue to flesh out the scope of the MAC. Nonetheless, in light of the financial crisis, there has been one observed change to MAC clauses: Some of these clauses now expressly override the Delaware holding that a MAC must be of a long-term durational nature and contractually include short-term effects. It remains to be seen if the MAC is further affected by drafting changes spurred by the financial crisis.

Regardless of the future of the MAC, by the end of fall 2007, the parameters of a MAC clause dispute had been set and the difficulty of establishing a MAC affirmed. These events would steer the next wave of deal failures, the private equity implosion.

Chapter 4

United Rentals, Cerberus, and the Private Equity Implosion

The unfortunate experiences of Accredited, Radian, and SLM were the first signs of significant disruption in the takeover market. As the credit crisis continued, they would be only three of many failed and renegotiated takeover transactions. At the time, though, these disputes appeared to be unique, a function of the nature of the company's business, in the case of Radian and Accredited, or the specific bargained-for wording of a MAC clause in the case of SLM. But as the August disruption continued, stock market volatility increased, the credit markets became increasingly illiquid, and the subprime mortgage crisis began to spread generally into the markets and the economy. These events turned public attention to the viability of pending takeover transactions in other industries. The bulk of pending takeovers were sponsored by private equity, the dominant force of that time. As of August 1,

2008, more than $250 billion in pending private equity transactions were awaiting financing and completion.[1]

A number of public commentators and news sources began to report on the optionality inherent in the private equity acquisition agreement, the reverse termination structure discussed in Chapter 2. Many of these reports questioned the willingness of private equity firms to complete these acquisitions. The first prominent news piece, published in the *New York Times* on August 21, 2007, was titled "Can Private Equity Firms Get Out of Buy-outs?"[2] The article, by Andrew Ross Sorkin, highlighted the reverse termination fee structure, detailed the current uncertainties of financing, explored the willingness of private equity buyers to terminate these transactions, and discussed the reputational constraints on the ability of private equity firms to do so.

Sure enough, beginning in August and through mid-November 2007, private equity firms in three pending public transactions with reverse termination fee structures did indeed attempt to terminate acquisitions agreed to prior to the summer credit crisis. These involved the already discussed buy-out of SLM Corporation and two others: the $3 billion buy-out of Acxiom Corporation, the marketing services provider, and the $8 billion buy-out of Harman International, Inc., the legendary audio company, still run by its 89-year-old founder Sidney Harman. In each case, the private equity buyers did not invoke the reverse termination fee provisions negotiated in their transaction agreements. These private equity buyers instead asserted real or ostensible MAC claims to terminate their obligations.

The presence of a reverse termination fee would work to alter the traditional mechanics of the MAC dispute. This was illustrated in both Harman's and Acxiom's cases. In each of these deals, the grounds for the MAC assertion were never made clear, at least publicly. But the buyers in each obviously felt that the deal no longer made economic sense or otherwise could not be financed. These buyers therefore exercised the MAC clauses in their agreements for at least three reasons: First, the deterioration in the markets and general economy provided a colorable basis to make this assertion. In the cases of Acxiom and Harman, there were also specific claims that each company had deteriorated disproportionately to their peers.[3] Second, a MAC claim provided reputational cover. Instead of being labeled as walking on their contractual obligations, a MAC claim provided historically legitimate grounds for a buyer to terminate the transaction. It is generally perceived as acceptable for a buyer to invoke a MAC. Third, a MAC claim provided negotiating leverage to the private equity firm. Under the terms of each of these agreements, if the private equity firm was successful in claiming a MAC, it could terminate the agreement without any required payment to the target.

Moreover, the maximum liability of the private equity firms if their MAC claim failed was capped at the reverse termination fee. It would otherwise be zero if a MAC claim could be proved. Thus, any negotiation between the parties would start at the maximum number set by the reverse termination fee and go only down. This last dynamic would affect the incentives of private equity buyers to renegotiate the transaction. As discussed in the preceding chapter, in a traditional MAC dispute, the terms of the acquisition agreement placed pressure on the buyer to renegotiate because the buyer feared losing the dispute and paying a full purchase price for the target. This never became an issue in a private equity agreement with a reverse termination fee. The reverse termination fee served as a significantly reduced cap on the maximum liability of a buyer, approximately 3 percent of the deal value. The negotiation thus revolved around how much of the reverse termination fee the buyer would pay and not on a renegotiation of the transaction. The settlement incentive present in ordinary, strategic transactions was thus markedly lower.

The failed Harman and Acxiom deals proved this point. Both transactions were ultimately terminated through an agreement among the parties. The Acxiom deal was terminated on October 1, and Harman was terminated officially on October 22. The legitimacy of these MAC claims and the effect of the reverse termination fee provision on the settlement were reflected by the amounts the private equity firms ultimately paid to the targets to terminate the transaction. This amount was the parties' assessment of success in any litigation. This was good proof that the parties did not think that the MAC claims would succeed in litigation, but rather were instead brought to provide reputational cover for these terminations.

In the Acxiom termination, the two buyers, Silver Lake and ValueAct Capital LLC, paid $65 million to terminate the transaction. The Acxiom agreement provided for a two-tiered reverse termination fee. The lower fee of $66.75 million was payable if there was a failure of debt financing; the higher amount of $111.25 million functioned as a maximum cap on the buyers' liability.[4] It was never disclosed why the two buyers' payment was $1.75 million less than the lower fee. But the fact that the settlement approximated the lower fee probably meant that the lenders on the deal were balking at funding the transaction, providing a basis for the buyers to set their maximum liability at $66.75 million. This was subsequently confirmed by news reports that half of the fee paid to Acxiom was paid by Morgan Stanley and UBS, two of the three banks financing the deal.[5]

Meanwhile, the amount of the payment in the Harman termination was disguised; KKR and GS Capital Partners, the private equity buyers, elected to buy convertible notes worth $400 million in Harman yielding 1.25 percent per annum and initially convertible at $104 per share. The notes were clearly priced to provide an additional benefit to Harman, and though the benefit was difficult to calculate, the true payment appeared to approximate the reverse termination fee.[6]

In Federalist Paper Number 15, Alexander Hamilton observed that reputation is a "less active influence" constraining behavior when a nefarious deed is done by many. Hamilton's observation aptly applies to the events surrounding the fall 2007 wave of private equity acquisition terminations. Initially, no single private equity firm was willing to stain its reputation and harm its competitive position in the buy-out market by invoking a reverse termination fee provision. Instead, in the Acxiom and Harman deals, these firms asserted MAC claims to publicly justify termination and avoid being labeled as walking on their transactions and as an untrustworthy future buyer. However, as the fall progressed, the reputational forces on private equity firms to complete buy-outs became diluted as the credit markets remained illiquid and the number of terminated private equity deals increased. The early fall MAC cases like Accredited had also illustrated the high hurdle a buyer had to jump to establish even a colorable MAC claim. These forces would combine to shape the next wave of failed private equity acquisitions.

The Cerberus–United Rentals Dispute

On November 14, 2007, a private equity fund controlled by Cerberus Capital Management LP, the hedge fund and private equity firm, suddenly attempted to terminate its $5 billion agreement to acquire United Rentals Inc., the rental equipment provider. Cerberus did not assert a MAC to justify its action. Cerberus actually went out of its way to note that no MAC had occurred and confirmed this to United Rentals at the time it terminated the agreement.[7] Rather, the shell subsidiaries owned by Cerberus who were the parties to this agreement simply invoked the reverse termination provision in the acquisition agreement.[8] Cerberus argued that this provision permitted it to terminate its obligations for any reason upon payment of a $100 million reverse termination fee.

Cerberus had decided that any reputational impact was overcome by the declining economic return of the transaction. In assessing the reputational damage, Cerberus was no doubt influenced by the prior failure of private equity transactions in Acxiom, Harman, and SLM and the atmosphere they created, which diminished the reputational impact for simply walking on a transaction. Cerberus itself was also operating under a tarnished halo, as only a few weeks before, it had abruptly terminated preliminary negotiations to buy out Affiliated Computer Services, Inc. This and Cerberus's status as a nontraditional private equity investor—its roots were as a hedge fund—may have made it only easier for it to spurn United Rentals.

United Rentals sued the Cerberus shell subsidiaries in Delaware Chancery Court, challenging their attempt to terminate the agreement. United Rentals argued that the acquisition contract allowed United Rentals to force the shell subsidiaries to specifically perform their obligations. In other words, the parties' dispute centered on the type of reverse termination fee structure they had negotiated, the pure reverse termination fee or specific performance structure. United Rentals argued that this contract provided for specific performance of the shell subsidiary entities' financing commitments (i.e., United Rentals could force the shell subsidiaries to take the actions agreed to in their agreement). Only if the financing then failed could the entities terminate the agreement. The Cerberus shell entities argued that the same language of the contract barred specific performance and that their only liability was for $100 million.[9]

These were diametrically opposed arguments. Under Cerberus's argument, it could walk at any time and for any reason, simply by paying

$100 million. United Rentals argued that the same acquisition agreement provided United Rentals the right to force Cerberus to complete the acquisition. The problem was that both were arguably right. The contract language was ambiguous and could reasonably be interpreted to support either position. This was remarkable. The contract on the $5.4 billion deal had been negotiated by two top law firms, Simpson Thacher, & Bartlett, LLP and Lowenstein Sandler, PC, yet you could not definitively determine the parties' rights to terminate it. If you read the language, it did appear that United Rentals had the better argument, but it was not clearcut by any means. Unlike Acxiom, Harman, and SLM, Cerberus had the real possibility of having to do more than pay a reverse termination fee. They may actually have been required to complete the transaction.[10]

It would later be rumored that a settlement was not reached because of Cerberus CEO Stephen Feinberg's insistence that there be a meaningful reduction of the purchase price and United Rentals refusal to accede to this request.[11] The trial was held in Delaware Chancery Court from December 17 to 19. When the notoriously secretive Feinberg testified, the *Wall Street Journal* blog The Deal Journal ran an image from his testimony under the heading "The Money Shot," stating that Feinberg was a "faceless tycoon no longer."[12]

The lawyers were in a particularly bad position. Both sides' lawyers had engaged in shorthand contract drafting as they negotiated and had drafted an ambiguous clause on the most important issue: When could Cerberus terminate the transaction? It appeared that one law firm or the other had made a mistake. Although we may never know the true answer, the court decision placed the mistake at Lowenstein's feet. According to the court's findings, Eric Swedenburg, the primary negotiating attorney at Simpson for United Rentals, had recognized the error and remained quiet, preferring to leave an ambiguous agreement rather than a fully negotiated one that was adverse to his client. Swedenburg, apparently with the blessing of his client, had appeared to come to the conclusion that raising the issue again would only have led to his side losing the argument. Leaving it ambiguous preserved a litigation position and an ability to challenge the termination in court, a situation the parties were in right now.[13]

Chancellor William B. Chandler, the judge in the Chancery Court, found that the contract language was indeed ambiguous. He then applied the principle of the "forthright negotiator" to find that Swedenburg knew that the contract was meant to be negotiated as a pure reverse termination fee deal and failed to disclose the drafting error. Under the "forthright negotiator" doctrine, Swedenburg should have disclosed this mistake, and the contract should be read as Cerberus intended. Chandler had applied standard contract interpretation principles to hold in favor of Cerberus's reading of the agreement.[14] When United Rentals announced that it would not appeal this decision, Cerberus promptly terminated the acquisition agreement and paid United Rentals $100 million.[15]

There were a number of lessons in this dispute that would emerge again throughout the financial crisis. First, shorthand or sloppy contract drafting could function as an unintentional landmine, lurking to create trouble. Second, the high-pressure atmosphere of takeover negotiations and the fast-paced timetable appeared to encourage mistakes, perhaps beyond a fault tolerance. Third, the mistakes made under this pressure were unlikely to come to light and tolerated by lawyers, but when they were discovered, they bit. It was doubtful whether the attorneys on either side enjoyed being put on the stand and having their ambiguous drafting parsed in the national news media. Fourth, complex agreements could never be complete in their terms. There would always be some omission or ambiguity. In the case of a litigation dispute, it would be fairly easy for one side to trump up a claim. Instead, what held these agreements together were extralegal factors like reputation. This was particularly true in the private equity context, where the deal was usually an optional one to begin with.

In the short term, the *Cerberus* ruling actually resulted in some bizarre negotiating techniques, as attorneys strained to avoid running afoul of the forthright negotiator rule. To avoid issues, some lawyers put a disclaimer of the rule in the agreement. Meanwhile, negotiations became more choreographed, with attorneys sometimes asserting their understanding of clauses in the negotiation. The goal was to obtain primacy of interpretation and leverage under the rule in any negotiation or future dispute. Attorneys on the other side were put in an unfortunate position, as they had to decide whether to challenge the statement or remain silent, hoping it would not count. The reaction showed the problems of the forthright negotiator rule in a world of sophisticated actors where ambiguity could not be eliminated.

In the longer term, the *Cerberus* decision was a watershed moment in private equity. After this litigation, it was now acceptable in the private equity market to simply walk from your deal. The reputational force that many sellers had thought would ensure that their transactions were completed had disappeared. In the period from December through February 2008, three additional private equity transactions would be effectively terminated: the pending acquisitions of PHH Corp. by Blackstone and General Electric Co., Reddy Ice Holdings, Inc. by GSO Capital Partners, and Myers Industries, Inc. by Goldman Sachs Capital Partners. In each case, no MAC claim was publicly asserted, but instead the buyer merely exercised the reverse termination fee provision in its agreement to exit the transaction. Each of the buyers could do this, since their agreement clearly permitted this action.

Thus, by early 2008, the fundamental understandings of the parties in private equity agreements appeared to have fallen by the wayside and the inherent optionality in this type of a reverse termination fee structure was realized. A reverse termination fee provision had become exercisable without significant reputational impact or other external normative constraints. At this, one had to laugh, or maybe cry, at the slogan of the now rejected Reddy Ice, the nation's largest provider of packaged ice: "Good times are in the BAG!"

The Implosion of Private Equity

The economics and parameters of the pure reverse termination fee structure were largely redefined by the fall 2007 wave of collapsed private equity acquisitions. By 2008, most of these deals had either been terminated or consummated in accordance with their terms. However, the public impact of private equity firms' reneging on their agreements was large. Private equity's image and reputation were significantly tarnished by the perception that private equity had walked on a number of transactions in the fall. Private equity firms were viewed as having failed to honor their implicit promise to complete acquisitions.

Into 2008, a number of multibillion-dollar private equity transactions also remained pending. The completion of these transactions was delayed into the winter of 2008 on account of regulatory or financing issues. At the time, many speculated that these deals remained outstanding in part because of their less optional structures. Most of these transactions were structured along the lines of the deal United Rentals argued it had agreed with Cerberus. The private equity firms could not terminate the agreement unless financing became unavailable and the targets could sue to force the buyers to specifically perform their obligations. In the other transactions, the private equity firms could terminate for any reason and pay the reverse termination fee, but these fees were so large that termination was not an economic option. Trapped, the private equity firms waited, hoping the credit and stock markets improved sufficiently to make the economics of their transactions again viable.

The credit crisis continued unabated, though, and focus narrowed to five transactions, which I hyperbolically labeled in my *New York Times* DealBook column as the buy-outs of the apocalypse:

- Blackstone's pending $7.5 billion purchase of Alliance Data Systems, Inc.
- Thomas H. Lee Partners LP's and Bain Capital's pending $19.4 billion purchase of Clear Channel Communications, Inc.
- Hexion's pending $10 billion purchase of Huntsman
- Fortress Investment Group and Centerbridge Partners LP's pending $8.4 billion purchase of Penn National Gaming, Inc.
- The largest private equity deal ever, a consortium led by Ontario Teachers' Pension Plan's pending $48.5 billion purchase of Canadian BCE, Inc.[16]

All of these transactions had been agreed to before the market crisis. There was no doubt that the prices the private equity firms had agreed to pay were much higher than these companies were now worth. The stock market had declined and would later savagely fall in September and October 2008. Furthermore, the banks financing these transactions would bear the brunt of this decline, losing billions if these transactions were completed. Given this, even at the beginning of 2008, market spectators wondered whether these transactions would be completed, and they were right.[17] Each of these deals would subsequently collapse or be renegotiated. The failure of these five large transactions would expose the weakness of private equity agreements and bank financing arrangements, as well as the failure of law and contract. Their collapse would also show the fragility of any agreement against the determined efforts of a buyer or lender.

The Alliance Data Systems (ADS) transaction was the first of these deals to implode. ADS was one of the nation's leading credit card service providers. The company had agreed to be acquired by Blackstone on May 17, 2007. At the end of January 2008, it was disclosed that the Office of the Comptroller of the Currency (OCC) was refusing to grant a required regulatory approval for ADS to be acquired by Stephen Schwarzman's Blackstone. The OCC justified its refusal on the grounds that the postacquisition leverage of ADS would leave it insufficiently capitalized to support its national bank subsidiary. The OCC did, however, ultimately express a willingness to reverse its position if the acquiring Blackstone fund itself provided a backstop, a $400 million guarantee of ADS's bank liabilities effective upon completion of the sale. Blackstone refused, stating that it was not required to provide this guarantee under the acquisition agreement. Blackstone's refusal was no doubt a product of the declining market and ADS's vulnerable credit card businesses. If Blackstone paid the price it had agreed to, it would suffer a substantial loss on the deal, even if it could still force the banks to honor their own agreements to finance the transaction.[18]

ADS sued in Delaware Chancery Court to compel Blackstone to provide this guarantee. ADS had negotiated an acquisition contract that provided that ADS could sue to specifically force performance of the Blackstone shell subsidiaries' obligations under the agreement. This arguably included the subsidiaries' agreement to use "reasonable best efforts" to obtain any necessary regulatory approvals, including OCC clearance, for the transaction. ADS argued in court that the requirement to use reasonable best efforts by the shell subsidiaries required them to sue the Blackstone fund itself, their parent, to compel it to issue the OCC requested guarantee.[19]

Blackstone countered that ADS had entered into the acquisition agreement only with thinly capitalized shell subsidiaries, a fact that ADS was fully aware of at the time it entered into the agreement. Blackstone's only obligation was under its equity commitment letter issued to these subsidiaries and its own guarantee of the reverse termination fee. Therefore, the shell entities could not force Blackstone to provide the OCC guarantee, and since these entities could not provide the guarantee required by the OCC, the transaction could not be completed.[20] In the anonymous words of a Blackstone representative at the time: "It's not a suicide pact. It's a merger agreement."[21]

Blackstone's response highlighted a fundamental limitation of the specific performance form of private equity structure. The private equity shell subsidiaries are corporate limited liability entities whose only real assets are their financing commitments and agreement to acquire the target. If regulators or other events require the shell subsidiaries to act beyond these assets, specific performance becomes meaningless because no assets are available. The agreement thus effectively becomes unenforceable unless the private equity fund voluntarily agrees to support any such arrangements.

ADS attempted to sidestep this dilemma by arguing that the reasonable best efforts clause in its acquisition agreement contemplated more, a fact that the parties were aware of at the time of the agreement's negotiation. This clause, standard in every acquisition agreement, obligated the Blackstone shell subsidiaries to use their reasonable best efforts to complete the transaction. The shell subsidiaries could be required under this clause to sue their parent Blackstone fund for any additional sums or contractual requirements required to satisfy regulatory demands. However, the meaning of reasonable best efforts under Delaware law had yet to be addressed substantively in any court and was therefore uncertain.

Vice Chancellor Strine, the judge assigned to adjudicate ADS's complaint, openly questioned ADS's argument in a hearing. He noted that Blackstone was not contractually bound to provide the OCC demanded guarantee in this structure. The grounds for any suit by the Blackstone subsidiaries against their parent would probably be slim.[22] In the wake of Strine's comments and his apparent favorable view of Blackstone's arguments, ADS withdrew its complaint. At the time, ADS cited Blackstone's public statements that it was still committed to completing the transaction as the reason for this withdrawal.[23]

ADS was probably just using these statements as a face-saving excuse to withdraw a suit that appeared to be on shaky legal grounds. At the time, most thought that Blackstone would continue to talk nice publicly but privately do nothing until the agreement termination date, that is, the date after which either party could terminate the agreement. This is what happened, and the agreement was terminated on April 18, 2008. ADS still sued again to collect the $170 million reverse termination fee, but lost before Vice Chancellor Strine on the grounds previously stated.[24]

The ADS litigation exposed the limits of the private equity structure. Under the traditional private equity agreement, a target could not force the actual fund to do any act to assist the buy-out. If the private equity firm's assistance was necessary to complete the transaction, and they did not want to provide it, the acquisition would fail. This provided a wide out for the private equity firms, particularly with respect to acquisitions that underwent extended regulatory review or needed special regulatory approvals.

As ADS's deal collapsed, the market attention turned to another buy-out, Clear Channel's $19.4 billion purchase by Thomas H. Lee Partners LP and Bain Capital. The Clear Channel buy-out had had a rocky road. The deal had been pending since November 16, 2006, and the private equity buyers had agreed to raise the purchase price in the interim to forestall shareholder rejection of the transaction. In early February 2008, the deal finally received all regulatory clearances, and the period to complete the marketing of the debt necessary for the transaction began to run in anticipation of a March closing. Given the state of the debt and equity markets, it was feared that the private equity firms would now balk at paying this high price or that the lenders on the transaction would refuse to finance it. The banks had good reason to be hesitant. Documents would later show that the financing banks stood to lose more than $2.6 billion if the transaction were completed.[25]

The first hints of trouble in this deal came from a dispute involving the sale of Clear Channel's TV station business to Providence Equity. As part of its own buy-out, Clear Channel, the owner and operator of more than 1,200 radio stations, had agreed to sell at a price of $1.2 billion 56 TV stations to Providence Equity, a private equity firm, to satisfy antitrust regulators. The sale of the TV stations was a necessary predicate to the main sale. Now that both sales appeared imminent, the lenders and buyers in the TV station transaction appeared to step back from the transactions. The rumor in the market was that Clear Channel and Providence Equity were renegotiating the transaction price.

No agreement was reached at that time. Instead, on February 15, 2008, Clear Channel preemptively struck. Clear Channel sued the Providence Equity shell subsidiaries in Delaware Chancery Court to force them to litigate against Wachovia Corporation to enforce their debt commitment letter and equity commitment letter.[26] The agreement for the TV station sale was of the specific performance type. Clear Channel had a right to force Providence Equity to sue to enforce the financing.[27] The rumors were true, and the parties were renegotiating the price, but Clear Channel still sued because of its continuing doubts about Providence Equity's willingness to complete the transaction. Wachovia, one of the financing banks on the transaction, then countered. On February 22, 2008, Wachovia sued the Providence Equity shell subsidiaries in a North Carolina court to terminate its obligations under its debt commitment letter to finance the subsidiaries' acquisition of the Clear Channel TV business. Wachovia asserted that any possible renegotiation of the purchase price constituted an "adverse change" under its debt financing letter. Providence Equity was clearly stuck in the middle.[28]

The deal was a jurisdictional morass. It highlighted the difficulty of enforcing the specific performance model of the private equity structure. The legal availability of specific performance in a cash transaction was still an uncertainty in many states, including Delaware. And the dual litigation due to the disharmony in the forum selection clauses in the financing documents and acquisition agreement raised the real possibility that the structure could completely collapse. In other words, not only could the private equity firm breach their financing commitment letters, but the financing banks could as well. This would create a situation where a target would be forced to sue the shell subsidiaries and, through some type of judicially ordered mechanism, arrange a suit on behalf of the subsidiaries against the banks and/or private equity firms to obtain necessary financing. The suits would have to be in different jurisdictions due to the differing forum selection clauses. Although a target could theoretically perform such acrobatics, the Clear Channel transaction appeared to be collapsing under its own weight at this point.

This problem was discussed at a February 26 hearing in the *Clear Channel TV* case before the ubiquitous and brilliant Vice Chancellor Strine, who didn't seem terribly troubled. He mused that in such circumstances, a remedy of specific performance could set free the shell subsidiaries.

The shell subsidiaries' obligation to use reasonable best efforts to obtain financing would thus be interpreted to include a search by parties for financing and funds other than to the recalcitrant private equity firms. It would also include a right and obligation to sue the banks to collect the financing.[29] The issues were never resolved, as this litigation unfolded and was settled in a few weeks. On March 14, Providence Equity agreed to pay a reduced price of $1.1 billion, but Clear Channel contributed $80 million in cash to the sold stations, thereby lowering the final price to $1.02 billion.[30]

The troubles of Clear Channel with Wachovia were ominous for two reasons: First, they did not portend well for Clear Channel's own private equity buy-out. Wachovia had agreed also to finance Clear Channel's buy-out. Wachovia's litigation here appeared to be a test run for its attempts to escape that second, larger deal. Second, Wachovia's actions marked the first public attempt of a bank to escape its financing obligations. There had been prior hints, though, that banks were balking at financing private equity deals.

In the fall of 2007, lenders in the HD Supply, Inc. and Reddy Ice Holdings, Inc. private equity acquisitions had aggressively worked to escape from their financing commitments. In both HD Supply and Reddy Ice, the private equity firms had renegotiated their deals with their targets, and the banks had used this change in terms to attempt to escape from their financing obligations. In each of these deals, the banks had asserted that the renegotiation of the transaction constituted a material adverse change under their debt financing letter, entitling the bank to terminate that letter. The Reddy Ice transaction ultimately was terminated through payment of the reverse termination fee by the private equity firm, and the banks' position forced a renegotiation of the HD Supply transaction. In both instances, these disputes remained private and did not result in any litigation or public dispute. Similarly, in the Acxiom termination, the payment of part of the reverse termination fee by the banks hinted at their recalcitrance, but their role in the termination was not publicly disclosed by the parties.[31] The Wachovia suit changed all this. It was now acceptable for lenders, as well as private equity firms, to openly challenge their commitments. Reputation did not particularly matter anymore.

The fears about Clear Channel's main deal turned out to be right. But things unfolded in a much different manner than anticipated. Instead, Bain Capital and Thomas H. Lee (THL), Clear Channel's buyers, came out fighting to complete the acquisition. On March 26, 2008, 12 days after resolution of the first Clear Channel litigation, Bain Capital and THL sued their financing banks in New York Supreme Court.[32] In their complaint, the private equity firms alleged that the banks had breached their commitment letters by demanding unreasonable terms that were onerous and unusual. The banks made these demands in an attempt to terminate their obligations under the commitment letter, something the banks were incentivized to do in light of their possible $2.65 billion loss.

The private equity firms asserted that the language proposed by the banks violated the requirement in the debt commitment letter that the final debt "contain the terms and conditions set forth in this Commitment Letter and shall be customary for affiliates of the Sponsors."[33] This "sponsor precedent" clause was considered quite friendly to the private equity firms because it narrowed the scope of precedent to be referenced to that in which the sponsor, another name for the private equity firm, had previously agreed to.

This was a different scenario than what unfolded in the Clear Channel TV station litigation. Here, it appeared that the private equity firms wanted to complete the transaction. They were, after all, suing. But the Clear Channel main agreement contained a $500 million reverse termination fee. The private equity firms could walk at any time simply by paying this fee.[34] Given that the private equity firms stood to lose probably more than $500 million if the deal went through on its current terms, people questioned the motives of the private equity firms' suit as a renegotiation ploy. The private equity firms could appear to publicly be the good guys while privately pressuring Clear Channel to settle. In a worst case scenario, the private equity firms would lose the litigation but could still walk from the transaction by paying the fee. But Clear Channel knew the private equity firm's options, so they would be likely to work with the private equity firms to settle the dispute with the banks by reducing the price the private equity firms paid. Still, to the credit of THL and Bain Capital, there was no doubt that the private equity firms were litigating. Scott Sperling, managing director of THL, even went on CNBC to tell TV reporter Erin Burnett why THL was fighting this battle and to proclaim his firm's commitment to acquiring Clear Channel.

The banks countered that the 71-page debt commitment letter they had issued to THL and Bain Capital was unenforceable because it contained too many open, yet to be negotiated terms. It was an agreement to agree, unenforceable under the laws of New York. Only with final documentation would the contract be sufficiently complete to be enforceable. In addition, the banks argued that a specific performance remedy was unavailable to the private equity firms; they were limited to money damages because specific performance could be awarded only when money damages were an inadequate remedy that could not be calculated. Here, the damages were easily calculable as the cost of finding alternative financing.[35]

However, the banks also argued a catch-22 for THL and Bain Capital. The banks claimed that specific performance was unavailable but then asserted that money damages would also be unavailable under the terms of the debt commitment letter. The reason was that the letter barred monetary damages. In any event, the banks also asserted that the acquisition agreement limited the private equity firms' monetary damages to $500 million, the amount of the reverse termination fee. Finally, the banks argued that the sponsor precedent language cited by the private equity firms was essentially meaningless since, due to the state of the market, no transaction was customary or similar.[36]

The dispute entered into discovery with the parties making the same arguments. Some of the banks' arguments appeared strained. In particular, the inclusion of sponsor precedent language seemed to nullify their argument that these were simply unenforceable agreements to agree. The sponsor precedent language provided a road map to document the final terms. And these letters had been standard in acquisitions for almost three decades—at no time before had a party asserted they were unenforceable. Despite the apparent weakness of the banks' case, there was substantial risk that the entire deal could blow up.

Settlement negotiations were hampered by anger; as one person put it: "The companies and lenders were hating each other so intensely that if it were in person, we would have needed an armed guard."[37] However, the risks were too great, and the parties "had to wipe away the emotional issues and come to a pain-sharing agreement."[38] An initial meeting at a hangar in a Westchester airport was arranged, and from there on the eve of trial on May 13, 2008, the deal was renegotiated. They indeed did share the pain. Clear Channel agreed to a lower price, and the private equity firms agreed to an increase in their equity commitment and the interest rate they were to pay on their bank debt and a decrease in the amount of debt financing provided by the banks. The transaction closed on July 30, 2008.[39] Nonetheless, the banks were proven right in their resistance; by December 2008, some of Clear Channel's debt was trading at less than 20 cents on the dollar.

At this point, it was clear that there had been a wholesale breakdown in the mechanics of private equity transactions. First, the structure of the deal between private equity and its targets was a fragile one. The pure form of these deals—those with a reverse termination fee and a bar on specific performance—allowed a buyer to walk for any reason now with little reputational constraint. The second form of this deal, the specific performance version litigated in the ADS and Clear Channel TV station litigations, was quite difficult to enforce. It required a target to sue the buyer and then potentially force the buyer to sue the lender, creating two different suits in two different jurisdictions. This was even before the fund itself decided whether to renege on creating a third suit. Moreover, banks were now disputing the enforceability of their debt commitment letters. This was shocking. In their struggle to escape from these bad loans, the banks were arguing that their agreements meant nothing. In taking such extreme actions, the banks were showing not only their dominance in their relationship with private equity, but their willingness to take reputational and relationship hits in pursuit of their own economic interests.

In the wake of the collapse of the ADS transaction and the renegotiation of Clear Channel, the market stood on edge waiting for what would happen to the Penn National and Huntsman buy-outs. It was not a happy ending for either. The end to the $8.4 billion Penn National buy-out came rather· quickly in July 2008. Penn National, a gaming company, was thought to have a very tight acquisition agreement. It was of the specific performance variety and included an unusual right for Penn National to directly sue Fortress to force it to perform its obligations under its equity commitment letter.[40]

The settlement came in the form of a discounted preferred stock investment by Fortress in the amount of $1.25 billion and a payment of the reverse termination fee of $225 million. It was clearly valued above the $225 million reverse termination fee set forth in the acquisition agreement but left Penn National trading at $28 per share, well below Fortress's initial offer price of $67 per share. When announcing the settlement, Penn National's management emphasized that the prospect of litigation against Fortress and the banks forced them into settling. Penn National CEO Peter M. Carlino stated, "This transaction represents the Company's best alternative to the uncertainty of litigation."[41] Targets had lost confidence in the enforceability of their agreements.

The Huntsman and Hexion result was even worse. As discussed in Chapter 3, on June 18, 2008, Hexion had sued Huntsman, claiming that it was permitted to terminate their $10 billion deal on account of the occurrence of a MAC to Huntsman and the insolvency of the combined entity. It was a daring litigation strategy for Hexion, as the insolvency claim blew up its own financing arrangements and, if Hexion's claim failed, was likely to leave it without the money to acquire Huntsman. Huntsman responded forcefully against the claims and countersued Apollo and its key executives Leon Black and Joshua Harris, as well as Credit Suisse and Deutsche Bank, the two banks financing the acquisition, in Texas state court, claiming tortious interference of contract, namely the agreement between Huntsman and Hexion. Huntsman also claimed that these companies and individuals had tortiously interfered with Huntsman's contract to be acquired by the Dutch chemical company Basell Industries AF. Huntsman had spurned that bid on July 12, 2007, and an extra $2.75 a share to be acquired by Hexion, a decision on the eve of the subprime crisis that at the time was appropriate but in hindsight seemed particularly regretful.

Huntsman was attempting to invoke the demons of the seminal case of *Pennzoil v. Texaco* In that case, Pennzoil Co. had an alleged informal, binding contract with Getty Oil Co. to purchase the company. Texaco, Inc. intervened with its own proposal, and in a San Antonio court, Pennzoil won a $10.53 billion jury verdict against Texaco on a tortious interference claim. Texaco was forced to declare bankruptcy and eventually paid a lower negotiated amount of $3 billion.[42] With its claim of tortious interference of contract, Huntsman was putting the pressure of a possible Texas-size jury verdict on Apollo and the banks.

The Texas case, though, was a stretch legally, and at the time commentators speculated that a renegotiation of the price was the most economical route for both parties. The parties did not settle, and the trial began on September 8, 2008. Jon Huntsman on the eve of trial spoke to the *Wall Street Journal* personally, attacking the head of Apollo, Leon Black, for reneging on his word. This was probably why no settlement was forthcoming at the time. The Huntsmans were simply still too angry over Leon Black and Apollo's conduct. Jon Huntsman would state:

> I will fight this until the day I die. . . . Private-equity firms have taken over America, and we will fight it. These guys are getting away with dishonest behavior, and I won't tolerate it.[43]

Vice Chancellor Lamb provided the Huntsmans some solace when he ruled forcefully against Hexion. He denied the MAC claim and found that the agreement with Huntsman did not provide a financing out for Hexion, nor did it contain a reverse termination fee provision. He did not therefore need to determine at that time whether the combined entity would be insolvent. He found Hexion in breach of the agreement, leaving Hexion in a bad position.[44] Hexion was now facing a damages claim that it could not pay and banks who could rely on Hexion's own allegations to refuse to fund the transaction. Huntsman had shown how the strength of an agreement could make a difference. Their lawyers at Shearman & Sterling and Vinson & Elkins LLP had negotiated a nontraditional private equity agreement that looked more like a strategic one. The result was to provide Huntsman a successful litigation position.

Hexion had initiated a very aggressive litigation strategy that appeared to be backfiring. On October 29, it was forced to sue its financing banks, who indeed now refused to fund the acquisition based on Hexion's own insolvency claims. Nonetheless, a month and a half later on December 14, 2008, Hexion and Huntsman announced a settlement with Apollo and Hexion. The headline figure for the settlement was $1 billion, but it was actually lower, as it included $250 million in 10-year convertible notes that would have to be repaid.[45] In the wake of the settlement, Huntsman's market capitalization fell to approximately $700 million, meaning the market assigned almost no value to the Huntsman business itself. Notably, Huntsman did not at this time settle its suit against the two banks—this would come later in June 2009. At that time Huntsman settled with Credit Suisse and

Deutsche Bank for $632 million in cash and $1.1 billion in subsidized financing.

The settlement with Hexion was a surprise as it appeared to be in an amount below the Penn settlement, despite Huntsman having a more favorable agreement and litigation position. The rumor was that Huntsman was forced to the table by its own liquidity problems. It no longer had the funds to survive to pursue litigation. Moreover, given its shaky claims against Apollo, Huntsman would be forced to seek a remedy from Hexion, rendering Hexion insolvent and providing Huntsman with little monetary compensation. This theory was later provided support when Huntsman obtained a similar recovery against the less culpable banks in June 2009, a time when Huntsman was much more stable.

It would also be later disclosed that Jon Huntsman, the man who had vowed to "fight this until the day I die," was paid $15 million by Huntsman for negotiating the settlement. The payment raised a conflict of interest issue: Was it appropriate for Huntsman to pay this fee to a large shareholder who already had a significant incentive to negotiate on behalf of Huntsman? In defense of Jon Huntsman, Nolan Archibald, a director of Huntsman, has asserted that the payment was quite justified and was for "singlehandedly negotiate[ing] this settlement" and "sav[ing] the company in doing so."[46]

Apollo and Hexion had succeeded in their gambit, but this entire episode tarnished Apollo's reputation as well as that of Joshua Harris and Leon Black, its executives. Apollo's investors no doubt also sweated the prospect of a Hexion bankruptcy and significant damages. In Apollo's case, it had adopted a litigation strategy that was quite risky and ultimately succeeded only by luck. Many questioned whether they would have been better off from the start simply waiting for the inevitable bank suit to provide them a cleaner motive for attempting to escape the transaction. But this was more speculation, and presumably Apollo took on this risk knowingly.

Huntsman's board appeared particularly dumbstruck. The deal will be cited for years in this more troubled age for the principle of taking a more certain deal as opposed to a higher bid with financing risk. In the end, Huntsman's board spurned a bid by another suitor, Basell, for a few extra dollars a share, leaving Huntsman with little. Of course, the Huntsman board made this decision in much better times and without foreknowledge of the financial crisis, but it still was a sobering, going-forward lesson on the risks of delay in an acquisition during times of financial crisis rather than the sunnier times of July 2007 when such delay meant little.

The final death song of the private equity era was BCE Inc., the Canadian telecommunications giant. The BCE buy-out, the largest private equity buy-out ever agreed to, went through twist and turn. It was almost felled by an adverse decision in bondholder litigation; then it was resurrected by a reversal of that ruling by the Canadian Supreme Court.[47] It was renegotiated in July and appeared on track toward a December closing. Then, a few weeks before the closing, BCE's handpicked accountant, KPMG, asserted that it could not provide the solvency opinion required under the acquisition agreement. KPMG's refusal to issue the solvency opinion allowed its buyers to refuse to complete the transaction. This they did, and the deal was terminated on December 11. The parties are still litigating whether the buyers are required to pay a $C1.2 billion reverse termination fee.[48]

Fault and the Failure of Private Equity

Who is to blame? The refrain has been repeated throughout the failure of many of these deals, as targets, private equity firms, investment bankers, banks, and lawyers were variously censured for the serial implosion of so many private equity transactions. Here, criticism of the private equity structure was principally directed at the optionality and the resulting uncertainty it created. In its purest form, the reverse termination fee structure created an option. The private equity firm had the discretion to exercise this option, and if the firm did so, it could terminate the transaction and pay the reverse termination fee. A private equity buyer could thus assess the benefits of the transaction before completion and decide whether it was more economical to complete the transaction. Otherwise, the firm could pay the reverse termination fee and terminate the acquisition agreement.

This option was not calculated according to any option pricing method. Nor did it appear to be calculated by reference to the damage incurred by a target in the event it was exercised by the private equity firm. The amount ultimately paid also did not deter buyers from exercising it in many instances. Rather, the amount of the reverse termination fee was set normatively by reference to the termination fee typically paid by targets, approximately 3 percent of the transaction value. Setting the fee at 3 percent for buyer and target made for a symmetrical penalty.

But this type of penalty was completely different. The termination fee was capped by Delaware case law and was designed to deter competing bids and compensate bidders for the costs associated with making a trumped offer. The same principles did not apply in the reverse termination fee context. The fee in a number of prominent instances did not deter exercise of the option, and in hindsight, the amount appeared to undercompensate targets for the losses incurred by the target company and its shareholders. Evidence of this came from the posttermination share trading prices of targets against whom these provisions were invoked. In the months after the exercise of this provision, the share prices of these companies traded significantly below the preoffer price.[49]

So why did targets and their advisers agree to this type of provisions? Here is what probably happened:

First, the reverse termination fee structure provided more closing certainty than the structure it supplanted. In the pre-2005 structure described in Chapter 2, the structure was wholly optional. The target entered into an agreement with thinly capitalized shell subsidiaries, and the agreement itself contained a financing condition. If the subsidiaries refused to perform or financing failed, the target was left with no compensation or recourse to the private equity firms except through a veil piercing or other creative litigation argument.

Second, reputation mattered. Private equity was a multiplayer game. It was assumed that the reputational incentive to close would keep them from exercising the reverse termination fee option and being perceived as reneging on their deals. The penalty for failure to follow this norm would be a higher price paid in future transactions to compensate targets for this failure and increased risk, as well as any other public approbation for this action.

Third, and related to the second point, the economic incentives of private equity firms push them to complete the acquisition. In other words, private equity firms initially enter into the transaction because of a desire to acquire the company. The transactional costs incurred to enter first into this agreement also pressure private equity firms to complete their transactions.

Fourth, private equity lawyers relied on prior precedent. In this regard, SunGard provided a precedent for the structure, one that private equity attorneys rapidly adopted. A deviation from what became the market norm at the time would likely be seen as off-market and therefore unlikely to be proposed by attorneys or accepted.

These four reasons provide an explanation for why a different, more certain structure has historically been utilized for strategic transactions, acquisitions made by a functioning company rather than a private equity firm. Strategic transactions lack the optional nature of private equity acquisitions. In strategic transactions, the structural norm is to eschew financing conditions and reverse termination fee structures. Instead, target companies obligate the buyer to specifically perform the acquisition in case of a breach of the acquisition agreement. Unlike the private equity context, this agreement is secured by the assets of the buyer.

The traditional reason offered for this dichotomy in structure is a financing rationale. In a strategic transaction, a buyer has assets to secure its obligations and is not dependent on the vagaries of the financing market to complete its transaction. But many strategic buyers employ substantial leverage to effect acquisitions while private equity funds do have assets—the contractual agreements of their investors to fund the buyout. A stronger explanation is that a strategic buyer is not in the business that private equity firms are—acquiring companies. If a strategic buyer reneges on its acquisition agreement, the reputational loss is likely to be less because it is not consistently in the acquisition market, and stronger contractual protections are justified.

All of these forces combined to make the private equity structure, though optional, acceptable. Similarly, when lawyers were negotiating the rest of the structure, it was papered over as the best bargain that could be achieved. The deal would obviously go through because of the forces pushing it to close. The flaws in this structure or even any mistakes made would thus not matter due to these other forces. This is the best possible explanation for the other errors in structure, such as the drafting mistakes litigated in the United Rentals/Cerberus dispute. Unfortunately, the harsh winds of the credit crisis changed this assumption. Table 4.1 lists the significant terminated private equity deals during 2007–2008. It is a sobering list.

Table 4.1 Failed and Renegotiated Private Equity Transactions 2007–2008

Announcement Date	Acquirer	Target	Outcome
11/16/2006	Bain/Thomas H. Lee	Clear Channel	Renegotiated
3/15/2007	GE Capital Solutions/Blackstone	PHH	Terminated
4/16/2007	JC Flowers/Consortium	Sallie Mae	Terminated
4/20/2007	Providence Equity Partners	Clear Channel TV Stations	Renegotiated
4/24/2007	Goldman Sachs Capital Partners	Myers International	Terminated
4/26/2007	KKR/Goldman Sachs Capital Partners	Harman	Terminated
5/16/2007	ValueAct Capital/Silver Lake	Acxiom Corp.	Terminated
5/17/2007	Blackstone	Alliance Data Systems	Terminated
6/4/2007	Lone Star Funds	Accredited Home Lenders Holding Co.	Renegotiated
6/15/2007	Fortress Investment Group/Centerbridge Partners	Penn National Gaming Co.	Terminated
6/30/2007	Providence Equity Partners/ Madison Dearborn Partners	BCE	Terminated
7/2/2007	GSO Capital Partners	Reddy Ice Holdings	Terminated
7/12/2007	Hexion/Apollo	Huntsman	Terminated
7/23/2007	Cerberus Capital Management	United Rentals	Terminated
7/23/2007	Merrill Lynch Global Private Equity	Cumulus Media	Terminated
9/28/2007	Bain/Huawei	3Com	Terminated

SOURCE: Steven M. Davidoff, "The Failure of Private Equity," 82 *Southern California Law Review* 101, at Ex. A (2009).

These failures are only one part of a much bigger failure. The collapse of private equity occurred in the postcredit bubble hangover. The deals reached in those headier times were made in an atmosphere that did not expect the collapse that occurred. In hindsight, the companies who did agree to these exits and whose deals did not implode proved to have made a very good decision, however questionable it may have been at the time. The burden of those deals mostly fell on the private equity firms and more significantly their lenders. The private equity firms could pay so much because the lenders made loans at insufficient interest rates and with too much leverage. Thus, the principal failure of the private equity industry in the period leading up to August 2007 was the failure of financial institutions to properly price their loans and financial instruments. This allowed private equity firms to acquire a vast portfolio of companies at low interest rates, with too flexible credit terms, and with minimum money invested. This particular failure is part of a broader credit crisis that has had astounding economic implications for our world economy as many of these portfolio companies struggle under the weight of this debt.

In the end, this was simply a product of misplaced incentives. The banks were no longer in the *It's a Wonderful Life* mode, where they saw their lenders in person, assessed their credit, and were penalized when a creditor defaulted on its loan. Rather, in the sixth wave, lending became a matter of securitization and the ability of banks to securitize and sell leveraged buy-out and other debt.

The banks' focus in their risk management and lending committees was whether the debt could be securitized and sold to third parties. Whether it was paid back or not, once sold, it became someone else's problem, a factor that the banks simply did not take into sufficient account. And that is what got us into the mess the economy is in.

The failure of these private equity deals showed the strength of banks and their dominant role in the private equity process. In each of these collapsed transactions, it was the banks rather than private equity that had the most to lose. When they could no longer act from behind the scenes after the easy deals had cleared in the fall of 2007, the banks emerged with a vengeance to escape transactions that no longer made economic sense. In doing so, the banks showed that in the private equity relationship, they were the ones that called the shots.

This left targets to suffer at the hands of the reverse termination fee and lawyer practices in agreements (such as agreeing to reverse termination fees) that appeared inexplicable. In retrospect, they were a product of lawyers' overreliance on extralegal forces to close transactions. In other words, lawyers relied on private equity's reputation and need to close transactions to paper over fundamental errors and mistakes in agreements, as well as an optional closing structure. In particular, lawyers failed to vary the reverse termination fee dependent upon the closing risk of a particular transaction, instead preferring to leave at 3 percent no matter the deal's characteristics. But when the economic incentives were no longer there, the banks and private equity firms no longer felt bound by these extralegal constraints and instead struggled mightily to find or invent any reason to escape from their legal obligations.

In a sense, this failure was a failure of lawyers and targets of prescience. Who could have predicted such a maelstrom? The failure also exposed the errors of lawyers in the process, errors that were normally hidden and should not have been made. It also uncovered the failure of lawyers to vary deal terms depending upon deal risk, failures that likely should have been compensated for regardless. Ultimately, in the post-August 2007 litigation, private equity firms always appeared to be able to find some clear or less than clear contractual or legal basis to attempt to terminate their agreements. The failure of private equity shows the importance of extralegal forces in gluing together transactions. In complex transactions, there will always be limits to what attorneys can do. At some point, further additions or revisions to the contract are constrained by the limits of imagination or are otherwise hampered by time constraints. This may mean that there is some hook that a buyer can always find to attempt to terminate a transaction.

In other words, when a dispute arises, lawyers are always reasonably certain in the complex contract context that they can find some flaw to litigate. This type of behavior was clearly on display in the private equity failures of the past year. The consequence is that in the private equity context and likely complex acquisition contracts generally, reputation and trust are an important and inescapable component of a contract. In future deals, parties would do well to remember this. Nonetheless, they should also remember that a tight, well-drafted agreement can provide benefits. One need only compare the settlements of Penn National, which had a tight albeit partially optional agreement, with United Rentals, which ultimately had a more optional pure reverse termination fee structure. Both were spurned by their would-be private equity buyers, but the former received more than a billion dollars, and the latter only $100 million.

The Future of Private Equity

The serial collapse of private equity deals and the market conflagration left private equity firms reeling. The market for private equity deals disappeared. In 2008, globally only $109.9 billion worth of private equity acquisitions took place, down from $512 billion in the prior year.[50] This was only 3.8 percent of total takeover volume, a level not seen since 2001. It was even worse in the first quarter of 2009—globally, only $7.9 billion worth of private equity acquisitions were announced in the entire quarter.[51] Putting this in perspective, worldwide activity for the quarter was less than a fifth of the TXU acquisition alone.

The lack of deal-making activity gave private equity needed time to devote attention to its 2004 through 2007 crops of increasingly distressed acquisitions. The number of troubled portfolio companies seemed to expand on a daily basis and included such luminaries as Chrysler, Clear Channel, Freescale Semiconductor, Inc., GMAC LLC, Harrahs, Linens 'n Things, and Realogy. The burden of these failed acquisitions would no doubt weigh on private equity returns for their new millennium funds.

Private equity firms pushed the limits of their latitude under their previously negotiated debt in attempting to salvage these companies and their investments. Unfortunately, though, for already burnt debt holders, private equity firms often structured these workouts at the expense of debt leveraging off the relatively slim terms banks had agreed to during the credit bubble. The result was litigation in the case of Realogy's and Freescale's debt restructurings and a continuing deterioration in private equity's reputation.[52] In the next round of acquisitions, banks and the purchasers of securitized private equity debt will no doubt respond by demanding significantly tighter terms. The private equity firms probably knew this was coming anyway and felt that playing hardball with debt holders during these workouts would not change the inevitable.

Private equity firms began to downsize. Blackstone laid off 7 percent of its workforce in December 2008.[53] Investors also began to become wary of their investments and future commitments. The Harvard

University endowment, for example, put out to bid a third of its private equity portfolio valued at $1.5 billion.[54] It received no acceptable bids. And Stephen Schwarzman, the king of private equity and now a significantly poorer man, disappeared. One reporter relayed this exchange when he inquired at Blackstone's offices in December 2008 for an interview of Schwarzman:

> "Mr. Schwarzman's office," said the receptionist, "is no longer taking calls."
>
> "Ever?"
>
> "Not for the foreseeable future, I've been told."[55]

Private equity was not out forever. Unlike hedge funds, private equity had long-term commitments with its investors. As of January 2009, one estimate put at $472 billion the amount private equity firms globally still had in uncommitted funds that it could draw down.[56] This number was likely to be an overestimation, as private equity investors, already suffering from losses, will probably struggle to avoid fully honoring these commitments. Still, this provided the firms who were not fully committed with some level of funds to make distressed investments during the storm and to ride it out. The ones who were fully committed were less fortunate, faced with a never-ending sea of workouts and an inability to raise future funds. Private equity also had a 30-year track record of excess returns to continue to raise money on. In future fundraisings, it would no doubt claim the financial crisis as an unexpected aberration to be discounted. Moreover, the collapse of the investment banking model left firms like Blackstone and KKR in a better position to offer boutique investment banking services in competition with middle-market investment banks, a topic I explore further in Chapter 12.

Private equity was largely returned to its position of the early 1990s, albeit with a significantly smaller war chest and a number of headaches to deal with. The days of the $40 billion dollar mega private equity deal have probably passed. Meanwhile, private equity firms unwilling to continue to subject themselves to the harsh scrutiny of the public markets are likely to unwind the publicly traded structures they had created in headier times. But for deal-making to return in force, private equity will need to repair its deteriorated relationship with financing banks and targets.

In the wake of private equity's collapse, there was also a marked shift in deal structure. First, lawyers, not surprisingly, went back to basics. They attempted to clean up forms and draft more clearly and simply in response to the apparent drafting errors that had come to light. There was a focus on reading and rereading contract drafts to catch errors, and all parties put in significant efforts to negotiate tighter contracts. Lawyers simply became more important to the deal process.

Many also expected targets to negotiate more certain deals. This has not happened thus far. Instead, the private equity structure has shifted in the opposite direction toward a model more favorable to private equity. Approximately 80 percent of U.S. private equity transactions announced in 2008 utilized a pure reverse termination fee structure.[57] This is a telling response. The nature of this shift again marks a recognition that the drivers to closing in a private equity transaction substantially exist outside the contract language. It also represents a collapse of the bargain between private equity firms and target companies, which permitted more rigorous forms of the reverse termination fee structure to exist.

It also reflects the nature of credit in these troubled times. Credit is hard to obtain and, until drawn, is in danger of being pulled by the banks. Private equity firms were simply unwilling to do deals with credit risk and, in any event, were often unable to obtain credit. Attorneys were unable to find some way to bridge the gap. Instead, in the new distressed takeover market, targets self-selected. It is no surprise that the few 2008 private equity deals were in industries less affected by the market disruption. Targets justified using the reverse termination fee structure because of their stable cash-generative business models, which would make them less resistant to any adverse impact by the economic crisis. This would ensure that their business remained stable and the private equity acquisition would complete.

Private equity attorneys have not come up with a better way to structure transactions than through use of the reverse termination fee. The result is that many sellers will not do business with private equity because they cannot offer completion certainty. For now, this is a function of the credit market, but as a recovery takes hold, the question is what will private equity agreements look like? In the short term, there may be higher reverse termination fees to adjust for the closing risk. The private equity reverse termination fee in the pre-August 2007 vintage transactions was in hindsight set too low and too mechanically at the 3 percent norm.[58]

Targets will attempt to ensure closing certainty by making the penalty for walking significantly higher. This may lead to bifurcated reverse termination fees: a higher fee for a buyer's breach of the agreement or a financing failure, and a lower one in other circumstances. We may also see the return of nonrefundable deposits or escrow arrangements to ensure that a target obtains some recompense for a failed deal.

In addition, private equity may attempt to make deals more certain by trying to negotiate complete credit agreements with banks beforehand. Finally, MAC clauses may perversely become even broader, as sellers grapple with the problems of a MAC clause and its interaction with a reverse termination fee. Here, targets would be attempting to make MAC claims harder in order to prevent private equity from using these clauses for reputational cover against invocation of a reverse termination fee. Of course, the true solution to the MAC issue is to simply eliminate the MAC clause in private equity deals, but this is likely to be too extreme a step for lawyers.

None of these solutions bridges the gap and provides more certainty to targets while providing private equity firms latitude to walk in case of a financing failure. This gap could be bridged by demanding bigger equity infusions from private equity firms or in smaller deals actually obtaining full equity commitments from private equity funds for the entire purchase price. It could also be met by targets and buyers demanding that financing be committed at signing. In the meantime, private equity will continue to suffer as it is unable to complete deals on account of the lack of certainty. This drag will become remarkably clear when market conditions return to normal and sellers are able to negotiate from a stronger position. Who, after all, and if given the choice, would do a deal with Apollo after its conduct in Huntsman? Not me.

But solutions to this certainty gap are likely only to definitively appear once the takeover and credit markets fully heal. For the time being, private equity has been able to leverage its bargaining position in a distressed market to obtain pure reverse termination provisions when it can find financing to do a deal. This lack of certainty, however, and private equity's inescapable dependence on its dominant force, financing banks, have also significantly hampered the private equity industry. Meanwhile, banks themselves were suffering as they fell behind in their race to write off bad debt brought on by the credit bubble. But the banks' fervent attempts to raise capital in the winter of 2008 showed another possible way for private equity: alternative capital sources such as sovereign wealth funds.

Chapter 5

Dubai Ports, Merrill Lynch, and the Sovereign Wealth Fund Problem

S overeign wealth funds burst onto the world scene in the fall of 2007. Their emergence was not so coincidentally timed with the first stirrings of the credit crisis. In the fall of 2007 into the winter of 2008, U.S. financial institutions eagerly solicited capital from these funds and paid millions to lobbyists to grease the regulatory wheels for this investment.[1] The money initially flowed. In 2008, global sovereign wealth fund investment in financial institutions was $32.7 billion. This capital was a lifeline for financial institutions struggling under the weight of real estate and leveraged buy-out debt. It was not just financial institutions. That same year, sovereign wealth funds globally invested $47.2 billion. This was a decrease from 2007, when $77.7 billion was invested, but still a 434 percent increase over the $10.9 billion invested in 2004.[2] (See Figure 5.1.)

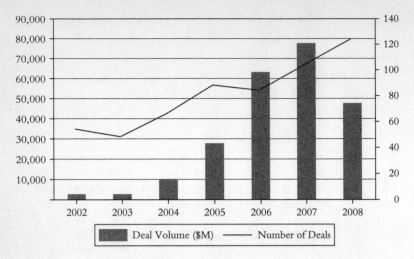

Figure 5.1   Sovereign Wealth Fund Global Investment 2002–2008
Source: Thomson Reuters

Sovereign wealth funds may have helped save the world, but their emergence was not without controversy. Sovereign wealth funds are government-sponsored investment funds created to invest their country's foreign currency reserves. As such, these funds are mostly creatures of countries that have unduly benefited from economic globalization and the now-past commodity boom, namely, oil producers or exporters of goods to the United States, most prominently China. In 2008, 7 of the 10 largest sovereign wealth funds were held by non-Western oil producers: Algeria, Kuwait, Libya, Qatar, Russia, Saudi Arabia, and the United Arab Emirates.[3] China had one of the largest funds, capitalized initially in 2007 by the Chinese government with $200 billion.[4] None of these countries are democracies, and some are possible U.S. enemies. Many in the United States expressed concern that these countries would use these investments to wield undue political influence on U.S. corporate interests, as well as to overtly appropriate U.S. technology.

As these funds grow, the issues surrounding sovereign wealth funds are likely to increase over time. Sovereign wealth funds currently have an estimated $2 trillion to $3 trillion in assets. Merrill Lynch and Morgan Stanley estimated in 2007 that these funds may have more than $7.9 trillion in assets by 2011 and $10 trillion in assets by 2015, respectively.[5] These numbers will probably be far less, now that the commodity bubble has deflated and the global recession has taken its toll on

exporting economies. Still, the secular trend is toward further accumu-
lation of reserves in these funds, particularly China's. (See Figure 5.2.)
The United States even had its own fund popularized in the past election by the nomination of Governor Sarah Palin as the Republican
vice presidential candidate. The $28.3 billion Alaska Permanent Fund
holds and invests Alaska's oil wealth on behalf of that state's residents.[6]

Tied into the concern over sovereign wealth funds is a recent,
heightened sensitivity to foreign investment in the United States, particularly in light of the economic downturn. The bizarre 2007 uproar
over an attempt by Dubai Ports, a company controlled by the United
Arab Emirates, to acquire control of a number of U.S. ports spurred
Congress to legislate heightened requirements for national security
review of foreign acquisitions. The sovereign wealth fund investment
spurt came after this controversy and legislation, but the Dubai Ports
incident highlights the complexity surrounding the issue of growing
foreign investment in the United States.

This chapter is about the increasingly important role foreign investment plays in deal-making and the U.S. capital markets. It is particularly about the wave of sovereign wealth fund investment and its future
direction and regulation. Regulating foreign investment is always a
struggle among irrational xenophobia, legitimate national interests, and
the need for and benefits of foreign direct investment. Sovereign wealth
funds raise even more particular concern as a direct government investment, but this type of investment also highlights the changing nature of
the financial marketplace. Sovereign wealth funds stand to become an
alternative capital provider for deal-making, albeit in a likely accompanying rather than direct role. Yet foreign investment will continue to be
a place of nuanced risk and reward, where the public relations aspect of
the deal machine particularly matters and regulators will continue to
play a heightened role. To understand why, it is necessary to begin by
discussing the nature of sovereign wealth fund investing.

The Financial Wave of Sovereign Fund Investment

Not surprisingly, the initial prominent sovereign wealth fund investment was tied into the private equity boom and Blackstone. In May
2007, China Jianyin Investment Company, a Chinese government
agency, purchased a 9.3 percent interest in Blackstone for $3 billion.

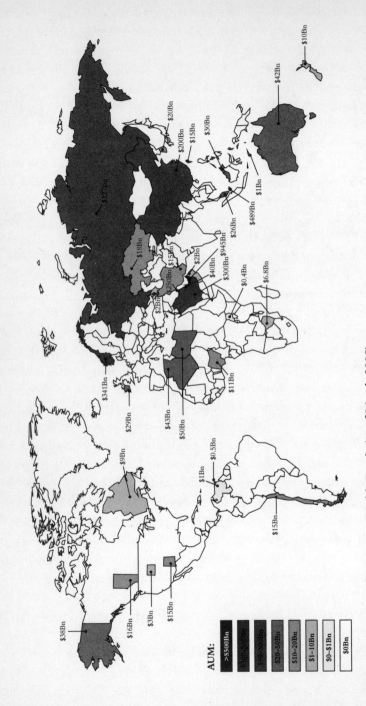

Figure 5.2 Map of Sovereign Wealth Funds (as of March 2009)
SOURCE: Morgan Stanley

At the time, Blackstone asserted that it accepted the investment for strategic reasons. A relationship with the Chinese government would provide Blackstone superior access to the Chinese market. China probably had a similar rationale for this investment; the government could now steer Blackstone's investment capital further into China. In addition, China now also had access to the financial expertise of Blackstone's Schwarzman and his partners, as well as a 9 percent ownership stake, albeit nonvoting, in one of the largest privately held companies in the United States. The investment marked China's first sovereign wealth investment. Indeed, the Blackstone investment would herald the formation, on September 29, 2007, of an official Chinese sovereign wealth fund, China Investment Corp. Ltd (CIC). The China fund was capitalized by the Chinese government with approximately $200 billion, backed by the approximately $2 trillion in Chinese dollar currency reserves, and it provided a soft government mandate to earn a return of 5 percent on invested capital.[7]

The Blackstone investment was the first significant sovereign wealth fund investment in a U.S. financial institution. It was also a creature of the private equity boom. The Chinese government purchased a nonvoting stake in Blackstone at a price that even at the time appeared heady. But highlighting the issue surrounding these investments, the economic returns may have been secondary to the strategic and technical benefits China gained from access to Blackstone. After all, why else would China pay full price for a nonvoting stake at a time when market observers were calling a private equity bubble?

In hindsight at least, the full price CIC paid for Blackstone was indeed too much. But into the fall of 2007, the continuing credit crisis drew in sovereign wealth funds looking to profit from the stock market decline and the visible distress of financial institutions. In September, Mubadala Development Company, the investment arm of the Abu Dhabi government, purchased a 7.5 percent stake in the Carlyle Group for $1.35 billion.[8] Also in September, the Borse Dubai, the stock exchange controlled by Abu Dhabi agreed to, purchase a 19.99 percent stake in the Nasdaq Group Inc. and in connection with that purchase also agreed to acquire Nasdaq's 28 percent stake in the London Stock Exchange Group PLC.[9] The investment accelerated toward the end of 2007. In November through January, Citigroup, Merrill Lynch, and Morgan Stanley alone collectively raised $37.8 billion with over three quarters of that coming from sovereign wealth funds.[10] (See Table 5.1.)

Table 5.1 Share Price Performance of Selected Sovereign Wealth Fund Public Financial Investments 2007–2008

Investor	Institution	Investment ($B)	Date	Share Price at Initial Investment	Share Price at 2/27/2009
Government of Singapore Investment Corp.	UBS	9.8	Various	$51.66	$9.05
Government of Singapore Investment Corp.	Citigroup	6.88	1/15/2008	$26.94	$1.50
Abu Dhabi Investment Authority	Citigroup	7.5	11/26/2007	$30.70	$1.50
Temasek Holdings (Singapore)	Merrill Lynch	5.9	Various	$20	$3.40
China Investment Corp.	Morgan Stanley	5.579	12/19/2007	$50.08	$19.54
China Development Bank	Barclays Plc	3.08	7/23/2007	$60.35	$5.14
China Jianyin Investment Company	Blackstone Group	3	6/21/2007	$29.60	$4.87
Dubai International Capital	Och-Ziff Capital Management Group	1.26	10/29/2007	$30.50	$5.16

Merrill Lynch was acquired by Bank of America on Jan. 1, 2009. The Merrill share price at Feb. 27, 2009 is the effective share price converted from Bank of America's closing share price on that date.

In 2008, sovereign wealth funds announced $23.7 billion worth of investment into the United States. Financial institutions were the top targeted industry, with $32.7 billion in global investment. The next two investment categories were not even close: oil and gas with $7.1 billion and real estate with $4.4 billion of investment.[11] By investing in financial assets, such as investment banks, sovereign wealth funds were taking advantage of the market distress to obtain access to the highest reaches of the institution's management. Sovereign wealth fund investments were thus of a very different type than those made in the 1980s by the Japanese. Back then, the Japanese for the most part bought cyclical assets at the top of another bubble, purchasing trophy properties such as Pebble Beach and Rockefeller Center.[12] Sovereign wealth funds appeared in part to break with the investment pattern set by the Japanese, focusing instead on distressed financial institutions and operating companies.

Investment in financial institutions opened up access for the sovereign wealth fund to a bigger menu of investments. It also provided the funds greater opportunity to channel investment into their own countries to nurture domestic businesses and industries. The Blackstone investment was not unique; these financial institution investments appeared to be generally made for more than just a return. Moreover, purchasing an interest in these financial companies was a means for the managers of sovereign wealth funds to access the world's leading investors and their investing skill.

Many of these sovereign wealth funds are newly created. Two prominent exceptions are the Kuwait Investment Office, which has been around in some form since 1953, and Norway's Government Pension Fund, established in 1990.[13] The people running sovereign wealth funds are smart but often relatively inexperienced global investors. The sovereign wealth funds were attempting to cover this deficit by purchasing investment and financial acumen. As such, these were also strategic investments made for long-term gain beyond an economic return. These funds may have been willing to earn a lower return than other investors might have sought, due to the funds' other investment purposes. Sovereign wealth funds generally target a low return in any event because of their government origin, lower cost of capital, and the tax-free status of their investing due to their sovereign nature.

What do financial institutions gain from this relationship? To understand the benefits to each party and the corporate flight to these funds,
it is worth looking at the terms of a particular investment: Temasek
Holdings' Christmas Eve 2007 $4.4 billion purchase of a 9.4 percent
interest in Merrill Lynch. This was viewed as a coup for now-tarnished
ex-Merrill CEO Jonathan Thain. At the time, Temasek purchased this
interest at $48 dollars a share, received no special corporate govern-
ance rights, and agreed to a standstill that prohibited it from purchasing
more than 10 percent of the company.[14]

The Temasek investment was typical for the time. The paradigmatic
fund investment in a public company in the past two years has been a
5 to 20 percent stake in a financial institution. In many of these investments, the securities purchased by the fund did not have a voting ability or provide the fund with seats on the company's board of directors.
In other words, sovereign wealth funds during this time made largely
passive, noncontrolling investments. *Passive* here refers to the actual
rights the funds are receiving, not any soft influence they now wielded
due to their stakes.

Merrill took Singapore's money, first, because it could be raised
fast. Sovereign wealth funds here offered a compelling advantage
as willing investors who could quickly deploy money in a capital-
starved world. Merrill also benefited from Temasek's willingness to
take a noncontrolling, passive interest. Keeping the stake below 10
percent had regulatory advantages. In particular, at the time of this
investment, there was a general view that a passive stake of this nature
was not subject to review by the U.S. government for national security purposes.

The question, though, was who was fooling whom? Were the banks
taking advantage of the funds, or was it vice versa? The banks accepted
capital from these investors in part because of the funds' willingness
to quickly make passive, noncontrolling investments in a manner that
sidestepped extensive regulatory review. However, at the time of these
investments, the public markets remained open enough to raise equity
or other capital. For example, in January 2008, Bank of America Corp.
raised $12.9 billion through a public offering of preferred stock.[15]
Hedge funds, private equity, and other U.S. institutional investors also
remained possible investors.

These other institutional investors, though, would probably have wanted a measure of control rights along with their large investments. In contrast, a sale to a sovereign wealth fund largely meant that the investor would be a passive one. Even if Temasek had negotiated management rights, it was unlikely that the government of Singapore would launch a proxy contest to unseat the Merrill board or otherwise attempt to overtly influence the company. Instead, any influence was likely to come through soft power, steering business and investment expertise to these countries. Sovereign investment also insulated management from any unsolicited takeovers or other shareholder activity. The net result was that sovereign wealth fund investment was preferable to management because it was likely to leave them with much wider latitude to operate their business.

In the short term, the returns have been horrible (see Table 5.1). It appears that the banks have gotten the better of the funds.[16] And the wave of government investment starting in the fall of 2008 significantly diluted this wave of sovereign wealth fund investment. Here, some funds benefited from negotiating more sophisticated investment rights. Temasek, for example, had negotiated a repricing right if Merrill raised equity at a lower price within a year of their initial investment. On July 29, 2008, Merrill announced plans to raise another $9.8 billion in capital. At that time, Merrill's stock price was about half of what Temasek paid for it, entitling Temasek to $2.5 billion of compensation. However, Temasek agreed to reinvest this amount and purchase another $900 million in Merrill common stock without any future reset protection.[17]

This provision ultimately saved Temasek money but did not spare it from a loss. At the time Merrill was sold to Bank of America, it was said to have an estimated loss on paper of $2 billion. Since its Merrill investment, Temasek has suffered even further losses on investments in Barclays Plc and Bank of China and a general decline in the value of its fund on account of its 40 percent concentration in financial assets.[18] Temasek's most recent return figures calculated as of November 31, 2008, reveal that Temasek's investments were worth about $85 billion, a decline of 31 percent from March 31, 2008.[19]

Citic Securities, a top state-controlled investment bank in China, was one fund that dodged a bullet. Citic had yet to invest the $1 billion in Bear Stearns it had agreed to and therefore was able to cancel its investment and save its government a billion dollars when Bear Stearns collapsed. But overall, the sovereign wealth fund investments during this time have been much less fortunate. For example, China's $3 billion investment in Blackstone had by early 2009 lost four-fifths of its value. Notably, CIC has since renegotiated its agreement with Blackstone to obtain another 2.6 percent of the company, without any additional investment of funds.[20] In hindsight, sovereign wealth funds moved too early to invest in financial institutions, and more experienced investors benefited by waiting. Mitsubishi UFJ, for example, invested $9 billion in Morgan Stanley in October 2008. The price was effectively $25.25 per share, less than half the effective per-share price, ranging from $48.07 to $57.68 per share, CIC had paid in December 2007 to invest in that company.[21] Sovereign wealth funds may have been investing for purposes other than economic returns, but the losses meant that they paid quite dearly for these opportunities.

These funds, though, appear to be long-term investors, and the true returns will only be known years from now. Saudi Arabian Prince Alwaleed bin Talal made billions investing in Citigroup back during its last financial crisis in the early 1990s (money he largely lost in this financial crisis). The sovereign wealth funds certainly know this, though they clearly would have preferred to get into their investments during the September 2008 crash. Moreover, the funds are learning. Whereas some of these early investments such as in Blackstone were in non-voting equity without a guaranteed return, later investments have been made in the form of preferred investments that assure a minimum return. For example, when CIC invested in Morgan Stanley, it did not purchase common stock. Rather, CIC sought some assurances on its investment by purchasing equity units that were mandatorily convertible into common stock on August 17, 2010. In the meantime, the equity units yielded 9 percent on their investment, a way to ensure a more certain return than an investment in common stock.[22] Of course, in hindsight, CIC still has on paper lost a tremendous amount of money on that investment, but it could have been worse.

Sovereign wealth fund investment has thus had mixed results for the funds themselves. Most did not pan out as the financial sector further deteriorated. In August and September 2008, when the financial firms reached a breaking point, the sovereign wealth funds were nowhere to be seen. Instead, licking their wounds, these funds have begun to invest in different areas. For example, in one week in September 2008, the sovereign wealth fund of Abu Dhabi bid $354 million for the English soccer team Manchester City and announced that it was investing $1 billion in Hollywood, Bollywood, and entertainment.[23] Sovereign wealth funds thus remain active although quite wary after the losses of the past years. Their investment will probably continue, albeit at a quieter and more subdued pace. This was illustrated by the 2009 Davos gathering. Sovereign wealth funds had been the star of the 2008 conclave and a source of heated debate, but by 2009, their presence was muted in light of the financial crisis and their significant losses.[24]

Individual countries still remain significant holders of sovereign assets. These funds will continue to remain a force in investing. Their trillions will eventually begin to flow into other industries and investments beyond financial institutions. For example, Aluminum Corporation of China, the Chinese state-controlled aluminum company known as Chinalco, together with Alcoa in 2008, announced the surprise acquisition of a $14 billion stake in Australian miner Rio Tinto. This investment made in the midst of BHP Billiton's bid for Rio Tinto was generally viewed as a means for Chinalco to cement a source of supply for its aluminum factories.[25] It was a commodity boom deal and yet another one where China will in the short term lose significant sums. Nonetheless, the transaction showed the potential direction of sovereign wealth funds. These funds will gradually move beyond their current passive stakes to larger purchases, often flowing to the greater strategic benefit of the country. Chinalco would attempt in February 2009 to follow up with another $19.5 billion investment in Rio Tinto by purchasing $12.3 billion of Rio Tinto's mining assets as a joint venture and $7.2 billion of convertible bonds.[26] This second investment was cancelled amidst public angst and outcry in Australia over excessive Chinese investment in key Australian assets. Still Chinalco's first investment would constitute the largest outward investment transaction from China to date.[27]

Sovereign wealth funds are also liable to specialize, depending on their origin. Mideast funds are likely to focus on petrochemical and similar investments that leverage their oil-driven economic expertise. Meanwhile, Chinese and other exporter country sovereign investment funds are likely to focus on cementing their supply chain and generally building up their financial and technical expertise. The difference may lie in whether they begin to become more like investment banks in nature, investing funds but also serving as capital providers and arrangers. This may indeed come to pass for some of the larger funds. However, it will take time for these funds to build the necessary expertise and apparatus to provide quick, regular capital funds. This process is likely to be further slowed by the funds' investing losses and short-term needs to finance their own country's declining economies. In fact, the slowdown of many of these commodity-driven and trade-driven economies is likely to diminish the sovereign wealth "problem" to a handful of funds as these entities are depleted for domestic purposes.

The mad dash of 2007 and 2008 to send investment bankers and lawyers to these regions was thus an overreaction, but at least some of these funds will still be on the prowl, investing strategically in the United States and elsewhere. Their experiences of the last two years will mean that they will continue to look for investment expertise, either through investment or internal hiring. Evidencing such a trend in February 2009, Temasek replaced its own CEO, a Singapore national, with Charles "Chip" Goodyear, the U.S.-born ex-CEO of BHP Billiton, the global mining company.[28] Sovereign wealth funds will also continue to serve an ancillary rather than primary role, making smaller investments and facilitating larger ones. In doing so, these funds will increasingly seek to guarantee a minimum return in order to assure that the failures during the financial crisis are not repeated. Given the difficulties with banks that private equity firms have had over the past year and a half, this may be a source that private equity firms cultivate. In fact, sovereign wealth funds may become locally vigorous competitors to private equity funds using their resources and local influence to dominate their markets.

Sovereign wealth funds are often young, though, and controlled by their governments. This will make investors wary of taking capital when these funds are deemed too political. For example, in December 2008, Dow Chemical was badly burned when the government of Kuwait decided to terminate the $17.4 billion chemical joint venture between Dow and Kuwaiti-owned Petrochemicals Industries Company. The joint venture had been agreed to only the month before but was scuttled by the Kuwaiti government after political protests in Kuwait against the investment.[29] This type of overt political decision making hurts sovereign wealth funds, but it also shows the parameters of their possible regulation and differentiation.

The Sovereign Wealth Fund Problem

The 2007–2008 wave of sovereign wealth fund investments stirred tremendous public controversy. Detractors highlighted the risk that these fund investments were not made for economic purposes. Rather, sovereign wealth funds would use their funds and investments to overtly or subtly act against Western interests. Alternatively, sovereign wealth funds would invest for very good economic purposes contrary to Western industry and business. Here, the anxiety was that sovereign wealth funds would use their ownership interests in U.S. and European companies to direct capital or valued technology to their own countries. In other words, they would steal our secrets. Despite these concerns, there was no concrete evidence that any of this conduct was occurring. The fears concerning sovereign wealth funds appeared to be simply, at this point, a fear, though possibly a well-founded one.

Perhaps pointing toward an overreaction, the public response to the sudden increase in sovereign wealth fund investment was similar to other waves of high-profile foreign investment in the United States. In the 1980s, it had been Japan. The concern was that the Japanese, and their growing investment in the United States, were going to threaten the economic well-being of America. People like Steven Forbes, a future failed presidential candidate and publisher of *Forbes*, and Lester Thurow, at the time dean of the MIT Sloan School of Management, raised a public alarm.[30] The result was a tightening of the national securities investment laws and a variety of forced restrictive trade pacts and quotas upon the Japanese. The worry turned out to be overinflated, as Japan's economy suffered from its own economic crash in the 1990s. Nonetheless, it did produce one of the most lovable of Michael Keaton's movies, *Gung Ho*, about a Japanese company taking control of a U.S. auto factory. In that movie, the Japanese were portrayed as friendly people seeking to understand American culture. But as the 1980s wore on, the public mood changed. The 1992 Michael Crichton book and movie *Rising Sun* portrayed the Japanese as sinister, bent on taking over the United States.

The fear of sovereign wealth funds seemed to be affected by xeno-phobia, like the reaction against Japanese investment. This response was no doubt spurred by general fears about the rise of the Chinese economy and the growing power of Middle Eastern Islamic nations. In defense of sovereign wealth funds, though, their investment provided tangible benefits to Western countries. Capital investment is a good thing. The American railroads and the industrial economy in the Gilded Age were built in large part with British funds (i.e., foreign capital).[31]

In the case of sovereign wealth funds, their U.S. investment has the virtue of recycling currency into our country. The United States continues to run the world's largest trade deficit as it continues to purchase cheap, imported goods and commodities from other countries. So at a minimum, this investment recycles money back to the United States in the short term to hopefully bridge the gap toward our country closing this trade deficit. Furthermore, in these particularly troubled times, foreign capital is particularly necessary to restart our economy in a world of scarce credit. Sovereign wealth fund investment absent nefarious influence can provide a source of capital to further grow the economy.

The trick is to balance the desire for this capital against the fears, real or imagined, surrounding sovereign wealth fund investment. It may be true that sovereign wealth funds have yet to cause any particular trouble, but the potential for mischief is there. The appropriate measure of caution will drive the need for sensible regulation and set the tension between attracting this capital and appropriately regulating it. As the Sultan Ahmed bin Sulayem, chairman of the United Arab Emirate's sovereign wealth fund, stated to the BBC: "We are investors and we are free to go wherever we want. If you squeeze us, we will go elsewhere."[32] The irony in the sultan's statement is that these countries, including his own, almost all regulate and restrict foreign investment in their own jurisdictions. Nonetheless, the point has validity; any regulation must not only be appropriate but also not drive capital inappropriately toward other less regulated jurisdictions.

The sovereign wealth fund controversy and the drive to regulate such investments during 2008 focused on their governance. These funds are largely run by governments that are not known for their transparency. The funds historically have largely mirrored this practice, holding their investments and investment goals private. They are dark pools of capital. For example, the Sovereign Wealth Fund Institute publishes a transparency index rating each sovereign wealth fund on a scale of 1 to 10. Saudi Arabia's sovereign wealth fund receives a 2, which is particularly troublesome when you look at the scoring system: A fund receives one point for publicly disclosing its main office location address and contact information, such as telephone and fax. Moreover, a score of 8 is needed to be considered adequately transparent. The only non-Western fund to receive a score this high is the Azerbaijani one.[33]

At this point in time, this is perhaps the most legitimate source of concern about these entities. To address these governance issues, the United States and other Western countries have focused on erecting voluntary codes of conduct to ensure openness and professional investing by sovereign wealth funds. Nudged to adopt these codes, presumably these funds would be transformed into professional investing institutions immune from the political pressures of their controlling sovereign. This would have the secondary effect of ensuring that their investment was legitimate and economically based.

In the fall of 2007, the European Community privately circulated a draft voluntary code, and the International Monetary Fund, at the request of the United States, Germany, Italy, Japan, Britain, France, and Canada, took the lead in leveraging this code into an international one.[34] On September 2, 2008, the IMF through the International Working Group of Sovereign Wealth Funds announced that an agreement had been reached in Santiago, Chile, on a voluntary code with 26 countries, including China, Kuwait, Qatar, Russia, and the United Arab Emirates. The code was known as the Santiago Principles, and its 24 principles covered transparency, governance, and accountability. The code was modeled on the open practices of the Norwegian fund, requiring disclosure and reporting of investments and returns, transparency in investing intent, investment for only economic and not political purposes, and good governance.[35]

However, this voluntary code had a number of problems. One of the first problems was definitional. What is a sovereign wealth fund? People agree it includes a state-controlled pool of money designated for investment purposes, like Abu Dhabi's $875 billion fund. The Santiago Principles similarly define sovereign wealth funds as "special purpose investment funds or arrangements, owned by the general government."[36]

But this definition excludes state-controlled companies like Chinalco. In a world where capital can easily be transferred and many of these sovereign wealth funds have massive state-owned industrial complexes, countries can merely reallocate this capital to these enterprises, thereby avoiding even the application of these principles. Moreover, many of the same issues of uneconomic or inappropriate strategic investment arise in the case of these state-controlled industrial companies.

Another problem with a voluntary code is that it is voluntary. The governments agreeing to the Santiago Principles code already publicly state that they comply with many international norms and treaties they appear to blatantly ignore in practice. Does the West really expect these governments to follow the code of conduct they agree to or to otherwise keep investing if it is too rigorous? Here, one need only again peruse the Santiago Principles. The voluntary code uses the term *should* 37 times, including a requirement that "there should be clear and publicly disclosed policies, rules, procedures, or arrangements in relation to the SWF's general approach to funding, withdrawal, and spending operations."[37] This may sound fine on paper, but in practice, the Western nations risk giving up much—recognizing the unique problems of these funds and more direct regulation of legitimate concerns—and gaining very little. In fact, it may create an excessive amount of false comfort.

All this begs the question, though. What is the real problem that any code or proposed solution is addressing? Presumably, it is to track this foreign investment, monitor it, and implement safeguards to ensure that there is no inappropriate activity. If that is the case, a code of conduct, voluntary or otherwise, may not be necessary, at least in the United States. In the United States, we have the basic elements of such a system already in place. The keystone is CFIUS approval. CFIUS is the Committee on Foreign Investment in the United States, an interagency committee chaired by the Secretary of Treasury. It is charged with administering the Exon-Florio Amendment. This law grants the president authority to block or suspend a merger, acquisition, or takeover by a foreign entity if there is "credible evidence" that a "foreign interest exercising control might take action that threatens to impair the national security" and existing provisions of law do not provide "adequate and appropriate authority for the President to protect the national security in the matter before the President."[38] The president has delegated this review process to CFIUS.

The statute was enacted in 1988 in response to the 1987 attempt by Fujitsu Ltd., a Japanese electronics company, to acquire Fairchild Semiconductor Corporation. Again, that was back in the 1980s, when fears of Japan ruled the day. Congress struck back at this menace by passing the Exon-Florio Amendment.[39] In July 2007, Congress passed the National Security Foreign Investment Reform and Strengthened Transparency Act, known as FISA.[40] FISA further enhanced the CFIUS review process and adds to the factors for national security review critical infrastructure and foreign government-controlled transactions. In either instance, CFIUS can initiate a mandatory review. Like the 1988 bill, this amendment was a response to perceived foreign investment threats. This time it was the acquisition of Peninsular & Oriental Steam by Dubai Ports and the ensuing political brawl and heavy congressional protest, which led to Dubai Ports terminating the U.S. component of its acquisition.

The problem is that sovereign wealth funds weren't on Congress's horizon back in July 2007. The 2007 amendments dealt largely with the problem of foreign-controlled entities acquiring controlling stakes in U.S. companies. But the Exon-Florio review process applies to acquisitions of only "controlling" interests. Control is not defined, but it has generally been considered under the securities laws to be a 10 percent or more voting stake. This is generally why the round of sovereign wealth fund investment in 2007 and 2008 was designed to be under this threshold; the parties were attempting to avoid CFIUS review. In response, CFIUS promulgated new regulations in November 2008 to specify that even 10 percent or lower interests could trigger CFIUS review, depending on the way soft and hard control were exercised.[41]

The CFIUS process, together with other foreign investment reporting requirements set up by the Department of Commerce, provides a skein that imposes only incremental regulatory burdens on sovereign wealth funds and investments by companies controlled by foreign governments.[42] It is a scheme that creates the clearance, monitoring, and tracking function that a voluntary code would largely produce while not unduly infringing on the operation of these funds. This is a scheme, a monitoring one, that appears likely to be more effective than a voluntary code of conduct.

The trick is in setting the correct level of review under the CFIUS process and ensuring that it does track and monitor these investments.

A status quo solution seems particularly appropriate in light of the fact that sovereign wealth funds have yet to show any significant harm. In fact, their 2007 and 2008 investments have thus far subsidized U.S. companies significantly, as these funds overpaid for their investments. In a remarkable turn, in October 2008, the Treasury Department Deputy Secretary Robert Kimmitt actually toured the Middle East seeking further sovereign wealth fund investment to assist capital-deprived U.S. corporations.[43] Kimmitt's tour reflected the desperate U.S. need for this capital during the financial crisis.

Moreover, to the extent that sovereign wealth funds do act on an overtly political basis, as the government of Kuwait did with Dow Chemical, they risk alienating the companies who would otherwise solicit them for investment. This will provide a modest, though not complete, check on their behavior. There are still troubling aspects to sovereign wealth funds, their lack of transparency being the most prominent. These problems, though, can be addressed through the data collection features provided under the CFIUS process and through the Department of Commerce. A voluntary code is gravy in these circumstances—certainly to be paid heed to and pushed for, but otherwise to be backed by a real regulatory process. In fact, the primary role of a voluntary code of conduct may be in forestalling backlash. Western political leaders can show their political constituency that they have some gains and forestall harsher, perhaps uneconomic legislation.[44]

There is still the problem of soft power exercised by these funds. And management may favor this investment because sovereign wealth funds are typically passive investors. Sovereign fund investment may therefore be more acceptable to management in that it strengthens their power. A monitoring program as I described does not address this type of power, yet this has been the typical investment made by sovereign wealth funds during the financial crisis. However, as discussed in Chapter 7, these soft power issues are present with normal institutional investing and even more overtly political state pension plan investments. Thus, this problem may be unavoidable, perhaps mitigated by other institutional shareholder pressures by hedge funds and at this point best met with a firm monitoring process. As time progresses, it can then be ascertained if more restrictions on sovereign wealth funds are necessary. In particular, this monitoring process should fluctuate, depending upon the country and fund. It is questionable whether Norway's sovereign wealth fund needs the same monitoring as China's. In fact, as the commodity boom fades and the financial crisis depletes and distracts many sovereign wealth funds, the sovereign wealth fund problem is likely to transform into a Chinese problem to the extent that China keeps accumulating assets at the expense of the United States.

In the meantime, it is important to take perspective and view this is a learning process for both sides. As these funds grow, we will undoubtedly receive more information on their conduct, goals, and even investing skill. We should actively seek to do so. More aggressive steps do not appear either justified or apt to produce more than is needed or provide a structure that incentivizes these funds to invest appropriately in the United States. Reciprocally, sovereign wealth funds' need to show measured returns will also force them to naturally evolve structures and policies to guide their burgeoning wealth outside codes of conduct. A firm monitoring and disclosure process in the United States and Europe should push this process in the right direction. In the future, as sovereign wealth fund investment grows and becomes more professional, the sovereign wealth issue will probably be encapsulated increasingly around the appropriateness of foreign investment generally.

CFIUS and Foreign Investment

The sovereign wealth fund controversy is the latest one arising from five years of sustained foreign investment. In 2007, non-U.S. buyers made $365.6 billion in U.S. acquisitions, accounting for 23 percent of all U.S. takeovers. Even in the down year of 2008, non-U.S. buyers made $289.1 billion in acquisitions, accounting for 29 percent of U.S. takeovers. These figures are a marked increase from the $73 billion in non-U.S. acquisitions in 2002.[45] The list of prominent foreign U.S. acquisitions during this time is long, including InBev's 2008 $52 billion hostile offer for Anheuser-Busch, Saudi Basic Industries Corporation's 2007 $11.6 billion acquisition of GE Plastics, and Vivendi's 2007 $9.8 billion acquisition of Activision.

The growth in non-U.S. acquisitions was due to a number of reasons: a decline in the U.S. dollar during this period, which made U.S. acquisitions more economical for foreign buyers; the industrialization of countries in the Mideast and China, as well as India, Brazil, and Russia, which created significant corporate enterprises in these regions bent on expansion into the United States; the globalization of the economy and the creation of transnational corporate entities, which led to more cross-border acquisitions; and the continuing prominence of the United States as a profit-making center for business, which served to attract this capital (see Figure 5.3). These forces combined to increase foreign direct investment in the United States and probably mark a continuing U.S. dependence on foreign investors for lifeblood in the deal market. Again, this dependence will be exacerbated because of the financial crisis due not only to the capital needs of the United States but also to its perceived status as a safe haven for global investment.

Despite the rise of the BRIC (Brazil, Russia, India, China) and Mideast countries, foreign capital has still largely come from more traditional sources. In 2008, 6 of the 10 largest foreign buyers were European. The other four were Japan, Israel, Canada, and India. The largest buyer

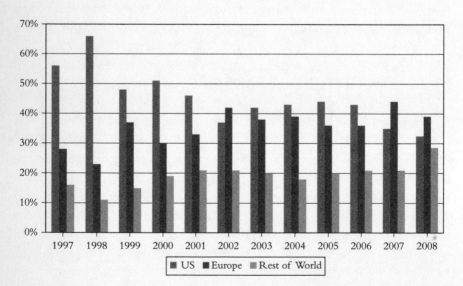

Figure 5.3   Global Takeover Volume by Region 1997–2008
SOURCE: Thomson Reuters

was Belgium, due to the InBev transaction; the second largest was Switzerland. Ironically, the Japanese were particularly acquisitive in 2008, acquiring $36 billion worth of U.S. companies, including three significant bids made on a hostile basis. Moreover, the largest non-Western buyer on the list of foreign investors was India, with $5.02 billion in acquisitions. Notably, China was not among the 10 largest buyers but was the fourth largest recipient of U.S. takeover funds, with $13.23 billion worth of acquisitions. While non-Western acquisitions are in an embryonic stage, due to their increasing industrialization, when economic normalcy returns, they are likely to be the growth areas for non-U.S. to U.S. takeovers (see Figure 5.4).[46]

This investment has raised public outcry like that against sovereign wealth funds. The most significant protest seemingly appeared out of nowhere in 2006, when Peninsular & Oriental Steam Navigation Company (P&O) based in Great Britain, agreed to be acquired by Dubai Ports. Dubai Ports was based in the United Arab Emirates and controlled by that country. P&O had provided contract services under long-term contracts at over 20 ports in the United States, including New York, New Jersey, and New Orleans. The deal did not initially raise any concerns. CFIUS cleared the transaction without an extended review

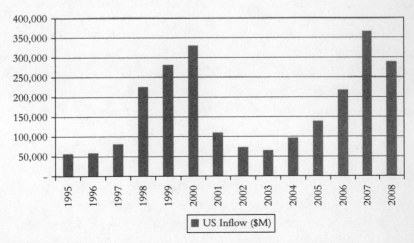

Figure 5.4   Non-U.S. Buyers Acquiring U.S. Targets (Value in Millions) 1995–2008
SOURCE: Thomson Reuters

under its normal process. However, one of Dubai Ports' potential business partners under the new arrangement, Eller & Company, objected to the deal and began lobbying Congress. A firestorm soon erupted as New York Senator Chuck Schumer and others openly questioned the deal, asserting that it would harm U.S. national security. On March 8, 2006, the House Appropriations Committee voted 62 to 2 to block the deal. Dubai Ports then capitulated and announced that it would sell these ports to a "U.S. entity," which later turned out to be an asset management division of AIG, Inc.[47]

The dispute was puzzling: Dubai Ports was acquiring an English company with port operations in the United States, and Dubai Ports is headquartered in the United Arab Emirates, one of our strongest allies in the Middle East. Television interviews with the representatives of Dubai Ports at the time showed their frustration, but the undertone of Dubai Ports' opponents was clear: The Middle Eastern country could allow some type of weapon to be smuggled into the United States. Dubai Ports could not be fully trusted. Here, the concerns seemed overstated and inappropriate, given the fact that the United Arab Emirates frequently and reciprocally allowed the use of its territory by U.S. military forces.

Congress won its victory against Dubai Ports and retained its interest in national security and foreign acquisitions. Congress turned its attention to the Exon-Florio Amendment. On February 28, 2007, the U.S. House of Representatives passed FISA by a vote of 423 to 0. Who, after all, would vote against increased national security? As already noted, the bill heightened congressional oversight of the review process, mandated CFIUS review of any transaction where the acquiring entity is owned or controlled by a foreign government, and broadened the scope of potential review areas.[48]

Still, the bill was relatively mild. It only slightly heightened U.S. supervision of foreign investment. However, the real test would be in implementation. The rhetoric surrounding the congressional action had poisoned the atmosphere for foreign investment, despite the fact that U.S. companies were the larger beneficiaries of foreign investment. In 2008, U.S. companies made $189.4 billion in non-U.S. takeovers, significantly lower than the $289.1 billion in U.S. takeovers by foreign companies.[49]

In the wake of this new law, CFIUS has indeed stepped up its review of foreign transactions. In 2008, CFIUS conducted 22 full transaction reviews, a contrast with only 2 such reviews in 2004.[50] Nonetheless, despite an uptick in formal reviews, the true scope of CFIUS review is still largely unknown, as national security review remains a murky world and the transparency of CFIUS review limited. The reason is that many deals do not enter the formal review process but instead are found wanting prior to any extended review and abandoned.

The most prominent example involved the 2005 proposed acquisition by CNOOC Ltd., the Chinese oil company, of Unocal Corporation, the U.S. oil company. There the U.S. government privately blocked a bid by CNOOC for Unocal, citing inappropriate access by Chinese government to Unocal's specialized drilling technology. This was that CNOOC's bid was reportedly $2.1 billion higher than a competing successful bid by the American oil company Chevron Corporation, and that the majority of Unocal's oil assets were located outside the United States. CNOOC never even had a chance to plead its case before CFIUS, though to be fair, its bid may not have been as firm as the media led people to believe.[51]

To date, only one transaction has been officially blocked under the Exon-Florio Amendment. Not surprisingly, this also involved China. In 1990, the president unwound the acquisition of MAMCO Manufacturing, an aircraft parts manufacturer, by the China International Trust & Investment Corporation (CITIC). CITIC supposedly had a significant relationship with the Chinese army—more formally, the People's Liberation Army of the People's Republic of China. CFIUS unanimously recommended that President George H.W. Bush order the divestiture of MAMCO by CITIC, an action the president promptly took, citing the fact that this acquisition threatened national security because of CITIC's relationship with the Chinese military and the "unique access" to U.S. aerospace technology CITIC would obtain.[52]

President George H.W. Bush's action was unusual, though, and most buyers realize the futility of their acquisition well before a presidential recommendation is made under the CFIUS review process. More typical of CFIUS regulatory action is CFIUS's review of Hong Kong–based Hutchison Whampoa Ltd.'s attempted acquisition of Global Crossing Ltd., the fiber-optic network company. CFIUS initiated a second-stage 45-day review of the pending acquisition. In the wake of this investigation, Hutchison Whampoa terminated the acquisition.[53]

The growing role of CFIUS highlights the importance of public relations and media in transactions, particularly those with a regulatory component. A singular example of this in the modern age came with the agreement of Bain Capital and Huawei Technologies Co., Ltd. to acquire 3Com Corporation, announced on September 28, 2007. In a conference call with the CEO, Edgar Masri, on the day of the transaction announcement, an analyst inquired about the Huawei component of the investment. Instead of answering the question, Masri stonewalled, refusing to say whether the transaction was conditioned on CFIUS clearance or what Huawei's stake in the combined company would be. This information would later be publicly disclosed, but 3Com would never disclose whether the deal was conditioned on CFIUS clearance. Nor would 3Com ever publicly disclose the postacquisition governance rights of Huawei over the company.

Unfortunately for 3Com, Huawei had a bad reputation with the U.S. government. Huawei had extensive ties with the Chinese military and was promoted by the Chinese government as a national champion, and 3Com had reportedly neglected to make pretransaction announcement inquiries with the U.S. government beforehand. The government balked at clearing the transaction, and on February 20, 2008, 3Com announced that it, and its agreed buyers, Bain Capital and Huawei, had agreed to withdraw their application for clearance of the acquisition under Exon-Florio.[54] Both parties subsequently attempted to terminate the acquisition agreement.

On March 20, 2008, 3Com also announced that it intended to pursue the $66 million reverse termination fee from Bain Capital. The odd silence from 3Com about the involvement of Bain Capital and the need for Exon-Florio clearance extended to the acquisition agreement, which provided that Bain Capital and Huawei were required to pay 3Com a $66 million termination fee if "a U.S. Federal regulatory agency (that is not an antitrust regulatory agency) has informed [Bain Capital] or [3Com] (or their Representatives) that it intends to take action to prevent the Merger."[55] Presumably, this was meant to pick up the Exon-Florio clearance. However, the fact that it was the regulatory approval that dare not speak its name in the acquisition agreement shows the length 3Com and its buyers were going to keep the Exon-Florio process private.

Bain Capital disputed the applicability of this provision to a failure to achieve Exon-Florio clearance, and the parties are now in litigation over the termination fee. Ultimately, 3Com's failures highlight the importance of public relations in deals, as well as government cooperation and early communication. In this deal, 3Com came off as hiding something, and the national security apparatus reacted badly to 3Com's secretive conduct.[56] In the wake of 3Com's failure, it replaced its CEO with Robert Mao, who ironically announced his intention to be based in Hong Kong in order to grow the company's Chinese operations.[57] Mao's relocation illustrated the difficulty of cabining off technology and expertise in a global age.

In addition, 3Com's failures illustrates the political nature of the national security process. Foreign buyers, including sovereign wealth funds, need to be alert to both regulatory realities and political sensitivities. The stumbles of Bain Capital and 3Com show the importance of obtaining public relations and government presence early in the process. As foreign investment grows, these controversies are likely to continue. However, in today's age of $700 billion bailouts, foreign money is needed to sustain the United States. So, public outcry is likely to be muted by the U.S. government's limited desire to intervene and be seen as hostile to this investment.

Certain countries such as China will still continue to receive heightened scrutiny. And while CFIUS review and U.S. public outcry at foreign acquisitions have focused on non-Western buyers, our allies in Europe and elsewhere in the West are not immune. For example, CFIUS imposed extensive restrictions as a condition to its clearance of the French telecommunication company Alcatel SA's acquisition of Lucent Technologies Inc., and in Chapter 8, I talk about the public outcry over Belgium-based InBev's proposed acquisition of Anheuser-Busch, the American beer-maker.

The process with 3Com and Bain Capital also shows the often hazy difference between sovereign wealth funds and foreign investors, suggesting that the distinction between the two may be overstated. This may change if sovereign wealth funds truly become more like investment

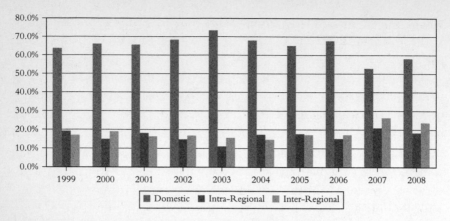

Figure 5.5   Cross–Border Takeover Activity 1999–2008
SOURCE: Morgan Stanley; Thomson Financial 2008 figures as of April 30, 2008

banks and function as alternative capital providers. But right now, this is a potential that has not blossomed. The result is that the jurisdiction of origin of investment is likely to continue to be more important than the form of capital. This may be borne out in future CFIUS reviews.

Absent a 1930s wave of recessionary protectionism, capital will continue to become increasingly global. Foreign investment will only increase and become a more significant source of investment. This is to the advantage of global investment banks, attorneys, and others who have a global presence. It will also make for new sources of capital, perhaps breaking traditional routes such as bank finance. The future depends upon America's continued openness. The CFIUS process, as shrouded in mystery as it still is today, must come out into the open, making its process clear and transparent. In doing so, CFIUS can work to counteract prior U.S. actions that have put off foreigners on U.S. investment. In the end, the United States has a choice. It can be like France, which has protected its yogurt-maker Danone SA from outside takeover by designating it a national champion, or it can move toward a prudent, more welcoming stance.[58]

The choice is driven by the growing globalization of the takeover market (see Figure 5.5). In 2008, European takeover activity at $1.3 trillion exceeded U.S. activity at $1.08 trillion. In that year, Asian take over activity was at $502 billion, only a 10 percent decrease over 2007.

Meanwhile, cross-border takeovers continued to be an important part of the market. In 2004, cross-border takeovers amounted to $589 billion, and by 2008, the amount had risen to $1.14 trillion, a decline of 36.3 percent from 2007's figure of $1.79 trillion.[59] The continued, sustained worldwide rise of takeover activity will continue to drive cross-border activity toward and away from the United States. The global nature of the takeover will be a driving force in deal-making in the coming decades, particularly when more stable economic times return. In these troubled times, this trend should be encouraged.

Chapter 6

Bear Stearns and the Moral Hazard Principle

Into March 2008, the markets remained snarled in a credit crunch. In the period from December 2007 through February 2008, financial institutions had undertaken a massive recapitalization globally, raising $155.1 billion in new capital from investors.[1] Sovereign wealth funds were the largest single type of investors, supplying $24 billion of total domestic investment.[2] For a time, the stock market continued to trade near its fall 2007 highs. However, the relatively stable equity markets hid turmoil in the credit markets, as banks continued to struggle under the weight of the housing crisis and the mortgage-related assets on their balance sheets. Meanwhile, private equity firms remained hard-pressed to keep in place preagreed financing to complete their pending acquisitions. As credit remained scarce, the U.S. economy was undergoing something it had never experienced in modern times: a credit-driven rather than equity-driven market correction.

It was amid this backdrop that Bear Stearns imploded the week of March 10. It would be a historic and important event with significant ramifications for deals and deal-making. The saving of Bear Stearns would be a case study of how deal lawyers structure deals both within and up to the bounds of the law.

Saving Bear Stearns

In March 2007, the state of the investment bank Bear Stearns was best categorized as troubled. The battering was clear enough. In June 2007, two hedge funds advised by Bear Stearns and created to invest in sub-prime mortgage-related assets had become insolvent. Their failure had required Bear Stearns to commit approximately $3.2 billion to bail out one of the funds and had also made market participants particularly wary of the investment bank's exposure to mortgage-related assets.[3] Moreover, Bear Stearns was the most highly leveraged of the five large investment banks, with an approximate 33:1 debt to equity ratio.[4] Bear Stearns was considered to have the largest exposure to mortgage-related assets. The bank had already taken $1.9 billion in write-downs related to its ownership of these types of assets in the fourth quarter of 2008.[5] But the news was not all bad. At the beginning of March, Bear Stearns's long-term debt, despite downgrades, was still rated investment grade by Standard and Poors.[6] On Friday, March 7, 2008, its stock price closed at $70.08 per share—far down from its all-time high of $171.51 in January 2007, to be sure, but the market was not predicting Bear Stearns's collapse.

The week of March 10 changed all this. It was the week that Bear Stearns's luck ran out, but it was also an incredible illustration of the public trust necessary for any financial institution to survive. In that week, over the course of five days, a panic hit Wall Street. It would unfold around Bear Stearns, as rumors doubting the firm's solvency began to spread. It would end with the sudden downfall of one of Wall Street's bulge bracket banks. The failure would become almost commonplace by the next September, but at the time it was extraordinary.

It began on Monday, when rumors began to spread in the market that a major investment bank had rejected a standard $2 billion repurchase loan request from Bear Stearns.[7] From there, rumors increasingly spread that Bear Stearns was in financial difficulty. Counterparties become hesitant to trade with Bear Stearns and otherwise demanded collateral for their preexisting and future trades. Asset managers such as hedge funds began to move funds to other financial institutions.[8] Bear Stearns was forced to put out a press release stating: "There is absolutely no truth to the rumors of liquidity problems that circulated today in the market."[9] Nonetheless, the market remained skeptical of Bear Stearns's health, and credit default swaps for the company's debt began to trade up sharply, going for more than $1 million for every $10 million piece of 10-year debt.[10]

Rumors of Bear Stearns's perilous state continued to spread on Tuesday. Market traders heard the scuttlebutt, and hedge funds and other institutional traders continued to withdraw their trades and assets from the firm. In an ominous sign, the credit default swap market for Bear Stearns shut down. No one was willing to insure against a Bear Stearns collapse.[11] Bear Stearns management recognized the crisis and attempted to strike back. On Wednesday, Alan Schwartz, the recently appointed CEO of Bear Stearns, went on CNBC. The purpose of his appearance was to dampen rumors that Bear Stearns was suffering liquidity problems.

In a seminal exchange, David Faber, the CNBC host, asked Schwartz about counterparty risk and rumors that the investment bank Goldman Sachs would not trade with Bear Stearns. Schwartz responded: "There's been a lot of volatility in the market. . . . We are in a constant dialogue with all of the major dealers and the counterparties on the street and we are not being made aware of anybody who is not taking our credit as a counterparty . . . Our liquidity position has not changed at all. Our balance sheet has not weakened at all. . . ."[12]

The exchange was cited as Bear Stearns's first public death blow. Banks run on trust and confidence, and Faber's remark was seen as publicly alerting the markets to a growing lack of confidence. But it is unfair to pin Bear Stearns's fall at this point on Faber's questions. The rumors were gathering, and a storm was about to hit. Bear Stearns was in that precarious of a position. Thursday was when it all ended for Bear Stearns. By that day, the rumors were rampant, traders were en masse refusing to conduct business with Bear Stearns, and asset managers, particularly hedge funds, continued to rush to pull funds from the bank. The hedge fund D.E. Shaw & Co. alone had withdrawn $5 billion in cash. More perilously, Bear required daily financing of approximately $75 billion to function. These funds were obtained in the short-term repurchase (repo) market, with Bear putting up collateral assets in exchange for cash liquidity. On Thursday morning, Bear was unable to obtain approximately $20 billion of the $75 billion required.[13]

By Thursday night, Bear Stearns's liquid reserves had dropped from $18.3 billion the week before to $5.9 billion, and it owed Citigroup $2.4 billion.[14] The next day's available borrowings in the repo market looked ready to decline even further. The rapid decline of Bear Stearns's liquidity showed the perils of using prime brokerage accounts (i.e., hedge fund deposits) and daily repo lending for liquidity purposes, as Bear Stearns had done. These funds could be pulled at any time by these sophisticated clients and lenders. When that happened, Bear Stearns concluded on Thursday that without outside assistance it would have to file bankruptcy the next day.[15] Bear had experienced a classic run on the bank driven primarily by a collapse in repo lending with an able assist due to prime brokerage account flight.

After the market close, Schwartz contacted JPMorgan CEO Jamie Dimon and Timothy Geithner, then president of the New York Federal Reserve. Schwartz's sober news: Bear Stearns was going to be insolvent in the morning unless a lifeline was put together. Faced with the sudden collapse of Bear Stearns and the shock it would cause to the financial markets, the Federal Reserve overnight decided to guarantee a 28-day loan from JPMorgan to Bear Stearns in the amount of $30 billion.[16]

The Federal Reserve had no choice. The markets were shaky as it was, and a quick collapse of Bear Stearns would be likely to bring on a chain reaction that would cause a wave of financial institution collapses. Bear Stearns was saved, and it now thought it had 28 days to find a lifeline. Additionally, the market thought that Bear Stearns's situation was likely to be achieved through a stockholder-friendly resolution. Bear Stearns's stock closed that Friday at $30 a share.

The decision did not sit well politically with Secretary of the Treasury Henry Paulson. Moreover, Bear Stearn's financial situation appeared to be further destabilizing that Friday, and according to Geithner, the run even accelerated.[17] That Friday evening, Schwartz was informed by Paulson and Geithner that the guarantee and loan would be terminated in 72 hours by the Fed, leaving Bear Stearns to find an alternative transaction by that time or declare bankruptcy.[18] The reasons for the government's reversal of course on Bear Stearns still remain somewhat murky, though the government has since adamantly claimed that it had no choice due to the continuing deterioration of Bear Stearns. The next move by the government was less mysterious.[19] It apparently already had an idea about a buyer for Bear Stearns.

There were two prospective bidders: JPMorgan and a consortium led by private equity firm J.C. Flowers. The Fed and the Treasury Department, which were both actively involved in structuring this bailout, were unable to commit to provide the approximately $20 billion in financial assistance J.C. Flowers required to make an acquisition, essentially locking the J.C. Flowers group out of the process.[20] Furthermore, Treasury pushed JPMorgan to offer as low a price as possible for Bear Stearns, a company that on Friday had closed at $30 a share and on Monday had closed at $70 a share. Under Secretary of the Treasury Robert Steel would later testify that Secretary Paulson encouraged this low price in order to prevent future moral hazard by financial institutions.[21]

JPMorgan had maximum leverage, and Secretary Paulson deliberately encouraged JPMorgan to price the transaction low. When the final per-share price was announced, it was shocking. JPMorgan agreed to pay $2 a share for a company that a year ago was trading as high as $172 a share. The Federal Reserve had also agreed to continue guaranteeing Bear Stearns's liabilities up to $30 billion. The Fed's subsidy was a pure wealth transfer to JPMorgan's shareholders. On that Monday, JPMorgan's stock closed up 10 percent as the broader market declined. The stock price rise increased the bank's market capitalization by more than $12 billion. This was the market's measure of the amount of money JPMorgan had earned on its acquisition.

For those who follow their history, this deal was similar to the Goodbody one. In 1970, Merrill Lynch was picked as the biggest banker on Wall Street to pay $15 million to take over Goodbody & Company. In the process Merrill demanded, and received, a backstop guarantee of $30 million from the rest of the Wall Street community and made tremendous profits in securing Goodbody's brokerage operation. This time, the Federal Reserve had put together a similar bailout, with benefits going to the market leader.[22]

The market erupted in frenzied debate over the implications of this bailout with many decrying the bargain basement price forced on Bear Stearns. Others criticized the help provided, insisting that Bear Stearns should have been allowed to collapse. For deal watchers, though, the most interesting thing about the Bear Stearns deal was not the price, but its terms. Over the weekend, the lawyers for JPMorgan—Wachtell, Lipton, Rosen & Katz—had managed to negotiate a number of unique provisions in the acquisition agreement to ensure that the deal would be completed.

JPMorgan and its lawyers were attempting to address two problems: First, the deal price offered was so low that Bear Stearns's shareholders might revolt and simply decide that bankruptcy was a preferred option. Second, the employees of Bear Stearns were unlikely to welcome JPMorgan's takeover and needed firm oversight even before deal completion. The agreement Wachtell negotiated pushed the legal envelope, going much further than Delaware law typically allows for deal protection devices. But in their haste, Wachtell would soon prove too clever. The agreement had several features that were designed to ensure that Bear Stearns could not escape JPMorgan's embrace, but these provisions would soon turn out to be more beneficial to Bear Stearns than to JPMorgan.

JPMorgan's Grip

The acquisition agreement placed Bear Stearns in a tight grip until the acquisition closed. It provided JPMorgan the right to direct the business of Bear Stearns in its reasonable discretion, down to having a veto right on Bear Stearns's ability to hire, promote, or terminate "employees in the position of vice president or above."[23] This was highly unusual. Acquisition agreements typically contain negative control rights over a company. So, for example, a typical acquisition agreement would contain provisions preventing the target from selling material assets or declaring unusual dividends. But these agreements seldom contained affirmative rights like those JPMorgan had obtained. The reason was that these provisions probably violated Delaware law as an undue delegation of corporate control by the target's board to the buyer. Bear Stearns was incorporated under the laws of the State of Delaware, and so Delaware law governed the validity of the Bear Stearns board's actions in agreeing to this transaction.

Bear Stearns's Put

Delaware law requires that the shareholders of an acquired company in a merger have a vote, and so the acquisition agreement provided for Bear Stearns to hold a shareholder meeting for its shareholders to approve the transaction. If Bear Stearns's shareholders voted no, the acquisition agreement required that the companies negotiate a restructuring of the transaction and resubmit the deal to Bear Stearns's shareholders for approval at the same $2 a share price. This obligation lasted for a full year until March 16, 2009. Moreover, the agreement only permitted the Bear Stearns board to change its recommendation if a higher bid emerged. The Bear Stearns board could terminate the agreement only after one year. JPMorgan thus had the option of waiting a full year before Bear Stearns could terminate its agreement to accept a higher proposal.[24]

The provision was designed to ensure that JPMorgan would have a second, and possibly a third, bite at the apple if Bear Stearns's shareholders voted no. It was highly unusual. Almost always in the case of a no vote, a target can terminate the acquisition agreement with its only obligation being a possible termination fee payment to a buyer. The net effect was still probably favorable to Bear Stearns's shareholders. The provision effectively provided Bear Stearns's shareholders a put right for a year to JPMorgan. During that time, Bear Stearns's shareholders could theoretically keep voting no while waiting for a better option to appear and for Bear Stearns and the markets generally to stabilize.

The Bear Stearns Headquarters

In 2001, Bear Stearns had built a beautiful 47-story headquarters building in Midtown Manhattan, which was named one of the best new skyscrapers for that year. Under the agreement, JPMorgan was granted an option to purchase Bear Stearns's headquarters for $1.1 billion.[25] An asset option of this type was not unusual in distressed sales. Dynegy Inc. had negotiated an option to purchase Enron's Northern Natural

Gas pipeline when it agreed to a distressed purchase of that company and an investment of $1.5 billion. The option was eventually exercised, even though Dynegy escaped buying Enron, which ignominiously fell into bankruptcy.[26]

The JPMorgan building option was a weaker form than Dynegy's and exercisable in circumstances where the acquisition agreement was terminated and Bear Stearns's board had either changed their recommendation or the agreement was terminated after the one-year anniversary thereof and another bid was pending at the time. This was actually a relatively minor form of deal-protection device. It applied only in confined circumstances and allowed Bear Stearns to keep its building if Bear Stearns's shareholders voted no simply because of an objection to the $2 a share price.[27]

The Uncapped Option

In connection with the execution of the acquisition agreement, Bear Stearns issued JPMorgan an option to purchase 19.9 percent of Bear Stearns at $2 a share. The option was limited to only 19.9 percent of Bear Stearns because of the requirements of New York Stock Exchange Listing Rule 312. Rule 312 prohibits a company listed on the NYSE from issuing 20 percent or more of a listed company's voting stock without prior shareholder approval.[28]

This type of option is not unusual. It first arose as a form of termination fee that also functioned to kill pooling accounting. In prior times, the exercise of the option and issuance of such a significant number of shares meant that a subsequent bidder could use only purchase accounting in their acquisition, not pooling accounting. This was a significant deterrent because the use of pooling accounting meant that a buyer did not have to write off good will to its earnings. Pooling accounting had been eliminated in 2001, but these options continued to linger, particularly in bank deals. The reason is that they provide a cash-free form of compensation if the option is exercised since the bidder is compensated in shares of the target.

In Bear Stearns's case, it probably did conserve cash, but the option contained a unique feature. It was an uncapped option; in other words, if a higher bidder emerged, then JPMorgan's compensation on the option was not limited. This type of option, one where the payment could presumably exceed the 3 to 4 percent maximum limit generally imposed by Delaware law, had in other circumstances been ruled an inappropriate deal-protection device for a company involved in a change of control in the seminal case of *Paramount v. QVC*.[29]

Appraisal Rights

Finally, JPMorgan offered stock consideration to Bear Stearns's shareholders instead of cash. Presumably, this was done to avoid providing appraisal rights to Bear Stearns's shareholders under Section 262 of the Delaware General Corporation Law.[30] Appraisal rights allow a shareholder to go to the Delaware court and have the court independently assess the value of his or her shares. The shareholder receives this court-ordered amount, which can be higher or lower than the consideration offered by the buyer.

If JPMorgan had offered cash, these rights would have been available, and Bear Stearns's stockholders could go to a Delaware court to seek a determination of the fair value of their stock. Given the bargain basement price being paid here, there was a real risk that appraisal rights could provide Bear Stearns's shareholders substantial compensation. The distinction highlights a flaw in the appraisal rights statute. Simply by altering the consideration, parties could take away the right. The distinction here made no sense, but was leveraged by JPMorgan to its advantage.

JPMorgan's Out

In exchange for agreeing to these deal protections, Bear Stearns negotiated an equally tight death grip on JPMorgan. The acquisition agreement did not have an out for any further deterioration of Bear Stearns and particularly did not have a MAC clause.[31] Unless Bear Stearns deliberately breached the agreement or the guarantee, JPMorgan was bound to complete this deal.

Bear Stearns's Fury

In the ensuing uproar after announcement of the deal, Bear Stearns's shareholders and employees claimed that the government had not only forced Bear Stearns into the arms of JPMorgan but also done so at a penalizing price. Two days after the acquisition agreement was signed, James Dimon, JPMorgan's chief executive, ventured out in the rain to Bear headquarters to speak to the wounded Bear employees. Landon Thomas Jr. and Eric Dash of the *New York Times* relayed this exchange:

"In this room are people who have built this firm and lost a lot, our fortunes," one Bear executive said to Mr. Dimon with anger in his voice. "What will you do to make us whole?"

The packed room of senior managing directors applauded.

Mr. Dimon responded gingerly. "You're acting like it's our fault, and it's not. If you stay we will make you happy."

But the Bear employee was not satisfied. "I think it's galling you come into our house and you call this a 'merger,'" the Bear executive went on.

This time, Mr. Dimon was silent.[32]

This debate missed the only other alternative for Bear Stearns, given the government's position: bankruptcy. Given Bear Stearns's substantial assets, the question was whether its equity holders would reap more than $2 a share in bankruptcy. This may have been a possibility for an industrial company with hard assets like factories, but Bear Stearns was principally a brokerage operation. Brokerage operations are not permitted to file bankruptcy under Chapter 11, which permits a reorganization and allows a bankrupt company to keep any going concern value. Rather, brokerages are required to file under Chapter 7, which requires that they sell off their assets and liquidate. The rule is designed to protect the security holders who have deposited securities with the brokerage. However, here it significantly handicapped Bear Stearns. It would have to find enough cash to keep the brokerage operating until it could be sold and otherwise sell off other assets to do so while the main holding company entered into bankruptcy.

This made the bankruptcy option substantially more uncertain than normal. Bear Stearns would ultimately decide not to pursue this option, claiming that there was insufficient liquidity in its operations to manage such a sell-off. In fact, reports of the board deliberations would later emerge indicating that only ex-Bear Stearns CEO James Cayne would support a bankruptcy filing, and only as a means to punish the U.S. government for its conduct.[33]

But another force was working to benefit Bear Stearns's shareholders. The agreements Wachtell had designed to tightly bind Bear Stearns to JPMorgan and prevent its escape were having a different effect.

JPMorgan's Dilemma

JPMorgan's problem arose from the interaction of its guarantee with the voting provisions in the acquisition agreement. Under the acquisition agreement, Bear Stearns had a year to keep the deal outstanding, during which time its only obligation was to repeatedly hold shareholder meetings to approve the transaction. JPMorgan's guarantee required JPMorgan to keep guaranteeing Bear Stearns's liabilities incurred during that time period. That is, even after the rejection from Bear Stearns's shareholders, JPMorgan's guarantee would continue to apply to any liabilities Bear Stearns accrued up to the date the agreement was terminated.[34]

The provision allowed Bear Stearns's shareholders to seek a higher bid while Bear Stearns could still trade safely in the shadow of JPMorgan's guarantee. Although the guarantee would not apply to liabilities accrued after termination of the acquisition agreement, it may have been much broader than JPMorgan and Wachtell meant it to be. This is because the guarantee was retroactively terminated only if there was a change of the recommendation by Bear Stearns's board, not a negative vote by Bear Stearns's shareholders. The language in the guarantee also suggested a scenario where an offer could be made and the board could recommend that shareholders reject the third-party offer, but still permit shareholders to tender into the new offer. So, Bear Stearns's board could simply sit tight, wait for its shareholders to reject the deal for a year, and then when things had stabilized, seek a better transaction.[35]

Apparently, over the course of the week after the announcement of the deal, JPMorgan began to realize this issue and the unintentional option it had provided Bear Stearns. This was confirmed by news reports stating that Dimon was "apoplectic" at Wachtell for negotiating these provisions and was seeking to have the guarantee modified.[36] Publicly, JPMorgan stated things differently. They asserted that the uncertainty as to JPMorgan's acquisition was creating continued liquidity problems with Bear Stearns, and so the guarantee needed to be tightened. Nonetheless, the *Wall Street Journal* relayed this conversation between Dimon and the CEO of Bear Stearns Alan Schwartz over the guarantee:

"Don't you understand that we have a problem?" Mr. Dimon asked. Mr. Schwartz, who had been taking a beating over the low price, knew an opening when he saw one. "What do you mean, 'we' have a problem?"[37]

The guarantee appeared to be defective. Moreover, the shareholders and employees of Bear Stearns were seething. They had no incentive to support this deal. JPMorgan needed these shareholders to approve the transaction and, importantly, needed to keep the Bear Stearns employees satisfied. Otherwise, it would significantly destroy the value JPMorgan had agreed to pay for. JPMorgan had another option. It still had the power to direct Bear Stearns's operations in its reasonable discretion. It might attempt to use this power to prevent Bear Stearns from incurring new liabilities if the deal appeared on the verge of collapse. This would be questionable under Delaware law, but JPMorgan might still try it.

Probably because of its need to assuage the Bear Stearns employees, JPMorgan decided not to go this route. Instead, the issue was resolved that weekend when JPMorgan agreed to raise its offer to $10 a share for Bear Stearns. JPMorgan used the opportunity to rework the arrangement and lock up Bear Stearns definitively. In doing so, JPMorgan and its attorneys at Wachtell stretched the bounds of Delaware law past any normal limitations. To understand why, though, it is first necessary to go through the changes implemented by these new agreements.

The Share Exchange

The most controversial and significant revision to the deal was the elimination of the 19.9 percent option and its replacement with a share exchange agreement. The agreement provided that JP Morgan would be issued a 39.5 percent interest in Bear Stearns without prior approval of Bear Stearns's shareholders. In exchange for this interest, Bear Stearns received shares of JPMorgan. JPMorgan presumably issued shares instead of paying cash in order to avoid providing additional liquidity to Bear Stearns. Moreover, the shares issued to Bear Stearns by JPMorgan were unregistered and could not be sold in the market to otherwise raise cash.[38]

New York Stock Exchange Rule 312, though, still applied, requiring that Bear Stearns's shareholders approve the share issuance. There is an exception under Rule 312, however, if "the delay in securing stockholder approval would seriously jeopardize the financial viability of the enterprise."[39] Bear Stearns relied on this exception to issue these shares to JPMorgan. The NYSE didn't argue with Bear Stearns's request and granted the exemption.

The 39.5 percent interest placed JP Morgan at a significant advantage to obtain stockholder approval. But JP Morgan was not taking any chances this time. On March 24, the day after the parties agreed to recut their deal, JPMorgan acquired 11.5 million Bear Stearns shares in the open market, all of them at $12.24 a share. This constituted an additional 8.91 percent of Bear Stearns. JPMorgan would subsequently acquire a prevote 49.43 percent interest in Bear Stearns.[40] This would mean that the Bear Stearns shareholder vote would become a certainty. After all, only 0.57 percent of the shares needed to approve the transaction after the JPMorgan interest was counted.

JPMorgan probably structured this share acquisition in two separate tranches in order to build a litigation position. In *Omnicare v. NCS HealthCare*, the Delaware Supreme Court by a 3–2 vote struck down a locked-up deal.[41] There, the court reviewed the deal under the *Unocal* standard, which requires that deal-protection devices not be preclusive or coercive and be reasonable in proportion to the threat posed. The Delaware Supreme Court held that under the *Unocal* standard, the agreement of approximately 65 percent of the shareholders to vote for a transaction, together with a force-the-vote provision, a provision that required the company to hold a shareholder vote, was preclusive and coercive. The merger protections were both preclusive and coercive because "any stockholder vote would have been robbed of its effectiveness by . . . [the] predetermined outcome of the merger without regard to the merits of the…transaction at the time the vote was scheduled to be taken."[42] The court ordered this despite the full auction of NCS and its near insolvency at the time. The opinion was criticized by academics and practitioners because of the failure of the Delaware court to provide sufficient latitude to the board to agree to a transaction in such circumstances.

Thereafter, in the Delaware Chancery Court case of *Orman v. Cullman*,[43] the Chancery Court upheld an agreement for a controlling shareholder to vote in favor of the merger. However, the controlling shareholder also agreed that for 18 months after termination of the agreement, the shareholder would vote against any other transaction. Notably, the shareholder vote was conditioned on approval of a majority of the minority, and the judge relied on this fact, that it was not a fait accompli, to make this decision. Since *Orman*, takeover practitioners have generally advised that so long as a deal was theoretically possible, *Omnicare* wasn't implicated. Delaware practitioners have subsequently settled on the "40 percent rule" to set a limit on the highest share threshold a lockup could be under *Omnicare*. This was a rule of thumb. Nowhere had Delaware law validated this measure.

Nonetheless, *Omnicare* was viewed at the time as highly likely to be overturned. The composition of the Delaware Supreme Court had changed since that time. Justice Myron Steele, who dissented from *Omnicare*, was now the chief judge, and Justice Joseph Walsh, who voted to overturn these deal-protection devices in *Omnicare*, was now retired. Later in 2008, Vice Chancellor Stephen Lamb, a judge on the lower Delaware Chancery Court, would even go so far as to assert that "*Omnicare* is of questionable continued vitality."[44]

Nonetheless, it appears that the 39.5 percent figure for the share exchange was set with this 40 percent rule of thumb in mind. The separation of the two events into a share exchange and open market purchase thus preserved a litigation position. If a shareholder ever challenged JPMorgan's actions, JPMorgan could argue that the 39.5 percent issuance was valid and only the market share purchases should be nullified or were otherwise inappropriate, and vice versa.

Other Lockup Arrangements

The revised acquisition agreement and guarantee contained four other significant new provisions designed to further lock up the transaction.

- The $1.1 billion option on Bear Stearns's office building was expanded. JPMorgan could now acquire the building if Bear Stearns's stockholders did not approve the deal at the first shareholders' meeting. This was a powerful incentive for Bear Stearns's shareholders to vote yes for the deal. Otherwise, Bear Stearns would not have any offices to run its business from.
- JPMorgan obtained significantly more control over the day-to-day operations of Bear Stearns, further stretching the Delaware law on this matter.
- The force-the-vote provision was now qualified by new termination rights. JPMorgan and Bear Stearns could now terminate the transaction if the first shareholder approval was not obtained and 120 days elapsed. JPMorgan was also able to negotiate some additional insurance providing it the right to terminate this agreement after the 120 days if a court enjoined JPMorgan from receiving or voting the 39.5 percent in Bear Stearns's interest.
- Finally, the guarantee was amended in a manner that made clear that JPMorgan's guarantee was probably flawed under its original terms. The guarantee now terminated 120 days following the failure of Bear Stearns to receive the approval of Bear Stearns's stockholders for the transaction at any shareholder meeting. This was a significantly shorter period than the one year that Bear Stearns could keep the guarantee in effect.[45]

The Fight for Bear Stearns

Bear Stearns was now cornered. JPMorgan had almost a majority stake and a host of other deal-protection devices in place that made it almost certain that it would obtain the minuscule 0.53 percent yes vote they needed. There were many questions still to ask, though, of the Bear Stearns board's conduct in negotiating this second deal. Did Bear Stearns's board act in due deliberation approving this deal and agreeing to a number of features that made the sale all but a certainty, or did the board sell too hastily? The Bear Stearns board had obtained a higher price but in doing so had seemed to bargain away any chance of any other opportunity. Moreover, why $10? The price was clearly being dictated at this point by negotiating leverage over the contract and the wishes of the government rather than the actual value of Bear Stearns.

This may have been a calculated and correct assessment of its chances without JPMorgan's support. However, the day after the announcement of the revised transaction, the price of Bear Stearns's stock traded above the $10 a share price. The market was predicting that the offer would be raised yet again. Former Bear Stearns CEO and then Bear Stearns Chairman James Cayne quickly took advantage of this fact, selling his remaining shares in the week the new agreement had been announced and pocketing $61 million. Paul A. Novelly, another Bear Stearns director, also disclosed on April 1 that he had sold all of his stock. The market may have been betting on a higher price, but some members of the Bear Stearns board clearly were not.[46]

Given JPMorgan's new agreement, the only out for Bear Stearns left was if a court enjoined the transaction by finding that JPMorgan had overreached in negotiating its deal-protection devices. Five actions were filed between March 17 and March 20 in New York state court. Meanwhile, on March 20 and 24, two more lawsuits were filed in Delaware against Bear Stearns, its directors, and JPMorgan Chase & Co. The race was now on to judicially halt this transaction before JPMorgan voted its shares to complete it.

The first judicial events in these disputes occurred in Delaware. The plaintiffs filed for a preliminary injunction to prevent JPMorgan from voting its acquired shares at the meeting. The plaintiffs argued that the motion should be granted on three separate legal grounds.[47]

Undue Infringement on the Shareholder Franchise

The plaintiffs first argued that the JPMorgan share issuance was inequitable under the seminal case of *Schnell v. Chris-Craft Industries Inc.*[48] In *Schnell*, the Delaware Supreme Court found that management had utilized the corporate machinery "for the purpose of obstructing the legitimate efforts of dissident stockholders in their rights to undertake a proxy contest against management." The court there held that such an action was for an "inequitable purpose, contrary to established principles of corporate democracy."[49]

The primary question under the *Schnell* doctrine was whether Bear Stearns acted inequitably or was merely trying to prevent a bankruptcy and preserve the only deal available. But at what point should this be measured from? Clearly, Bear Stearns was about to go bankrupt before it entered into deal one. But the share issuance here was only in connection with the recut deal. Bear Stearns may have been in a better situation by then, though Bear Stearns would later claim it would have gone bankrupt without the renegotiated deal. It was also unclear whether the *Schnell* doctrine applied at all to a vote on a takeover. *Schnell* took place in the context of a battle to replace directors. The plaintiffs in the Delaware lawsuit were arguing to expand the doctrine to the takeover context.

Lacking a Compelling Justification

The plaintiffs next claimed that the share issuance violated the Delaware Supreme Court's holding in *Blasius Industries Inc. v. Atlas Corp.*[50] The Delaware Supreme Court in *Blasius* held that where an action is taken for the sole or primary purpose of impeding the effectiveness of the shareholder vote, it is deeply suspect and can be sustained only upon the showing of some compelling justification.[51] In their motion, the plaintiffs relied primarily upon the case of *Commonwealth Associates v. Providence Health Care, Inc.*,[52] which applied *Blasius* in the context of a contest for board control. There, then Chancellor William T. Allen had invalidated an issuance of a 20 percent voting interest in a corporation that, together with a 30 percent interest controlled by a friendly party, would have effectively prevented an insurgent from replacing the board of directors. The court found no compelling justification for this issuance.

Bear Stearns and JPMorgan argued that the compelling justification was Bear Stearns's imminent bankruptcy. Moreover, *Providence* was distinguishable by the fact that in *Providence*, a majority voting bloc was being put in place. In Bear Stearns, a no vote was still theoretically possible. A compelling justification may have existed when the first deal was struck on March 16, when Bear Stearns was on the verge of bankruptcy. In the renegotiated, second deal being challenged, Bear Stearns already had the benefit of a one-year guarantee from JPMorgan. If compelling justification was assessed on the change from deal number 1 to deal number 2, it was not so certain. JPMorgan countered this argument by arguing that Bear Stearns was about to go under a second time before deal number 2 was reached. In addition, it was unclear whether and how the *Blasius* doctrine, a species of the *Schnell* test, applied to a vote on a takeover transaction. In prior cases, the Delaware courts had come to different conclusions, a split that has yet to be resolved.[53]

The Bear Stearns Stock Issuance as Preclusive or Coercive

The most interesting thing about the plaintiffs' arguments was that at no point did they even cite the controversial case of *Omnicare* around which this share issuance had no doubt been structured. This was smart lawyering. By ignoring *Omnicare*, the plaintiffs avoided the whole dispute of whether *Omnicare* was rightly decided. Instead, the plaintiffs resorted to the *Unocal* doctrine applicable to actions taken by the board to protect itself against a corporate threat. The plaintiffs cited the case of *Paramount v. QVC* to argue that the sale was preclusive and coercive under the *Unocal* doctrine discussed more fully in Chapter 8 and so invalid. The plaintiffs made this argument implicitly, not by citing the intermediate standard of *Unocal* but instead by using its language, which prohibits preclusive or coercive action by a board of directors in the face of a danger to the corporation. The plaintiffs were probably correct, however, that the issue was that the *Unocal* doctrine required a threat to be triggered. Here, there arguably was no other willing bidder and no threat. The plaintiffs attempted to get around this argument by asserting that the threat was that the stockholders would vote no.

In *Paramount Communications v. QVC Network*, the court held that "when a corporation undertakes a transaction which will cause: . . . a change in corporate control; or . . . a breakup of the corporate entity, the directors' obligation is to seek the best value reasonably available to stockholders."[54] These are called *Revlon* duties after the case of *Revlon, Inc. v. MacAndrews & Forbes Holdings, Inc.* and are a form of *Unocal* duties that are generally considered to impose strict scrutiny on a board's actions when applicable.[55] Delaware courts have never applied *Revlon* duties to a stock-for-stock merger. The reason is that posttransaction control is generally considered fluid, and therefore no change of control occurs. However, if there ever was a case for this doctrine to apply, this was it. The JPMorgan acquisition was clearly a change of control. Unfortunately, the implications of such a finding would upset Delaware doctrine substantially by allowing for target shareholders in stock-for-stock mergers to litigate the issue in future cases.

In normal times, the plaintiffs' arguments would almost certainly have prevailed. The deal was coercive and possibly preclusive and also draconian, though the actual existent threat was uncertain. However, in its public filings, Bear Stearns asserted that it would have been forced to declare bankruptcy without the first JPMorgan deal. Moreover, Bear Stearns also asserted that without the firmness provided by the second JPMorgan deal, the company would have had to declare bankruptcy yet a second time, since other parties were still refusing to do business with it. Bear Stearns was arguing that the insolvency justified all of these provisions either within each doctrine or as a new, untested insolvency doctrine. Ultimately, there was validity to their arguments. Bear Stearns probably had no time to adhere to the niceties of Delaware law due to its insolvent or near-insolvent status.

This was shaping up to be a fight between Delaware and the federal government. The federal government had orchestrated a deal that it wanted to go through on terms that punished the Bear Stearns shareholders. This posed a dilemma for the Delaware courts. If they found these measures invalid, they would be criticized for endangering the capital markets system and come into direct conflict with the federal government. Alternatively, they could issue an opinion that upheld them but risked stretching the law of Delaware and providing bad precedent and doctrine for future cases.

A hearing was held on March 31. It became clear at that hearing that the main issue was whether Delaware should abstain entirely from the case and defer to New York. Delaware typically defers to first-filed cases under the *McWane* principle, which states that a Delaware court, when considering staying a case in deference to a first-filed action in another jurisdiction, should rule:

freely in favor of the stay . . . in a court capable of doing prompt and complete justice, involving the same parties and the same issues; that, as a general rule, litigation should be confined to the forum in which it is first commenced. . . .[56]

Here, the cases were filed so close together as to be considered contemporaneous, providing judicial flexibility to the Delaware court to retain jurisdiction. Vice Chancellor Donald F. Parsons, Jr., the judge in this case, ultimately ruled that Delaware would abstain under this doctrine for the New York proceedings. In doing so, he cited the federal issues involved:

> Rather, I find the circumstances of this case to be sui generis. What is paramount is that this Court not contribute to a situation that might cause harm to a number of affected constituencies, including U.S. taxpayers and citizens, by creating the risk of greater uncertainty.[57]

Delaware would not risk coming into conflict with the federal government. Vice Chancellor Parsons's ruling also confined any harm that the case might inflict. If New York issued any bad law to uphold these deal-protection devices, it would not be binding on Delaware. The ruling went against Delaware's penchant to attempt to grab jurisdiction in as many cases as possible, but here, as Professors Kahan and Rock have described it, it could be viewed as simply a strategic decision designed to prevent Delaware from harming itself.[58] It was a clear lesson in a judging tendency to rule with regard to political reality. Parsons quite wisely was not about to be the one blamed for upsetting the entirety of the global capital market by challenging the federal government and allowing Bear Stearns's possible failure.

The case against Bear Stearns fizzled out after that. The plaintiffs saw the impediments to halting the transaction, withdrew their preliminary injunction motion before the New York court, and decided to pursue a monetary damages claim. Presumably, they decided that a monetary damages remedy, if any, would be more palatable to the court then enjoining the transaction and destabilizing the financial system. The plaintiffs' attorneys were wrong. Their claim was subsequently dismissed by the New York court on December 4, 2008.[59]

On May 31, JPMorgan acquired Bear Stearns. At the time, it was greeted with great publicity and fanfare worthy of a funeral, but the public did not yet know what was to follow. Bear Stearns was only the first of a number of failed and acquired investment banks heralding the eventual destruction of the model. In hindsight, Bear Stearns's shareholders were lucky to get their measly $10 or so a share.

Lessons Learned from Bear's Fall

The Bear Stearns case said as much about deal-making as it did about government intervention. First, the Bear Stearns case again displayed the importance of personality in deals. Bear Stearns's fate was ultimately decided by Treasury Secretary Hank Paulson acting in tandem with then-President of the New York Federal Reserve Timothy Geithner. Paulson's desire to avoid moral hazard and pay heed to political pressure by punishing the Bear Stearns shareholders led to the first low price. Paulson's personality would play an important part in the government's "regulation by deal" approach first used in Bear Stearns but then applied to a host of other bail-out transactions, a topic discussed in full in Chapter 10.

JPMorgan CEO Jamie Dimon's forceful personality was similarly on display. The acquisition was his recrowning as one of the kings of Wall Street after departing from Citigroup years ago in a dispute with then Citigroup CEO Sandy Weill. Dimon's desire to acquire Bear Stearns drove the Wachtell lawyers to implement the heavy deal-protection devices placed in the second deal.

The Bear Stearns transaction also showed the importance of extrinsic factors such as employee satisfaction in driving a successful deal. It was not enough for JPMorgan to pay a bargain basement price for Bear Stearns. In the wake of the $2 a share price, the employees, seething in anger, initiated a slow-motion revolt at Bear Stearns's ignominious demise. Integrating these employees would have caused significant losses for JPMorgan. This no doubt drove JPMorgan's decision to assuage this employee dissatisfaction by paying a higher price.

Moreover, the lawyers for Bear Stearns, backed up by the federal government, had stretched the bounds of permitted deal-protection devices under Delaware law. But they did so only hesitantly. At first, they merely adopted the typical bank acquisition model with a few revisions that made it favorable to JPMorgan. In their haste to graft on these new changes, they provided a large unintended consequence, giving Bear Stearns a possible out. In the deal's second iteration, JPMorgan's lawyers further innovated pushing the deal to the limits of Delaware law. The negotiated structure paid enough heed to that law to survive, but did no more. The deal shows the remarkable innovation that deal lawyers given free rein can undertake. At the end, the JPMorgan lawyers could and did structure this second deal to push the envelope around Delaware law and the NYSE rules. The fact that this deal went through is testament to that creativity.

In structuring the transaction in this manner, JPMorgan's lawyers also revealed many of the remaining open issues in Delaware law applicable to takeovers, including:

- **Revlon:** Does the *Revlon* doctrine apply to a stock-for-stock transaction where a change of control is clear on its face?
- **Omnicare:** Is the *Omnicare* doctrine still a viable one?
- **Unocal:** What is the type of threat that implicates *Unocal* and leads to an application of its review? Did a third-party bid have to be outstanding or only the potential of one?
- **Insolvency:** What are a board's duties to equity holders, if any, when the company is considered technically insolvent?

I talk more about these open issues and Delaware law in later chapters. However, the number of questions showed the perpetual indeterminacy of Delaware law. The Delaware courts have a preference for keeping these questions open in order to allow market and judicial leeway.[60] Some of these questions may be resolved in the coming years, but in their resolution will lay new ambiguity to provide this flexibility. The abstention of Vice Chancellor Parsons showed that Delaware was not above using this flexibility to arrive at a predetermined political outcome.

More tellingly, the Bear Stearns story is the first of what would be a series of government-initiated deals. At the first instance, despite the legal-stretching that occurred, the structure of the Bear Stearns deal showed the limits of government's authority to act in the crisis. The

Treasury and Federal Reserve lacked any authority actually to seize Bear Stearns, an authority that bank regulators normally have over their regulatory charges. Instead, the government was forced to cobble together a deal that attempted to achieve its goals but required the cooperation of a private actor, JPMorgan, and pushed the limits of the law to effectuate. This limitation would come sharply into focus in the fall of 2008, a topic I discuss further in Chapter 10.

The Bear Stearns transaction was also the first of a number, including the bailouts involving AIG, Fannie Mae, and Freddie Mac, where the government attempted to penalize shareholders. The words thrown around at the time were "moral hazard," "to prevent future misconduct," and "the shareholders needed to be punished." That may be part of it, but the government's focus missed the point about the boards and officers of these entities. In the case of Bear Stearns, the government appeared to be avoiding penalizing its officers and directors. The government allowed JPMorgan to indemnify the Bear officers and directors for their conduct prior to the acquisition. Bear Stearns director and former Bear Stearns chief executive Alan C. Greenberg, who headed Bear Stearns's risk committee, took a new job at JPMorgan as vice chairman emeritus. Meanwhile, former Bear Stearns CEO Jimmy Cayne still pocketed $61 million in stock in addition to any compensation he earned in prior years. It was on his watch that Bear Stearns made the risky business decisions that ultimately led to its demise.

If the government was going to punish moral hazard, then it should have set up a system that clawed back this compensation and prevented this indemnification. This would punish the real parties responsible for Bear Stearns's demise. Perhaps the shareholders also needed to be disciplined, but the focus on them to the absence of the officers and directors of Bear Stearns missed the entire point. Then again, this was also an authority that the government for the most part lacked, and the shareholders were a much easier target. The government needed the cooperation of the Bear Stearns management and board. And ultimately, the failure of Bear and what followed are such extreme events that their occurrence is something that is unlikely to be a calculus in a future manager's mind. This is a view the government would also eventually adopt.

Bear Stearns also had much to say about systemic risk and the investment banking model. The fall of Bear Stearns illustrated the hazard of a financial institution losing market trust. There was no doubt that Bear Stearns's liquidity vanished because of the market's loss of confidence. Bear Stearns's failure also symbolized more. It showed the riskiness of the investment banking model that placed leverage at 30:1 ratios and above on their balance sheets, all the time relying on short-term lending and deposits for liquidity. In times of crisis, this meant that there might not be enough equity to carry the day and keep the confidence of counterparties and lenders.

This problem was reinforced by the opaqueness of these banks' financial positions, which encouraged counterparties and lenders to assume the worst. Bear Stearns's downfall also illustrated the riskiness of the investment bank model and its overreliance on trading profits. Bear Stearns suffered from too-large bets in mortgage-related assets, and it suffered accordingly.

More tellingly, Bear Stearns illustrated the problems with traditional models of corporate governance as applied to financial institutions. Bear Stearns was a complex financial beast that was poorly understood even by its own chief executive officer. It was the prototypical modern financial corporation with a trading operation that yearly engaged in hundreds of thousands of sophisticated financial transactions. However, these transactions were the realm of advanced mathematics not operational management.

The operations of Bear Stearns required little input from the Bear Stearns board of directors. This was for multiple reasons, but primarily because the nature of Bear Stearns' business—complex financial alchemy—was beyond traditional comprehension. The board was simply incapable of monitoring Bear Stearns' trading operations, let alone able to serve a decision-making or information-aggregating function with respect to the Bear Stearns business. The story of Bear Stearns is thus one of limits, the limits of board and shareholder governance and ultimately people themselves. If one is going to create a proper oversight and monitoring mechanism for a complex financial institution, it is likely not going to arise from traditional corporate governance models or metrics involving the board or shareholders. Instead, it is likely to come from regulatory and other forces that can directly intervene in and comprehend the financial institution architecture.

Even so, Bear Stearns's management had been remarkably hands-off in the months before its demise, as had its board. Cayne, then CEO of Bear Stearns, was reported to be noticeably absent during the July and August 2007 beginning of the market crisis, leaving on a helicopter on Thursday afternoons to play Friday golf at his New Jersey country club and spending 10 days in Nashville to play bridge.[61] Bear executives would later claim that they were stuck in a catch-22 of wanting to appear strong to the market but knowing that if they raised needed equity they might then be seen as in a deteriorating position. The result was that they took no action. Bear Stearns's rapid downfall illustrated the need for quick action in corporate governance and the resolution of this possible dilemma. It also illustrated the utility of a strong and proactive market regulator. Had such a regulator existed, then Bear Stearns might have been assisted earlier.

Instead, Bear Stearns was largely unregulated, primarily subject to voluntary compliance with the Consolidated Supervised Entity program under the SEC's oversight. When Bear Stearns rapidly failed, the SEC was nowhere in sight to aid the investment bank, and instead Bear Stearns became subject to the vicissitudes of the Department of Treasury and Federal Reserve. In the wake of Bear Stearns's and Lehman Brothers' failure, the SEC would ultimately shut down the CSE program, and ex-Chairman of the SEC Christopher Cox would famously state that "voluntary regulation does not work."[62]

Chapter 7

Jana Partners, Children's Investment Fund, and Hedge Fund Activist Investing

T he demise of Bear Stearns caused a significant shock to the financial system. In the days after Bear Stearns's fall and forced acquisition, stock market volatility increased, and the credit markets once again froze up. Bear Stearns's implosion had provided a fright to the equity markets, but the economy, though weakening, appeared stable. A $168 billion stimulus package passed by Congress in February 2008 was about to be distributed to taxpayers, and initial economic reports would state that the economy would grow less than 1 percent in the first half of 2008.[1] It would, of course, turn out that this appearance was terribly wrong. These false reports of growth and the stimulus were hiding the credit-driven market correction occurring outside public view. This correction would emerge in September 2008 to hit the global economy like a category five hurricane.

This would come only later. Instead, during the false stability of the spring of 2008, the equity markets experienced significant activity in three areas. The first two would be a relative rise in activity by strategic buyers, as well as in hostile takeover offers, topics for the next two chapters. The third would be the emergence of hedge fund activist investors in a number of high-profile shareholder disputes. Notably, many of these hedge funds utilized new financial instruments and techniques to implement their dissident campaigns. This development was not met with joy by all, and targeted corporations struggled to resist this onslaught. The ensuing battles and inevitable litigation engendered two important judicial opinions on the regulation of shareholder activism. These opinions, respectively, arose from Jana Partners' targeting of CNET Networks, Inc., the Internet media company, and Children's Investment Fund's and 3G Capital Partners' targeting of CSX Corp., the railroad operator.

The hedge fund as activist investor is a new species, more activist and interventionist than other institutional investors, such as mutual funds. Hedge funds may have the capacity to change the corporate governance of companies and drive increased deal-making activity in ways other institutional investors have not. This will be particularly true in the coming years because of heightened shareholder focus on executive compensation and proxy access in light of the perceived failings of management leading up to the financial crisis.[2] To understand why and how this is the case, as well as the future of hedge fund activism in distressed times, we must first briefly discuss the problem of corporate governance and the potential of activist investors.

A Brief Overview of the "Agency Problem"

A fundamental corporate governance problem for public companies is agency costs. Public corporations are run by agents. Officers are selected by directors, who are elected by shareholders. The officers and directors are agents of the real owners of the corporation, the shareholders. Ownership of the corporation is thus separated from control, resulting in a cost to owners known as agency costs. What are agency costs? At its most basic level, agency costs are the salaries paid to officers and directors, the cost of hiring these agents to operate the business.

There are also other less economic costs these agents impose. Officers may take advantage of their position to rent-seek, which is an economic term for obtaining their own private benefits at the expense of the corporation and its owners. They may pay themselves excessive amounts that do not correlate with their performance, or they may arrange to receive perks that are otherwise inappropriate. The former problem is exemplified by CEOs who, in hindsight at least, received shockingly excessive compensation. The poster boys for this issue are Countrywide Financial Corp.'s founder and ex-CEO Angelo Mozilo, ex-Merrill Lynch CEO Stanley O'Neal, and ex-Citigroup CEO Charles Prince, who collectively were paid $460 million between 2002 and 2006 despite the billions in losses their companies subsequently incurred from their wrong decisions.[3]

A paradigm example of the perk problem is the corporate jet, which until the financial crisis was a seemingly mandatory part of any pay package. The perk aggravates shareholders who are still stuck flying commercial. Some have argued that perks like these are simply cheaper, indirect forms of compensation and so justified. This may be true, but their class-separating nature clearly results in avoidable shareholder resentment and friction with officers and directors.[4]

Sometimes, agency costs are more direct, and managers may have outside competing interests that divert them from the corporate enterprise. The problem is particularly acute in the takeover context. Delaware law allows a board to just say no and to implement takeover-protection and deal-protection devices. Management can use these protections to attempt to entrench themselves, thereby depriving shareholders of a takeover premium. Agents can also be outrightly disloyal, entering into arrangements that explicitly benefit them at the expense of the company. The activities of the Rigas family with Adelphia Communications Corp. are one such example. There the Rigas family, led by Adelphia founder John Rigas, conspired to conceal about $2.3 billion in Adelphia's debt and appropriated approximately $100 million from Adelphia for their own purposes, including purchase of a golf course.[5]

The problem of agency costs, and particularly executive compensation, has occupied corporate governance experts for decades. One remedy proffered for the agency cost problem is the existence of substantial shareholders. The theory is that a controlling shareholder will provide a monitoring function and have an economic incentive to undertake this task because it has a significant interest in the company. The substantial shareholder will also ensure that officers and directors do not unduly profit. However, these types of shareholders have not proven themselves in practice. For example, Sumner Redstone, the controlling shareholder of Viacom and CBS Corporation, has awarded himself more than $80 million in compensation over the past three years while engaging in disputes with two of his children over their shareholdings in the two companies' parent, National Amusements Inc. As of February 2008, the stock prices of Viacom and CBS had declined 52 percent and 71 percent, respectively, since 2007.[6]

In this vein, a substantial or controlling shareholder can reap private benefits to compensate them in outsize proportion to the value they bring to the corporate enterprise. From 2001 to 2006, the CEO of Ford Motor Company was Henry Ford's great-grandson, William Clay "Bill" Ford Jr. He was paid more than $63 million during that time, all while refusing to accept a salary until Ford turned a profit. Fortunately for Bill Ford, stock awards and options did not count as salary.[7] Did he receive this job because he was the most qualified? Or was it because his family still controls 40 percent of the voting stock in Ford? And perhaps this "salary" was indeed justified given that Ford has thus far been the only one of the Detroit three automakers to avoid government assistance. This may have been due to the outsize attention the Ford family provides to Ford.

Controlling shareholders can thus serve a monitoring function, but they raise their own problems of undue influence. Because of this, the focus in this arena has been on institutional investors. Institutional investors are mutual funds, pension funds, endowment funds, and other professional investing groups. This investor historically does not acquire a controlling interest but rather takes a sizable minority stake in the company. In the early 1990s, many thought that these institutions were the answer to the corporate governance problem. These institutions would provide an independent monitoring function without exacting their own private benefits.[8]

This has not come to pass. Instead, mutual funds, the largest investors, have remained passive. The reasons for passivity remain diverse, but largely relate to their desire not to be seen as agitators, regulatory constraints that prevent them from taking sizable stakes in companies, and compensation mechanisms that do not adequately award them for this activism. Meanwhile, pension funds in particular have often acted for political purposes rather than economic ones. There are of course, prominent exceptions to both of these general statements, such as the California pension fund CalPERS, which historically has been both political and active as an investor. In the past few years, the new president of that $176 billion fund has notably disavowed the notorious political use of the fund by the prior president, Sean Harrigan, but has continued its activist stance.[9] For the most part, though, institutional investor activism has consisted of voting in accordance with corporate governance advisory service recommendations.

By the spring of 2008, the corporate governance movement was in flux. Prior solutions to the agency cost problem had appeared to fail to cure excessive executive compensation in particular. In fact, the agency problem increasingly appeared to be a struggle about curbing exorbitant executive compensation. This jibed with the arguments of some that the agency problem was overstated. After all, the current structure had created our $14 trillion economy; it must be doing something correctly. Against this argument, the financial crisis, though, once again highlighted the problem of compensation and agency costs generally. Executives earned short-term profits for a year or two and then left their institutions in a terrible situation; they profited at their institutions' expense. The windfalls of Mozilo, O'Neal and Prince are apt illustrations.

It was into this mix, in the spring of 2008, that hedge funds had their most active proxy season ever.

The Rise of Hedge Fund Activism

Hedge fund activism is a legacy of the 1980s exploits of corporate raiders. These were individuals such as Ronald O. Perelman, Carl Icahn, and T. Boone Pickens. They would launch hostile contests to acquire companies in order to engage in a restructuring or liquidation. Fearful companies would oftentimes instead simply repurchase the raider's shares at

a premium, so-called greenmail. The aggressive conduct of these raiders would provide hedge funds a road map, albeit a somewhat outdated
one, for their conduct. In fact, many of these self-same raiders, such as
Carl Icahn, reappeared in this new guise, portraying themselves as shareholder champions, a much better public relations moniker than corporate
raider.[10]

Hedge fund activism prominently emerged in the years after the
Internet bubble. During that time, firms such as Bulldog Investors, Jana
Partners LLC, Pershing Square Capital Management LP, Pirate Capital
LLC, and Third Point, LLC began to create a network for hedge fund
shareholder activism (see Table 7.1). In 2007, 501 dissident events
occurred, with hedge funds participating in 54 percent of all campaigns
announced, up from 48 percent in 2006. This number would slightly
decline to 479 dissident events in 2008, or approximately 53 percent of
all activity. The first six months of 2008, though, actually saw an increase
over 2007, but the economic crisis diminished activity in the second

Table 7.1 Major Activist Hedge Funds and Lifetime Dissident Campaigns
(through 2008)

Activist Fund	Total Number of Campaigns
JANA Partners LLC	27
Icahn Associates Corp.	76
Pirate Capital LLC	24
Bulldog Investors	94
Crescendo Advisors LLC	19
Harbinger Capital Partners	35
Pershing Square Capital Management LP	38
GAMCO Investors	247
Third Point Management Co. LLC	44
Greenlight Capital, Inc.	23
Sandell Asset Management Corp.	18
Steel Partners, LLC	113
ValueAct Capital Management LP	61

SOURCE: Factset SharkWatch

half of the year.[11] There was no doubt that hedge funds were driving activist shareholder dissident activity.

Hedge funds initiating a dissident campaign typically followed a set pattern. In its most prominent incarnation, the hedge fund would accumulate a position in a company above the 5 percent threshold. This would require the hedge fund to report this interest on a Schedule 13D filing with the SEC. In this filing, the activist would announce its intentions with respect to the target, either in the filing itself or by attaching a previously written letter, known as a poison pen, to management outlining the hedge fund's agenda.

The poison pen accounted for 54 percent of campaigns initiated in 2007.[12] Typically, the hedge fund's poison pen would include proposals for change to the company, including restructurings, sales, and executive replacements. Certain hedge funds, such as Third Point, run by the colorful Daniel Loeb, adopted the aggressive tactics of the 1980s corporate raiders and turned the poison pen into legendary screeds against management. He has branded a CEO a CVD, or chief value destroyer; referred to two great-grandsons of one company's founder as part of the Lucky Sperm Club; and in a letter to Irik Sevin, CEO of fuel distributor Star Gas Partners LP, wrote: "Do what you do best: Retreat to your waterfront mansion in the Hamptons where you can play tennis and hobnob with your fellow socialites."[13]

The public announcement of the hedge fund's proposal was important, and not just because it publicly notified management of the hedge fund's agenda. This first filing also often attracted other hedge funds from the activist network to take stakes in the company and join the campaign. This type of pack mentality was common in activist campaigns. One study found that hedge funds coordinated their efforts in 22 percent of a sample of campaigns.[14] In many circumstances, the dissident hedge fund would attempt to negotiate with management to initiate their proposed changes. However, if these attempts failed, the hedge fund would often launch a proxy contest for board seats on the targeted company board in order to more directly assert control.

The hedge fund response depended on the reaction of the targeted companies, which varied. One study found that with respect to hedge funds, "target companies choose to accommodate the activists 29.7 percent of the time, to negotiate 29.1 percent of the time, [and] to fight/

resist 41.3 percent of the time."[15] It appears that hedge fund activism was met with more resistance by companies than other activist interventions. In 2007, 108 such events or approximately 21 percent of all events resulted in a proxy contest. In that year, hedge funds accounted for 56.5 percent of these contests (see Figure 7.1).[16] The hedge funds had adopted the old hostile tactics of the 1980s corporate raiders.

The hedge funds, though, differed from the corporate raiders in the nature of their ownership. The median maximum ownership of activist hedge funds involved in dissident campaigns was only 9.1 percent of the company.[17] The reason for this was probably liquidity. Larger controlling stakes are harder to quickly dispose of for regulatory and market reasons. Hedge funds typically also did not seek to obtain a majority of the board seats of the company. Nor did they seek to acquire all of the company's shares. Instead, the typical hedge fund would run a campaign for a minority position on the board. The corporate raiders attempted to seize the entirety of the profits by acquiring the entire company for restructuring, partial dismemberment, or liquidation. In contrast and due to their own liquidity needs, activist hedge funds were willing to share the benefits of their activities with the remaining public shareholders (see Figure 7.2).

The growth in hedge fund activity was due to a simple economic fact: Hedge fund dissident campaigns appeared to work (see Figure 7.3). A paper first released in 2007 looked at the stock returns of companies targeted by hedge funds for shareholder activist campaigns from 2001

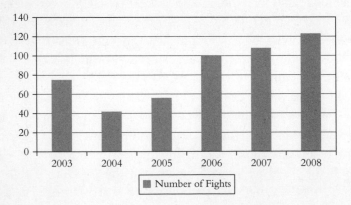

Figure 7.1 Domestic Proxy Campaigns Fights 2003–2008
SOURCE: Factset SharkWatch

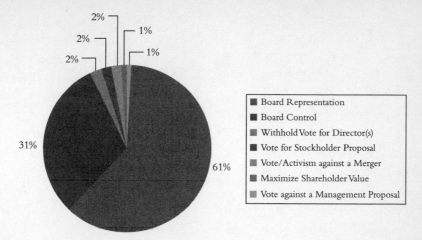

Figure 7.2   Primary Campaign Type Domestic Proxy Fights (All Proxy Fights in 2008)
SOURCE: Factset SharkWatch

through 2006. The writers found that activism that targeted the sale of the company or changes in business strategy returned 8.54 percent and 5.95 percent, respectively. Moreover, this paper also found that hedge funds that regularly engaged in this type of activity or other hostile activity also experienced higher returns.[18] Other papers found similar beneficial effects.[19]

This was remarkable. Activist hedge funds earned returns that substantially exceeded the costs they incurred by engaging in this activity. Public shareholders participated in these gains. Hedge fund activism was found to have other beneficial effects, such as overall improved performance, including increased return on assets and operating margins. It also resulted in reduced executive pay, the bête noire of the agency theorists. The 2007 paper found that the year before the hedge fund activity occurred, the target companies' average CEO pay was $914,000 higher than the average CEO compensation at the targets' peer companies. In the year after the hedge fund's dissident activity, CEO compensation was reduced to a level in line with the target's peer companies (see Figure 7.3).[20]

This activism and validating returns created its own self-perpetuating cycle. Announcements of shareholder activism by hedge funds would result in stock price increases. Meanwhile, new entrants, seeing value, entered the field. By January 2008, one estimate put the number of "event-driven" hedge funds that specialize in this type of activity at more than 75, with

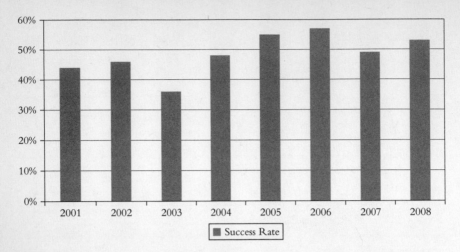

Figure 7.3   Success Rate for Dissident Domestic Proxy Fights 2001–2008
SOURCE: Factset SharkWatch

combined assets under management in excess of $190 billion dollars. This compared with only $95.6 billion in 2004.[21] Though the entrance of money validated prior hedge fund activism, it raised the possibility that the easy gains were no longer there and that hedge fund activism would become less focused and earn lower returns.

Targets and some academics also expressed concern about hedge fund activism. Their primary focuses were twofold. First, the hedge funds were looking for short-term benefits at the expense of the long-term interests of the company. Here, one estimated calculation of the median hedge fund activist position during the period from 2001 through 2006 was for one year.[22] Second, the hedge funds would use their board positions to obtain their own private benefits at the expense of other shareholders.

Cries of short-termism have always surrounded hedge fund activities and activist investing generally. In the case of hedge funds, some have proposed that special fiduciary duties to the targeted company should be imposed on hedge funds.[23] Yet, the early statistics have not shown any undue impact by their activities. Rather, the benefits for companies appear to be widespread. The nature of the typical hedge fund position, a minority one on the board of directors, also provides a mechanism for oversight of hedge fund activities. The remaining majority directors can not only look out for the interests of the company but also prevent any private gains from accruing to the hedge funds' activities.

A recent Delaware case, *Portnoy v. Cryo-Cell Int'l, Inc.*, also showed the extent to which the Delaware courts will monitor hedge fund activities and any compromises reached between the company and a dissident shareholder.[24] In that case, Vice Chancellor Strine held that the Delaware courts would deferentially review a board compromise that gave a dissident stockholder two board seats. However, he also held that any benefits given by the corporation to a stockholder to compromise a proxy contest would probably be subject to heightened review for entire fairness and good faith to ensure that the company's shareholders were protected.

Heading into the 2008 proxy season, hedge funds had shown themselves to be disrupters. They were changing the nature of shareholder activism, providing the dissident voice often asked for on boards, and increasingly influencing the corporate governance debate. But hedge funds are also sophisticated financial entities. In their desire to maximize returns and conceal their preliminary efforts, hedge funds innovated by using the tools of the financial revolution. Instead of actually buying the shares of a company, hedge funds began to purchase cash-settled equity derivatives. The use of these derivatives meant that the hedge funds did not purchase the actual stock in the company. Instead, the hedge fund merely placed a bet with a counterparty that the company's stock would move one way or the other. Presumably, the investment bank counterparty would then also hedge the transaction by purchasing the actual stock. The hedge fund, though, never owned any stock, and the trade was settled for cash.

This was a powerful innovation that permitted the hedge funds to accumulate a large interest in a company without being subject to the usual accompanying regulatory requirements. Normally, a stockholder who beneficially owns 5 percent or more of a public company's equity securities is required under Section 13(d) of the Exchange Act to report that interest on a Schedule 13D filed with the SEC. The form is required to be filed within 10 days of the buyer going over this threshold.[25]

Cash-settled equity derivatives, though, are separate from the ownership of common stock. The hedge fund simply has a bet with an investment bank that the stock price will rise. The hedge fund has no right to dividends in the stock or to vote on the election of directors.

The hedge fund owns no interest in the company. On this basis, hedge funds took the position that the Section 13(d) reporting requirements did not apply. A hedge fund could therefore acquire a large interest in a target without alerting the market. The hedge fund could then quickly convert this derivative position into actual stock because it was likely that the investment bank counterparty would have taken a position in the target's stock to hedge its risk. This tactic would put hedge funds in the spotlight in the 2008 proxy season, as they were repeatedly accused of using these cash-settled equity derivatives to avoid the early-warning requirements of Section 13(d).[26]

The 2008 Proxy Season

The 2008 proxy season was expected to be an eventful one. It did not disappoint (see Figure 7.4). In the period from January 1 to February 1, 2008, 79 dissident events occurred, compared with 49 in the comparable period in 2007. In particular, there were 123 proxy contests in 2008 compared with 108 in 2007. Again, activist hedge funds were the focal point of this activity. Hedge funds initiated 273 dissident events, and 53.7 percent of proxy fights involved hedge funds.[27] I have set forth the more significant hedge fund activist campaigns during this time in Table 7.2.

During this time period, the two most prominent instances of shareholder activism were Jana Partners' targeting of CNET Networks, Inc. and Children's Investment Fund and 3G Capital Partners' targeting of CSX Corp. These two dissident actions would reshape the securities laws and alter the way these contests would unfold in the future. They would also show the perils, potential, and limitations of hedge fund activist investing, as well as provide a case study of the modern hedge fund activist campaign.

Jana versus CNET

Jana Partners is a $5 billion event-driven hedge fund founded by Barry Rosenstein. It specializes in activist shareholder investing and is most

Table 7.2 Significant Domestic Proxy Campaigns 2008

Target/Dissident	Date	Action
Amylin Pharmaceuticals, Inc. / Carl C. Icahn	5/22/2008	Proxy Fight (Board Representation)
Biogen Idec Inc. / Carl C. Icahn	8/11/2008	Proxy Fight (Board Representation)
Charming Shoppes, Inc. / The Charming Shoppes Full Value Committee (Crescendo Partners LP & Myca Partners Inc.)	1/15/2008	Proxy Fight (Board Representation)
Circuit City Stores, Inc. / Wattles Capital Management LLC	1/22/2008	Proxy Fight (Board Control)
CNET Networks, Inc. / JANA Partners LLC, Sandell Asset Management Corp.	1/7/2008	Proxy Fight (Board Control)
CSX Corp./Children's Investment Fund & 3G Capital Partners	12/19/2007	Proxy Fight (Board Representation)
Motorola, Inc. / Carl C. Icahn	1/31/2008	Proxy Fight (Board Representation)
Office Depot, Inc. / Levitt Corporation	3/17/2008	Proxy Fight (Board Representation)
The New York Times Company / Harbinger Capital Partners and Firebrand Partners LLC	1/25/2008	Proxy Fight (Board Representation)
Yahoo! Inc. / Carl C. Icahn	5/15/2008	Proxy Fight (Board Control)

SOURCE: Factset SharkWatch

famously known for partnering with Carl Icahn in 2005 to force the energy company Kerr-McGee Corp. to restructure. Jana's actions ultimately resulted in the sale of Kerr-McGee and a more than $160 million profit for Jana. Rosenstein is also known as one of the more level-headed of the shareholder activists; he is a devotee of vinyasa yoga, a more active form of the discipline.[28]

In the case of CNET, Jana began its battle early in the 2008 proxy season. On the morning of January 7, 2008, Jana filed a Schedule 13D with the SEC.[29] Jana's Schedule 13D was loaded with new information for the market. First, Jana disclosed that it owned 8.1 percent of CNET's stock. Second, Jana disclosed that it was a party to cash-settled equity derivative contracts equivalent to another 8.2 percent of CNET's stock. Third, Jana announced that Sandell Asset Management Corp. had agreed to support Jana's efforts. Sandell itself also disclosed a 3.4 percent interest in CNET through cash-settled equity derivatives as well as a beneficial ownership stake of 1.31 percent of CNET. Through their use of cash-settled derivatives, Jana and Sandell had an approximate 21 percent economic interest in CNET, but only a 9.4 percent ownership stake.

Jana's 13D filing also stated that Jana had had contacts with CNET management in October through December about implementing a restructuring program. The discussions had gone nowhere, and on December 28, 2007, Jana delivered a notice to nominate 7 new directors to CNET's board. CNET had a staggered board provision in its bylaws requiring that only a portion of its eight directors be put up for election in any given year. In 2008, 2 CNET directors were up for election, and Jana nominated replacement directors for those two seats. In this notice, Jana also proposed to amend CNET's bylaws so that the board would be expanded by 5 directors, bringing the total to 13 directors. The other 5 directors Jana was nominating would fill these new positions. If Jana were successful, it would obtain control of the CNET board.[30] This was a highly aggressive move by Jana. Instead of nominating a minority slate of directors, Jana was deviating from the hedge fund playbook to take full control of CNET.

CNET rejected the Jana nomination and proposal by relying on a strict reading of the advance notice provision in its bylaws. Article III.6 of the CNET bylaws stated with respect to director nominations that:

> Any stockholder of [CNET] that has been the beneficial owner of at least $1,000 of securities entitled to vote at such meeting for at least one year may submit a director nomination to the Board of Directors or, if designated by the Board of Directors, a Nominating Committee.[31]

Jana's bylaws contained a second provision limiting stockholder proposals along the same grounds. CNET thus rejected Jana's proposals and nominations by claiming that Jana was not the beneficial owner of at least $1,000 worth of stock for at least one year. Jana had first acquired shares of CNET in October 2007, far from the one-year deadline.

Jana's argument in its complaint was twofold. First, Jana offered a differing interpretation of that bylaw. Jana argued that the bylaw stated that shareholder "may seek" to nominate directors through the board and that *may* is a permissive word. The bylaw did not prohibit shareholders from making proposals outside this process. Jana thus argued that so long as Jana filed and circulated its own proxy and did not seek to submit the proposal to the CNET board, then the bylaw restrictions did not apply.

Second, Jana argued that, to the extent the bylaw did apply, the holding period requirements were discriminatory and unreasonable and improperly permitted the CNET directors to be gatekeepers for director nominations. Shareholders were the only persons who could nominate directors. In contrast, the CNET bylaws impermissibly placed this power with CNET's directors.

Jana's second argument was also a good one. In other circumstances, Delaware courts had held that application of a bylaw governing the shareholder franchise is appropriate if it is not applied inequitably and so long as it is reasonable. However, under Delaware law and doctrine as annunciated under the *Blasius* standard, bylaws must on their face offer a fair opportunity for shareholders to nominate candidates. Here, if this bylaw was interpreted as CNET wanted, it functioned to make the board the gatekeeper of all director nominations. The Delaware courts are protective of the shareholder right to nominate and elect directors. If all nominations were centered through the board, it was probably an unreasonable restriction on the shareholder franchise.

Ultimately, Jana won a full victory. Referring to Lewis Carroll and the "Bloody Shirt of *Blasius*," Chancellor William B. Chandler, the judge presiding over this case, held that the CNET bylaws were unambiguous in favor of Jana.[32] He interpreted the corporate bylaws as a contract between the corporation and stockholders. Siding with Jana, he did not find any ambiguity. Rather, he found that, because of the "may" language, these bylaws applied only if Jana sought to include the proposals in CNET's proxy. Because Jana was going to self-finance its contest, it would, therefore, not be subject to this bylaw. The result cleared the way for Jana to run this contest and was a blow to CNET, which was left bloodied and facing a difficult proxy contest.

Lost in this bitter legal battle between the two sides was the actual performance of CNET. CNET's operational performance had been lackluster for several years prior to Jana's involvement. Its stock price had dropped by 50 percent over the past two years, its projected revenue growth remained weak, and financial observers believed that CNET was overstaffed and poorly managed. On October 3, 2007, Henry Blodget, the infamous ex-analyst from Merrill Lynch, wrote on his blog Alley Insider that CNET was "geriatric." He suggested that a private equity firm buy the company, stating that "the company's growth has stalled, its tech-news dominance has been usurped, and its stock is barely clinging to $8."[33]

It was likely that Jana would win its contest if CNET could not find a legal hook to defeat Jana. This explained CNET's opposition, though it did not excuse its battle against its own shareholders' arguments for improvement. However, CNET did not wait until its shareholder meeting. On May 15, CNET announced an agreement to be acquired by CBS for $11.50 a share or $1.8 billion in total.[34] Jana had purchased its shares at an approximate price of $7.50 a share. The quick profit of Jana was no doubt a boon for future activist shareholders.

In the long run, the *Jana* case will have a significant impact on campaigns to replace board directors. The *Jana* opinion shows that Delaware courts will strictly construe bylaw amendments against the targeted company. This was a forceful reminder that companies should update their bylaws to make any nomination or shareholder proposal requirements and restrictions clear and unambiguous. This is an update that indeed occurred as companies prepared for the 2009 proxy season. Law firms used the *Jana* case as a marketing opportunity, flooding clients with memos and sample bylaws to be adopted to clarify bylaws, restrict the nominating process, and force greater disclosure upon hedge funds engaging in dissident activity. Here, law firms generally recommended that companies adopt bylaws requiring the reporting of any ownership of cash-settled equity derivatives and wolf pack activity with other hedge funds. The deal machine was acting to protect its steady corporate clients over a select group of hedge fund activists.

Companies responded to these missives. Morgan Stanley, Sara Lee Corporation, and Coach, Inc., for example, have each in the past year revised their bylaws to ensure that they provide the companies greater latitude to exclude hedge fund proposals.[35] Each of these companies also acted to enhance disclosure by any activists, including requiring the disclosure of cash-settled equity derivatives. Other companies have even amended their poison pills to include cash-settled equity derivatives for purposes of determining whether the pill has been triggered. But this was dangerous business, as it could presumably lead to an undue trigger for these pills.

Companies undertaking these defense enhancements did so with the *Jana* case and hedge fund activism in mind. Many explicitly imposed clear and extended holding periods for shareholders wishing to nominate directors or make shareholder proposals. However, the *Jana* case did not address whether CNET's holding restriction, if applied, would be inequitable and invalid under Delaware law. In other words, is a one-year holding period appropriate under Delaware law?

The Delaware legislature acted in 2009 to partially address this open question. The legislature enacted a new Section 112, which allows the bylaws of a Delaware corporation to provide that the corporation may be required to include nominations by individual stockholders. The provision also allows the bylaws to implement mandatory holding periods and minimum ownership thresholds. It remains to be seen, though, how Delaware courts will view the effect of this new statute on the question of how long a holding period is appropriate.

The *Jana* case was ultimately a good illustration of how bitter these fights can become, as well as how they could turn on legalities. In this battle, the actual issue at hand, the performance of the company, appeared immaterial. The Jana proxy contest was also a good exemplar of how these contests can end in the sale or restructuring of the target company. Jana's use of cash-settled equity derivatives and coordinated activity with another hedge fund also foreshadowed the battle for CSX.

Children's Investment Fund versus CSX

Children's Investment Fund is a London-based hedge fund headed by Chris Hohn. It has a publicity-friendly name due to the allocation of a portion of its revenue to a related charitable foundation for children.[36] Children's is also one of Europe's largest hedge funds, with more than $5 billion in assets under management. It has periodically ventured into shareholder activism in Europe, most recently in the ABN Amro Bank N.V. dispute, where it pressured the company to split up, eventually leading to ABN Amro's sale to a group of banks including Royal Bank of Scotland Plc, Banco Santander SA, and Fortis Holding SA/NV.[37]

Children's first set its sights on CSX in the second half of 2006. It took an interest in the company on October 20, 2006, by purchasing cash-settled equity swaps. The following months were filled with intrigue, as Children's repeatedly approached CSX about a restructuring of the company, inquiries that were repeatedly rebuffed. The hedge fund 3G appeared on the horizon, also taking a stake in CSX. During this period, the two funds met several times to discuss investments, though both would later claim that CSX was not discussed at these meetings.

Children's had decided to target CSX because it believed that its management was ineffective and that CSX had substantial legacy contracts that were undervalued by the company.[38] In addition, CSX had a number of noncore assets ripe for disposition, including the famous Greenbrier resort in West Virginia, described in the *Wall Street Journal* as one of the nation's "most lavish and historic resorts," which CSX had owned since 1910.[39]

On December 19, 2007, Children's was finally ready to go public. The fund announced that it was going to launch a proxy contest with 3G to nominate directors to the CSX 12-member board. At the same time, Children's and 3G filed a Schedule 13D showing that they had a combined 8.3 percent interest in CSX and that they had agreed to act cooperatively. They also announced a collective 3.5 percent economic interest in cash-settled equity derivatives.[40]

CSX's response was not welcoming. On March 17, 2008, seven days after the Children's group filed their proxy statement to elect five directors to the CSX board, CSX sued Children's and 3G in the Southern District of New York, claiming that they had failed to file a timely Schedule 13D reporting (a) Children's entry into cash-settled derivative swaps above a level equivalent to 5 percent of the outstanding CSX stock and (b) that the two hedge funds were acting as a group as early as February 2007 and had failed to jointly file a Schedule 13D at that time.

The issue gripped Wall Street: Were cash-settled equity derivatives subject to Section 13(d)'s beneficial ownership reporting requirements under Section 13(d), triggering joint reporting of their holdings? And when could two hedge funds acting together be deemed to be a group? In answering these questions, the court would decide the future playing field for hedge fund activism.

A two-day bench trial was held in New York on May 21 and 22, 2008. Three weeks later, on June 11, Judge Lewis A. Kaplan of the Southern District of New York issued his opinion. He ultimately ruled that Children's entered into the swap transactions to avoid reporting under Section 13(d). He also found that 3G and Children's had formed a group at least 10 months before they publicly stated they were one and filed a Schedule 13D. Since they formed a group earlier, their securities holdings were aggregated at that time for purposes of 13D, topping the 5 percent threshold. Another violation thus arose—the failure to jointly file a Schedule 13D reporting this group interest.

This has always been a troublesome issue under Section 13(d). When do two actors form a group acting in concert trigger the Section 13(d) filing requirements? Section 13(d)(5) provides: "When two or more persons act as a partnership, limited partnership, syndicate, or other group for the purpose of acquiring, holding, or disposing of securities of an issuer, such syndicate or group shall be deemed a 'person' for the purposes of this subsection."[41] In such circumstances, the "group's" holdings will be aggregated for purposes of the Section 13(d) filing requirements, and they will be required to jointly file as a group any required Schedule 13D.

To find the funds were a group, Judge Kaplan found that the close relationship of the parties, patterned buying, and references to the other in e-mail messages created an inference of a group. This is a tough call. Children's and 3G met, knowing the danger of acting as a group, and appeared to structure their conduct accordingly, trying desperately not to form a group and even stipulating that they were not a group at the beginning of their few meetings. The alleged group conduct here was rather light and mostly drawn from inferences and patterns. In this case, it was primarily based on the judge's finding that the two funds had a prior close relationship.

Going forward, this presents a dilemma for any hedge fund. How do you communicate with other shareholders without running afoul of these rules? This is particularly true when any finding of a group appears so subjective and at the mercy of a judge's broader views of the funds' conduct. Generally speaking, the purpose of these shareholder communications is to share information that each may act upon. This may then appear to the outside world as coordinating, and it very well may be. But in the hands of a judge and the broad Section 13(d) standards, this effectively means that any contact creates liability under Section 13(d) if no joint Schedule 13D filing is made.

Despite his ruling for CSX, the decision was a victory of sorts for Children's and 3G. Judge Kaplan found a violation of the Section 13(d) requirements but ordered that the remedy be curative disclosure by Children's and 3G.[42] Here, he was hampered by a precedent that limited the remedy to this type of cure and foreclosed harsher penalties such as disgrogement. CSX had argued that Children's and 3G be forced to divest their shares or that they otherwise be prohibited from voting at CSX's upcoming election of directors. Precedent dictated a different outcome. Judge Kaplan was forced to limit CSX's remedy, but he clearly didn't like it and in his opinion practically begged CSX to appeal the case to overturn this precedent and more harshly punish Children's and 3G.[43]

Nonetheless, the consequences of Judge Kaplan's ruling are likely to be broad. Holders will now tend to read this opinion as forcing them to report cash-settled derivative swaps. The alternative is not to file a Schedule 13D and risk a court battle and adverse judgment, hopefully safe in the knowledge that the court's injunctive remedy for finding a violation is apt to be a weak one—more disclosure. This will trouble hedge fund general counsels for a while. And it is because of this that the main effect of this decision is likely to be to push the SEC to act and propose Section 13(d) reforms to address the issue of reporting cash-settled derivatives.

Shortly thereafter, CSX held its board election. Instead of its usual luxury location at the Greenbrier or a similar place, CSX held the meeting at a remote location in a railroad yard outside New Orleans. The maneuver did not deter shareholders from attending and voting. After a four-hour meeting, four Children's group directors were elected to the board.[44]

Children's victory came in the wake of a recommendation by the proxy advisory service RiskMetrics for its candidates, again showing the power of these services. Importantly for future contests, RiskMetrics premised its recommendation on the poor performance of CSX but made this conclusion based on CSX's "aggressive" response to Children's and 3G.[45] Many criticized RiskMetrics for this finding, as the service was endorsing a set of candidates that had been found by a court of law to be less than truthful. But RiskMetrics had presumably weighed this factor in its opinion and come down against a hostile company response.

The Children's group's win was based on receiving the vote of the shares CSX sought to have Children's and 3G disgorge. If Children's and 3G's shareholders didn't count, then the CSX board's two nominees would be seated instead. CSX was, at this time, appealing the lower court ruling, arguing that Children's shares should be excluded for purposes of this election. Notably, CSX did not dispute the election of the Children's other two nominees, Gilbert H. Lamphere and Alexandre Behring. These two would have been elected with or without Children's interest.[46]

On September 15, 2008, the Second Circuit rejected Judge Kaplan's plea to enjoin Children's and 3G from voting shares of CSX stock.[47] Children's two other directors were thus seated, and the hedge funds took control of one-third of CSX's board. The final outcome of this dispute, though, was less successful for the hedge funds. As of March 2009, the stock price of CSX was down almost 66.7 percent since September, and the famous Greenbrier had been put into bankruptcy. Faced with these significant loses, Chris Hohn decided not to again seek reelection to Children's board in order to maintain flexibility to sell the fund's remaining CSX shares. At the time Hohn was quoted as saying: "Quite frankly, activism is hard."[48] This was true—and it also required staying power.

The Future of Hedge Fund Activism

The Jana and Children's battles show the perils and potential of hedge fund investing. In both instances, the companies appeared to have limited defenses and lagging historical performance against their peers. In Jana's case, a nice, quick profit was also had. Companies saw these dissident contests and, aware of their own vulnerabilities, responded. But they did not do so with welcoming arms or corporate restructuring

and reform. Rather, most companies responded by adopting amendments to their bylaws to impose significantly increased shareholder disclosure and other restrictions on shareholder activism.

These actions will probably have their intended result and chill
activity. Companies argue that these measures prevent short-termism.
However, hedge fund activity has resulted in increased shareholder
value and reduced excessive executive pay. Thus, the battle over hedge
fund shareholder activism seems more about hedge fund tactics than
about their results. Here, the recommendation of RiskMetrics in the
CSX battle is likely to affect companies' response. Although companies
may arm themselves and even attempt to fight off hedge fund activism, they will probably do so in a manner that appears to be at least
receptive to the ideas of their new hedge fund shareholders. The consequence is to again make the public relations campaign, and the choice
of a PR firm, one of the central elements in these battles.

Hedge funds may become a more sustained force, but there are
countervailing trends that probably mean they are unlikely to become
ubiquitous. First, there are a limited number of easy targets. Second,
activist hedge funds have been terribly hurt by the financial crisis.
These funds typically invest in distressed companies to begin with, and
the returns in 2008 were not pretty on account of the exacerbated
impact of the financial crisis. Children's results were negative 42.8 percent for the year.[49] Most spectacularly, Bill Ackman's specialized $2
billion fund to invest as an activist shareholder in retailer Target Corp.
lost 89.5 percent of its value in less than two years.[50] These are hardly
encouraging returns to fund significant expansion, despite the increased
opportunity. In the wake of these returns and the financial crisis, many
funds were also hit by investor redemptions, and Jana alone was rumored
to have redemption requests for 20 to 30 percent of its assets.[51] These
hits are likely to set back the growth of these funds by several years and
may result in the liquidation of many funds.

Still, despite the general economic downturn and the huge losses
sustained by many corporate activist funds, the 2009 proxy season experienced the sustained activity of 2008. As of March 25, 2009, there were
already more shareholder proposals than in the comparable period a year
ago. So far, 283 shareholder proposals were disclosed, compared with 252
for the same period last proxy season. In the most contentious arena,

proxy contests, it appears that as of March, the pace was set to surpass 2008's record total. As of March 25, 2009, 71 proxy fights for board seats at U.S. companies have been announced. At the same point in 2008, 69 had been announced.[52]

These numbers point to the likely staying force of hedge fund activism. Even in the down year of 2009, with many shareholder activists leaving the arena, new activists appear to be springing up to take the mantle from those driven away or in hibernation. These new activists will exist side-by-side with the older ones who remain or return in the coming years. Bill Ackman, for example, appeared unchastened, initiating an unsuccessful proxy contest in 2009 to elect five nominees to the Target board, despite the prior significant losses in his fund.

This secular trend towards greater hedge fund activism will be assisted by the proxy advisory services. These services have been criticized for the arbitrariness of their proxy recommendations, which appear to import notions of civic democracy into the corporate realm without firm economic basis.[53] Nonetheless, these services have substantial power and appear prone to recommend dissident slates for diversity purposes if for no other reason. This provides comfort to any dissident hedge fund that the substantial expense of a campaign will prove successful.

As for the bugbear of the agency theorists, executive compensation, the financial crisis appears to be forcing boards to rethink the topic. Many of the largest pay packages were paid by financial institutions that received federal government assistance and became subject to compensation restrictions imposed as a condition to their receipt of bailout money. Meanwhile, the public outcry at excessive pay to CEOs whose companies subsequently lost billions increased the focus on reworking financial compensation to emphasize pay for performance and reduce pay that rewarded short-term performance over long-term losses. In the wake of these outcries, many boards cut back on compensation and restructured their pay packages to ensure longer-term pay-for-performance. The ultimate impact and sustainability of this trend remain unknown and may be strongly affected by possible government regulation.

Thus, for the short term and to the regret of those who decry agency costs and view the institutional investor as the perennial solution, hedge funds may turn out to have more potential than pervasive systemic impact. However, when they do act, they are likely to play an increasingly important part in corporate governance and provide a new force to cajole directors to take an active and dissident voice in the corporate enterprise. Their potential to act may therefore be even more game-changing by forcing companies to conduct themselves in anticipation of possible criticism and hedge fund action. And hedge funds are likely to be increasingly successful on account of majority voting requirements and brokers who increasingly divvy up nonvotes among candidates rather than just voting them for the board's nominees.

Hedge funds thus appear to be the missing actor to spur companies to change and reduce agency costs. Hedge funds also appear to be willing to spend the money to do so. This is not to say that there are not dangers. Hedge funds are acting for their own private interests and do not seem shy about taking contentious positions. Nonetheless, their conduct thus far has not merited increased oversight. Instead, because they usually seek minority board positions, they can be monitored by other board members and by the Delaware courts.

The deal machine has been less receptive to these funds. Instead, the large law firms and investment banks have largely served their traditional corporate clients by arguing for increased disclosure of cash-settled equity derivatives and bylaw amendments to damper this activity. This opposition is likely to decline as hedge fund activism becomes a more traditional part of the capital markets.

Hedge funds will also engender deal-making in a number of ways. First, hedge funds will drive companies to maximize value through a sale or other corporate transaction. Second, hedge funds themselves can provide capital and operational advice. Here, we may even see the rare occasion where hedge funds are actually invited to invest in companies and serve on their boards. In this regard, expect to see partnering of activist hedge funds and private equity funds as these hedge funds take longer investing stances and begin to resemble private equity funds. This trend will be facilitated by the events of 2008. The mass flight of capital during this time from hedge funds has led some of these funds to adopt private equity strategies like lockups, which allow hedge funds to retain capital for longer periods of time. To the extent that activist hedge funds adopt this feature, it will allow more sustained shareholder activism.

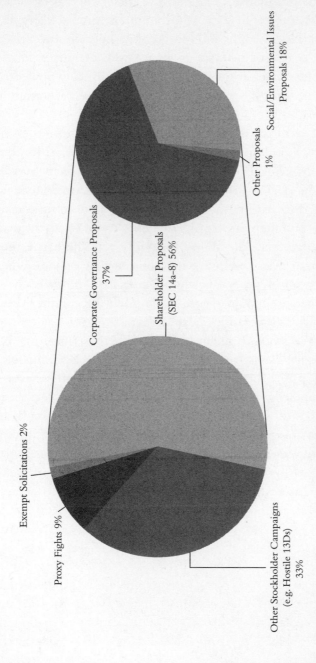

Figure 7.4 Shareholder Activism against U.S. Companies 2008
Source: Factset SharkWatch

Exempt Solicitations 2%

Proxy Fights 9%

Other Stockholder Campaigns
(e.g. Hostile 13Ds)
33%

Shareholder Proposals
(SEC 14a-8) 56%

Corporate Governance Proposals
37%

Other Proposals
1%

Social/Environmental Issues
Proposals 18%

Corporations still fight hedge fund activism, though, often arguing the funds' tactics and menacing potential rather than the facts. In the contests of the future, the Section 13(d) requirements are likely to be a central battlefield. The CSX case showed the hampering role the group requirements of Section 13(d) can impose. Given the strict, subjective test the CSX case imposed on hedge funds, the SEC would do well to clarify this area with specific safe harbors so as not to entirely limit communication.

With respect to cash-settled derivatives, the CSX case is likely to be eclipsed by SEC rule making once the SEC's attention turns away from the financial crisis. If the SEC does so act, it is likely to require reporting of these derivatives on Section 13(d) as other countries like the United Kingdom have proposed.[54] There is a drive to further monitor derivatives, but there are strong benefits to these derivatives, as they provide hedge funds the ability to swiftly act. The harm, though, appears minimal at best. Disclosure may be the best remedy, but anything more is probably overkill. More generally, regulators for now should look at hedge funds as a potentially good force, rather than the nefarious one many corporations portray them as.

Ultimately, the story of hedge funds and activist investing is one of potential. Hedge funds have the capability to be a strong force in disciplining companies, but the industry is still in its infancy. As with mutual funds, the hedge funds may be derailed on the path to becoming a strong force in activist investing. Moreover, hedge funds themselves are transforming to become more like private equity funds. This may change both their tactics and their image as they take longer stakes and are more apt to offer strategic advice on a friendly basis. In other words, the story has a ways to go.

Chapter 8

Microsoft, InBev, and the Return of the Hostile Takeover

A notable burst of unsolicited, so-called hostile takeover activity occurred in the spring of 2008. The increase was the only highlight in an otherwise moribund deal market and reflected a continuing upward trend in hostile takeovers over prior years. In 2008, 71 unsolicited and hostile transactions comprising $150 billion in value were announced in the United States. This was an increase from $83.4 billion the year before and the highest number of hostile deals since 1999.[1] During 2008, 23 percent of all takeovers announced were hostile or unsolicited, and hostile activity rose in relative terms throughout the year, from 21 percent of deals in the first quarter of 2008 to 29 percent in the fourth quarter of 2008.[2]

The rise in hostile activity during this period was unsurprising. It was due to the confluence of three trends. First, would-be buyers made opportunistic bids for targets with significantly depressed share prices. Target boards resisted these offers. These targets claimed that the decline in their share prices was a short-term, quite downward turn that was due to the financial crisis rather than any fall in the target's intrinsic value. Even taking into account any share premium offered by the would-be buyer, targets argued that these bids undervalued the company.

Second, due to the efforts of corporate governance activists, companies were less defended than at other times in recent corporate history. For example, 302 companies in the S&P 500 had a staggered (also known as a classified) board in 2003 compared with 172 companies in 2008.[3] During 2006–2008, roughly 67 percent of S&P 500 companies with an expiring poison pill had allowed this takeover defense to expire rather than renewing their pill.[4] As a result, by the beginning of 2009, only 20.6 percent of S&P 500 companies had a poison pill, and only 34.4 percent had a staggered board in place.[5] (See Figure 8.1.)

The decline in staggered boards likely left companies more defenseless. As Professors Bebchuk, Coates, and Subramanian have argued the staggered board can be a more powerful antitakeover device because it requires a bidder to run multiple proxy contests over a span of two years to acquire control of a target.[6] The lapse of this takeover defense instead provided hostile bidders the ability to replace the target's entire board in a given year. Moreover, unlike a poison pill, a staggered board required that shareholders approve its adoption. The defense was therefore unlikely to be resurrected once forgone.

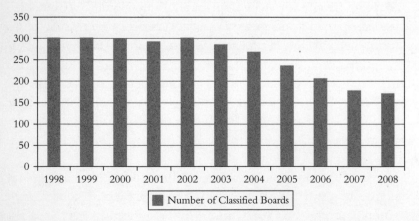

Figure 8.1   S&P 500 Companies with Classified Boards 1998–2008
SOURCE: Factset SharkWatch

Third, the nature and scope of a hostile bid had changed since the 1980s era of the corporate raider. The conventional wisdom from that time was that a hostile offer for a people-based business was notoriously difficult. This was because the target's human capital could exit at any time, and a hostile bid was viewed as an aggressive tactic that would negatively affect employee morale. This put a large number of companies safely outside the specter of any hostile takeover attempt, particularly technology-based companies that were heavy with people capital, namely, engineers and computer programmers.

This conventional wisdom changed with the success of Oracle Corp.'s hostile bid for PeopleSoft Inc., the enterprise application company, in 2003; Oracle's second hostile bid for BEA Systems, Inc., an enterprise infrastructure software company, in 2007; and the aging of technology companies. Technology was becoming akin to an old-line industry. It was less people-based and increasingly asset-rich, allowing for hostile transactions to occur. In fact, 7 of the 10 largest deals in the technology industry in 2008 began as hostile offers.[7] The reason for the high number of hostiles in the technology industry was probably due to arguments about value, but it was also attributable to the continuing presence in these companies of first-generation CEOs and management who were more resistant to a takeover for personal reasons. They did not want to see their beloved companies and their legacies disappear.

The rise of the technology hostile bid illustrated the changing nature of the hostile bidder. The hostile bid was becoming a tool of strategic buyers rather than more aggressive 1980s-type corporate raiders and financial buyers. Strategic buyers typically looked to preserve the targeted company and create synergies rather than dismember their targets. Strategic hostile bidders emphasized their friendliness to the company's employees and customers and publicly regretted their hostile activities as an unwelcome necessity. True hostile activity was now left for the activist hedge funds and the history books.[8] (See Figure 8.2.)

In the midst of this upswing in activity, two significant hostile offers were announced: Microsoft's hostile bid for Yahoo, the Internet media company, and InBev's hostile bid for Anheuser-Busch, the nation's largest brewery. These transactions would show the nature and potential of hostile transactions, the role of attorneys and legal maneuvers in the success of these offers, and the effect of takeover defenses in determining

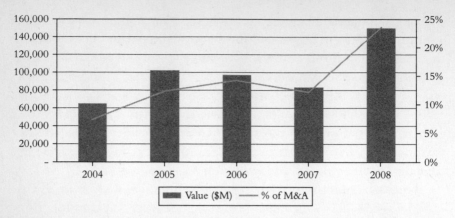

Figure 8.2   Domestic Announced Hostile Takeover Activity (Value and Percent of M&A Transactions) 2004–2008
SOURCE: Factset Mergermetrics

these contests. These two hostile offers would also once again show the importance of personality for deal-making.

Microsoft–Yahoo!

On February 1, 2008, Microsoft announced that its CEO Stephen A. Ballmer had delivered to the Yahoo board of directors a written proposal to acquire Yahoo for $31 a share. This type of letter is known as a bear hug letter. A bear hug letter is designed to put an unwilling takeover target on notice that it is no longer safely independent, but it is written to fall short of being overtly hostile. The hug is the offer, but the bear is the implicit threat that the buyer might go hostile if the hug is not returned. Ballmer's bear hug letter was no different. It contained all the make nice language you typically see in these letters, as well as a warning that there was a bear waiting to come out. Microsoft stated in its letter:

> Depending on the nature of your response, Microsoft reserves the right to pursue all necessary steps to ensure that Yahoo's shareholders are provided with the opportunity to realize the value inherent in our proposal.[9]

Despite the private address, Microsoft promptly made the letter public. Potentially hostile bidders typically do this to put public pressure on the target's board of directors to consider the bidder's proposal. Microsoft was no different, and its disclosure was designed to notify the public of its intentions and use public enthusiasm for a share premium to temper any adverse reaction from the Yahoo board of directors and Yahoo co-founder and then-CEO Jerry Yang. The reason was simple: Without Yahoo's cooperation, a bid would be significantly harder.

The advent of the poison pill in the mid-1980s transformed the nature of a hostile transaction. A poison pill effectively prevents a corporation from being acquired without the consent of the target's board of directors. The reason is that under Delaware law a board can just say no and refuse to accept a takeover offer. Only the target board's directors can redeem the pill and allow an acquisition to proceed. This provides the target board the ability to block a takeover. Hostile bidders, therefore, complement their hostile bid with a proxy contest to remove the target's directors and replace them with the bidder's chosen directors. When elected, these new directors then vote to remove the poison pill and agree to a transaction with the bidder.

The need to complement a hostile bid with a proxy contest thus drives the timing of hostile offers. It effectively means that a hostile offer must come at a time when a company's directors can be replaced. Opportunities to replace the board of directors can come at an annual meeting of the shareholders, a special meeting of the shareholders called for that purpose, or outside the annual or special meeting because of action by written consent of the shareholders. The majority of public companies, approximately 79 percent, either do not permit the calling of special meetings by shareholders or otherwise prohibit shareholders from acting by written consent. In particular, only 45 percent of U.S. public companies provide their shareholders with the ability to call special meetings, and only 30 percent allow their shareholders to act by written consent.[10] In companies that prohibit such actions, shareholders can remove directors only at the company's annual meeting. The annual meeting has its name because it happens only once a year. Thus in such a circumstance, a hostile bidder must time its bid to coincide with this meeting and allow the bidder to nominate directors. Targets know this timing necessity and so have the remainder of the year to plan for any impending proxy contest and hostile offer.

Yahoo was in the majority of U.S. companies. Yahoo's bylaws and certificate of incorporation prohibited actions by written consent and the calling by shareholders of special meetings. Yahoo also had a poison pill with a 15 percent trigger.[11] As a result, Microsoft could not effectively acquire an interest in Yahoo above that threshold unless it obtained prior approval from Yahoo's board.

HOW THE POISON PILL WORKS

The most popular type of poison pill plan, [is] a call plan, under which the holder has a contingent right to buy securities of the target or the acquirer at a deep discount from their market value. . . . There are two types of call plans, the older "flip-over/flip-in" plans and the newer automatic "flip-in" plans. . . .

To implement a call plan, a company issues to its stockholders one contingent share right for each share of common stock outstanding. The issuance is in the nature of a dividend authorized by the directors and need not be approved by the shareholders. The typical call right entitles the holder (once the right becomes exercisable due to a triggering stock acquisition) to buy stock at half price in certain situations. In the case of a merger between the rights issuer and acquirer, the rights holders can buy, at half price, the stock of the company surviving the merger (whether the survivor is the issuer or the acquirer), a flip-over. If an acquirer of the issuer's shares does not pursue a back-end merger but engages in certain kinds of self-dealing transactions with its new subsidiary, the rights holders can purchase shares of the target at half price, a flip-in. The call right thus allows the issuer's stockholders to block a squeeze-out second-stage merger or other methods of self-dealing.

The right is initially "stapled" to the common stock; that is, it trades together with the common stock. The rights vest 10 days after a third party acquires a specified percentage (often 15 percent or more) of the company's stock or has started a tender offer for 15 percent or more of the shares (the "triggering events"). Once vested, the company issues separate rights certificates, and the rights become exercisable and transferable separately from the common stock. The unvested rights have a stated term of 10 years and target directors may redeem them at a nominal price (for example, 10 cents) at any time before they vest. This means that the plans have built-in "sunset" provisions and must be periodically re-issued. The redemption feature allows the board to remove the plan to negotiate an acquisition of the company.

The vested rights permit holders to buy a share of the common stock of the issuer or acquirer (depending on the circumstances) at a price that is typically a multiple of the market price (usually three) of the common stock on the date of issuance of the right. This option is seriously out-of-the-money (the exercise price is much higher than the value of the underlying asset) and holders will not exercise it. . . .

The . . . more powerful call plans omit the "flip-over" feature entirely and eliminate the contingent part of the "flip-in" provisions. The flip-in rights become exercisable to buy stock of the issuer or an acquirer at a fraction of market value whenever the acquirer buys more than a threshold amount of the issuer's stock, even if the acquirer does not engage in any coercive or self-dealing transactions. The acquirer who triggers the options for the other shareholders does not have such an option herself. The other shareholders, exercising their new options, substantially dilute the value of the acquirer's stock. In extreme forms, the acquirer simply loses much of the value of the triggering stock purchase (at minimum, the value of fifteen percent of the voting stock). . . .

Excerpted From Dale A. Oesterle, *The Law of Mergers & Acquisitions* (3rd ed., 2005). Reprinted with permission of Thomson Reuters.

Microsoft's bear hug letter and offer were made in accordance with these time limitations. Yahoo's last annual meeting had been on June 12, 2007. In this case, it meant that the notice period for Yahoo director nominees began on February 13, 2008, and ended on March 14, 2008.[12] Microsoft thus had a window from mid-February to mid-March to make such nominations. Microsoft was acting strategically in the timing of its announcement. The bear would be able to appear in time to launch a proxy contest if Yahoo's board refused to negotiate or make a deal with Microsoft. Microsoft could then seek to replace the entirety of Yahoo's board.

Yahoo was particularly vulnerable. It did not have a staggered board, so all of its directors were up for nomination that year. In a contested election, Yahoo's bylaws also provided that directors were elected by a plurality of votes cast.[13] This was a low threshold, which would aid Microsoft in electing its own slate. Microsoft, though, would be acting in a novel manner if it actually launched a hostile proxy contest. Since 2001, there have been only 26 proxy contests in connection with a hostile bid by a strategic buyer.[14] The low figure reflected the historically low rate of hostile offers, but it also showed how bear hug letters typically ended the matter and forced a transaction with the bidder or a white knight. A white knight is a third-party buyer who comes along to save the target from the hostile bid by acquiring the target itself. In Microsoft's case, the logical white knight for Yahoo was Google. Google, though, was likely to be forestalled by antitrust laws from acquiring all of Yahoo.

Many thought Yahoo would quickly fall, given its weak defenses and the full price Microsoft was offering. Things unfolded differently. Yahoo publicly adopted a just say no defense. On February 11, 2008, Yahoo's board rejected the Microsoft offer, asserting that the bid "massively undervalued" Yahoo. Privately, though, Yahoo took the position that a price in the high 30s would be acceptable, one that most analysts thought unreasonably high. Many instead attributed Yahoo's implacability to the hatred often expressed toward Microsoft in Silicon Valley. In particular, Jerry Yang was said to be adamantly against any acquisition by Microsoft, taking every private occasion to heap scorn on Microsoft.[15]

In response to Yahoo's rejection, Stephen Ballmer and Microsoft appeared to be following the tactic used by Larry Ellison, ex-CEO of Oracle, in Oracle's hostile bid for PeopleSoft. Oracle had made an initial offer, then threatened to pull the offer, and eventually lowered its offer to force PeopleSoft into a deal. Microsoft's Ballmer repeatedly stated in interviews that Microsoft would not overpay. He also equivocated on whether Microsoft would acquire Yahoo if Yahoo demanded a higher price than Microsoft initially offered.

Yahoo bought time by announcing on March 4 amendments to its by-laws that effectively postponed its annual shareholder meeting to a date that eventually turned out to be August 1, 2008.[16] The effect of this maneuver was twofold. First, it bought time for Yahoo to bake another transaction. Second, it pushed back Yahoo's director nomination deadline, thereby keeping Microsoft at bay from actually nominating directors and going fully hostile.[17]

Yahoo's delaying strategy worked to a point. Microsoft did indeed refuse to ratchet up the pressure on Yahoo by formally launching a proxy contest. Over the weekend of May 3 and three months into the contest, Microsoft increased its bid to $33 a share, approximately $47.5 billion. Yahoo countered that it would take only $37 a share, a price many viewed as laughably high. There was also a rumor that the parties could not agree on who would bear the risks of an antitrust challenge. Microsoft then walked away, a move that Yang applauded by exchanging high fives on the Saturday afternoon he learned of Microsoft's withdrawal.[18]

The deal then devolved into farce. Initially, it was thought that Microsoft was simply being a tough negotiator. Ballmer, the driving force behind Microsoft's bid, had wanted to show that he was a deal-maker who could walk away from the table.[19] Carl Icahn sent a letter to Yahoo's Chairman Roy Bostock, stating that Yahoo "completely botched" the Microsoft talks and announced that he was going to run a slate of directors for the Yahoo board. Icahn's specific goal was to force Yahoo to take Microsoft's bid.[20] This raised a number of issues. What would be the board's negotiating power? The new board would need to familiarize themselves with Yahoo and then bargain and even decide whether to sell to Microsoft. Their bargaining position, though, would be from weakness, as they would be locked into an acquisition strategy.

Microsoft inexplicably stayed away, and Yahoo settled with Icahn, placing Icahn and two other directors selected by Icahn on Yahoo's board.[21] Yahoo instead turned to Google and negotiated an ad-sharing revenue pact. Yahoo was criticized for reaching that deal instead of negotiating in good faith with Microsoft, and when antitrust regulators objected to the arrangement, Google abruptly terminated the pact. The day after Google's termination of its agreement with Yahoo, Jerry Yang repented, stating: "To this day, I believe the best thing for Microsoft to do is buy Yahoo," and that Yahoo remains "open to everything."[22] Yahoo, in rushing into the arms of Google, had forgotten a cardinal rule of deal-making: "Marry in haste, repent at leisure."

Meanwhile, Microsoft's Ballmer acted more like a scorned lover than a businessman, publicly speculating about a deal, but Microsoft taking few steps to do so. Jerry Yang subsequently resigned on November 18, 2008, with his company's stock price trading at approximately $12 a share.[23] His replacement may have been an attempt by Yahoo to clear the air and appease a Microsoft that appeared no longer willing to deal with Yahoo in part due to Yang's conduct. To date, though, Microsoft has yet to act again with respect to Yahoo

InBev–Anheuser-Busch

The InBev hostile bid unfolded in a very different manner than Microsoft's bid for Yahoo On June 11, 2008, InBev, the Brazilian-Belgian brewer, publicly leaked its bear hug letter. The bear hug letter from InBev CEO Carlos Brito personally made a proposal to Anheuser-Busch CEO Augustus A. Busch IV to acquire Anheuser-Busch for $65 a share. The bid was valued at approximately $46 billion. This was a good price. It was 18 percent over Anheuser-Busch's all-time high reached almost six years before. InBev's letter also very much stressed its friendliness. In his letter, Brito stated: "We have the highest respect for Anheuser-Busch, its employees and its leadership, who have built the leading brewer in the U.S. and grown the iconic Budweiser brand. . . ."[24] Brito even made a video to accompany the letter. Despite the big hug in the letter, it still remained clear from its text that the InBev team would be persistent and that a bear lurked.

Anheuser-Busch had reason to be concerned. Anheuser-Busch's defenses were weak, but in a manner different from Yahoo's. Anheuser-Busch's annual meeting had already taken place in April. Normally, this would mean that InBev would have to wait until next year for a proxy contest to unseat Anheuser-Busch's directors. But Anheuser-Busch appeared to have a hole in its armor. Anheuser-Busch was in the minority of companies where the shareholders could act by written consent. These shareholders could act at any time to remove all of Anheuser-Busch's directors and replace them.[25]

Anheuser-Busch had also let its poison pill naturally expire in 2004 and begun a process to declassify its staggered board in 2006. The lack of a poison pill could be rectified; a board can adopt a poison pill at any time. This is something that is publicly misunderstood. Whether a company has in place a poison pill upon receipt of a hostile bid makes very little difference because the board can simply and rapidly adopt a poison pill in response. In fact, most companies have a shadow poison pill, a poison pill that is already drafted and ready to be adopted at a moment's notice.[26] The lack of a staggered board was more serious. Because of this, the Anheuser-Busch board could apparently be removed and replaced entirely and at any time by its shareholders.

On June 26, Busch rejected InBev's offer. In a letter to the InBev CEO Brito, Busch asserted that the bid "substantially undervalued" Anheuser-Busch.[27] The rejection was not surprising. Anheuser-Busch had been a family-led operation for 148 years, since its founding in 1860. The family was led now by Busch, who publicly opposed any acquisition. His opposition to the InBev overture was probably ego-driven. The Fourth, as he was known, did not want to be seen as losing the family heritage.

Busch, though, was viewed as a particularly weak leader of Anheuser-Busch. During his 19 months as company CEO, Anheuser-Busch's stock had stagnated. His past was even less stellar. When he was a college student at the University of Arizona, he had been driving his sports car from a night out at a bar when it flipped over, killing the woman passenger with him. Police found him at home eight hours later with blood still on him. After evidence was lost or damaged, police decided not to charge Busch with manslaughter. Then, two years later, he got into a car chase with police in St. Louis and allegedly attempted to run over at least one of the officers with his Mercedes. Busch was acquitted of assault charges brought in connection with the chase.[28]

Eleven days after Anheuser-Busch's rejection, InBev filed its consent solicitation with the SEC.[29] This was the document necessary to solicit written consents from Anheuser-Busch's shareholders to remove and replace the Anheuser-Busch directors. After the first consent was delivered to Anheuser-Busch, InBev would have 60 days under Delaware law to obtain sufficient consents to remove the Anheuser-Busch directors.[30] Unlike Microsoft, InBev was acting in a textbook manner to take over a target, sending a bear hug and then ratcheting up the pressure to the extent the target resisted.

On May 23, 2008, before the bid was announced, the *Financial Times* web site had contained a story stating that InBev was considering an offer to acquire Anheuser-Busch for $65 a share. Anheuser-Busch had taken this story seriously and so was already prepared when InBev's bear hug letter arrived a few weeks later. By that time, Busch had activated the deal machine, hiring an army of lawyers and bankers to fight any InBev bid and advise Anheuser-Busch in its defense.[31] Nonetheless, given the full price and its weak defenses, this left Anheuser-Busch with few options to counter the InBev bid and consent solicitation. Still, against InBev's determined offense, Anheuser-Busch quickly cobbled together a solid defense.

First, Anheuser-Busch took the offense on public relations. Anheuser-Busch was an American icon and a St. Louis stalwart. On the day of InBev's announcement, Missouri Governor Matthew R. Blunt asserted his opposition to the bid: "Today's offer to purchase the company is deeply troubling to me. . . . "[32] Anheuser-Busch played up to this sentiment and in subsequent press releases highlighted InBev's foreign origins. Anheuser-Busch also enlisted a host of Missouri politicians to proclaim the importance of Anheuser-Busch to the American economy and Missouri.

In a counterattack to InBev's actions, Anheuser-Busch also filed a federal lawsuit against InBev in St. Louis. The lawsuit accused InBev of violating the federal securities laws by failing to disclose the conditional nature of InBev's debt commitment letters for its financing. In addition, Anheuser-Busch asserted that InBev was misleading Anheuser-Busch shareholders by asserting that the acquired Anheuser-Busch would be the North American headquarters of the combined companies. This was allegedly misleading under the federal securities laws because InBev had operations in Cuba. Anheuser-Busch therefore could not legally have this operation under its domain under the U.S. laws boycotting Cuba. Hence, Anheuser-Busch would not be the North American headquarters.[33]

Both claims were a public relations maneuver more than anything else. The Cuban claim in particular was designed to highlight InBev's foreign nature. Anheuser-Busch's first claim concerning InBev's failure to disclose its debt commitment letters had a wider point, though. Buyers typically refused to reveal the terms of their commitment letters. The validity of this practice was dubious under the federal securities laws and, in any event, deprived target shareholders of the benefit of knowing the terms of the bidder's financing. InBev would attempt to meet this second complaint by subsequently lining up more committed financing when Anheuser-Busch eventually agreed to be acquired.

Second, like Yahoo, Anheuser-Busch took steps to control the process. On June 26, Anheuser-Busch amended its bylaws to allow the Anheuser-Busch board to set the record date for InBev's consent solicitation.[34] The record date determines who can provide consent to remove the board. All Anheuser-Busch shareholders on that date would be eligible. Without this maneuver, the record date would have been set under the Delaware default rule, which is the date on which the first consent is delivered.[35] Instead, Anheuser-Busch's board now had 10 days from the date of any shareholder request to set a record date. The Anheuser-Busch board could set the record date within 10 days of its date selection. Through this small maneuver, Anheuser-Busch bought an additional 20 days to fight off the InBev bid and the ability to set the record date with a mind to obtain the most favorable shareholder base for this consent solicitation.

Third, Anheuser-Busch took steps to defend its board. Anheuser-Busch publicly argued that its entire 13-director board was still a staggered one. Under Delaware law, directors of a staggered board can be removed outside the annual meeting only for cause. Here, there was not sufficient cause alleged by InBev. Anheuser-Busch's case was a technical one that essentially boiled down to an argument that Anheuser-Busch was in the process of destaggering its board, so until all of Anheuser-Busch's directors were elected at once, the entire board was still deemed to be staggered. This barred the removal of these directors except for cause. Anheuser-Busch was trying to deliver a death blow to InBev's bid. If the board was deemed unstaggered, then the directors could be removed at any time for any reason. If Anheuser-Busch's directors were staggered, though, they would be removable only for cause, and InBev would have to wait until next year's shareholder meeting to attempt to replace the Anheuser-Busch directors. InBev sought to counter Anheuser-Busch's arguments by filing suit for a judicial resolution of the issue in Delaware Chancery Court.[36]

Finally, there were also rumors that Anheuser-Busch was looking for an alternative strategic transaction, such as buying all of Grupo

Modelo S.A.V. de C.V., its business partner for the Corona brand, or undertaking a leveraged recapitalization.[37] This is a standard 1980s-type tactic that the Delaware courts have sanctioned since the 1989 case of *Shamrock Holdings v. Polaroid Corp.*[38] To fight off a hostile bid, the target can agree to an alternative transaction or arrange a leveraged recapitalization. In either case, the target is no longer as appealing to a buyer because it has lost crown jewel assets or has acquired new assets or debt that places a large amount of leverage on the company. If Anheuser-Busch could reach a deal to acquire all of Grupo Modelo, it would make itself too expensive for InBev to acquire.

From a weak hand, Anheuser-Busch had managed to put together an able defense. However, InBev appeared to have a good argument in Delaware that the Anheuser-Busch board was not staggered and could be replaced at any time. Anheuser-Busch's St. Louis case, in contrast, appeared to be a publicity stunt. On the strategic side of Anheuser-Busch's defense, an alternative transaction would be hard for Anheuser-Busch to justify to its shareholders, given the underperformance of Anheuser-Busch's management over prior years. Weighing InBev's rich offer, and Busch's continued nonperformance, shareholders were likely to go to Belgium. Nonetheless, the Fourth's opposition to the bid was considered InBev's main impediment.

Having fleshed out Anheuser-Busch's response, InBev moved in to finish the task. On July 9, InBev agreed to raise its price by $5 a share. In the face of limited options and continued shareholder pressure, Busch quickly capitulated, making the Missouri politicians who had run to his defense appear a bit foolish.[39] InBev had acquired Anheuser-Busch through a textbook application of hostile strategy. It had launched its bid and taken legal and strategic steps to steadily increase the pressure on Anheuser-Busch until a final face-saving raise resulted in Anheuser-Busch's capitulation.

The Elements of a Successful Hostile Takeover

The two deals and their markedly different outcomes illustrate the uniqueness of each hostile transaction. Hostiles are snowflakes, and each is different, depending on the target's defenses and strategic situation, as well as the subsequent actions of the target and bidder. The Microsoft and InBev hostiles ably show this but also highlight the common elements to a successful hostile transaction in today's modern age.

Publicity

A coordinated, preplanned publicity strategy is a necessity. From the beginning, InBev worked to counter claims that it was a foreigner buying a beloved domestic company. InBev promised to keep its North American headquarters in St. Louis and accompanied that promise with assurances on job retention in Missouri. InBev's initial and subsequent statements to this effect allowed InBev to fight off Anheuser-Busch's attempts to spur xenophobic opposition to InBev's acquisition. In contrast, Microsoft's public relations strategy appeared to lack a message and flittered about as Microsoft appeared to be unwilling to commit to a transaction. Microsoft came off as acting to massage its ego and failed to implement a sustained publicity strategy to corner Yahoo This may have been Microsoft's strategy, to appear to be fickle in order to bring Yahoo to the table, but the varying messages Microsoft put forth appeared incoherent to the public.

Personality

The personalities of Stephen Ballmer and Jerry Yang clearly mattered in the outcome of Microsoft's bid. Microsoft's fickleness appeared to come from Ballmer's need to appear strong and in control and for the market to perceive him as having reached a good deal. Meanwhile, Yang was visceral in his initial reaction against a Microsoft deal. Yang appeared to be out to defeat the Microsoft bid at all costs, solely because it was Microsoft. This, no doubt, added fuel to the fire and made Ballmer all the more focused on achieving a public win that made him appear strong and humiliated Yahoo Lost in all of this were the economics of a deal. In contrast, Anheuser-Busch first resisted InBev, but InBev worked to accommodate Anheuser-Busch's CEO, Augustus Busch IV, by providing him a face-saving exit. As part of this strategy, InBev offered Busch a postacquisition compensation package that included a continuing consulting assignment to InBev. Busch would be paid a lump sum of $10.35 million and $120,000 a month through December 31, 2013.[40]

Defenses

A good hostile offer is designed from the announcement to box in a target and force it to capitulate. In setting this strategy, the timing and implementation of the offer is set by the target's defenses. This principle was ably on display in the Yahoo and Anheuser-Busch bids. The targets' lawyers also manipulated the process and legal institutions to buy as much time as possible and control the process. Meanwhile, the bidders clearly planned their strategies to work within the shareholder election and consent timing as set by the target's defenses and response. Although ultimately a target may not be able to save itself through legal tactics, these legal maneuverings can certainly work to buy time. In Yahoo's case, the extension of their meeting date and the date for director nominations functioned like Anheuser-Busch's maneuver to postpone the record date for a consent solicitation. Both actions bought time for the target to find an alternative transaction and enhance their defenses.

The Target

To be victorious, a hostile bidder must win the confidence of the target's shareholders. This is ultimately accomplished by paying the right price, but a bidder is ably assisted in this regard if there is a leadership gap at the target. Both Anheuser-Busch and Yahoo were governed by less than perfect CEOs. Anheuser-Busch, in particular, had suffered under the Busch family, and its stock had underperformed against the market and its trading peers. Meanwhile, Yahoo's CEO, Terry Semel, had recently resigned and co-founder and then-CEO, Jerry Yang, was seen as an interim choice. Yahoo was also struggling and losing ever more market share to Google. In both cases, this put the targets in a significantly weakened position and made the premium offered by the bidders more acceptable. InBev succeeded, and had Microsoft more ardently pursued Yahoo, it would no doubt have completed its own deal.

Credibility

Larry Ellison pioneered the threatening technology hostile. He artfully maneuvered between offense and defense, backing off from a deal or otherwise lowering the consideration in successful bids for PeopleSoft and BEA Systems. Ellison also knew when to come back to the table and raise his bid to close. Microsoft initially seemed to be following the Ellison strategy but then took a wrong turn and appeared to act out of petulance. Microsoft's strategy ultimately reduced Yahoo to begging for a deal, but this left Microsoft looking more like it was trying to get its ego massaged rather than reaching an economic bargain. In short, both Microsoft and Yahoo appeared to be incompetent, not executing a pre-planned economically driven strategy.

The Limits of Defenses

The just say no defense can work to forestall a hostile. This may be a particularly potent defense when a company has a staggered board. In fact, I am not aware of any bidder ever successfully running a two-year proxy contest to surmount a staggered board if a board does adopt a just say no defense. Here, though, shareholder pressure and the rise of independent boards may be an increasing force working against targets where bidders actually decide to launch a bid and run a proxy contest against a staggered board. This, though, remains to be a subject of future study and events.

For boards without a staggered structure, though, a just say no defense is at best a delaying tactic until the shareholder meeting. Against an adamant hostile bidder, this defense typically serves only to allow the target to find an alternative transaction. Quite often, this still ends in an acquisition of the company by the bidder or a white knight. In one sample dating to 2002, 66 percent of companies who do not have staggered boards do not retain their independence after a hostile bid emerges.[41]

A just say no defense, though, is not without its risks and can drive away bidders and offers that in hindsight were acceptable, even at the initial price offered. In 2008, companies like Yahoo, Take-Two Interactive Software, Inc., Diebold, Inc., and Acxelis Technologies, Inc. were left with seller's remorse as their just say no strategy worked all too well, leaving their share prices trading at historic lows. This may have been due to the disjointed market during this period. There is no doubt, though, that their share prices traded significantly down after their would-be buyers walked away from the table, and the targets were unable to find an alternative transaction.

Flaws in takeover defenses can also work against a target. For example, in Roche Holding, A.G.'s 2008 hostile offer for Ventana Medical Systems, Inc., Ventana's lawyers had failed to put Ventana's staggered board provision in the certificate of incorporation, instead placing it in the company's bylaws. This allowed Roche to seek shareholder approval to amend Ventana's staggered board to expand it.[42] In contrast, if the staggered board is in the certificate, the board must approve its amendment. This would allow Roche to gain control of Ventana in a single year and circumvent the staggered board. Similarly, in InBev's bid for Anheuser-Busch, the ambiguity over the state of Anheuser-Busch's staggered board benefited Anheuser-Busch, but had it been explicitly spelled out, Anheuser-Busch would have had much more leverage with InBev. This flaw also shows that takeover defenses must be viewed in total rather than individually. The fact that Anheuser-Busch's shareholders could act by written consent was probably satisfactory to Anheuser-Busch when its board was staggered and its directors could be removed for cause. This ability, though, would work in a very different manner once Anheuser-Busch's board was destaggered.

Federalism

Yahoo and Anheuser-Busch were both incorporated under the laws of Delaware. Delaware law allows a company to just say no and refuse a hostile offer, leaving the bidder to pursue a proxy contest if it still desires to take over the target. This can be a high hurdle but a possible one to leap. Other states have much stricter antitakeover laws. Not surprisingly, the strictest are those in rustbelt states such as Ohio and Pennsylvania. Notably, studies of Pennsylvania firms have found that they declined in value in the wake of the passage of these laws.[43] The reason is that these laws entrench management. The companies in these states are significantly harder to take over, and even winning a proxy contest may not be enough. This is even before any political element is accounted for. Legislatures in states other than Delaware may also be quite willing to intervene and rejigger the landscape to protect a local company. The outcome of the InBev offer may have been far different if the company had been incorporated in Missouri instead of Delaware.

Price

Any hostile bid will be for naught if the price offered is not acceptable to target shareholders. As the statistics show, a good price can, and historically has, overcome even the most able defenses. This has led many hostile bidders to strategically increase their bids until the target's board breaks from the pressure. In 2008 alone, 63 percent of hostile bidders ended up increasing their original bids, and target boards responded by recommending the takeover 40 percent of the time. For hostile bidders that do not follow this advice, the results are somewhat predictable. There has been a rejection rate of nearly 100 percent, at least in almost every year since 2004.[44]

The Yahoo and InBev transactions point to the future of hostile offers. These transactions will be the pinnacle of deal-making, where tactics and strategy make a difference, and a coordinated implementing approach is a key to success. The current upward trend in hostiles is likely to continue, but hostiles will continue to remain only a minority portion, but very public, component of the takeover market. Despite their confined place in the market, these deals will also continue to be the area where dealmakers look to soar. These deals will continue to be viewed as battles, where the barbarians at the gate can surmount a target's defenses and win the prize. Hostiles will thus be the area of takeover where personality continues to dominate and uneconomic takeovers are more likely to occur. This is particularly true because buyers have essentially unfettered freedom to engage in these takeovers. Nonetheless, the question remains whether the good governance trend and other actors such as hedge funds become a strong counteracting force to this ego. This appears to be anecdotally the case, but has yet to be confirmed empirically.

Delaware and Hostile Takeovers

The Microsoft and InBev hostiles reveal the peculiar role of Delaware law in regulating hostile takeovers. Delaware law sets forth an array of standards to review a target board's decision when it is faced with a takeover decision. Finding a guiding point in this thicket is often hard, but these standards provide a special role for the Delaware courts to regulate takeovers. As we saw in the InBev offer, this means that litigation in Delaware is a component of most hostile offers. It allows the target and bidder to put forth both a public relations agenda and a legal defense or offense as the Delaware courts review a board's action for compliance with its doctrine.

Revlon Duties

The principal standard governing a target board's consideration of a takeover offer is *Revlon. Revlon* duties, as they are commonly known, were first set forth in the seminal 1986 case of *Revlon, Inc. v. MacAndrews & Forbes Holdings, Inc.*[45] This case arose from the hostile bid by Ronald O. Perelman for Revlon discussed in Chapter 1. *Revlon* duties today require that a board facing the inevitable breakup or change of control of the company obtain the "highest price attainable."[46] A Delaware court will strictly scrutinize a board acting under *Revlon* duties. If a target board attempts to forestall a higher, competing bid, their actions will be suspect and enjoined to the extent they violate *Revlon*'s price-maximizing dictates.

Revlon duties are triggered only if the board affirmatively decides to initiate a sale or breakup process. This is the part about just say no that is often thrown around in takeovers. Because *Revlon* applies only in this limited circumstance, a target board of a company that has not put itself into play by deciding to sell or break up the company can otherwise refuse to accept a takeover offer. Instead, it can adopt or refuse to redeem a poison pill and force the bidder into a proxy contest to acquire the company.

The only countervailing case law is principally Chancellor Allen's 1988 opinion in *City Capital Assocs. Ltd. P'ship v. Interco.*[47] In that case, Allen forced a board adopting a just say no strategy to redeem its poison pill. The validity of *Interco* in light of subsequent Delaware decisions is probably limited applicability at best. There was a possibility, even rumor, that Vice Chancellor Strine was going to order PeopleSoft to redeem its poison pill in the Oracle battle. The case settled before a decision when PeopleSoft capitulated. But to date a just say no strategy has yet to be upended after *Interco* and is likely to be upheld in Delaware unless the company is simply pursuing the status quo and the shareholder ballot box is not open.[48]

This does not mean that the target board can blindly ignore an offer. Rather, a board must be mindful of the procedural requisites of its duty of care and allow enough time for it and the company's officers to consider the proposal and the board's financial advisers to analyze the offer.[49] But this is a procedural requirement that is often just a formality for a board to document its true wishes. *Revlon* duties, in the context of a hostile bid, thus more often come into play when a target has already agreed to a friendly transaction and a second bidder arrives to attempt a trumping bid. In the next chapter, I discuss the board's duties in those circumstances. In that context, Delaware law has seen much movement, and market practice is actively affecting how Delaware reviews board conduct under *Revlon* once a trumping bid has been made. Without a sale or breakup decision, though, the validity of a just say no defense appears to be settled Delaware law.

The Unocal *Standard and Takeover Defenses*

It is because of *Revlon*'s limited applicability that other standards under Delaware law primarily guide a board's conduct in their response to a hostile offer. The Delaware courts outside of *Revlon* duties have promulgated two standards to analyze board defensive conduct, the *Unocal* and *Blasius* standards discussed in Chapter 6. The 1985 decision of *Unocal Corp. v. Mesa Petroleum Corp.*[50] arose out of T. Boone Pickens's bid for Unocal. In that bid, T. Boone Pickens's Mesa Petroleum had bought 13 percent of Unocal in the market and subsequently offered to pay $54 in cash for approximately 37 percent of Unocal's outstanding stock, providing Mesa with majority control of Unocal. The remaining 49 percent of Unocal's shareholders would receive debt securities and preferred stock, which Pickens claimed were worth $54 per share.

Unocal rejected the offer and claimed that it was coercive. Shareholders would rush to bid to receive cash; if they did not, they would instead receive debt securities in the now highly leveraged Unocal. And these securities would be subordinated to $2.4 billion in debt taken on by Unocal to refinance existing debt and the initial cash purchase of Unocal shares. The battle was nasty, and at one point Pickens criticized Unocal CEO Fred Hartley for having a piano installed on one of Unocal's corporate airplanes. Pickens would later state in his autobiography about Hartley that "never has a company been more dominated by personality."[51]

Unocal responded by launching a self-tender offer for its own stock at $72 a share in debt securities, which would be triggered only if Pickens purchased the initial 37 percent. Most shareholders would therefore not tender into Mesa's offer and would instead wait for the richer back-end offer by Unocal itself. Moreover, if they did indeed tender, the company would be almost impossibly overleveraged with an additional $6.1–6.5 billion of debt, making an acquisition by Pickens unpalatable. To be sure that Pickens and Mesa did not attempt to take advantage of the back-end offer, Mesa was prohibited from tendering.

Pickens and Mesa sued, challenging the board's defensive conduct, and lost. The Delaware Supreme Court held that a target board decision to take defensive action, in light of an unsolicited takeover offer, was governed by an intermediate standard of review. This standard requires that the defensive action be "reasonable in relation to the threat posed."[52] Here, the Unocal board's response was reasonable in light of the coercive nature of Mesa's bid.

Unocal, again as with *Revlon*, could also be painted as a crafted response to the SEC's antitakeover stance in the 1980s. The Delaware court's decision to regulate, and put a limit on, takeover defenses was an olive branch to prevent greater SEC action in this arena. Then in 1995, after the battles of the 1980s had passed and long after the SEC lost interest in takeover regulation, the Delaware Supreme Court relaxed *Unocal*'s strictures on takeover defenses in *Unitrin, Inc. v. American General Corp.*[53] *Unitrin* held that a Delaware court should first ascertain whether a target board's takeover response was preclusive or coercive. If not, then the court should review the decision under a "range of reasonableness."[54]

The true impact of *Unitrin*, though, was in its facts. In *Unitrin*, the Unitrin board had initiated a self-tender that had the effect of raising the target directors' holdings to a blocking threshold, preventing any merger transaction with a 15 percent or greater shareholder (i.e., the hostile bidder in the case, American General). Unitrin had also adopted a poison pill with a 15 percent threshold, limiting any subsequent bidder's acquisition of the target's shares. The Delaware Supreme Court reversed a lower court finding that this response was unreasonable in relation to the threat posed. The Supreme Court stated: "The adoption of the poison pill and the limited Repurchase Program was not coercive and the Repurchase Program may not be preclusive."[55]

The court then remanded the case for the lower court to consider whether the program made a bid "mathematically impossible or realistically unattainable" and was reasonable in relation to the threat at hand.[56] However, in other parts of the opinion, the court telegraphed the lower court's determination by strongly implying that the Unitrin board had met this new test. The *Unitrin* gloss on *Unocal* accordingly gave target boards wide latitude in their ability to adopt strong, potentially preclusionary takeover defenses, so long as they did not completely preclude a proxy contest.

Unocal review, as subsequently modified by *Unitrin*, is thus quite limited. By one count, the Delaware courts after *Unitrin* have overturned only four takeover defense responses as disproportionate or preclusive solely under the *Unocal* standard.[57] All except *Omnicare* were decided in the Chancery Court.[58] On the edges of *Unocal*, the courts, acting in their takeover supervisory role, repeatedly punished target boards who completely shut off a bid's potential for success, however remote, or who otherwise unfairly acted mid-contest to alter the rules of the game to the same effect. Thus, in two cases, *Carmody v. Toll Brothers, Inc.* and *Mentor Graphics Corp. v. Quickturn Design Systems, Inc.*, the Delaware courts struck down no-hand and dead-hand poison pills.[59] Then in *Chesapeake Corp. v. Shore*,[60] the Chancery Court held that a bylaw provision adopted in the middle of a takeover battle that effectively frustrated an unsolicited bidder after its successful proxy battle was not sustainable under *Unocal* and *Unitrin*. However, these decisions were islands in a sea of permissiveness. The Delaware courts have largely upheld the vast majority of takeover defensive action, largely confining *Unocal* to a test of preclusiveness. In the wake of this constriction, two academics have labeled the *Unocal* standard as "dead."[61]

The result is twofold. First, litigation remains an element of any hostile as the potential, if not the actuality, for a violation of *Unocal* is present. Delaware courts thus retain their oversight review of hostile transactions. Second, given the Delaware court's strict reading of *Unocal*, the defensive actions that a board can take today outside *Revlon* are vast.

SIGNIFICANT TYPES OF TAKEOVER DEFENSES

White Knight—A friendly buyer who purchases a target subject to a competing hostile bid.

White Squire—Similar to a White Knight but the friendly buyer purchases a significant interest in a target instead of the entire company.

Poison Pill—See sidebar on pages 192–193.

Pac-Man Defense—A tactic where the target turns the table on a bidder by making a bid for the bidder itself. The most famous example occurred in the bidding war between Bendix and Martin Marietta in 1982.

Leveraged Recapitalizations—To fight off an unsolicited bidder, the target will borrow a significant amount of funds to pay a dividend or repurchase its shares. If successful, this makes the target too leveraged for a bidder to acquire using debt financing.

Crown Jewel Sale—A sale by the target of a key asset to make it unattractive to an unsolicited bidder.

Golden Parachutes—Benefits provided to employees, typically senior executives, of a target upon a change of control of the target. This typically takes the form of cash payments and accelerated vesting of restricted stock and stock options.

Greenmail—The repurchase of a block of stock at a premium from an unwanted shareholder.

Shark Repellents—Charter and bylaw provisions that discourage takeover activity. Examples include staggered board, fair price, supermajority voting, and expansive nomination notice provisions.

State Antitakeover Laws—Since the 1980s, most states have put in place laws that make a hostile takeover more difficult and, in some states such as Pennsylvania, almost impossible without target consent. Examples of these statutes include "control share," "fair price," and "business combination" statutes. Control share statutes typically mandate that a majority of disinterested target stockholders preapprove the acquisition of bidder control. Fair price statutes generally require that a business combination with a person holding 10 percent or more of the corporation's stock be approved by a supermajority of the bidder's disinterested stockholders unless certain exemptions were met (primarily approval of the disinterested directors or payment of a fair price). Business combination statutes usually prohibit bidders from engaging in a business combination with a target for preset period upon the bidder's acquisition of 15 to 20 percent or more of the target's equity unless the purchase was preapproved by the target's board or a specified percentage of disinterested target stockholders.

The Blasius *Standard and Shareholder Voting*

The Delaware courts also review target board defensive actions under the holding of *Blasius Indus., Inc. v. Atlas Corp.*[62] The standard in *Blasius* is applied when "the primary purpose of the board's action is to interfere with or impede exercise of the shareholder franchise and the shareholders are not given a full and fair opportunity to vote."[63] There has been substantial debate about the continued existence of this standard and its fit with the *Unocal* standard. However, the Delaware Supreme Court reaffirmed its validity in the 2003 case of *MM Companies, Inc. v. Liquid Audio, Inc.*,[64] when it held that a defensive action to expand a board from five members to seven in order to prevent an insurgent from taking control of the company lacked compelling justification under *Unocal*. The court applied a *Blasius* analysis within an application of the *Unocal* standard because "the defensive actions of the board only need to be taken for the primary purpose of interfering with or impeding the effectiveness of the stockholder vote in a contested election for directors."[65]

The advent of the poison pill and the effective requirement that a hostile bidder conduct a proxy contest are likely to mean that *Blasius* will continue to play a prominent role in regulating hostile takeovers for corporate control. Illustratively, in the recent case of *Mercier, et al. v. Inter-Tel*,[66] the Chancery Court applied *Blasius* outside the hostile context to a vote on a merger transaction. In that case, a special committee had postponed on the day of the meeting a shareholder vote on an acquisition proposal because it otherwise would have been defeated. Vice Chancellor Strine asserted that the *Blasius* standard was inappropriate. Instead, the standard should be incorporated into *Unocal*'s reasonableness standards. However, acknowledging that such a change could only be effected by the Delaware Supreme Court, he applied the standard in the alternative to find that the postponement had a compelling justification due to a corporate governance firm's possible change of recommendation, among other factors, and the board's "honesty of purpose."[67] This holding is one of only two cases so far where the Delaware courts have actually applied the *Blasius* standard and found the action to pass muster.[68]

In reality, *Blasius* is not often implicated in hostile takeovers, probably because boards are now regularly advised that they have limited ability to affect the proxy machinery during a pending hostile transaction as well as the Delaware court's preference to review target responses to hostile bids under *Unocal*. *Blasius*'s effect is thus as a regulating force that is seldom invoked but is followed by target boards fearful of the high threshold it imposes. The question remains, though, whether Vice Chancellor Strine's attempt to rewrite the *Blasius* standard takes hold and, if it does, whether it applies to all takeover votes. Given the corporation's control of the proxy machinery and the head start their positions and control provide, such a move is likely to be ill-advised, and *Blasius* should be generally applied to votes on all takeover transactions.[69]

The Future of Hostile Takeovers

Vice Chancellor Strine's attempt to rewrite the *Blasius* standard points to a movement in Delaware law. There are many academics and even Delaware judges who want to simplify the multiple standards Delaware imposes on takeovers. They advocate instead that Delaware largely rely on independence and reasonableness tests. So long as directors act reasonably and independently in the context of a takeover, their actions should be upheld. The movement has yet to see success, but it may eventually result in a consolidation of Delaware standards.

This movement belies a more obvious fact. Even under the current standards, Delaware courts rarely rely on any of these standards to intervene in hostile takeover battles. Instead, Delaware courts increasingly regulate takeover contests through their state's disclosure requirements. When the Delaware courts find a violation of these obligations by either the target or the bidder, they tend to then order only corrective disclosure. This allows the Delaware courts to tell a moral story: What you, the target directors or the buyer, did was bad and must not be done again. Practitioners and academics then write about these lapses and presumably clients are advised not to repeat these mistakes. But the deal itself is little affected once the corrective disclosure is made. Delaware courts will truly act to substantively intervene only when a target board takes action to completely foreclose an offer. The Delaware courts are hesitant angels rather than active umpires.[70]

In recent years, at least, the process appears to have worked. Delaware courts have maintained a level playing field for wealth-maximizing bids. A board can refuse a takeover and just say no, but it cannot preclude bids and access to the proxy mechanism to force a change of control. Delaware thus allows the soft force of shareholder pressure to work to substitute the court's judgment in these deals and overcome the deterring effects of management control and the possibility of a proxy contest. The soft force of shareholder power has purchase in effecting sales of the company and forestalling the adoption of takeover defenses. This trend is likely to be enhanced in light of the appearance of more activist hedge funds and other shareholders who will work to take advantage of these events. And this is presumably why majority substantial number of hostile bids result in a sale of the target.

Thus, Delaware's easy hand on takeover defenses allows many devices that impede takeovers, such as the poison pill, to exist. However, this may not be, in effect, a bad thing. It allows a board to actually fulfill the purpose of the poison pill and takeover defenses, to prevent advantaging underpriced bids, while allowing shareholder pressure to function in preventing management entrenchment. Theoretically, the force should work. The InBev and Microsoft offers are illustrative and reflect the increasingly important role of shareholders and shareholder activists. Nonetheless, as in Yahoo, in the past year the just say no defense has backfired, as many bidders simply withdrew their bids before shareholder pressure could take effect. It remains to be seen, though, whether this was simply a function of market conditions or a secular trend.

Evidence that shareholder power may be working comes from the
rise in hostile activity. It is clear that hostile activity in recent years has
been significantly diminished from 1980s levels. Some have connected
the diminished takeover activity to Delaware's relaxing its review of takeover defenses. The rise in activity in the last few years has correlated with
the rise of activist hedge fund shareholders and good corporate governance campaigns. It may be that this soft shareholder force is indeed the
tonic for the relaxed Delaware standards that otherwise seem too permissive. In such a circumstance, Delaware's focus through *Blasius* on preserving access to the shareholder ballot to effect takeovers makes sense.

None of this will do away with the staggered board. This takeover
defense appears to more strongly work against shareholder interests and
entrench management. As Bebchuk and his co-authors have argued, a
staggered board can act as a deterrent on hostile takeovers.[71] The reason
is simple. A hostile takeover against a company with a staggered board
can take two years to obtain majority control and complete. Many companies are unwilling to expend the time and effort for such an uncertain
outcome. In this light, studies have largely found that staggered boards
deter bidding and result in fewer successful bids.[72] The studies are more
mixed on whether a staggered board results in a higher takeover premium due to the need to overcome the target's strong defenses.[73]

Some argue that the rise of independent directors and higher management stakes will work against the staggered board.[74] In particular,
the ability to win the first shareholder election and elect a short slate—
that is, one-third of the board—provides substantial ability to pressure
a company. Here, the examples most often cited are Weyerhaeuser Co.'s
acquisition of Willamette Industries Inc. and AirTran Holdings Inc.'s
failed acquisition of Midwest Air Group Inc. In both cases, the bidder elected a short slate of directors, forcing the target to enter into
a change of control transaction. Willamette agreed to be acquired by
Weyerhaeuser, and Midwest sold itself to a white knight, TPG.

Nonetheless, even assuming that a staggered board results in higher
premiums, by reducing success rates, shareholders of companies with
staggered boards probably lose out in the aggregate and on the edges.
Although poison pills and other takeover defenses may deter takeovers,
today only the staggered board appears to be a truly effective deterrent. The more activist shareholder agenda may indeed counteract the

staggered board, but that will have to wait for further studies. The staggered board may be an appropriate tool for other value-creating reasons, such as preserving board independence and providing long-term perspective. But in the takeover realm it is for now a suspect device.

In the first five months of 2009, the uptick in hostile activity continued. During this time period, 27.78 percent of all U.S. activity was hostile compared to 20.8 percent during the same period in 2008.[75] If hostile activity continues its rise, companies may also push back, attempting to counteract this shareholder force. In the past two years, companies aware of their relative weakness began to arm themselves as quickly and best as they could. In 2008, 122 companies adopted their first poison pills to fend off takeovers. Only 71 companies adopted poison pills for the first time in all of 2007.[76] The sizable increase in poison pill adoptions was most likely an attempt by companies, particularly small ones where a significant percentage of the company could be acquired in the market without a filing under antitrust laws, to signal to the market that they would resist a hostile takeover attempt. Although poison pills do not forestall an offer, these adoptions foreshadow a more aggressive response by targets in the future and perhaps a return of the more aggressive takeover defenses of the 1980s. This response may push the takeover laws further into target management's favor, collapsing the balance that Delaware law has perhaps unwittingly arrived at. In other words, the soft power of shareholders is a fragile one at best.

Ultimately, takeovers have come a long way from the first true blue-chip hostile, International Nickel Company of Canada's 1974 unsolicited offer for ESB, Inc., then the country's largest battery maker.[77] The wild times of the 1980s corporate raiders are not likely to return. The days when Goldman Sachs and other investment banks and law firms refused to participate in hostiles because of their aggressive nature are also long gone. The hostile probably achieved full legitimacy in 1995, when IBM launched its landmark and textbook hostile against Lotus Corporation.[78] Since that time, hostiles have become an accepted part of the marketplace, another facet of the deal machine. They are no longer the coercive bids of the 1980s launched by raiders to take over and carve up companies. Now, the hostile is the domain of strategic buyers using terms like *synergies* and *growth*. It is a trend that is part of the mainstreaming of the strategic transaction, the subject of the next chapter.

Chapter 9

Mars, Pfizer, and the Changing Face of Strategic Deals

T he fervent activity and wallets of private equity overshadowed strategic buyers in the sixth wave. During the period from 2004 through 2007, strategic transactions—transactions where the buyer is an operating company rather than a financial buyer such as a private equity firm—were 71 percent of announced U.S. takeover transactions.[1] Strategic transactions still comprised the majority of deal-making, but their profile and role was limited by private equity's aggressive tactics and willingness to bid for almost any company.

In this environment, sellers could attract a large number of private equity bidders to compete with a strategic one. Company auctions became a more frequent means to sell companies, as sellers favored competitive bidding contests. Private equity came to these auctions in full strength. The free availability of easy credit meant that private equity could finally compete with strategic buyers. In prior times, strategic buyers could almost always trump a private equity bid. Strategic buyers could do this by paying higher amounts due to the cost savings and synergies that they could obtain by combining their operations with a target.

Private equity lacked these advantages because private equity purchased companies on a one-off basis. But the determining factor in auctions and acquisitions changed. Now, it became which buyer could tolerate the highest possible debt load. As private equity grew, these firms even began to create their own strategic buyers, leveraging the advantages of being a private equity bidder with the ability to obtain the cost savings and synergies of a strategic buyer. The most notable example was certainly Apollo's Hexion Specialty Chemicals. Hexion outbid the strategic buyer Basell Holdings BV for Huntsman in a $10 billion deal with near-fatal results for both Huntsman and Hexion.[2]

The deal machine accommodated this financing trend, and investment banks began to successfully lobby targets to offer stapled financing in these auctions. Stapled financing is prepackaged financing offered by a target's investment banker in an auction. The financing is encouraged for use by any bidder. Stapled financing allowed targets to level the playing field among buyers by homogenizing bid financing. It also allowed investment banks to doubly profit by representing both the target and the buyer. Shareholders complained that this was a conflict of interest, but the practice continued, with some targets hiring a second investment bank to paper over the conflict claims, producing yet more fees for the investment banks.[3]

The availability of cheap credit and the presence of private equity also changed the nature of the consideration buyers offered in the sixth wave. Cash came to dominate as an acquisition currency. This marked a strong turn from stock, the preferred currency of the fifth wave, the technology bubble. The increased use of cash by strategic buyers also heralded a more conservative approach to deal-making. In the technology bubble, many buyers had made dilutive takeovers with their company's stock, takeovers that then proceeded to fail miserably. The ultimate example was the 2001 merger of AOL and Time Warner, which resulted in Time Warner shareholders losing up to $220 billion in value. The use of cash was viewed as a disciplining force in acquisitions. Stock could be freely issued, but managers would have to work diligently to ensure that the cash borrowed to finance an acquisition would be paid back.

This sentiment was a reflection of an intermittent focus during the sixth wave on disciplined acquisitions in light of the ill-fated deals of the prior years.

Disciplined takeovers became a cherished goal advocated by shareholders and market observers to some success, but the social aspect of deal-making became a less important factor during this time period. In strategic transactions, one of the primary concerns is social integration. The buyer must not only complete the deal but also then effectively merge the target's business, management, and employees into the buyer's own corporate culture. In the fifth wave, this had been a significant issue as large merger-of-equals transactions predominated. In these transactions, there was no designated buyer. Instead, the companies claimed that they were equals and peers combining for purely strategic reasons. Unfortunately, in a number of these transactions, such as Morgan Stanley's $10 billion merger of equals with Dean Witter & Co. and Citicorp Inc.'s $37.4 billion merger of equals with Travelers Group Inc., trench warfare subsequently broke out, as the executives of each company fought for control and the cultures failed to effectively integrate.[4] Companies in the sixth wave had learned from these difficulties. Merger-of-equals transactions became less commonplace, and buyers self-selected for more appropriate targets that would fit within the buyer's own culture.

Targets themselves became less concerned with preserving their own culture through contractual agreement. The two notable exceptions during this time were the acquisitions of Pixar and Dow Jones & Co. When the Walt Disney Co. acquired Pixar in 2006 for $7.4 billion, the parties agreed to strong measures to preserve the separate Pixar culture, including a requirement in the acquisition agreement that "Pixar's operations will continue to be based in Emeryville, California. The Pixar sign at the gate shall not be altered."[5] And when Rupert Murdoch's News Corp. acquired Dow Jones for $5 billion in 2007, the parties established a five-member independent special committee of "distinguished community or journalistic leaders." This committee was provided postacquisition approval rights over the *Wall Street Journal* managing editor and editorial page editor and the Dow Jones managing editor. This was a unique arrangement driven by the distrust of the tabloid-owning Rupert Murdoch and the leverage of the selling Bancroft family, who controlled Dow Jones.[6]

Strategic transactions during the sixth wave were also strongly influenced by the globalization of deal-making discussed in Chapter 5. Cross-border transactions rapidly rose in value during this time, from $589 billion in 2004 to $1.79 trillion in 2007.[7] Groundbreaking domestic transactions also occurred. Most prominently, Hewlett Packard Co.'s landmark acquisition of Compaq Computer Corp. spawned its own proxy contest, as HP's shareholders revolted against the takeover. The transaction morphed into a referendum on the tenure of Carly Fiorina, then CEO of HP, as former HP director Walter Hewlett led an insurgency against the deal. Fiorina won, and the combination was approved by HP's shareholders.[8] She then proceeded to write about this victory in a memoir titled *Tough Choices*.[9] The HP shareholders lost, but their objections showed that buyer shareholders could wield their own power to forestall deals.

During this period, innovation in strategic transactions was reduced as the limelight stayed on private equity. There were only two truly significant game-changing legal shocks to the system during this time. The first was Vice Chancellor Strine's opinion in *In re IBP Inc., Shareholders Litigation* discussed in Chapter 3, which was decided in 2001, just before the sixth wave's beginning. In this decision, Strine provided strong guidance on the scope of a MAC and confirmed the availability of specific performance in an acquisition transaction.

The second was a 2005 decision in federal court decided by the Second Circuit Court of Appeals sitting in New York City: *Consolidated Edison, Inc. v. Northeast Utilities*.[10] In that decision, the court held that under New York law, a target could not sue for lost share premium in a failed acquisition transaction. Instead, the only remedy to the company itself was its out-of-pocket losses. The decision was an odd one. After all, what were buyers agreeing to do in these contracts, if not to pay the share premium? Still, the New York court relied on the particular no third party beneficiary language in the acquisition contract to make this decision.

The decision likely led even more buyers to switch their acquisition agreements to be governed by Delaware law, firmly cementing Delaware's role as the primary regulator of takeovers. However, the issue still remained whether a party, even under Delaware law, could obtain specific performance of their transaction, and if they could not, whether Delaware courts would apply the holding of the *Con Ed* case. This issue would arise in the private equity litigation of 2007–2008 but would not be definitively addressed in that time. As we will see in this chapter, though, this issue would again come into focus as Dow Chemical struggled to escape its obligations to acquire Rohm & Haas.

Strategic transactions had thus become a background affair during the credit bubble and the sixth takeover wave. In the ashes of private equity and the stress of the financial crisis, though, renewed focus would come to these transactions and their structure.

The Changing Structure of Strategic Transactions

The global credit crunch and the implosion of private equity did not leave strategic deals unaffected. Prior to this time, the structure of strategic takeovers was well set and defined. A buyer would typically agree in the acquisition agreement to specifically perform the transaction. In other words, the target could contractually force the buyer in a court of law to comply with its agreement and complete the takeover. This structure contrasted with the more optional nature of the private equity structure discussed in Chapter 2. In a takeover with a private equity buyer, the target would contract with shell subsidiaries created by the private equity fund. These agreements would typically limit specific performance and provide only for the payment of a reverse termination fee if the private equity buyer breached the agreement and refused to complete the transaction.

The historical reason for this difference was private equity's dependence on financing. Without financing, a private equity firm could not complete an acquisition. Accordingly, the private equity firms bargained hard to retain the ability to terminate their agreements if financing became unavailable. Otherwise, the private equity firm would be required to complete an acquisition when it did not have the funds to do so. In the wake of the financial crisis, these same forces undergirding the optionality of a typical private equity agreement began to worry strategic buyers. Strategic buyers began to fear that their financing might fall through, leaving them without sufficient cash to acquire a target. This fear was reinforced by the conduct of the banks in the Clear Channel and Genesco litigations. In those and other deals, banks had shown that they were not afraid of walking on their financing obligations, even if it resulted in the bankruptcy of their client, the buyer.

Fearful of any credit risk whatsoever, strategic buyers began in the spring of 2008 to negotiate the optional features common to private equity deals but previously unheard of in strategic transactions. The most notable of these was the first: Mars Inc.'s agreement to acquire Wm. Wrigley Jr. Co. for $23 billion. In the acquisition agreement for that deal, Mars negotiated a reverse termination fee. This provision allowed Mars the right to walk from the transaction at any time by paying approximately 4.5 percent of the equity transaction value, or $1 billion.[11] Mars no doubt demanded this optionality on account of its need for significant financing to complete the deal and its concern that this financing might fall through.

Wrigley probably accepted this provision because of the high price Mars was offering and the particular social problems surrounding the deal as a result of the Wrigley family. Wrigley was still controlled by the Wrigley family and the family members remained a pillar of the Chicago community. Wrigley's agreement to a reverse termination fee probably reflected the Wrigley family's ambivalence about the transaction and their unwillingness to force Mars to complete it. Moreover, Warren Buffett's Berkshire Hathaway Inc. was an investor in this transaction, investing $2.1 billion directly in the postacquisition Wrigley itself and providing $4.4 billion in financing.[12] The involvement of the legendary Buffett no doubt assuaged Wrigley of Mars's commitment to the deal but also highlighted the troubled financial market and consequent need for alternative sources for credit.

The Mars-Wrigley deal opened up the door for the negotiation of more optional deal structures in strategic transactions. In the wake of Mars-Wrigley, strategic buyers began to negotiate provisions that allowed the buyer to terminate the transaction if the financing for the transaction failed. In such circumstances, a reverse termination fee would instead become payable. This was a stronger provision than that in the Wrigley acquisition because it purported to allow the buyer to walk only if the financing became unavailable. In all other circumstances, the target could specifically force the buyer to complete the deal.[13] Examples of 2008 strategic deals with this feature included Third Wave Technologies Inc.'s agreement to be acquired by Hologic Inc. for approximately $580 million, Brocade Communications Systems Inc.'s $3 billion agreement to acquire Foundry Networks Inc., and Ashland Inc.'s $2.6 billion agreement to acquire Hercules Inc.[14]

The grafting of the reverse termination fee onto the strategic structure was problematical, though. It falsely equated private equity and strategic transactions. Unlike private equity firms, strategic buyers are not in the business of making acquisitions and for the most part are not repeat players in the takeover game. The reputational penalty for walking is thus not as substantial. Moreover, a strategic buyer must answer to its shareholders. An adverse public reaction by a buyer's stockholders to the announcement of an agreed acquisition could incentivize it to abandon or renegotiate the deal. This was proven by subsequent events. In at least two strategic deals with private equity features negotiated in 2008, buyers leveraged this optionality to attempt to renegotiate the transaction. The two were Foundry's acquisition by Brocade and i2 Technologies Inc.'s acquisition by JDA Software Group Inc. In the latter instance, i2 refused to renegotiate, leaving it with only the reverse termination fee as compensation for its failed deal.[15]

In the wake of these collapses, Pfizer Inc.'s acquisition of Wyeth Pharmaceuticals Inc. for $68 billion was announced in January 2009. The attorneys in that deal appeared to have learned from the travails of Foundry and i2. In the Pfizer deal, Wyeth negotiated a reverse termination fee of $4.5 billion. This was a substantial payment and 7.6 percent of the enterprise value of the transaction or approximately half the share premium being offered by Pfizer. Like the other strategic transactions following the Wrigley deal, this fee was payable if Pfizer's financing became unavailable.

The two key innovations in the Pfizer agreement, however, were the size of the reverse termination fee and the nature of the financing out. First, unlike other deals, where the reverse termination fee was small enough to be treated as an option payment, the fee in this case was sizable enough that Pfizer would be quite hesitant to walk on the transaction or otherwise attempt to trump up a financing failure to excuse its performance. Second, the parties narrowly drafted what would constitute a financing failure to encompass only a ratings downgrade of Pfizer

below investment grade. In all other circumstances, Wyeth could force
Pfizer to specifically perform its obligations under the agreement.[16]
This tight objective standard ensured that Pfizer could not trump up a
financing failure to escape its obligations.

A variation of the Pfizer–Wyeth strategic form subsequently appeared
in the March 2009 acquisition of Schering–Plough Corp. by Merck &
Co., Inc. In that transaction, if the financing was available and Merck
refused to complete the transaction, then Schering's only remedy was to
terminate the agreement and collect a $2.5 billion reverse termination
fee from Merck, plus expenses up to $150 million.[17] Otherwise, Schering
retained the ability to force Merck to specifically perform the transaction.

This was a variation of the Pfizer model with two important
distinctions. First, it was a lesser amount—Pfizer's reverse termination
fee was at 6 percent of deal value, compared with 6 percent for Merck.
Second, the Pfizer reverse termination fee was payable only upon a ratings downgrade of Pfizer. In all other circumstances, Pfizer was required
to close. Pfizer took the risk that it would lose the financing only if it
wasn't an investment grade company. In Merck's case, there was a wider
out, encompassing circumstances where the financing became unavailable for any reason—a proviso that included the possibility of a financing bank going bankrupt.

The Pfizer–Wyeth strategic model appeared to get it right and
will probably set the model in some variation for future deals. It also
showed the ability of attorneys to innovate and how such innovation
goes through iterative stages to arrive at a more stable deal model. Still,
the use of private equity types of features in strategic deals remains
unusual. The majority of strategic transactions in 2008 and 2009 were
structured in the traditional manner. These included InBev's $50.6 bil-
lion takeover of Anheuser, Dow Chemical's $15.3 billion agreed acqui-
sition of Rohm & Haas, and Altria's $10.3 billion acquisition of UST.
However, these three buyers were hit by the credit crisis in September
and October 2008, and Altria was forced to delay its acquisition
because of an inability to obtain financing.[18] The possibility was real
that financing could fail in a takeover, leaving a buyer in the sad state of
Finish Line in the Genesco acquisition and Hexion in the Huntsman
transaction. The buyer would be ordered to complete an acquisition
but without the cash to do so.

The Rohm & Haas deal in particular highlighted the perils of a lack of a financing out. The collapse of Dow's joint venture with the Kuwaitis in late December 2008 had left Dow struggling to finance its acquisition of Rohm & Haas without dismembering Dow itself, cutting its dividend, or undertaking a dilutive equity issuance. It was at this point that Dow, on January 26, 2009, simply refused to complete the acquisition. Rohm promptly sued Dow in Delaware Chancery Court to force it to specifically perform the agreement. From the prior MAC battles of 2007 and 2008, it was clear that Rohm & Haas had not suffered a MAC and that Dow had no financing out in the acquisition agreement.

Faced with few legal options, Dow decided to argue the issue of whether specific performance was available in a cash transaction. Despite having agreed in the acquisition agreement to specific performance, Dow argued that if it were forced to complete the takeover, it would significantly and adversely affect Dow and force it to slash costs, close plants, and lay off employees. Because of this, the Chancery Court should use its equitable discretion to ignore the language in the agreement, refuse to order specific performance, and instead award monetary damages. Dow then argued that the Delaware court should apply the Con Ed case and award Rohm & Haas only its out-of-pocket expenses.[19]

The case appeared to be more a public relations campaign than a legal argument. Dow CEO Andrew Liveris even went on CNBC to praise Rohm & Haas but argue that the deal no longer made sense despite Dow's legal obligations. On the eve of trial, Dow settled without a reduction of the purchase price but an agreement of two significant shareholders of Rohm to roll over up to $3 billion of the proceeds into a preferred share investment in Dow. The failure of Dow to obtain a reduction in the share price and the relatively high yield of 15 percent on the preferred showed the weakness of Dow's arguments.[20] The settlement appeared to be one that Dow may have been able to get without litigation.

Dow's failure to obtain a better settlement showed the hazards of a public relations campaign. By repeatedly and publicly claiming that it would be faced with possible default on its debt obligations if the transaction proceeded on its prior terms, Dow locked itself into a litigation strategy. Yet, the litigation case was weak, and on the cusp of trial

Dow was forced to recognize that. This forced it into a settlement as the alternative; an adverse judgment was only likely to now severely spook Dow's lenders.

Ultimately, the travails of Dow and the Pfizer precedent are likely to spur increased use of reverse termination fee provisions in strategic transactions. In negotiating these provisions, though, targets and buyers will continue to bargain over the scope of optionality. Targets will prefer the Pfizer model, and buyers will argue for a more traditional type of private equity reverse termination fee. The course of these negotiations will affect the future structure of strategic transactions.

The Phenomenon of the Distressed Deal

The financial crisis brought on another new development in the world of strategic transactions, the rise of the distressed takeover. During 2008 and through to 2009, the credit markets remained frozen. Because of this, distressed companies often could not obtain the necessary debtor in possession financing to continue their operations in a bankruptcy. Moreover, the so-called reforms implemented by the Bankruptcy Abuse Prevention and Consumer Protection Act of 2005 made it much harder for companies to reorganize in bankruptcy even with such financing. Instead, locked out of the normal bankruptcy restructuring process, these companies turned to strategic buyers to preserve their businesses and avoid liquidation.

But buyers were scarce, as companies were either unwilling to risk a troubled takeover or lacked the financing to make an acquisition. In some extreme instances, the lack of buyers led to reverse auctions, as companies competed with each other for a single buyer. A prominent example arose when Lehman's ex-CEO Richard Fuld Jr. repeatedly tried to reach Bank of America Corp. CEO Kenneth D. Lewis at his home in order to speak to him about purchasing Lehman. Lewis's wife told him that if Lewis wanted to speak to him, he would call him back. Lewis did not call back, and Lehman Brothers lost out on landing Bank of America as a buyer when Bank of America chose to acquire Merrill Lynch instead. Unable to find a buyer or obtain government assistance, Lehman was forced to declare bankruptcy and liquidate.[21]

Buyers confronting these distressed situations resurrected a number of legal tactics to drive hard bargains on both price and acquisition terms. Buyers sought to lock up targets as firmly as possible while simultaneously obtaining as much flexibility as possible to terminate the transaction before its completion if the target further deteriorated. In the pursuit of these dual goals, dealmakers during 2008 and 2009 would push the envelope of the law, negotiating terms that tested the bounds of Delaware and other states' law.

Perhaps the best example of this unfortunate development was MidAmerican Energy Holdings Co.'s agreement on September 19, 2008, to acquire Constellation Energy Group Inc. MidAmerican was a subsidiary of Warren Buffett's Berkshire Hathaway Inc. Constellation was on the verge of insolvency and agreed to accept a buy-out from MidAmerican for $26.50 a share, approximately $4.7 billion. In addition, to meet Constellation's near-term capital needs, MidAmerican also purchased $1 billion of Constellation preferred stock, yielding 8 percent.

In exchange for this near-term liquidity infusion, MidAmerican negotiated hard. MidAmerican's right to close was conditioned on Constellation's unsecured senior debt still being rated investment grade, a form of back-door MAC clause. MidAmerican also negotiated a due diligence termination right in the agreement. If, prior to closing, MidAmerican found a material deterioration of Constellation's business as measured from June 30, 2008, in an amount greater than $400 million, then MidAmerican had a right to terminate the agreement. This was a significant out. The sale of Constellation, an energy company, involved the transfer of Constellation's nuclear power plant. The state and federal regulatory approval process oftentimes can last longer than a year. By negotiating a broad due diligence out during this time period, MidAmerican received substantial protection for an extended period of time over and above a MAC clause.

In addition, MidAmerican negotiated a force-the-vote provision that required the Constellation board to hold a shareholder vote even if a third party made a superior bid. Once the vote was held and the merger approved, Constellation could not terminate the agreement to accept a higher bid. If the Constellation shareholders voted no, Constellation was required to pay a $175 million termination fee to MidAmerican.

The MidAmerican acquisition agreement also had a reverse termination fee, and the maximum liability of MidAmerican under the acquisition agreement was capped at $1 billion. Finally, in case of a successful competing bid, MidAmerican was entitled to approximately 20 million shares of Constellation Energy common stock, representing 9.99 percent of outstanding shares, and approximately $418 million in cash.[22] If paid, MidAmerican would receive well over a billion dollars in cash and securities. MidAmerican had used Constellation's desperation to negotiate a very tough bargain. The end result in the Constellation bid was actually favorable to Constellation. Three months after MidAmerican's liquidity infusion, EDF Group proposed a superior offer, a joint venture, and Buffett's MidAmerican yielded, but took its billion-dollar payday with it.[23]

The Constellation deal showed how far a bidder would and could go in securing a distressed deal.[24] Other distressed deals began to pattern themselves on the Constellation deal, as buyers sought and received due diligence conditions, reverse termination fees, force-the-vote provisions, and higher break fees than normal. For example, Bank of America negotiated a force-the-vote provision in its agreement to acquire Merrill. Bank of America also negotiated a provision that Merrill's board could change its recommendation on the transaction only if a third party made a superior bid. This provision was a constriction of the board's fiduciary duties. It was also probably invalid under Delaware law as unduly restrictive on the board's decision making. In the Merrill deal, the termination fee implemented through a stock option agreement could also rise to 4 percent of the deal value, or $2 billion, a higher sum than normal.[25]

In more extreme cases, when the buyer did not want any taint of the target's bad investment decisions, there were asset purchases. Asset purchases allow the buyer to purchase only selected assets and liabilities. The buyer can therefore choose to leave with the target the liabilities the buyer does not want to assume. An asset purchase is thus a time-honored way to acquire troubled companies. For example, JPMorgan Chase & Co., chose to purchase Washington Mutual Inc.'s assets and selected liabilities, but not the company itself. This allowed JPMorgan to avoid taking on liabilities it would prefer not to assume, namely, mortgage-backed securities and loans related to real estate.[26] Left with little, WaMu itself filed for bankruptcy.

Toxic convert rights were often also negotiated by buyers purchasing equity stakes in distressed companies, but who did not purchase the entire company. Toxic convert rights typically involved an automatic resetting of the per-share price to be paid if there was a decline in the target company's stock after the purchase. Because of the huge potential for diluting out other shareholders, these types of investments are accepted only by the most desperate sellers. In this environment, though, buyers were forcing through these provisions in unexpected circumstances.

TPG's ill-fated investment in Washington Mutual was one example. Much earlier in 2008, when things looked a bit more stable for WaMu, TPG negotiated a right that allowed it to reset its investment value to any lower per-share price at which WaMu issued new equity. Ultimately, this protected TPG at the expense of WaMu, inhibiting it from raising additional capital until TPG waived the right. TPG eventually did waive this right, but that action came too late to save TPG's assets from being seized by federal regulators and sold to Bank of America. TPG's right had worked against it, and TPG lost $1.3 billion on its investment in WaMu.[27]

Finally, in two prominent deals, the target had so little leverage that the buyer negotiated a force-the-transaction provision. The Bear Stearns deal discussed in Chapter 6 is one deal. Another was in Wells Fargo & Co.'s $15.1 billion purchase of Wachovia. In that takeover, Wells Fargo negotiated a share issuance of 39.9 percent of Wachovia's voting stock to Wells Fargo. The shares were issued to Wells Fargo before the Wachovia shareholder vote on the transaction, providing Wells Fargo with the ability to push the transaction through despite shareholder objections.[28] Dealmakers were pushing the edge of the law on permissible deal-protection devices, justifying these maneuvers on account of the distressed nature of their targets.

Do Takeovers Pay?

The more disciplined takeover approach in the sixth wave belied a more fundamental question that many were asking in the wake of the fifth wave. Do takeovers even pay? The conventional wisdom is that they do not. Targets gain from takeover transactions but buyers lose, and on the whole, they result in a net destruction of value. In support of this proposition, classic deals from hell such as Time Warner's merger with AOL or Chrysler's merger with Daimler-Benz AG are cited. In addition, there are equally classic studies that are often wheeled out to support this proposition. One study by KPMG analyzed a sample of 700 mergers and found that only 17 percent created "real value."[29] An infamous McKinsey & Co. study found that "less than a quarter [of mergers] generated excess returns on investment."[30]

The thesis that takeovers do not pay for buyers supports the ego theory of deal-making. It justifies the conception that deals are creatures of personality. After all, why would takeovers still occur if they were value-destructive for buyers? The personality-driven model of deal-making persists even after these studies, but the skeptical light thrown on acquisitions has, at least anecdotally, driven CEOs in the sixth wave toward more careful, planned acquisitions.

But the evidence on takeover returns is more complex and supports a different viewpoint than the conventional wisdom. This alternative view is informed by over 135 studies, and 5 surveys on the matter. A review of this evidence finds that takeovers do indeed create value for both targets and buyers. More specifically, targets obviously win in takeovers; their shareholders receive a share premium. For buyers, the statistics are less certain. Two-thirds of studies find that takeovers create or conserve value for buyers, and one-third find the opposite. Based on this much more substantial evidence, Professor Robert F. Bruner finds that the disputes over whether takeovers pay mainly arise from defining how value is measured for buyers in takeovers. He notes that most studies conclude that the majority of buyers earn their cost of capital on acquisitions. However, the returns are widely distributed, and some buyers lose or gain substantially. A deal from hell and personality factors can not only adversely affect the poor buyer but also bias the study of takeover gains.[31]

Based on all the evidence, it appears that takeovers do pay but that the synergies, cost savings, and value creation necessary for successful deals can be hard to realize. In other words, takeovers are hard work. They need to be entered into with a firm plan for postacquisition integration that accounts for the culture of the acquired company.

Haphazard takeovers based on empire building or other notions of conquest are unlikely to have the necessary discipline.[32] Here, we have a good example from industry: private equity. Although the jury is still out on whether private equity in the aggregate pays, and certainly the vintage 2004–2007 acquisitions are troubled, very disciplined firms like Kohlberg Kravis Roberts and the Blackstone Group have earned extraordinary returns over extended periods. KKR had an annual average return of 20.2 percent net of fees on its first 10 private equity funds, and Blackstone has earned an annual return of 30.8 percent on its investments gross of fees since the firm began in 1987.[33]

The sustained takeover activity even in these turbulent economic times points to the value of takeovers. The forces toward disciplined takeovers and the rise of the distressed deal may also result in more value being produced in takeovers. Against these forces, the egos of corporate executives and the deal machine will continue to encourage uneconomical takeovers. This is a battle that will be never-ending and continue to shape strategic transactions in the coming years.

Delaware Law and Strategic Transactions

Like hostile transactions, strategic takeovers are also guided by the standards Delaware law imposes. The key question is again whether *Revlon* duties—the duty of a target board to obtain the highest price reasonably available—apply. In the 1989 case of *Paramount Communications, Inc. v. Time Inc.*[34] and the 1994 case of *Paramount Communications, Inc. v. QVC Network Inc.*,[35] the Delaware Supreme Court restricted application of *Revlon* review to a board's decision making upon the inevitable breakup or change of control of a target. These two decisions effectively eliminated stock-for-stock acquisition transactions from review under *Revlon*. The reason given by the Delaware court is that in such transactions, both buyer and target stockholders share ownership of the merged entities and therefore control is almost always indeterminate. *Revlon* duties are accordingly inapplicable, and the board's conduct is subject to review under *Unocal* or *Blasius*. These decisions heavily influenced the structure of fifth wave transactions and spurred the widespread use of stock consideration. Participants could now characterize their stock-for-stock transactions as mergers of equals and avoid application of *Revlon*.

The widespread use of the stock-for-stock merger structure in the fifth wave was accompanied by an increase in the use of lockups. Lockups are deal-protection devices negotiated by a target and buyer to ensure that their transaction is not interfered with by a third-party bidder. Examples of lockups include stock options, break fees, asset options including crown jewel lockups, force-the-vote provisions, no-talks, and no-solicits.

EXAMPLES OF SIGNIFICANT TRANSACTION DEFENSES (LOCKUPS)

Break Fee/Termination Fee—Fee paid by a target to an acquirer to terminate their agreement. Typically, this fee is payable if the agreement is terminated by the target to accept a third-party offer or the shareholders of the target reject the acquisition and subsequently accept within a specified period of time thereafter a third-party offer.

Stock Option—An option granted by a target to a buyer to purchase shares of the target. Typically, this option is for 19.9 percent of the target's shares and is triggered upon the termination of the agreement in similar circumstances where a break fee would be payable.

Asset Option (Crown Jewel Lockup)—An option granted by a target to a buyer to purchase a key asset of the target. This option is also triggered in similar circumstances as a break fee or stock option. The price for this option can be discounted, but the purpose is to ward off a subsequent bid because the first bidder will be assured of receiving the target's crown jewel asset.

Shareholder Support Agreement—An agreement with a target's significant shareholders to support the acquisition through a voting agreement to vote in favor of the merger or a tender agreement to tender into a tender offer.

No-Talk—A provision in an acquisition agreement that neither a target nor its representatives will speak to other third-party bidders. In its most common form, a target is allowed to talk to other potential bidders only if the target predetermines that the dialogue is, or is reasonably likely to lead to, a superior offer.

No-Solicit—A provision in an acquisition agreement that neither a target nor its representatives will solicit third-party offers.

Force-the-Vote Provision—A provision in an acquisition agreement that a target is required to hold a shareholder vote on the acquisition, even if a higher competing bid emerges.

In their study of lockups from takeovers from 1988 through August 31, 1999, Professors John C. Coates IV and Guhan Subramanian found: "In friendly U.S. mergers greater than $50 million in value, lockups appeared in 80% of deals in 1998, compared to 40% of deals a decade ago."[36] They also determined that in their sample "all-stock deals are much more likely to have stock lockups than cash deals (39% vs. 12%) or deals involving mixed consideration (18%), but are not more likely to have breakup fees than cash deals (46% vs. 47%) or mixed deals (55%)."[37] The aggregate result was that "lock-up incidence is significantly higher in all stock deals (governed by *Unocal*) than in all-cash deals (governed by *Revlon*)."[38] The difference was probably attributable to the applicable standard of review. Lockups in cash deals are reviewed under *Revlon* because they involve a change of control. In contrast, lockups in stock deals are subject under Delaware law to lower standards of review. Targets were aware of the distinction and so used their perceived latitude to negotiate more lockups in stock deals. This provided targets greater latitude to ensure that their company was acquired by their chosen buyer.

This trend was buoyed by the Delaware courts in 1997 in *Brazen v. Bell Atlantic*.[39] In *Brazen*, the Delaware Supreme Court upheld the validity of a $550 million termination fee agreed in the negotiated stock-for-stock merger-of-equals transaction between Bell Atlantic and NYNEX. However, the Supreme Court's holding was arguably at odds with the decision in *Time*, which had held that "structural safety devices" in non-*Revlon* transactions were to be reviewed under *Unocal's* proportional standard. Nonetheless, the court refused even to scrutinize under fiduciary duty principles the board decision to agree to the fee, instead applying a liquidated damages contractual analysis to uphold the fee under reasonableness grounds. Henceforth, buyers agreeing to transactions without the specter of another bid would arguably be able to avoid even *Unocal* review.

These targets would thus have wide latitude to agree to potentially preclusive lockups. For example, in *In re IXC Communications Inc. Shareholders Litig.*, Vice Chancellor Steele, then sitting in the Chancery Court, reviewed a number of lockups and found them valid, stating that:

> enhanced judicial scrutiny does not apply…[as] [n]either the termination fee, the stock-option agreements, nor the no-solicitation provisions are defensive mechanisms instituted to respond to a perceived threat [by] a potential buyer.[40]

In other words, absent a competing bid, it appeared that Delaware courts would not even find a threat necessary to review the devices under the *Unocal* standard and would instead subject these lockups to deferential review under the business judgment standard.[41] In *Omnicare*, the court rejected *IXC*'s proposed standard and instead held that lockups should be reviewed under the *Unocal* standards.[42] This may not make a difference, though, as Vice Chancellor Strine, at least, has implied that review under the business judgment rule contemplated by *IXC* would not be in a materially different spirit than *Unocal* review.[43]

Brazen also firmly places termination fees, the main form of lockup utilized these days, under a different standard of review as liquidated damages. The net effect of all of this is to make intervening bids more difficult and costly. This also provides a head start to a target board's choice of buyer. Here, Professor Coates and Subramanian have argued that in the strategic context when another "buyer is present, a lock-up more than doubles the likelihood of completion for the first buyer."[44] On this basis, they conclude that "foreclosing lockups do exist, and, more generally, that lockups do influence bid outcomes."[45]

Targets could thus agree to transactions and negotiate protections that ensured that their chosen buyer completed their deal. In the wake of these liberalizing rulings in the 1980s and 1990s, the use of termination fees, in particular, began to become the norm. According to one study, termination fees were rare in 1989. At that time, they accounted for only 2 percent of all takeovers. However, by 1998 these provisions were in more than 60 percent of all takeovers.[46] In the wake of *Brazen*, these fees became even more commonplace as targets attempted to affect the course of their acquisition. They also became the lockup de jure as targets and buyers less frequently utilized stock and asset lockups.

Then in *Omnicare v. NCS Healthcare, Inc.*[47] the Delaware courts limited the ability of a majority stockholder to agree to a stock lockup when the target had agreed to a force-the-vote provision. In the end, though, the Delaware courts never addressed the fundamental question of lockups per se, and their use post-*Omnicare* remains widespread, albeit subject to the restrictions set forth in *Omnicare*, the oversight of the Delaware courts, and the arguments of some academics that these provisions deter subsequent bids. Moreover, the Chancery Court strictly construed the scope of *Omnicare* in *Orman v. Cullman*, sharply reducing its impact.[48]

In another 2008 opinion referred to in Chapter 6, Vice Chancellor Stephen P. Lamb even further restricted *Omnicare* to almost meaninglessness. "Omnicare is of questionable continued vitality," stated Vice Chancellor Lamb of Delaware's Court of Chancery in *Optima International of Miami v. WCI Steel, Inc.*[49] In *WCI Steel*, Vice Chancellor Lamb declined to halt the acquisition of WCI via a merger by Severstal. The dispute centered over the mechanics of the approval of the deal. WCI's directors had approved the acquisition, and the acquisition agreement had been signed. The merger was then approved by the stockholders of WCI by written consent that very same day. In fact, the acquisition agreement permitted Severstal to terminate the transaction if this did not occur. Optima, a competing bidder who had bid $14 million more than Severstal, sued. Optima argued that this immediate shareholder vote was a lockup that violated *Omnicare*. More specifically, by approving and agreeing to the merger and arranging for shareholder approval that day, the WCI board breached *Omnicare*'s requirement that there be a meaningful fiduciary out and no fully locked-up deal.

Vice Chancellor Lamb rejected this argument. First, he made the comment just quoted about *Omnicare*'s continued validity, though he also noted that he was not in a position to overturn it. He then stated: "Nothing in the [Delaware General Corporation Law] requires any particular period of time between a board's authorization of an acquisition agreement and the necessary stockholder vote."[50]

The result was a win for the opponents of *Omnicare*. *Omnicare* can now be said to apply in the narrow circumstance where controlling shareholders can't act by written consent immediately or the extreme circumstance of Bear Stearns, where a board of a company attempts to pass control to an unaffiliated third party without a shareholder vote. Given that in most situations, this is not the case, *Omnicare* today has limited applicability, and the Delaware Supreme Court may not even get the chance to overrule it because of the unique facts required to implicate it.

The result of these cases is to classify strategic transactions into two modes, cash or stock. Cash deals are reviewed under higher *Revlon* standards. In effect, the vicissitudes of *Revlon* and the lower standard of *Unocal* matter only if a company agrees to sell. A company has wide latitude to just say no. Once it says yes, it can agree to lockups that potentially preclude other bidders. Again, the only limitation is what the company must do if a higher bidder comes along. If acting under *Revlon*, then the company must keep itself up for sale, arguably up to a shareholder vote on the transaction. If the deal is for stock consideration, the company can simply agree to these protections and fight off a higher bidder. The consequence is that buyers and targets have every incentive to structure a deal as a stock transaction in order to avoid this differential.

Delaware thus allows wide latitude for targets to negotiate these lockups in deals outside *Revlon*. Buyers also have every incentive to push for the most restrictive lockups possible in the form of break fees. This has resulted in an average break fee of 3.5 percent and 3.53 percent in 2008 and 2007, respectively. But 22 percent and 23.2 percent of deals in 2008 and 2007, respectively, had a break fee higher than 4 percent.[51] Compare this with an average break fee of 2.8 percent before *Brazen*.[52] The effect of these lockups is enhanced because shareholders almost never vote down acquisition proposals put forth for their approval. From 2003 through 2007, only nine takeovers were rejected by shareholders.[53] To some extent, this reflects the fact that these votes almost never occur when defeat is certain. Still, the result is the apparent rise in more restrictive lockups cited by Professors Coates and Subramanian. Whether this conduct actually forecloses alternative deals, as Professors Coates and Subramanian claim, or will otherwise be countered and adequately curbed in the future by shareholder activism remains an open question.

In the meantime, Delaware would do well to maintain a hard focus on these lockups, largely limiting break fees to a 3 percent range and putting forth a coherent reason for a liquidated damages provision at this level or above as truly incentivizing bidding. In addition, break fees payable upon a shareholder no-vote should be strictly scrutinized as limiting shareholder choice. Bidders should be compensated for bidding, but when lockups forestall a bidding competition and overcompensate, this is detrimental to shareholders. This is particularly true outside the *Revlon* process where a board can just say no to the hostile bid, erecting a double wall to any acquisition. A strict court policing of lockups is thus likely to be beneficial.

Revlon *and the Market Check*

If a board decides to sell in a cash deal, then *Revlon* duties apply to regulate the board's conduct vis-à-vis any competing bids. In repeated cases, the Delaware courts have acted under *Revlon* to erect a level playing field. In the case of competing bids, *Revlon* duties come into play to keep the playing field further level. First, *Revlon* duties serve to regulate the type of deal-protection devices a company can agree to with a buyer. Second, in this context, *Revlon* operates to regulate what a board, deciding to put itself up for sale, must do to satisfy *Revlon*'s price dictates.[54] This latter requirement has unfolded around the question of what type of market check a Delaware company must undertake, if any, once it decides to sell, and if the company does not perform a market check, what deal protection devices it can adopt. A market check is a procedure whereby a target's investment bankers canvass the market for potential bidders before a target agrees to an acquisition with a preselected buyer.

The need for a market check under Delaware law has always been debated, but in cases from the 1980s, the Delaware courts have refused to pigeonhole companies on the procedures it must use to shop itself or otherwise require an auction of the company when it is put up for sale.

Instead, in a string of cases through *In re Pennaco Energy, Inc. S'holders Litig.*[55] and *In re MONY Group S'holder Litig.*,[56] the Delaware courts held as reasonable deal-protection devices combining no-solicit provisions with approximately 3 to 4 percent termination fees by equity value, and in both cases these provisions were agreed to prior to the target's solicitation of any competing offers. In other words, in these cases the courts validated these lockups despite the lack of a market check.

In this regard, the Delaware courts allow termination fees to be set within a range of value that is typically within 2 to 4 percent of the transaction value, though the question of whether transaction value is based on the equity or enterprise value of the company remains open. This permissibility is effectively equivalent, though perhaps slightly stricter, than that allowed for termination fees in strategic transactions not subject to *Revlon*. This principle was reconfirmed in 2005 in *In re Toys "R" Us, Inc. S'holder Litig.*[57] In Toys-R-Us, Vice Chancellor Strine upheld a termination fee of 3.75 percent of the target's equity value and 3.25 percent of the target's enterprise value agreed to prior to a market check.[58]

A board acting under *Revlon* duties can thus preagree to a deal and also agree to relatively strong transaction defenses under Delaware law without preannouncement contact of other bidders. The board would need to negotiate a fiduciary out, subject to these breakup fees and other transaction defenses, if a higher, competing bid emerges and is superior. But this provides a board substantial latitude to negotiate protection for their current deal.

Starting in 2003, a modified form of market check began to appear, mostly in private equity transactions. This was the go-shop. The go-shop in its standard form allowed a 30–60 day period after announcement of the transaction for the company to speak to other bidders. In other words, to go-shop. Thereafter, the normal provisions that prohibit the target from soliciting other bids would apply. In addition, during this time period, the breakup fee would often be reduced from approximately 3 percent of transaction value to 1 percent.

The go-shop saw widespread utilization in private equity deals. Despite practitioner sense that these provisions were cosmetic, designed to provide reputational cover to done deals, one study has found that these provisions add value in the context of buy-outs where management was not involved.[59] Moreover, in the *Netsmart* case, the Delaware

Chancery Court held that a board breached its *Revlon* duties by, in the context of a go-shop, limiting its solicitation to private equity buyers and excluding strategic buyers. In that case, the court endorsed a go-shop as one part, though not a necessary part, of a market check.[60] *Netsmart* followed the Delaware courts' penchant to strike down no-talks. No-talks are provisions that disallow a target from speaking to a postannouncement third-party bidder even if the bid is superior.

This leaves boards in *Revlon*-land with limits on termination fees and no-talks similar to strategic transactions outside *Revlon*. But ultimately, the difference between *Revlon* review for cash deals and *Unocal* review for stock deals appears limited. For boards acting under *Revlon* review, it principally appears to be an open playing field requirement and perhaps tighter requirements upon break fees and lockups. The board cannot place any arbitrary limitations and must run an open sale process that includes consideration of all reasonable bids. Delaware seems moving toward endorsing go-shops more explicitly, but given the limited evidence of their efficacy, it is unlikely to be a strong tendency. Instead, go-shops are likely to remain a modestly used device limited primarily to the private equity sphere.

The result is that strategic buyers and targets will still have modest incentives to structure their deals around *Revlon*. This is a historical advantage that strategic buyers enjoy over private equity buyers, who can only offer cash. This advantage went by the wayside in the sixth wave due to the credit bubble. The end of easy credit will restore this advantage and further put strategic buyers ahead of the bidding curve with respect to takeovers. Again, though, the extent of this advantage and whether it is curbed by shareholder activism and a rise in no-votes on acquisition proposals remains a story yet to unfold. But excessive lockups may be one area where shareholder activism may not be sufficient to curb management entrenchment, given the historical penchant of, and forces upon, shareholders to approve acquisition transactions.

The Future of Strategic Transactions

The deal machine and personality-driven deal-making has been hit terribly by the financial crisis and the rapid collapse of many companies and emperors, such as Sumner Redstone's Viacom and CBS and Sandy

Weill's Citigroup. Both of these empires were created through deal-making by driven, ego-driven CEOs, and both stumbled hard in the credit crisis. The accusations against John Thain and Ken Lewis in the sale of Merrill Lynch to Bank of America have further illustrated the perils of personifying strategic deals.

In the Merrill sale, John Thain, former CEO of Merrill, was accused of concealing from Bank of America a $15.3 billion loss and paying an inordinate sum in bonuses to Merrill employees prior to the closing. Meanwhile, Ken Lewis was accused of forcing through the transaction and concealing Merrill's troubles from his own share-holders in order to obtain their necessary approval of the transaction. In the haze of spin, it was unclear whether the accusations were true, but they left a terrible tarnish on both men's reputations. Thain's image particularly suffered in light of the disclosure that he had spent $1.22 million redecorating his office suite at Merrill, including purchasing a commode for $35,000.[61] A commode, by the way, is a fancy name for a toilet. Thain subsequently repaid this amount but the public tarnish, whether justified or not, remained.

The personality-driven model remains intact, but it is more limited than in prior years. The focus on disciplined takeovers in the sixth wave will continue to affect the course of strategic transactions. The trend is toward this discipline, particularly in light of the greater shareholder activism spurred by hedge funds and other activist investors. However, the continuing latitude buyers enjoy to acquire companies will work to keep personality an important force in strategic takeovers.

The big deal, though, is unlikely to be a prominent feature of the takeover landscape for the foreseeable future. Rather, strategic transactions will tend to be bolt-on deals, incremental acquisition upon existing businesses. Private equity will eventually return to deal-making. But private equity will return in a submissive role, once again unable to outbid strategic bidders, and as a smaller part of the market. The end result is that strategic transactions are likely to dominate private equity in the coming years of diminished deal-making.

In this market, stock will again probably become the preferred acquisition currency. The principal reason is that stock is a readily avail-able acquisition currency, whereas cash financing is often unobtainable in this credit market. Moreover, in an economic downturn, buyers prefer to maintain their cash reserves. In a depressed market, paying with stock also allows the buyer to keep target shareholders in the game and provide them with a right to participate in the future upside of any acquisition. These trends have already begun to take effect. In both 2007 and 2008, more than 66 percent of all announced takeovers consisted of cash. However, in 2008 takeovers with only stock consideration rose approximately from 12 percent in 2007 to 17 percent in 2008.[62]

The principal problem with paying stock consideration in any financial crisis is that stock fluctuates in price. If the market is moving 1 to 5 percent in any given day, then pricing is impossible for any acquisition. In such a situation, companies try to bridge the gap. They do so by negotiating collar mechanisms that limit the maximum and minimum amount of stock that can be issued. In 2008, 34 percent of transactions offered stock consideration either alone or with cash, but only 9.2 percent of those had a collar.[63] This number should rise as collars become more frequently used in response to a continuing volatile market.

Still, valuing stock in this environment is difficult, and so other exotic instruments such as contingent value rights (CVRs) have begun to emerge to bridge the valuation gap. CVRs pay upon the occurrence of particular events. In 2008, they saw particular use in pharmaceutical deals. Buyers would pay a set price together with a CVR that paid further consideration only if a certain drug or other product met certain financial goals or was otherwise approved by the Food and Drug Administration. By offering these alternative securities, deals in this difficult environment were able to bridge the consideration gap. Still, CVRs had only a very confined use.[64] Buyers otherwise struggled to find a stable acquisition currency in this market as collars and alternative consideration only partially filled the gap.

The struggle over pricing and consideration reflects wider change in the world of strategic transactions. The financial crisis is spurring a rethink of the structure of strategic deals, leaving a number of unanswered questions, answers that are likely to come only in future years:

- **The Structure of Strategic Deals.** Buyers, particularly in more significantly sized transactions, are likely to increasingly demand more optionality in acquisitions where financing is necessary. Targets will continue to resist, but their level of resistance will

depend upon the market and their bargaining power, power that
is substantially diminished in a distressed market. It is likely that
in this world, optionality with respect to financing will continue
to creep into strategic agreements. But still the bigger question is an open one. What will happen when market normalcy
returns? Will strategic buyers revert to more certain structures
to show their greater closing willingness than private equity
firms? Alternatively, will buyers fearful of the credit problems of
the prior years continue to insist on optionality along the Pfizer
model or variations of it?

- **The Scope of a Market Check.** The scope and parameters of
  a market check are still also very much in flux. Delaware has confirmed that postsigning market checks are acceptable. But go-shops
  have become the norm, at least in private equity deals and deals
  with management involvement. While this standard is likely to
  remain, the question remains how widespread outside this context
  go-shops become and whether their use serves as a simple cosmetic
  to cement a certain deal or otherwise facilitates higher bidding by
  buyers.

- **Distressed Deals.** The current extreme deal-making for distressed
  targets has reflected the changed bargaining leverage between targets and buyers. The extreme provisions have the potential to seep
  into normal strategic transactions, further enhancing optionality
  in the strategic context. In pushing the envelope on structures to
  guarantee deal certainty, buyers are also setting up the Delaware
  courts to again address the permissible scope of lockups in distressed acquisitions and beyond.

- **Limits on Buyers.** Notable in Delaware law is the lack of limitations on buyers making deals, good or bad. Although the force
  of shareholder pressure, good corporate governance, and conventional wisdom about takeovers is likely to continue to provide a
  heightened monitoring process, the deal machine and issues of ego
  will continue to counteract these influences. Delaware, though, is
  unlikely to act for practical if not theoretical reasons. How would
  one even begin to monitor these decisions? The end result is that
  buyers will continue to have unrestricted discretion for takeovers,
  limited only by these economic and social forces.

- **Shareholder Activism.** Shareholder activism and good corporate governance practices as encouraged by the proxy services have proven effective in eliminating company defenses and encouraging the adoption of majority voting. The continued rise of these forces, led by hedge fund activist investors, may continue to put pressures on deal-making, affecting the course of deals and the scope of lockups. In particular, the continued rise of these forces may substitute for more searching, needed review of lockups by Delaware courts.

The answers to these questions will affect the course of strategic transactions and deal-making generally. But the strategic transaction will probably remain not only dominant but also the focus of change in coming years. This is particularly true in the case of distressed strategic transactions. These transactions are likely to spur innovation in structures and terms, innovation that is likely to seep into more ordinary strategic deals. The return of strategic deal-making to prominence, though, is subject to a significant caveat. The activities of the biggest dealmaker in history, the federal government, will continue to overshadow private deal-making, even as strategic transactions continue to return to the forefront.

Chapter 10

AIG, Citigroup, Fannie Mae, Freddie Mac, Lehman, and Government by Deal

The government moved full force to save the financial system in September 2008. Deal-making did not disappear during this time. Instead, deal-making took on new forms, as distressed acquisitions became common and the biggest dealmaker of all-time entered the market—the federal government led by Treasury Secretary Henry "Hank" Paulson Jr. and his team of former investment bankers. This chapter is about this activity, the incredible story of the government's frenzied attempt to save the financial system. In four short months, the government would allow Lehman Brothers, IndyMac Federal Bank, FSB, and Washington Mutual to fail; arrange bailouts or shadow bailouts for Bank of America, Citigroup, and Morgan Stanley; nationalize AIG, the Federal National Mortgage Association, more commonly known as Fannie Mae, and the Federal Home Loan Mortgage Corporation, also known by the nickname Freddie Mac; force the sale of Wachovia; arrange for the passage of the $700 billion Emergency Economic Stabilization Act of 2008, otherwise known as the TARP bill; and implement a controversial program to save General Motors Corporation, Chrysler L.L.C., and each of their financing units. A list of the significant financial institution government investments during this time is set forth on Table 10.1.

The government's response, as awesome as it was, would be criticized as haphazard and seemingly hesitant. At first, the government ignored the credit crisis, structuring the bailout of Bear Stearns and then proceeding to later bailouts on a one-off basis. Then, in the wake of Lehman Brothers' and AIG's collapse, the government changed course and obtained congressional blessing for the $700 billion TARP program. This programmed, systematic response would be short-lived. The government would soon revert back to form, structuring bailouts on a unique, one-off basis, in the case of Bank of America and Citigroup.

The government's apparently inconsistent response left many puzzled as to what the government's plan was. Some even speculated that there was no plan. But there is an explanation for the government's conduct first revealed in the Bear Stearns transaction. Professor David Zaring and I have written a separate paper, *Regulation by Deal: The Government's Response to the Financial Crisis*, in which we theorize that the government, led by a team of ex-investment bankers, was doing deals. These deals showed all the good and the bad of deal-making and the deal machine. The government structured bailouts as dealmakers do, preferring private solutions to government ones. The government dealmakers and their lawyers used the enormous power of the government to structure some truly novel deals that stretched the law to the breaking point at times.

Other times, as in the sad case of Lehman Brothers, the government did what dealmakers do: walk away from the table to show authority or otherwise because the law or politics constrained their action. As dealmakers, the government concluded its deals and moved on; conclude it and forget it is the deal-making term. Precedent was important for structuring the next deal, but as dealmakers, the government was not looking for consistency but rather a completed transaction structured to its political and other interests. The government's deal-making showed the mistakes, the resort to loopholes, and the overreliance on precedent that all too frequently characterizes private deal-making.

More telling, though, government by deal exposed a fallacy of the government's program. Financial panics are a product of asymmetric information and fear. People, lacking the information to value financial institutions or their assets, move their own assets to other institutions in a mad rush for safety. The key to restoring equilibrium is to defeat this panic by inspiring confidence in suspect institutions and the financial system generally.[1] The government's haphazard strategy, though, worked against confidence building. Instead, the government left a wake of deals that made the government appear to be lurching, struggling to respond to the crisis instead of controlling it. The government saved the financial system, but its approach may have hindered a fuller recovery from the panic of fall 2008.

However, this criticism must be leavened by the cold reality that the government lacked the statutory power in many cases to take more holistic action. The federal government lacked the ability to seize non-bank financial institutions in a quasi-bankruptcy process. The government also lacked a broad "lender of last resort" power that could provide it wholesale ability to salvage these institutions. Instead, the government was forced to work among the laws that existed at the time, mainly statutes dating from the 1930s. This partially explains why the government adopted a "government by deal" approach. It lacked the ability to otherwise save the financial system and in the fall of 2008 it choose not to go to Congress for wider authority other than the TARP Bill. Deal-making thus became the government's only real choice.

In the government's actions are also lessons for deal-making and deals. It is an incredible illustration of the potential of deal-making. In pushing the limits of the law, the government has created precedent for extreme deal-making situations. This is precedent not only for future government action to stem systemic panic, but also for private deal-makers structuring deals.

Table 10.1 Significant Government Financial Institution Investments
Sept. 2008–March 2009

Announcement Date	Target	Value ($Bn)
16–Sep–08	American International Group	85
10–Nov–08	American International Group	40
8–Oct–08	American International Group	38
2–Mar–08	American International Group	30
28–Oct–08	Citigroup	25
28–Oct–08	Wells Fargo	25
28–Oct–08	JPMorgan Chase & Co.	25
16–Jan–09	Bank of America	20
24–Nov–08	Citigroup	20
28–Oct–08	Bank of America	15
14–Oct–08	Freddie Mac	13.7
28–Oct–08	Merrill Lynch	10
28–Oct–08	Goldman Sachs	10
28–Oct–08	Morgan Stanley	10
24–Oct–08	PNC Financial Services Group	7.7
14–Nov–08	US Bancorp	6.6
29–Dec–08	GMAC	5
14–Nov–08	Capital One Financial	3.6
14–Nov–08	SunTrust Banks	3.5
16–Jan–09	Chrysler Financial Services Americas	1.5

The AIG totals include investments made to pay off prior government investments and does not
include all government expenditures related to AIG. As of March 2, 2009, the Government
Accountability Office has reported that the total government commitments to AIG were 182.5
billion (excluding commercial paper commitments).
SOURCE: Thomson Reuters.

The Nationalization of Fannie Mae and Freddie Mac

It began the summer of 2008.

On July 11, 2008, the Office of Thrift Supervision ominously closed the IndyMac Bank and placed it into conservatorship with the Federal Deposit Insurance Corporation (FDIC). This was the second largest bank failure in the history of the United States. Particularly troubling for the government was that even after the bank was seized, people lined up in the thousands to withdraw their money, despite the existence of federal insurance for their deposits.[2]

After Indy Mac, attention turned to Fannie Mae and Freddie Mac, the two government-sponsored enterprises (GSEs) responsible for the bulk of securitized mortgage lending in the United States. Going into August 2008, these two GSEs were battered by the housing downturn. The government urged the two institutions to recapitalize, but their stockholders resisted the dilution, and investors, wary perhaps of an equity-destroying Bear Stearns–like bailout, stayed away.[3]

In late August, the ratings agencies downgraded the preferred stock of Fannie Mae and Freddie Mac because of their continuing inability to raise capital.[4] Capital was still not forthcoming. Instead, the downward market pressure on Fannie Mae and Freddie Mac stock produced by the rating agency downgrades ironically made raising capital more difficult, as the market lost confidence in the two entities. Meanwhile, investors in the debt securities of both institutions were beginning to back away from them and the spread on their debt over U.S. treasuries began to widen.

Fannie Mae and Freddie Mac had lost the market's support, and the weekend of September 5, 2008, they also lost the government's confidence. Government auditors discovered that the accounting records of Fannie Mae and Freddie Mac significantly overstated their capital. According to these accounting reevaluations, the GSEs, thinly capitalized in the best of times, were technically insolvent. The government then concluded that whatever efforts the GSEs were making to recapitalize were failing. In a meeting that weekend with Secretary Paulson, Fannie Mae CEO Daniel H. Mudd and Freddie Mac CEO Richard Syron pleaded not to be nationalized. Paulson rejected the petition, and the government seized the enterprises, placing them into conservatorship.[5] The CEOs of the GSEs were each fired and replaced. In addition, the Federal Housing Finance Agency (FHFA), the GSEs' regulator, would later cut the exit packages of Mudd by $8 million and Syron by $15.5 million.[6] This last act would be the sole example thus far of the government acting to claw back executive pay in connection with a bailout.

To increase the GSE's capital, the Treasury also entered into senior preferred share purchase agreements with Fannie Mae and Freddie Mac for each of them to issue up to $100 billion of senior preferred stock to the Treasury Department.[7] The GSEs initially issued only $1 billion of preferred stock but were permitted to each draw greater amounts, up to this $100 billion limit, as needed. The issued preferred shares were ranked senior to Fannie Mae's and Freddie Mac's existing preferred shares and paid the Treasury a 10 percent yield if paid in cash and 12 percent if paid in kind. This yield was below the approximate 15 percent yield on the GSEs' other outstanding preferred. The terms of the preferred prevented each GSE from paying any dividend on the GSE's equity securities while any part of the government's preferred interest remained outstanding.[8]

The Treasury also received a warrant to purchase 79.9 percent of the outstanding common stock of each of Fannie Mae and Freddie Mac. The warrant was exercisable for a 20-year period and had a nominal exercise price.[9] Through this mechanism, the government effected a transaction to significantly, but not completely, dilute the holders of these securities and significantly reduce their value. But the government did not place its ownership interest higher into the capital structures of each GSE in order to penalize or otherwise wipe out the secured or subordinated debt of these entities.

This was probably done for both political and economic reasons. The secured debt was issued by Fannie Mae and Freddie Mac to finance mortgage lending and had historically been viewed as having an implicit (now effectively explicit) government guarantee. The amount outstanding was more than $5.14 trillion in mortgage-backed securities and guarantees, and the Treasury could not eliminate it or otherwise impair this debt without risking significant, if not catastrophic, disruption to the mortgage market.[10]

The subordinated debt was generally thought not to have the same government guarantee. This debt was utilized by Fannie Mae and Freddie Mac to finance their riskier, nonconforming loans and for trading capital. However, the subordinated debt, like much of the secured debt, was held by foreign financial institutions and sovereigns. It was privately viewed that if this debt was impaired, it would drive away foreign lenders from U.S. debt at a time when the U.S. required this money to service the federal deficit.[11] Thus, the government limited its actions to impairing the value of the GSEs' preferred and common stock.

The government also did not completely wipe out the preferred and common shareholders of the GSEs. Rather, the government limited its interest to the 79.9 percent figure. The exact reasons for this limitation have yet to be disclosed, but it does not appear that this issuance was structured to maintain value for the security holders. Rather, it was probably done to comply with tax laws and accounting rules and maintain an argument that the GSEs were not nationalized but rather were still corporate entities distinct from the federal government and that their debt was not on the government's balance sheet.[12]

Whatever the reason, the government felt that it could not completely eliminate these security holders' interests. The government's desire, as in Bear Stearns, to seemingly act within the law had allowed the Fannie Mae and Freddie Mac preferred and common shareholders to retain a meaningful interest in the companies. Moreover, to the extent the government was fighting moral hazard, it would have presumably wanted to also impair Fannie Mae's $11.1 billion and Freddie Mac's $4.5 billion outstanding subordinated debt, which had no implicit government guarantee.[13] This did not happen. Instead, the government was acting as a dealmaker structuring a bailout using the law, but also acting within and to the limits of its political interests. This led the Treasury and the Federal Reserve to impair the preferred and common shareholders and led the FHFA to limit the severance packages of these CEOs, but it did not go so far as allowing the government to act purely in pursuit of its stated purposes. Even assuming that it had any bearing in a financial action of this enormity, moral hazard seemed a shaky principle to rely on to justify the government's structuring actions.

In connection with the conservatorship of Fannie Mae and Freddie Mac, the federal government had now become the owner or guarantor of approximately 42 percent of American mortgages, and the extent of the guarantees was only growing in size and scope.[14] Secretary Paulson announced that these entities' retained mortgage and mortgage-backed securities portfolio would be shrunk to a smaller size of approximately $850 billion in assets by December 31, 2009, and would continue to decline by 10 percent per year until each reached an asset portfolio size of $250 billion.[15] However, this would occur only in later years. Instead, Secretary Paulson announced that the government intended to grow these institutions over the next 15 months to provide assistance to the housing market.[16]

The Week the Investment Bank Died

In the wake of the partial nationalization of Fannie Mae and Freddie Mac, the already troubled credit markets began to completely freeze up. The government still did not directly act. Indeed, when the Federal Reserve met on September 16, it did not lower interest rates again; instead, it focused on the problem of commodity inflation, particularly high oil prices, to justify keeping rates at the then current level.[17] Still, it was apparent that the credit market remained disrupted. This was a very different animal than the equity declines that had typified the financial crises of the past century. Unlike equity crises, the credit crisis was something that was harder for the public and regulators to see. But it was all about to burst into the open.

The Bankruptcy of Lehman Brothers and the Sale of Merrill Lynch

During the weekend of September 13, 2008, Lehman Brothers suffered from the same self-fulfilling feedback loops as Bear Stearns. On September 10, 2008, Lehman Brothers had preannounced quarterly earnings, with a loss of $3.9 billion for that quarter and gross asset write-downs of $7.8 billion. Lehman Brothers also announced on that day plans to hive off its troubled commercial real estate-related and other assets into a separate "bad" bank.[18] The plan had been criticized as insufficient by many analysts.[19] Rumors began to again circulate of Lehman Brothers' inability to survive. These rumors quickly created their own feedback loop, as customers became concerned for Lehman Brothers' survival. They began to pull assets from, demand collateral on counterparty trades from, and refuse to provide short-term repo lending to Lehman Brothers. By the weekend of September 13, Lehman Brothers' liquidity position had significantly deteriorated to approximately $1 billion, and the company was facing a loan call by JPMorgan.[20] Lehman Brothers was the next financial institution faced with insolvency if it could not find a buyer or obtain government backing. Initially, Bank of America and Barclays were interested buyers.

But Merrill Lynch had its own problems emerging at this time. After Lehman Brothers, Merrill Lynch was perceived as the next institution at risk of the five investment banks. Merrill Lynch's CEO John Thain would later assert that if Lehman Brothers did not survive, his bank would be viewed as the weakest of the investment banks and subject to the same viral self-fulfilling feedback loops.[21] The perception of the viability of the investment bank model was now in question. In light of the market turmoil and higher leverage ratios of these investment banks than more regulated bank holding companies, market participants were fearful of doing business with, investing in, or lending to these institutions. Market investors aware of this wariness began selling their stock in the investment banks, once again making it harder for them to raise capital and assuage investors. This led to further concern about the survival of these institutions. The feedback loop was whirring.

Fearful of Merrill Lynch's survival and being stuck in such a loop, Thain, after heavy prodding by his own board, contacted Bank of America about an acquisition. Bank of America's Ken Lewis quickly turned his attention from Lehman to Merrill, a much bigger catch. That weekend Merrill Lynch agreed to be acquired in an approximately $50 billion transaction by Bank of America.[22] The acquisition agreement for Merrill Lynch, struck in this perilous time, was strangely normal and fairly typical of a deal struck in more normal times. Of course, the one thing that was probably different was the disclosure schedules. These are Merrill's own disclosures, which qualify the representations and warranties in the agreement. The events included on the disclosure schedules are deemed not to be a material adverse change. The disclosure schedules are also not made public. Merrill had probably thrown everything and the kitchen sink onto these schedules to assure that there was full disclosure and a complete deal with little room for Bank of America to escape its obligation to acquire Merrill.

This left Lehman CEO Dick Fuld without a choice. Ken Lewis was refusing to return his calls, and Barclays was now the only willing buyer of Lehman Brothers. Barclays refused to acquire Lehman Brothers without government assistance. However, Secretary Paulson did not want the government to serve as a backstop for all financial institutions. Likely due to political reality, personal preference, and legal limitations on the government's power, Paulson insisted that the private market find a solution to Lehman Brothers. Barclays was definitively thrown out of the race when its own British regulator, the Financial Services Authority, refused to approve an acquisition. Meanwhile, the major financial institutions refused (or were unable themselves) to assist Lehman Brothers directly.

Early Monday morning, September 15, 2008, Lehman Brothers' holding company filed for Chapter 11 bankruptcy.[23] Notably, most of Lehman Brothers' subsidiaries did not file for bankruptcy, and on that Tuesday, Lehman Brothers agreed to sell its U.S. investment banking operations minus certain troubled commercial real estate–related assets to Barclays for a fire sale price of $250 million.[24] Still-aggrieved Bear Stearns shareholders no doubt felt a bit better about the low price they received for their sale. At least they had gotten something.

Many observers would accuse the government of making a mistake in failing to bail out Lehman Brothers, leaving its bondholders without recourse, the credit insurance that it had underwritten meaningless, and its significant issued commercial paper worthless. It was estimated that the "unplanned and chaotic" bankruptcy of Lehman destroyed up to $75 billion in value within Lehman alone.[25] Lehman's failure also caused the oldest and largest money market fund Reserve Primary Fund to break the buck, setting off a stampede as investors raced to withdraw funds from money market funds. This triggered a chain reaction that almost shut down the entire capital markets. In short, the collapse of Lehman led to a near implosion of the commercial paper market, a sharp decline in the stock market, and a financial panic. Regardless of whether Lehman Brothers should have been allowed to fail, it is still unclear that the government realized the extent of Lehman Brothers' obligations. On the other hand, the drastic market reactions that flowed from Lehman Brothers' failure ultimately drove the government to attempt to adopt a more comprehensive approach to the crisis.

But that approach had to wait. Secretary Paulson would later publicly state that the reason the government did not bail out Lehman Brothers was that it "did not have the power," because Lehman Brothers lacked enough assets to provide sufficient collateral for a Federal Reserve loan.[26] The government was clearly hamstrung here by the failure to have the power to simply seize Lehman. However, given the broad reach the Federal Reserve had previously interpreted its statutory authority to make loans in the context of the Bear Stearns matter, and would later interpret it to be, this explanation is not creditable. The government may not have been able to seize Lehman but the Federal Reserve could loan it money. Instead, it appears that Paulson was restricted from acting politically and wanted to make a statement about his willingness to bail out all financial institutions.

In the wake of the Lehman Brothers bankruptcy and Merrill's agreement to be acquired by Bank of America, the investment banking model was shaky at best. On September 21, the final two remaining independent investment banks regulated by the SEC, Goldman Sachs and Morgan Stanley, left the agency's voluntary regulatory program to become bank holding companies, overseen by the Federal Reserve.[27] These two investment banks were pursuing a safe-harbor under the federal regulatory umbrella to boost investor confidence. They were also following a path toward stability by acquiring bank deposits, an ironic event as bank deposits were also short-term financing. Nonetheless, the market perception was that this model was more reliable than one that depended on short-term prime brokerage deposits and same-day repo lending for liquidity. These were financially sophisticated entities who could more speedily shift funds than ordinary Americans.

The Nationalization of AIG

As Lehman Brothers died and Merrill disappeared, another famous financial name independently teetered on the edge of insolvency. AIG, a global financial conglomerate with the largest insurance business in the United States, had suffered approximately $21.7 billion in losses out of its London subsidiary, which had been writing insurance and credit default swaps on mortgage-related assets.[28] AIG was principally an insurance company, not an investment bank. Nonetheless, AIG became caught in a different species of feedback loop, one driven by ratings cuts and mark-to-market accounting rules.[29]

The decline in AIG stock due to its losses and its inability to effectively raise capital due to these stock declines had led the rating agencies to cut AIG from its triple AAA rating to A-.[30] Under the $441 billion in derivative contracts AIG was a party to, AIG was consequently required to put up approximately $14.5 billion in collateral.[31] AIG had never anticipated that it would be downgraded, but the collateral requirement in the midst of a credit crisis rendered the company insolvent and showed the fallacy of AIG's assumption. Moreover, in connection with this collateral requirement, AIG's accountants reviewed its asset values, and AIG was forced to record mark-to-market losses of approximately $60 billion.[32] On Monday, September 15, 2008, New York State Insurance Commissioner Eric Dinallo permitted AIG to borrow $20 billion from AIG's own regulated insurance reserve funds in order to try to save the company.[33] It was not enough.

The federal government initially refused to provide financial assistance to AIG. But the Lehman Brothers treatment was short-lived. AIG held more than a trillion in assets and had $971 billion in liabilities, and if it defaulted on its obligations, there was every prospect of a sequence of many cross-defaults beyond the CDS market, which in turn would have forced not just losses but a significant number of corporations to refinance their debt in a credit market that was incapable of doing so.[34] AIG was not just too big to fail, it was too interconnected to fail. The Federal Reserve thus decided on September 16 to provide financial assistance to AIG. The Federal Reserve once again justified this extension of credit under a very broad reading of its authority under the Federal Reserve Act.

Once again, though, the government would be constricted by the limits of the law and the lack of a seizure mechanism in structuring its rescue. And once again, the government stuck to its developing game plan for deal-making, driving a hard bargain in the name of moral hazard. On that day, AIG disclosed: "In connection with the revolving credit facility, AIG issued a warrant to the Board of Governors of the Federal Reserve . . . that permits the Federal Reserve, subject to shareholder approval, to obtain up to 79.9 percent of the outstanding common stock of AIG (after taking into account the exercise of the warrant)."[35]

On September 26, AIG announced that it had entered into definitive agreements with regard to its government assistance.[36] The Federal Reserve extended an $85 billion loan on hard terms. The interest rate was approximately 12 percent on funds drawn and 8.5 percent on undrawn funds, plus a $1.7 billion commitment fee paid to the Federal Reserve. The credit agreement also required that all of AIG's free cash flow be paid over to service the Federal Reserve loan, as well as the proceeds of any of AIG's asset disposals or capital raisings. The loan terms were better than what AIG could get in the market but were still designed to force AIG to downsize or perhaps disappear in order to service the debt.

In exchange for providing this loan, the government received AIG preferred shares equivalent to a 79.9 percent voting and dividend interest in AIG. The GSE precedent in deals had become the norm. Though the loan was issued by the Federal Reserve, the preferred shares were actually issued to a trust for the benefit of the Treasury Department.[37] It is unclear why the interest was for the benefit of the Treasury and not the Federal Reserve; presumably, this was a matter of control and who would realize the profits. In addition, the government has yet to fully explain why the interest was placed into trust, rather than issued directly to the government. The presumption, however, is that the government did this in order to keep a distance between the government and AIG and provide some colorable pretext to prevent political meddling in the workings of the company. There was also the question of whether the Government Corporation Control Act, which requires Congressional authorization in certain circumstances for the government to own private companies, would be violated if the government took full control. When the trust instrument was released three months later, it provided the trustees almost complete control of AIG, an extraordinary delegation of the government's power.[38] Clearly, matters of open government and the ordinary controls an investor would desire were not the government's goals or perhaps within their grasp given the legal limitations.

The ordinary details of corporate law, though, were not the sort of hurdles that the government found very worrying. AIG did not have sufficient authorized common stock in its certificate of incorporation to issue warrants to the government, but it did have a blank check preferred provision in its certificate. This type of provision permits a corporation to issue preferred shares on such terms and with such rights as the board deems appropriate. This permitted AIG to issue out 100,000 shares of convertible participating serial preferred stock with rights to 79.9 percent of the votes and dividends paid on AIG common and preferred stock.[39] Once again, the lawyers had innovated to bring about a novel solution to meet the government's deal-making needs.

The New York Stock Exchange requirement that a company obtain a shareholder vote prior to the issuance of an amount equal to 20 percent or more of its common stock or preferred shares convertible into common stock would normally have required AIG, a NYSE-listed company, to obtain shareholder approval for this issuance. However, AIG, like Bear Stearns, relied upon the exception available if the delay in vote would "seriously jeopardize the financial viability" of a company.[40] The NYSE had permitted reliance upon this exemption before in the Bear Stearns transaction, and it did so here.[41] It appears that this rule was simply ignored in the case of Fannie Mae and Freddie Mac, with the NYSE taking no action.

AIG still was required under Delaware law to hold a shareholder vote to amend its certificate of incorporation to authorize the issuance of the common stock that the preferred is convertible into. AIG initially appeared to take the position that the government's preferred shares would be able to vote on the transaction, making approval a foregone conclusion. However, when a shareholder suit was brought, challenging this practice as violating Delaware law, which allowed for a separate class vote of the common shareholders, AIG backtracked and asserted that the common stockholders would separately vote to approve this conversion.[42]

In the months following, the AIG rescue would take up more government resources, showing the perils of an ad hoc bailout. Meanwhile, AIG's ousted ex-CEO, Hank Greenberg, was reportedly lobbying the government to ease the terms of its bailout.[43] On October 8, the Federal Reserve Bank of New York agreed to accept up to $37.8 billion in investment-grade, fixed-income securities from AIG in exchange for cash collateral. The exchange was meant to provide additional liquidity to AIG and allow AIG to exchange that cash for the securities it had lent to third parties. Then, on October 27, 2008, the Federal Bank of New York allowed four of AIG's subsidiaries to participate in the Federal Reserve's commercial paper program, up to an amount of $20.9 billion, and to use the proceeds of the loans to prepay money borrowed by AIG under AIG's $85 billion credit facility with the Federal Reserve Bank of New York.[44]

On November 10, the government announced another restructuring of its financial support to AIG, and the New York Federal Reserve announced two new lending facilities for AIG.[45] This brought the government's potential support for AIG up to $173.1 billion. The government's initial thought—that the bailout of AIG was merely a bridge to fund liquidity—was clearly mistaken. The new rejiggered bailout was a dose of reality. The government had initially failed to comprehensively deal with the AIG situation. Instead, the government's attempt to downsize AIG had harmed the company and only hastened its deterioration. The government's new approach was now designed to stabilize AIG rather than dismember it. But AIG would again return to the well for a third time on March 1, 2009, for another $30 billion. The government again reworked the terms of its bailout. AIG had become a black hole for taxpayer money and the government's aggregate specific commitments to AIG rose to $182.5 billion.

This would explode in public fury the week of March 17, 2009, over the payment of approximately $165 million in bonuses to executives at AIG's financial products business. This was the selfsame business that had entered into the now infamous CDS contracts that had destroyed AIG. The outrage over these inappropriately structured retention payments—they were paid regardless of performance—was justified. But the outrage was more. It reflected public anger at repeated, unexplained government action that appeared to benefit corporate executives at the expense of the wider public. In the wake of the extreme display of public discontent, President Obama ordered that the government attempt to obtain repayment of the bonuses.

Moreover, the claims by now Treasury Secretary Geithner that he learned of the bonus payments only a week before appeared incredible. These bonuses were agreed to back in early 2008, and the AIG bailout had been arranged by the New York branch of the Federal Reserve at a time when it was headed by Secretary Geithner. At best, the failure of the government to act beforehand to forestall the payments was incompetence. At worst, the government was willfully blind, or otherwise wanted the bonuses to be paid to ensure that the AIG business group continued to unwind AIG's trillions in derivative contracts.

The outcry missed the real issue with AIG, though. In the wake of the public scrutiny, AIG also disclosed that almost $60 billion in the government's bailout funds had gone to European banks to satisfy collateral calls. The $165 million was meaningless, compared with this $60 billion payment. And here, the question was why the United States was not asking the European governments to share their burden for salvaging European financial institutions.

The government had also allowed these European and American banks to be made whole at 100 cents on the dollar without value to the American taxpayer except for the decaying AIG businesses. In addition, it was also disclosed that the government had repurchased at notional value $62 billion worth of securities to unwind AIG's book of CDSs. This payment was made in connection with the November lending facilities and was made despite the fact that these were collateralized at about 57 percent of that value. This represented a pure wealth transfer from U.S. taxpayers to the banks. Goldman Sachs alone received an estimated $5.5 billion in excess value.

The payments may have been justified in order to ensure market confidence in AIG and the full repayment of the government funds. In other words, the government now needed to act to ensure that AIG stayed in a suitable operating condition to ensure that AIG repaid the tens of billions it still owed to the government. Nonetheless, the failure of the government to adequately justify these payments was yet another source of public discontent, at least for those few who took the time to try to understand the government's complicated Frankenstein-like bailout of AIG.[46] Luckily for the government, few did and the AIG uproar faded with the next news cycle.

The Forced Sale of Wachovia

The collapse and workout of Wachovia unfolded in a less orderly manner. As of the weekend of September 27, Wachovia appeared to be insolvent. In a hectic weekend, the FDIC, headed by Sheila Bair, selected Citigroup as the buyer for Wachovia's depositary assets. In choosing Citigroup, the FDIC refused to support a competing offer by Wells Fargo to acquire the entirety of Wachovia and a proposal by Wachovia itself to maintain it as a stand-alone entity. On Monday, September 29,

Citigroup and Wachovia executed an exclusivity agreement, pursuant to which the parties agreed to negotiate definitive documentation for Citigroup to purchase the depositary assets of Wachovia for $2.2 billion. Wachovia would remain a functioning company operating a rump business consisting of Wachovia Securities, which, combined with A.G. Edwards, is the nation's third largest brokerage firm; Evergreen Investments, which is Wachovia's asset management business; Wachovia retirement services; and Wachovia's insurance brokerage businesses.[47]

Citigroup's plans were disrupted, however, when Wells Fargo decided to again bid for Wachovia that Thursday. Wells Fargo likely did so because of the imminent passage of the TARP Bill, which would permit Wells Fargo to utilize $74 billion in Wachovia's carryforward losses, a tax advantage that now made this acquisition quite financially attractive. This time, the FDIC, over Treasury and Federal Reserve protests, apparently provided its approval to this transaction and, in fact, informed Wells Fargo that if a merger proposal was not signed by October 3, Wachovia's banking subsidiaries would be put into receivership. That Thursday night, Wells Fargo and Wachovia negotiated and signed an acquisition agreement for Wells Fargo to acquire the entirety of Wachovia for approximately $15.1 billion. Bair had acknowledged the legal reality that, under the agreements Citigroup and Wachovia had signed, Wells Fargo could still make a competing bid.[48]

Wells Fargo's lawyers were from Wachtell Lipton, the same attorneys who represented JPMorgan in the Bear Stearns acquisition, and they negotiated an agreement with features similar to the one in Bear Stearns. Wachovia agreed to a force-the-vote provision modeled on the one in the Bear Stearns agreement, which required the company to rehold its shareholder meeting to approve the merger repeatedly during a six-month period after a first no vote on the transaction.[49] Wells Fargo was also issued 10 shares of preferred stock equivalent to a 39.9 percent preferred share interest in Wachovia in exchange for 1,000 shares of Wells Fargo.[50] The power of a blank check preferred stock was clearly on display. Wells Fargo could use these shares to approve the transaction, and once again, as in Bear Stearns and AIG, Wachovia sidestepped the NYSE rules on a shareholder vote for this issuance by invoking the insolvency exception, asserting that Wachovia would have had to file bankruptcy without this transaction.[51]

Citigroup sued Wells Fargo and Wachovia in New York State Court that Saturday, and the parties litigated in state and federal court over the weekend as Citigroup attempted to salvage its deal in the courts. Citigroup had entered into an exclusivity agreement that provided that Citigroup and Wachovia would negotiate exclusively for a week toward a transaction on the basis of a nonbinding term sheet to complete definitive documentation. During that time, the exclusivity agreement required Wachovia to abstain from entering into negotiations concerning or agreeing to any acquisition proposal. An acquisition proposal was clearly what Wells Fargo made and agreed to, and they did so during this exclusivity time period.

Citigroup's case, though, was weak. First, there was the question of whether Wachovia had a fiduciary out on the term sheet. Normally, an exclusivity agreement would allow the Wachovia board to deviate if its fiduciary duties require it to do so. This agreement did not have such a provision, but normally courts will still read this into agreements to override any constraints the board agrees to. This is because the court will not sanction an action that violates fiduciary duties, instead declaring it void. Second, Wachovia could argue that exclusivity was meaningless at this point, because a deal would never be reached. Finally, damages were limited in any event because a shareholder vote would have been required. Citigroup's asset purchase was a sale of all or substantially all of the assets of Wachovia, which required a shareholder vote under state law. No rational shareholder would vote for Citigroup's less valuable bid. Here, Citigroup had neglected to even put a break fee in the exclusivity agreement in case of a shareholder no vote or other breach or failure to reach an agreement. This left Citigroup without a strong litigation position and was a lesson to lawyers everywhere on the perils of exclusivity agreements without meaningful penalties for their breach.[52]

On Tuesday, October 7, 2008, the FDIC privately intervened and forced the parties to halt their litigation and sign a tolling agreement in order to negotiate a resolution. The FDIC then attempted to mediate a deal, but when Citigroup and Wells Fargo couldn't agree on a resolution, Citigroup dropped its bid for these assets, and Wells Fargo proceeded to acquire Wachovia.[53] The government's preference in these matters for an ordered solution to a designated bidder had once again been in evidence.

Citigroup had in hindsight made a mistake in failing to lock up Wachovia, and Wells Fargo had forced the government to allow a market solution. Wells Fargo, given a measure of government endorsement, had once again showed that buyers in such circumstances were not afraid to push the envelope on the law. Here, Wells Fargo and its lawyers followed the path first trod by JPMorgan in its Bear Stearns acquisition. Again, a government-backed acquisition had substantially stretched, but not broken, the laws for the structuring of an acquisition, safe in the assumption that the courts would not want to intervene.[54]

The deal machine subsequently assigned winners and losers in this battle. The failure to acquire Wachovia left Citigroup's new CEO Vikram Pandit looking weak and Citigroup itself further debilitated. It was viewed as having been out-dealt by Wells Fargo and unable to afford a competing bid. Meanwhile, Wells Fargo CEO John Stumpf was viewed as a daring corporate executive. He had snatched a jewel of a corporate banking property from one of his rivals in the face of government opposition.

The Saving of Morgan Stanley

The last pre-TARP episode of the government as dealmaker occurred over the weekend of October 11. On Friday, October 10, 2008, it did not appear that Morgan Stanley would survive. The S&P 500 Index had declined 18 percent that past week, mirroring a decline with the rest of the general stock market. Morgan Stanley closed at the end of Friday at $9.68 a share, down 57 percent in the space of a week. The next Tuesday, October 14, Morgan Stanley was scheduled to close its $9 billion investment from Mitsubishi Bank for 21 percent of Morgan Stanley at a price of at least $25.25 per share.[55] However, the stock price of Morgan Stanley reflected market perception that this injection would not occur. Morgan Stanley was now trading with a market capitalization less than Mitsubishi's entire investment. Mitsubishi had signed a definitive purchase agreement to make its investment but over that weekend invoked the MAC clause in the agreement in an attempt to escape its obligations.[56]

The investor agreement between Morgan Stanley and Mitsubishi contained a buyer-friendly form of MAC clause.[57] It did not contain the large number of exclusions typical of these clauses, most notably an exclusion from the MAC definition for changes to stock prices and for general and industry economic conditions. Moreover, the investor agreement was governed by Delaware law and, as discussed in Chapter 3, Delaware strictly construes MAC clauses and requires that any adverse change must be long-term and durational to be an MAC. It was unlikely that a court would find a simple stock decline of this nature to be a long-term and durational event without more occurring. Unfortunately, for Morgan, there was more. It would later emerge that there was a massive withdrawal of prime brokerage deposits occurring at Morgan Stanley that was impairing Morgan Stanley's liquidity. It was caught in the same death spiral as Bear Stearns and Lehman Brothers.

Morgan Stanley's dilemma was not new. Back in the crash of 1987, Jardine Strategic Holdings had agreed to purchase 20 percent of Bear Stearns for $400 million. Jardine then claimed a MAC had occurred, based on trading losses by Bear Stearns of $100 million and a "precipitous drop" in Bear Stearns' stock price from $19 to $13, or more than 32 percent. The New York Supreme Court ruling under New York law in *Bear Stearns Co. v. Jardine Strategic Holdings*[58] held that a trial was necessary to determine the meaning of the MAC clause but also indicated that Jardine should have understood that Bear Stearns was in a volatile, cyclical business and the loss and stock price decline could not be considered a MAC.

Mitsubishi would face the same uphill battle unless it could find a substantial and actual long-term deterioration in Morgan Stanley's business due to the flight of capital. The bankruptcy of Morgan Stanley due to this capital flight would clearly be something material and adverse, but then the question would be whether, given the financial crisis, this was a known possibility at the time of Mitsubishi's investment. Against this uncertainty, the government acted to ensure a deal. Over that weekend, the Treasury Department reportedly privately assured Morgan Stanley that it would support the investment bank if the Mitsubishi investment failed. This addressed the liquidity issue.

The government also provided assurances to Mitsubishi that if it was subsequently forced to provide capital to Morgan Stanley, the government would not significantly dilute Mitsubishi's investment. The government's prior requirement that shareholders be significantly harmed in any bailout was beginning to inhibit private solutions as parties refused to invest, fearful of later government action. It was at this point that the government abandoned this position for future transactions. With these government assurances, Morgan Stanley and Mitsubishi agreed to a minor reworking of their transaction. On Monday, the investment was completed, and Mitsubishi invested the full $9 billion in Morgan Stanley.[59] The investment was deemed a big success for Morgan CEO John Mack, still thought to be one of the best dealmakers on the Street.

TARP, Citigroup, Bank of America, and Beyond?

By the time of the Morgan Stanley transaction, the government had already decided to abandon its deal-making model for a more holistic response in the form of the TARP. Secretary Paulson at first resisted a larger, more programmed response, but he reportedly changed his mind when Federal Reserve Chairman Ben Bernanke informed him that the Fed could no longer respond in an ad hoc manner.[60] The weekend of September 20, Paulson agreed and submitted a three-page bill for a $700 billion TARP to Congress. The outcry was immediate. Many claimed this was a power grab and cited the administration's poor history in Iraq, where Congress had also delegated the administration virtually unlimited power. Yet, the final bill actually gave Paulson more power than he had asked for.

In the initial version of the TARP bill, Paulson requested that the Treasury Department have authority to purchase up to $700 billion of "mortgage-related" assets. In the final bill, Congress gave Paulson far more authority. The bill did so in the following manner. First it defined "troubled assets" to include "any . . . financial instrument that the Secretary, after consultation with the Chairman of the Board of Governors of the Federal Reserve System, determines the purchase of which is necessary to promote financial market stability. . . ."[61]

Under this definition, troubled assets were essentially any financial securities the Treasury Secretary deemed appropriate. This was a much broader provision than the one restricted to mortgage-related assets that Paulson had asked for. Moreover, another provision defined the institutions who could participate in this program. These institutions were defined as "any institution ... established and regulated under the laws of the United States or any State."[62] Under this definition, Paulson could conceivably buy securities from any institution in the United States. This could be the dry cleaner down the block, credit card receivables, student loans, and the automakers. The last on this list would soon realize this benefit.

Paulson quickly put the money to use. On October 15, he ordered the CEOs of the nine largest financial institutions to Washington. In a several-hour meeting, he cajoled them to accept a $125 billion TARP injection. Reportedly, some of the CEOs objected to this forced government infusion. The injection was on generous terms, so their protestation could not have been that hard. The preferred shares issued would pay only a 5 percent dividend, going up to 9 percent after five years. The government would get minimal control rights, exercisable only in an event of default, and dividends would not be prohibited. At least initially, executive compensation restrictions were also minimal, limited mainly to restraints on golden parachutes. Finally, the government took a warrant equivalent to 15 percent of the value of the injection but priced the warrants on a 20-day look back, putting the warrant significantly out of the money from day one, due to the declining stock market.[63]

Secretary Paulson quickly burned through the first $350 billion of the TARP program. Another $40 billion went to AIG and the remainder to a variety of smaller banks.[64] The automakers and their financial affiliates also received $25 billion in late December and early January 2009 after a series of dramatic Congressional hearings and Congress' ultimate refusal to pass a separate bill bailing these institutions out. President Bush thereafter proclaimed his willingness to save the automakers, stating that to allow them to go under would not be "responsible." He directed that TARP funds be provided to them, funds that General Motors and Chrysler eagerly accepted.[65]

The last two bailouts in the waning days of the Bush presidency were of Bank of America and Citigroup, two of the three largest financial institutions in the United States. In these two bailouts, the Treasury showed that it was willing to change direction yet again as circumstances dictated. But it also showed that the Treasury Department could not kick the deal-making habit.

Citigroup was yet another bank to get caught in a death spiral. This time, the stock price went in the space of two weeks from about $14 a share to as low as $3 a share. But Citigroup was much more complicated. An inefficient behemoth in the best of times and referred to by some government officials as the Death Star because of its soulless capability to destroy the U.S. capital markets, it now appeared to be coming apart. The weekend of November 23, the Treasury stepped in again to stabilize the beast.

The Treasury, Federal Reserve, and FDIC collectively agreed to fund the off-balance sheet purchase of about $306 billion of Citigroup's troubled assets. This was essentially the bad bank model that Lehman Brothers had proposed; it also appeared to be modeled on the initial Wachovia–Citigroup deal. Treasury agreed to take the first $5 billion of losses, the FDIC the next $10 billion, and the Federal Reserve the remainder. All of this was subject to a loss–sharing agreement by which 10 percent of the losses were paid by Citigroup. In addition, Citigroup agreed to guarantee the first $29 billion in losses. Learning from AIG, the Federal Reserve agreed only to charge a relatively low interest rate on this loan of approximately 5.3 percent.[66]

In exchange for this maneuver, the government received $27 billion in preferred shares in Citigroup through an injection made by the TARP program: $20 billion for its direct investment and $7 billion as compensation for the loan guarantees. Citigroup would pay an 8 percent dividend rate on these shares. Unlike other beneficiaries under the TARP, this preferred barred paying dividends above 1 cent per share for three years and had a higher interest rate than the 5 percent paid on other TARP injections. Citigroup was being slotted in the middle bailout category, between the stable financial banks and the systemically failing ones like AIG. Finally, the Treasury received $2.7 billion in warrants. Again, though, these warrants were priced on a 20-day moving average, so the strike price was $10.61 per share, which was laughably out of the money compared with Citigroup's trading price of $3.78 the Friday before the deal announcement.

The Treasury took only 10 percent of the total preferred being issued by Citigroup in warrants, as opposed to the 15 percent it had taken in other transactions. The reason was undisclosed, but probably it was to keep the government's ownership interest below a certain threshold.[67] On January 2, 2009, the government created a new program, the Targeted Investment Program, to encompass bailouts like Citigroup that were neither investments in systemically failing or stable financial institutions.[68] The government was ex post facto justifying its conduct and abandoning its hollow moral hazard principles.

The Citigroup model and this new program would be used to bail out Bank of America in early January 2009. At the time, Bank of America claimed that its need for funds was related to a massive $15.3 billion loss at the newly acquired Merrill Lynch, a fact that Bank of America apparently learned of some time between late November and mid-December. In mid-December though, and after the December 5 vote of Bank of America shareholders on the transaction, Bank of America began to question the wisdom of the acquisition and began to claim that an MAC to Merrill had occurred. At that time Bank of America had had discussions with the government about providing further support to ensure that it did indeed acquire Merrill Lynch.

In a series of meetings and calls, the government had questioned the ability of Bank of America to walk from its transaction, given the strength of the agreement Merrill had negotiated. In addition, the government had implied a threat to Bank of America CEO Ken Lewis's job if he attempted to walk from the transaction. In the wake of these apparent government threats and their offer of a bailout, Lewis agreed to complete the Merrill acquisition. This may have been Lewis' strategy all along—knowing the weakness of his claim he claimed a MAC to win government support. Here, Lewis was a victim of the overly generous deal terms he agreed to in September to acquire Merrill. Unfortunately for Bank of America's investors, the company never disclosed these facts until January, on the cusp of its own bailout. The total TARP investment in Bank of America would amount to $45 billion, plus the offer of the FDIC and Treasury to enter into a loss-sharing arrangement with respect to $118 billion of Bank of America's troubled assets.[69]

At this point, "bailout creep" had become the norm as the government incrementally struggled to save the financial system along the way, arranging for bailouts of the automakers and small community banks. Meanwhile, in the waning days of the Bush administration, criticism was heaped on the Treasury for negotiating too generous terms and for its opaqueness. It was at this time that the Obama administration took office, promising a new, more consistent program, with heightened transparency and accountability. In February 2009, the Obama administration would announce a turn from deal-making again. Newly appointed Treasury Secretary Geithner would instead propose a program to purchase troubled assets directly, as Secretary Paulson had initially proposed.[70] The government would also proceed to renegotiate its prior bailouts, impose harsher executive compensation requirements, and restructure its assistance to both Citigroup and AIG as well as the automakers. In Citigroup's case, the government converted part of its preferred shares into up to 36 percent of Citigroup's common stock.

Assessing Government by Deal

In terms of halting systemic panic, the government's regulation by deal had its short-term benefits, ameliorating the pain and avoiding total collapse of the financial markets, but it is still unclear whether it cured the disease. Government by deal at times appeared to reduce confidence in the markets. The government's reactive response also failed to address the root cause of the distress, the housing crisis. Instead, the government, led by Secretary Paulson, lurched from deal to deal. First, the government acted out of a need to save institutions but punish shareholders in the name of fighting moral hazard. Then it acted more benignly to shareholders as the bailout progressed and the government realized that its stance on moral hazard was increasingly harmful. The government and Paulson were learning and limited by the law in acting in full force, but their ad hoc response appeared to fail to fully restore confidence to the system. Moreover, the rigid structures the government created led it to repeatedly restructure its bailouts.

Despite its broader failure, government by deal showed that dealmakers, given freedom by the government, could creatively order deals in the shadow of the law. In doing so, dealmakers would look to preexisting precedent but would be willing to create new deal structures. This spoke to the incredible power of the U.S. government as dealmaker, able to structure deals of this nature safe in knowing that no state regulator or court, such as Delaware, would challenge them.

But it also spoke to the power of deal-making and its ability to implement sophisticated solutions in high-pressure, time-sensitive environments.

The government's deal-making also showed the bad side of deal-making. At times, the government implemented their specific goal—a deal—to the detriment of wider purposes. And Paulson's deal-making spree showed the addictiveness of deal-making. In the heat of crisis, deal-making becomes a definable solution and the deal-junkie in every dealmaker rises to the occasion. But here a deal-making solution could not offer a permanent solution. The government, to some extent, appeared to recognize this at times, but other than the TARP program never sought wider legal authorization to seize and lend to financial institutions.

Government by deal also had a more pervasive effect on deal-making generally. The government's deals were modeled on normal strategic deals. But the government stretched this model, pushing for deal certainty and a structure meeting its own political needs. Learning from the government, private actors began to advantage themselves of these structures. The Wachovia deal is a good example. There, Wells Fargo took advantage of government backing to arrange a 39.5 percent share issuance by Wachovia to Wells Fargo to vote through Wells Fargo's acquisition. Coercive deal protections of this type would probably have been struck down by courts in normal times. Normal times will hopefully return, but some of these extreme terms are likely to creep into deal-making on a more permanent basis. The result is likely to stretch the scope of permissible deal protection devices under Delaware and other state laws.

Chapter 11

Restructuring Takeovers

The last 10 chapters have been a whirlwind tour of recent deals and deal-making. The final two chapters look to the future to ascertain how these recent events will foster change. This chapter explores the regulatory structure governing takeovers, the most prominent aspect of deal-making, and possible areas for reform and improvement. Chapter 12 synthesizes the lessons of the preceding years and traces the future direction of deals in this crisis and global age.

Takeovers are defined by many forces, but a principal one is their applicable regulations and regulators. The current regulation of takeovers is a product of our federal system. The federal government has promulgated both procedural and substantive regulation governing the conduct of public takeovers. This skein consists primarily of the 1968 Williams Act rules governing tender offers and the 1934 Exchange Act's proxy rules governing the solicitation of proxies for shareholders' votes. There are also special Exchange Act rules governing going-private transactions (i.e., transactions where a significant shareholder, officer, or director of the company squeezes out the remaining shareholders), Securities Act rules governing the registration of securities to be issued in connection with an acquisition, and rules embodied in Section 13(d) of the Exchange Act governing the reporting of acquired interests in a public issuer. Other federal laws also apply to the process, such as the Hart-Scott-Rodino Antitrust Improvements Act, providing an antitrust waiting and review period prior to the completion of a transaction, and the Exon-Florio amendments, providing national security review of acquisitions by foreign buyers.

Interposed with this federal scheme are state laws that regulate the actual decision of a company's board of directors to agree to a takeover transaction. State law primarily regulates this decision through the imposition of fiduciary duties on directors to a company's shareholders, standards that are heightened in change of control or conflicted circumstances. For companies organized under the laws of Delaware, these are the *Revlon* duties and the requirements of *Unocal* and *Blasius* discussed in earlier chapters. Delaware law also goes further, for example, by regulating the disclosure process for takeovers. Each state also has an appraisal option available in certain confined circumstances that permits a shareholder to dissent from an acquisition transaction and seek a judicial valuation of his or her shares.

In both the state and federal circumstances, the law could use some pruning and reworking. The federal law in particular was first promulgated in the 1960s and was built upon piecemeal by SEC rule making throughout the 1980s. However, since that time, there has been substantial change in the world and mechanics of takeovers. There has been no corresponding update to the federal takeover code. Instead, it regulates to the state of the takeover market circa 1983. This was a time when the poison pill did not exist, proxy contests were only one means to acquire a company resisting a takeover bid, Delaware was not the primary regulator of takeovers, and financial innovation had yet to become the force it is today. The federal law does not take these developments into account; it is due for modernization.

Federal Takeover Law

The principal problem with federal takeover law is the inappropriate distinction it makes between tender offers and mergers. To understand this distinction, though, it is first necessary to understand the choice a buyer makes when deciding between a tender offer and a merger.

A buyer attempting to take over a public target faces a decision: How will it structure this acquisition? Historically, there have been three choices:

1. A tender offer followed by a back-end or squeeze-out merger
2. A merger
3. An asset purchase

Each option has its benefits and detractions, but an asset purchase of a public company is quite difficult. In this scenario, the buyer actually chooses the assets and liabilities of the target it purchases. This has an innate advantage if you are, say, Bank of America purchasing the banking assets of Washington Mutual. If so, you can simply purchase the assets and leave behind selected liabilities. Nonetheless, asset purchases of entire public companies are rare because they can create adverse tax consequences for the buyer and seller's shareholders. Moving assets out of the publicly traded shell can also be quite difficult for logistical reasons as well as provisions in contracts that prevent their assignment. Because of these and other transfer problems, the typical acquisition structure is either a merger or a tender offer.

The advantage of a tender offer over a merger is that, as currently regulated under the Williams Act, it can be completed in a quicker time frame than a merger. A tender offer must be held open a minimum of 20 business days, meaning that it can be completed in about a month rather than the two to three months a merger takes on account of federal and stock exchange notice, mailing, and review requirements for the required proxy statement.[1] However, with speed comes more federal regulation. A tender offer is subject to the Williams Act restrictions, including the all-holders best price rule and Rule 14e-5.[2] The former rule requires that the tender offer be open to all stockholders and the highest price paid in the tender offer be paid to all holders. The latter rule prohibits share purchases outside the offer from the time of its announcement until completion.

Moreover, the short-form squeeze-out threshold in the 50 states is 90 percent of a target's outstanding shares. At this threshold, a vote of the target's shareholders is not required to squeeze out the remaining shareholders. The 90 percent owner can simply file a merger certificate accomplishing this without a vote.[3] If the bidder's tender offer fails to achieve acceptances from shareholders holding 90 percent of the target's outstanding shares, then the bidder must also do a so-called long-form merger, which requires that a proxy be prepared and the same two- to three-month wait after the tender offer period.

Buyers thus prefer mergers in two circumstances. First, a buyer may predict that it will have trouble reaching the 90 percent threshold. In such a circumstance, the longer period for a merger is justified because it assures that the buyer will obtain all of the publicly held shares in a quicker time frame. Conversely, if a buyer thinks that another bid is likely, a tender offer may be preferable even in such a circumstance, as a tender offer assures faster control but not complete ownership.

To ameliorate this issue, in the past few years buyers have been demanding and obtaining top-up provisions in agreed tender offers. A top-up provision provides that so long as a majority of shareholders tender in the offer, the target will issue the remaining shares necessary to put a buyer over the 90 percent threshold. The minimum number of shares triggering the top-up varies, but the target share issuance must be below 20 percent of the target's outstanding shares because of stock exchange rules. Of course, the penalty for violating this rule is delisting from the stock exchange, something that was going to happen anyway. This means that the only effective limit on shares issued under a top-up are the fiduciary duties of a target and the number of remaining authorized shares of the target. In 2008, 100 percent of negotiated tender offers included a top-up arrangement, up from 55.6 percent in 2006 and 35 percent in 2004.[4]

The second circumstance for a bidder to prefer a merger over a tender offer is when the parties know beforehand that the bid will take a longer time period to complete, meaning there is no benefit to the speed provided by a tender offer. Examples are where regulatory approvals are required, a process that can take several months to years, or in the private equity context, where there is a go-shop or financing required, in both instances requiring several months to complete. In both cases, control cannot be achieved until these clearances are obtained and these time periods pass, so a tender offer does not provide any real timing benefit.

Previously, there were two additional reasons buyers favored mergers over tender offers. First, the application of the all-holders best price rule to tender offers and not mergers created bias toward use of the merger structure. The reason is that courts, starting in the 1990s, began to broadly interpret the meaning of a tender offer to arguably encompass change of control and other payments to executives in connection with the transaction. If a court found that the payment was indeed in connection with the tender offer, then it would apply the all-holders best price rule and order the buyer to pay this differential compensation to all target stockholders. This is a risk that many buyers did not want to take, and so there was a strong bias against tender offers and toward mergers, where this rule did not apply. This bias has largely disappeared, however, since the SEC in 2006 promulgated rules to eliminate this issue and create an easier-to-follow bright-line rule for when the all-holders best price rule applies to change of control and other executive payments.[5]

Second, if stock as opposed to cash is the consideration offered, a merger was historically preferable because the buyer could not commence the offer until the registration statement for this stock consideration became effective, a process that could take months for the SEC review process. In 1999, the SEC attempted to eliminate this timing distinction by permitting preeffective commencement of exchange offers.[6] Nonetheless, despite expectations of its widespread use, the exchange offer has yet to be so utilized. In fact, in 2008 there were only four takeover offers made via an exchange offer.[7] This was probably due to the historical issue of the all-holders best price rule. It also probably had something to do with the fact that exchange offers, because they involve the preparation of a registration statement in a condensed amount of time, require a tremendous amount of resources and work for takeover attorneys.

In light of these SEC rule changes, though, the tender offer has experienced a resurgence. In 2008, 24 percent of agreed transactions were tender offers, compared with a range of 7 to 10 percent between 2004 and 2006.[8] This trend is likely to continue as private equity transactions, which typically were mergers due to financing requirements and margin rules, remain scarce due to the credit climate. Moreover, tender offers are likely to see increased use in troubled times where speed is essential. The rise in hostile transactions will also spur their use. Typically, a hostile bid is accompanied by a tender or exchange offer.

This allows the bidder to table a bid, albeit a highly conditional one, and show its seriousness. A bidder cannot launch a hostile merger, as the target board must agree to a merger, requiring that it be replaced in a proxy contest, whereas a bidder does not require target board approval to launch a tender offer.

Tender Offer and Merger Parity

Against this backdrop, the SEC still maintains a historical bias in favor of mergers over tender offers. This is because the federal takeover code has traditionally had its locus in the Williams Act regulation of tender offers, with mergers regulated via the proxy rules. The SEC traditionally justified this distinction because mergers were viewed as requiring less federal supervision. They were negotiated contracts between commercially sophisticated parties. Thus, the problematical, coercive aspects of tender offers were presumed absent. The initial federal regulatory focus upon tender offers was therefore defensible since in the 1960s the target could not negotiate the terms of a tender offer.

However, the existence of the poison pill and other takeover defenses has rendered this federal regulatory bias moot. A proxy contest is now the only viable way for a bidder to acquire a recalcitrant target. For example, both Microsoft and InBev staged their hostiles to advantage themselves with an accompanying proxy contest if necessary. Recent successful examples of joint proxy contests and tender offers include BASF's successful $5 billion bid for Englehard, the pigment and catalyst maker, and Oracle's successful $10.3 billion bid for PeopleSoft.[9]

The tender offer alone can no longer achieve corporate control in such situations. Yet Delaware law largely regulates proxy contests. Delaware companies can adopt staggered boards, thereby arguably deterring hostile bids. Moreover, Delaware notice and director removal statutes further regulate hostile contests.

The shift in focus in unsolicited takeovers to proxy contests implicates the entirety of the federal takeover code, including the proxy and tender offer procedural and substantive rules. Federal takeover law has traditionally distinguished in the scope and manner of its regulation of tender offers and mergers. However, the old, simplified reason for this distinction, the ability of a bidder to implement an unsolicited offer without target consent, is no longer valid. The death of the true hostile, functional requirement of target consent and other takeover developments has made many of these historical biases largely anomalous. More bluntly, there no longer appears to be any reason to continue the federal takeover code's general, disparate treatment of the two structures.

The most glaring example of this unwarranted discrimination is the undue timing advantage tender offers have over mergers. Again, the justifications for this distinction appear no longer relevant in a world where targets must ultimately consent to the takeover, as the target can negotiate its preferred takeover structure. There are other cases where discrimination seems no longer sustainable in light of a target's effective ability to control the takeover structure. The federal disclosure requirements in mergers and tender offers are distinct, with different and increased or lesser disclosure required for each.[10] The propriety of this differentiation on the whole no longer seems appropriate; harmonization should be considered. Moreover, the all-holders best price rule is applicable only to tender offers.[11] There is no longer a reason for this. If the rule is maintained, application of the rule to merger transactions (or elimination in the case of tender offers) may be appropriate to stem the bias that the rule, as currently interpreted, provides toward merger transactions. It was this distinction that permitted JPMorgan to openly purchase Bear Stearns shares in the market at a price higher than the one it ultimately paid to Bear Stearns's shareholders.

A second issue with the federal takeover code is its prohibition on purchases outside the tender offer. Since 1969, former Rule 10b-13 (now redesignated Rule 14e-5) has prohibited bidder purchases outside a tender offer from the time of announcement until completion.[12] The primary reason put forth by the SEC for barring these purchases was that they operate "to the disadvantage of the security holders who have already deposited their securities and who are unable to withdraw them in order to obtain the advantage of possible resulting higher market prices."[13] This is no longer correct; bidders are now obligated to offer unlimited withdrawal rights throughout the offer period.[14] Moreover, Rule 10b-13 was issued at a time when targets had no ability to defend against these bidder purchases. They were yet another coercive and abusive tactic whereby the bidder could obtain control through purchases without the tender offer, thereby exerting pressure on stockholders to tender before the bidder terminated or completed its offer on the basis of these purchases.[15] Of course, now there is the poison pill. In the wake of these developments, the original reasons underlying the promulgation of Rule 10b-13 no longer exist.

Moreover, Rule 14e-5, by its terms, acts to confine bidder purchases to periods prior to offer announcement.[16] However, a bidder's capacity to make preannouncement acquisitions has been adversely affected by a number of subsequent changes in the takeover code, such as the Hart-Scott-Rodino waiting and review period requirements. These have combined to chill a bidder's ability to make preannouncement acquisitions or forthrightly precluded such purchases. Consequently, one study has recently reported that "over the past three decades only two percent of more than twelve thousand bidders initiating a control contests for publicly traded U.S. target firms chose to purchase a toehold shortly (within six months) prior to making the offer."[17]

Recent research and study has found that a bidder's preannouncement purchase of a stake in the target, known as a toehold, can be beneficial. The toehold purchase defrays bidder costs and incentivizes the bidder to complete the takeover, by providing the bidder compensation if its offer is subsequently trumped by a third party.[18] This can lead to higher and more frequent bids. It also can serve as a substitute for a termination fee. Meanwhile, market purchases amid a tender offer can provide similar benefits while providing market liquidity and confidence for arbitrageurs to fully act in the market. And these purchases can be regulated by targets through the poison pill or other takeover defenses, as well as through bargaining with potential bidders. Since the initial premise for this rule is no longer valid and recent research supports encouragement of these purchases, the SEC and other governmental agencies should accordingly consider loosening restrictions on bidder toeholds and postannouncement purchases.

Finally, Rule 14e-5 has never applied to bar purchases while a merger transaction is pending. Presumably, this made sense in 1968 because a bidder in a merger situation requires target agreement; the target can therefore contractually respond to and regulate this conduct. Accordingly, a bidder who runs a proxy contest without a tender offer is permitted postannouncement purchases during the contest. In most cases, the target will have the buyer contractually agree to abstain from such purchases upon agreement to a merger. But this is a negotiated point among the parties. For example, again in the JPMorgan–Bear Stearns transaction, the parties deliberately did not include such a provision to allow for JPMorgan to make market purchases. Unsolicited bidders also initially characterize their offers as mergers in order to leave the option of such purchases. The result is preferential bias toward mergers over tender offers, discrimination that no longer makes sense in a world where a takeover transaction will not succeed unless the original or replaced target board agrees to it. Any prohibition on outside purchases should apply to both merger and tender offer structures or to neither.

Due Diligence and Disclosure

There is another significant issue with federal takeover law: the way it treats due diligence and disclosure in the takeover process.

In recent years, the SEC has administered disclosure obligations haphazardly to the detriment of shareholders. Continuing its undue distinction between mergers and tender offers, SEC disclosure requirement makes inappropriate distinctions between these two structures. Moreover, in the private equity context, the SEC has failed to force disclosure of debt and equity commitment letters for buyer financing. Although some confidentiality on pricing terms may be appropriate, the complete nondisclosure of these letters has left shareholders without information about the ability of buyers to draw on financing and complete acquisitions. This has resulted in situations like the Clear Channel litigation, where shareholders were unaware of the ability of the banks to assert a legal claim that they could walk under the letters until litigation erupted.

Meanwhile, the SEC has increasingly allowed bidders to refrain from fully disclosing the conditions to the completion of their acquisition or other seemingly material information. Instead, the SEC has allowed the parties to put this information in disclosure schedules to the acquisition agreement, a part of the transaction documentation that is typically kept confidential. The problem with this was readily apparent in the 3Com transaction. There, the CFIUS condition discussed in Chapter 5 appeared to have been put in the disclosure schedule so shareholders did not even know of its existence. Finally, the SEC has seldom acted to enforce its own disclosure requirements in the takeover context. The result has been an increasing trend for buyers to underdisclose and to avoid disclosure of key acquisition terms.

In particular, the SEC has not annunciated specific requirements for disclosure related to projections supplied to buyers by targets in the diligence process. Contrast this with the U.K. rule that requires all assumptions underlying disclosed projections to be specifically stated and the policies and calculations supporting them to be examined and reported upon by the buyer's accountants.[19] Accordingly, the parameters of required disclosure in the United States are vague, and buyers tend to underdisclose information received through the due diligence process. Projections relied on by buyers are often not disclosed or are disclosed in a summarized and thus rarely useful form. For example, in the acquisition of Guidant Corp. by Boston Scientific, the parties exchanged projections but did not disclose them in their proxy statement.[20] Even when the disclosure is made, it is often limited. For example, when Gillette Co. was acquired by Procter & Gamble, the parties exchanged projections, but the proxy statement disclosed only projected growth rates for sales, profits from operations, and earnings.[21] Shareholders are thus left at the mercy of their company to decide as to the quantity and quality of forward-looking information that is disclosed. And they often choose not to do so.

The consequence of the SEC's failure to adequately regulate the disclosure process is that Delaware has stepped into the breach. The Delaware courts regularly review disclosure in takeover transactions and increasingly require that corrective disclosure be made. The Delaware courts thus provide the active regulator that the SEC does not, but court-created rules for disclosure are vague and lack definition. In other words, what are Delaware's disclosure rules? There is no easy answer, and instead someone, a lawyer, must piece it together from the prior case law. The SEC should act to revise its disclosure rules into the modern age and correct the bad disclosure practices that have become all too common in takeovers.

A Modest Proposal for Reforming the Federal Takeover Code

Federal takeover law thus too often either misregulates or underregulates. This is in large part due to the SEC's withdrawal from active regulation of the takeover market at the end of the 1980s. This has left the takeover code frozen and regulating to a time that no longer exists. The SEC would do well to reenter the business of takeover regulation, rethink the entirety of the federal takeover law, and possibly repeal much of the Williams Act's substantive requirements.

The best route would probably be to form a takeover commission to study and rework the entirety of the federal code. The last panel of this type was back in 1983. Marty Lipton, one of the deans of the takeover bar, one of the inventors of the poison pill, and a partner at Wachtell Lipton, was on that panel and no doubt would serve on this one.[22] The goal would be to create a cohesive takeover code that regulates in conjunction with the current state of the market and takes into account the tremendous change in the market since that time. It would also be a flexible code that regulates to future developments.

Given Delaware's prominence, the federal law should also be fine-tuned to work better with Delaware law. For example, Delaware requires that a shareholder meeting be held within 13 months of the last annual meeting.[23] But if you are a company in the midst of an accounting restatement, you cannot file your proxy with the SEC for that meeting. This puts you within a regime of two competing rules. In a takeover contest, this can permit you to delay holding your annual meeting, something that BEA Systems did when it was in the middle of an options backdating investigation.[24] This allowed it to mount a back-door takeover defense to Oracle's hostile bid giving it an argument to avoid a proxy contest to unseat its directors. Any federal takeover regulatory reform will need to take into account Delaware law.

Delaware Takeover Law

Delaware now dominates the regulation of takeovers and corporate law generally. Delaware accounts for more than 50 percent of all publicly traded incorporations, and in recent times, up to 77 percent of all companies going public have chosen to incorporate there.[25] Moreover, the preferred choice of law and forum to govern acquisition agreements has become Delaware.[26] Delaware has become the primary arbiter of corporations as well as takeover battles and the regulator of takeovers. But how did this small state become the center of the corporate law universe? In part, it is due to the quality and efficiency of its courts.

Delaware is a quick, efficient, and well-helmed forum for litigation. Historically, the five judges who sit on the Delaware Chancery Court—the court charged in the first instance to hear these corporate law disputes—have been viewed as some of the best in the land. Delaware offers corporations certainty and the ability to obtain rapid adjudication. Because the court is small and capable, Delaware has been able to put forth a relatively coherent corporate law that is viewed as responsive to the demands of a changing market.

Delaware judges obtain a sense of this market by constantly speaking publicly about corporate law issues and appearing responsive to the corporate law bar. In fact, they are mini-celebrities, coveted for corporate law speaking engagements and at law schools. Vice Chancellor Leo Strine Jr., a judge on the Chancery Court, now even coteaches a mergers and acquisitions class at Harvard Law School.

The financial crisis of the past years showed Delaware's capabilities. Litigation is often viewed as a long slog of meaningless discovery and appeals taking years to complete. In contrast, during the past two years, Delaware acted quickly to decide these takeover battles soundly. Consider, for example, the litigation involving Cerberus Capital Management and United Rentals. In that case, United Rentals sued to force Cerberus to complete the $4 billion acquisition it had agreed to. Chancellor Chandler took the case from the first filing of complaint to trial and an opinion in about a month, siding with Cerberus and allowing it to walk away from the transaction.

Chancellor Chandler's opinion was generally considered to be a good and well-reasoned one. This was not unusual for these cases, as time and again the Chancery Court has bent over backward to adjudicate quickly. In the litigation between Hexion Specialty Chemicals and Huntsman, which took only two and a half months to go from complaint to trial, Vice Chancellor Lamb delivered his thoughtful opinion only a few weeks after completion of the trial.

It was not just in this takeover litigation that Delaware showed its ability in the past two years. JPMorgan Chase Co.'s agreement to acquire Bear Stearns posed a political landmine for Delaware. Bear Stearns was incorporated in Delaware, and the Bear Stearns deal and the mechanisms that JPMorgan negotiated with the federal government's cooperation were designed to force the deal through over any protesting Bear Stearns shareholders.

The terms of JPMorgan's acquisition skirted the edge of validity under Delaware law. But when push came to shove, the Delaware courts decided to abstain from ruling in the case, deferring instead to a pending New York suit covering similar issues. Delaware watchers laughed at this result. Delaware's refusal to rule on this suit was quite contrary to Delaware's penchant for retaining jurisdiction on the most tenuous hooks. However, abstention allowed Delaware to kick the case to New York and for it to be decided there.

Keeping it in Delaware would have forced Delaware either to stop the acquisition or to make bad law and uphold a legally uncertain takeover. The former would have brought Delaware into direct conflict with the federal government, which adamantly wanted the acquisition to go through. The judge who decided to abstain, Vice Chancellor Parsons, may have been on shaky precedential ground, but it shows the sensibility that Delaware judges bring to their cases. Delaware passed another test.[27]

Before 1913, New Jersey was the preferred site for incorporations. New Jersey's dominance ended when its governor at the time, Woodrow Wilson, led a successful push for stricter corporate regulation. Corporations promptly decided to abscond to a more favorable jurisdiction, Delaware. How Delaware has kept its dominance since that time is a puzzle for corporate law scholars. Is it because Delaware continues to pander to corporate managers by offering more lenient regulation? Or is it because Delaware's law is simply the best available, which removes the incentive to switch?[28] Perhaps it is simply inertia and the failure of any other state to compete effectively. The only real exception here is North Dakota, which recently legislated a new shareholder-friendly corporate code in an attempt to attract some of these corporations and the revenue they bring.[29] There has yet to be any corporate stampede north, though.

Nonetheless, Delaware caters to its interests—the corporations that incorporate there, the parties who select Delaware law for their agreements and disputes, and the lawyers and bar of Delaware. Delaware must account for those interests or otherwise lose the $600 million in annual revenue it receives from corporate franchise taxes.[30] This may be why Delaware has endorsed takeover defenses and otherwise adopted relatively promanagement policies. To be fair to the judges of Delaware, however, they have also cracked down on egregious conduct such as in the 2007 *NetSmart* case, where the CEO together with his board attempted to bias the process by excluding certain bidders.[31]

Moreover, Delaware cannot go too far in favoring management because of another of Delaware's fears: the always-pending prospect of federalization of corporate law. This fear was particularly acute at the time of the Sarbanes-Oxley Act of 2002. The legislation invoked cries of creeping federalization of corporate law and raised the prospect that Delaware could be displaced.[32]

The Delaware courts quickly reacted, appearing responsive to claims of corporate mismanagement in cases involving options backdating and executive compensation. As Professor Mark Roe has postulated, Delaware often judges in response to the federal government and the public mood at the time, attempting to avoid federal intervention.[33] This is probably why Delaware refused to intervene in the Bear Stearns deal, and why any litigation in Delaware challenging other federal bailouts is apt to go nowhere. Today, the fear has arisen again in the realm of executive compensation, as Congress has moved to actively regulate this area. It remains to be seen how Delaware reacts, but it is likely to respond with its own regulation in order to attempt to mitigate any federal response.[34] Nonetheless, corporate governance and regulation of corporations is increasingly affected by capital markets regulation, an arena dominated by the federal government. In the coming post-financial crisis regulatory reforms, Delaware is apt to lose some power to more central capital markets regulation.

Despite the federal threat, Delaware is still dominant in regulating corporations and takeovers. It is likely to remain so, and full federalization of corporate law is unlikely. The crises of the past year show that there really is no other substitute for this type of quick adjudicative response. Even when mistakes are made, the responsiveness of the Delaware judges, through their engagement with the corporate bar, ensures it is only a short misstep. It appears that this has made Delaware's takeover regulation a more coherent and responsive market code than other areas of its corporate jurisprudence.

But this does not mean that Delaware is a perfect takeover regulator. Its multiple standards of review and for litigation discussed in prior chapters have left even the most experienced litigators puzzled as to the likely outcome of a decision. Moreover, there are limits to Delaware's prominence. Delaware is a court-driven takeover regulator. It cannot issue out rules and instead decides cases based on the facts at hand. Because of this, there will always be ambiguity in Delaware's jurisprudence and a need for an overlaid federal system. Finally, Delaware is no angel, and there remain flaws in its takeover jurisprudence. I have discussed some of these throughout the book, including its seemingly too permissive approach to lockups and its need to set a proper balance on MACs. However, it is worth highlighting one area not yet discussed in this book, the regulation of management buyouts (MBOs).

Management Buy-Outs and Going Privates

Despite its many standards of review, Delaware has yet to set significant, distinct standards for MBOs. In the 1970s, there was a fierce struggle over the appropriate regulation for going-private transactions. In the process, heightened review standards on both state and federal levels were adopted. The federal going-private rules apply to both MBOs and to take privates by controlling shareholders of their subsidiary companies. Delaware's special rules also apply to both types of transactions, but there is an important procedural difference.

In instances of controlling shareholder-subsidiary going-private transactions, the Delaware courts will always review these transactions under the "entire fairness" standard.[35] Conversely, at least one Delaware Chancery Court judge has held that an MBO transaction can be subject to deferential review under the business judgment rule.[36] According to this court, this can occur if the transaction is with management, they do not have a controlling stake in the company, and the transaction is approved or ratified by a fully informed vote of the noninterested shareholders. The problems with a gap like this were ably on display in the recent 2008 failed MBO of Landry's Restaurants, Inc., the owner and operator of Landry's Seafood House, the Rain Forest Café, and a number of other restaurant concepts.

On January 28, 2008, Landry's Restaurants, Inc. announced that its CEO and chairman of the board, Tilman Fertitta, was proposing to buy the company. Fertitta, who already owned 39 percent of Landry's, proposed to pay $23.50 a share for the rest of it, for a total deal value of $1.3 billion. The amount he offered was a 41 percent premium over Landry's closing share price of $16.67 on the day before the bid was announced.[37]

The Landry's board then did what boards usually do in such situations. The board established a special committee to consider the proposal. However, the committee got off to a slow start and did not officially announce the retention of its financial adviser, Cowen & Company, until April 2. The reasons for the delay appear to be related to complications surrounding the retention of Cowen and the negotiations of Cowen's engagement and fee letter. But it may also have been a sign of the committee's inexperience.

On April 4, only one day after the special committee had begun to supply Cowen with information, Fertitta lowered the price he was willing to pay to $21 per share. In a letter to the special committee, he sought to justify these revised terms by citing the declining state of the market, drops in Landry's stock price, and the company's deteriorating results from operations. At the time, he stated that he was "fully prepared to proceed with the transaction in an expedited manner."

On June 16, Landry's announced that it had agreed to be acquired by an acquisition vehicle controlled by Fertitta for that same $21 a share. The total value of the transaction was approximately $1.3 billion, including approximately $885 million of Landry's outstanding debt. At the time, Fertitta announced that this acquisition vehicle had received a debt commitment letter from the investment banks Jefferies and Wells Fargo to fund the acquisition. In connection with the deal, Landry's retained a 45-day go-shop period that permitted it to solicit third-party bids after the agreement's announcement. If a third-party bid materialized during this time period, Landry's would be required to pay only a termination fee of $3.4 million. In addition, Fertitta could terminate the acquisition agreement until August 15 and pay only a reverse termination fee of $3.4 million. Thereafter, he could walk from the transaction at any time by paying a reverse termination fee of $24 million.

The terms were very beneficial to Fertitta and effectively gave him a cheap option to purchase the company. It was later disclosed by Landry's that Fertitta bargained hard for this deal and optionality. He threatened to revoke his offer if the company was shopped prior to the signing of an agreement with him, refused to neutralize his shares in any vote, and refused to allow a condition that the transaction be approved by a majority of the Landry's stock he did not control. In negotiating against Fertitta, it seemed the committee was able to gain very little. The one time they threatened to refuse to approve the deal if he didn't agree to their demands, they quickly caved when he refused to do so.

On August 1, Landry's announced that it did not receive any third-party proposals to acquire the company during the go-shop period. This was not surprising: Fertitta was the company's chief executive and chairman, and he controlled 39 percent of Landry's stock. Given his head start and voting advantage, a third-party bidder would be starting from behind in any bid, and at a distinct disadvantage.

On October 7, Fertitta informed the special committee that "in view of the closure of the company's properties in Kemah and Galveston [due to a recent hurricane], the instability in the credit markets, and the deterioration in the casual dining and gaming industries, the debt financing required to complete the pending transaction is in jeopardy at the current $21.00 per share price."

On the evening of October 19—at 6:17 PM, to be exact—Landry's issued a Saturday night special, a press release announcing that the acquisition agreement had been amended so that Fertitta would pay a reduced $13.50 per share. The price reduction was still not enough to save the deal. On January 12, 2009, the Landry's deal was terminated. The reason put forth by Landry's was a bit tortured and, frankly, odd. According to Landry's:

> The S.E.C. was requiring the Company to disclose certain information from a commitment letter issued by the lead lenders to Fertitta Holdings Inc. and Fertitta Acquisition Co . . . and [Landry's] about the proposed financing for the going private

transaction and for the alternative financing (in the event the going private transaction did not occur).[38]

Landry's asserted that the commitment letter had a confidentiality clause that prohibited this disclosure and that the lead lenders Jefferies & Company and Wells Fargo refused to waive the clause. Instead, the lenders stated that they would assert a breach if the SEC required this disclosure and would cite this breach to terminate their commitment letters.

According to Landry's, this left it with no choice but to terminate the acquisition in order to preserve the company's alternative financing if the transaction did not occur. Conveniently, since it was Landry's that terminated the transaction, the company was not even entitled to the $15 million reverse termination fee from Fertitta's affiliates that it might otherwise have been entitled to. It still remains unclear why exactly Landry's terminated the transaction in a manner that left the company without any recompense.

The deal not only left Landry's with substantial expenses but also put Fertitta in a substantially better position than when the process began. According to the Landry's filings, Fertitta owned 34.6 percent of Landry's as of August 27, 2007, and 39 percent by July 17, 2008, five days after the initial announcement of this deal. As of January 2, 2009, he held 56.7 percent of Landry's.[39] The special committee had failed to negotiate a standstill with Fertitta and allowed him to obtain majority control of this company while this failed deal was pending. This appears to me to be a spectacular lapse by the committee. I believe it harmed Landry's shareholders by depriving them of a change-of-control premium and leaving them with substantial unreimbursed transaction expenses.

In light of the abuses ably illustrated in the failed Landry's transaction, the special committee process may not provide sufficient protection for nonmanagement shareholders. After all, if there is a no vote, then what happens? There are examples where shareholders have said no, such as in the case of the Dolan family's repeated attempts to take Cablevision private. However, these cases are rare.[40] This is because a no vote is often seen as effectively firing your management, leaving shareholders with a rudderless company. Here, the Landry's committee may have simply felt it had no choice in negotiating such a beneficial deal to Fertitta. In other MBOs in the past year, management has similarly used its ability to walk and leave the company helpless to drive very hard bargains and then to renegotiate those bargains once the company had agreed to an acquisition. In 2008, these included the failed $1.3 billion MBO of CKX, Inc., the owner of the American Idol brand, and the subsequently completed MBO of Zones, Inc., an intellectual technology provider.

At one point in time, prominent academics called for a complete ban on MBOs and going-private transactions because of the inherent prospect for abuse.[41] It is clear that a board faced with a proposed management buy-out is in a difficult situation. If it says no, management will remain in place but sorely disaffected looking to replace the special committee at some point. But if the committee says yes, it is likely to be unable to attract other bidders because of the head start and insider knowledge that management has. This is why go-shops have been ineffective in transactions with management involvement.[42] Moreover, as in the Landry's case, management is significantly incentivized to bargain for tight deal-protection measures. Though further study is needed, I suspect this means that management is probably able to get a better deal on price than it otherwise would in a competitive bidding arena.

Because of this, Delaware should not go so far as to ban MBOs but should ensure that MBOs are treated like parent subsidiary going-private transactions and are therefore always subject to an entire fairness review. Moreover, the actions of a special committee, particularly in all going-private transactions, should be heavily scrutinized. They should be required to negotiate within this standard (a) for meaningful recompense if a transaction falls through and (b) for the disinterested shareholders to have a veto on the transaction. The ultimate goal in MBOs should be to make these contests open and allow for outside bidders who can serve as a market check on the actions of management.[43]

Deal-Making

Which leads us to the final question: Should deal-making itself be reformed? The events detailed in this book point to a more disciplined approach to deal-making by buyers. The failures of too many deals lie in hasty decisions based on personality rather than on solid economic foundations and hard work. The good corporate governance and the failures of deals from the fifth wave have increased the focus on disciplined mergers and acquisitions. But buyer decision to deal will largely remain the domain of market forces. Legal regulation of the buyer decision to make a deal is probably too difficult, and rising shareholder and board power should temper ill-advised CEO empire building in a substantial number of cases. Still, the need for a fully informed shareholder vote in significant acquisitions would aid this process. If a buyer issues more than 20 percent of its stock, then the stock exchange rules require such a shareholder vote. Alternatively, in cash deals there is no required vote under the laws of Delaware. In contrast, such a vote often is required for European companies under their local laws. One possible solution is that, for significant acquisitions, the stock exchanges should require a vote when a buy-out constitutes more than 20 percent of a company's assets and market capitalization. This would place the same shareholder discipline on companies in all circumstances. Given that shareholders almost always approve deals, this would likely be decried as a formality placing more procedural restrictions on companies and hampering acquisitions. But given the shareholder activism rise and potential to force a more disciplined "deal" decision, this requirement is likely appropriate. Mechanisms that encourage more disciplined deal-making without significant burdens are a worthy goal.

It is here where deal reform should come. Management should continue to plan strategically for deals. The deal machine will continue to be an irreplaceable part of deal-making, but it will also place its own pressures on CEOs to deal. If there are lessons from the past years, it is that the ability to say no or otherwise implement a deal in a coordinated, planned fashion is important. The deal machine must sometimes be ignored on behalf of common sense. Boards and CEOs should make deal decisions within procedures that create independence from the deal machine and foster thinking that can counteract the forces that drive deal-making for deal-making's sake.

Chapter 12

Deal-Making Beyond a Crisis Age

D oes deal-making add value? The question is one that must be asked in light of the financial crisis. I believe that the answer is that, on the whole, deals do add substantial value. Deal-making provides added value by structuring and combining assets more efficiently to reduce the cost of capital and create value through, among other things, synergies and cost savings.

The backdrop to this value question is a more controversial one: Do those who advise deal-makers add value to deals themselves or are they simply a regulatory tax or other transaction cost? Strangely, this debate comes up over the role of lawyers and not investment bankers. Investment bankers are presumed to add value by providing pricing certainty among other activities. This is per se assumed. In contrast, academics who study deal-making continue to debate whether lawyers are equally value-creating. I must admit, I find this somewhat puzzling. After all, why do clients pay millions of dollars and fight to retain the best paid legal talent and law firms to make deals? Surely, they must offer some value over and above other lawyers and value in and of itself. In a sense, this book is a testament to that value and perhaps an answer to the debate. Lawyers certainly are a necessary part of a trans-action given the increasing regulatory nature surrounding deal-making. This is a cost. But lawyers likely add more than they cost—they are in the words of Professor Gilson transaction cost engineers—people who design and erect deal structures that maximize value and mitigate and balance risk for their clients. In this mix lawyers provide other roles including a way of thinking and experience that provides sage advice to their clients.[1]

This is not to say that deal-making or deals are a nirvana of value and capital markets perfection. This book has also documented the wasting of assets that deal-making can produce as well as the way that those who advise deal-makers can make mistakes or act in their own interests adding agency costs to deals and destroying value. Here, of course, the question really is whether deal-making contributed to the current financial crisis. Certainly, the over-leveraging of private equity targets and the securitization process for mortgages led to undue risk and leverage in the economy. But this highlights the need to regulate these activities not the role of deal-making in them. I'm less certain about blaming of the deal-makers who structured these deals. They did so because they could and were smart enough to be able to do so. Certainly, deal-makers and their advisers are blameworthy for this but in the future regulation should focus on activities not persons. In other words, deal-makers will always find ways to structure and execute deals up to and sometimes beyond the bright-line law. The law should take this into account in its regulation of these activities and create incentives that do not permit deal-makers to externalize their mistakes or deals onto the public as happened in the financial crisis.

Moreover, the financial crisis has upended the world of deals and the deal-making machine. Three of the five independent investment banks have simply disappeared. The remaining survivors, Goldman Sachs and Morgan Stanley, have been forced to become bank holding companies, subject to heightened regulation, which will limit their trading and lending activities. Meanwhile, traditional banks have struggled under the weight of distressed assets and wounded balance sheets, and private equity firms are occupied with their attempt to salvage their troubled, overleveraged acquisitions, vintage 2004 through 2007. The securitization market, the pipeline for the necessary debt for deals, remains turgid and likely will become subject to increased regulation.

Amid this turmoil and as I complete this book, the takeover market remains quiet as buyers remain wary of assuming acquisition risk, private equity has vanished from the market, credit still remains scarce, and pricing for deals remains difficult in a volatile market. The global takeover model appears precarious, as currencies revalue and buyers hesitate to risk deal-making, let alone complicated, cross-border takeovers. Finally, even the lawyers and accountants, the workhorses of the deal machine, appear chastened by the events of the past years, something that will further hamper deal-making.

From these ashes, a new, transformed deal machine is likely to emerge. First, boutique investment banks such as Evercore Partners Inc., Greenhill & Co., and Lazard Ltd. are likely to benefit. Investment bankers will turn to these firms as they flee a more regulated and institutional culture in which their banks and sometimes salaries are subject to government regulation and supervision. In the shorter term, clients will turn to them for more independent advice—advice likely to be cherished, given the conflicts that arose during the private equity implosion between clients and investment banks providing both financing and financial advice. Faced with this conflict, these investment banks repeatedly chose their own interests to the detriment of clients. Ironically, private equity firms may also benefit from this trend, as their financial advisory arms expand to offer this unconflicted function to companies. Nonetheless, the large investment banks will continue to exercise their balance sheets and lending power to retain clients and deals. Their success will in large part depend upon coming regulatory reform and whether and how "too-big-to-fail" banks are limited in their trading and lending activities. In effect this would be a quasi-resurrection of the Glass-Stegall Act wherein investment banks were forced to compete on a level playing field without financing and regulatory subsidies. Nonetheless, the big investment banks will likely continue to play an important role in deal-making. The question is whether they will or should return to their dominance.

In this regard, the small boutique bank model has the virtue of becoming more stable and prudent than the big investment banking model of years past. In recent years, these large investment banks had abandoned their partnership model in favor of publicly traded capital structures.[2] The partnership model allowed investment banks to invest in the future and forgo short-term for long-term gains by providing for individual partners with a strong stake in the future enterprise. In the modern era, though, these banks became publicly traded entities ever more reliant on technology as opposed to human capital. The result was a failure of prudent risk modeling and a severe lack of loyalty among employees.

This led to the relationship model of investment banking being replaced with the institutional model. In the latter model, the primacy of the long-term benefit of the client guaranteed in the form of a strong personal relationship with the bank's managing directors was traded for the bank's financing capabilities.[3] But again, the financial crisis has exposed the conflicts inherent in the institutional model, a development likely to benefit the boutique banks that focus on relationships. Because the boutiques are more focused on individual employees and creating long-term relationships, they are likely to provide better-quality advice to companies while creating a more stable investment banking model more attractive to many investment bankers.

In light of these developments, the methods and means by which dealmakers raise capital are likely to shift. Both lenders and borrowers are terribly wary of each other at this point on account of the conflicts that arose during the financial crisis. In the short term, lending will become a more documented affair, as lenders and borrowers struggle for deal certainty and trade heightened contractual terms for missing trust. In a world of limited credit, this is likely to further hamper dealmaking as these parties fail to reach sufficient agreement to provide each other assurances to proceed with a transaction.

In the longer term, any new regulation placed upon the securitization process is likely to drive the creditor-lender relationship. Until then, deals are set back to the 1980s, as buyers are forced to piece together their capital structures from scratch and on an ad hoc basis. To the extent regulation restores credibility to the securitization market through enhanced disclosure requirements, this may be a good thing for all involved. The revival of the securitization market for dealmaking, created by private equity back in the 1980s, will be particularly important because capital requirements are likely to be heightened under any regulatory reform, further limiting bank-originated borrowing to the extent that it cannot be securitized and sold.

This strained credit relationship and reduced availability of credit will continue to drive the structure of transactions. It will ensure that private equity firms continue to demand maximum optionality in their transactions and that strategic buyers continue to attempt to incorporate such features into their own agreements. However, targets will continue to balk, and the inappropriateness of more optional features in strategic transactions will continue to be apparent. The result will be that strategic transactions will continue to shift in structure, as buyers and targets in financed transactions realize that their relationship is really a threesome, including the banks, and they structure and bargain among themselves to accommodate this added complexity.

In this mix, alternative capital sources are likely to become more important. Private equity, hedge funds, and sovereign wealth funds will continue to serve as one-off capital providers for deals. They will also serve as co-investors in strategic transactions where capital is unavailable. Until they become institutionalized, though, both hedge funds and sovereign wealth funds will continue to be only supporting characters with unfulfilled potential. These financial investors need to develop the mechanics so any capital they have can be quickly and regularly accessed. This may occur, but it is likely to be a gradual process. In particular, hedge funds will have to become more like private equity funds and seek longer commitments from their investors that allow them to provide a long-term capital and investing function. This is a process that is occurring, as hedge funds attempt to recover from the immense capital withdrawals of the past year.

The terms of debt will shift. After the 1989 RJR/Nabisco deal, when KKR structured its acquisition debt to take advantage of pre-existing bondholders, event risk covenants became standard to protect debt holders. In the credit boom of 2004–2007, these went by the wayside as covenant-lite debt and PIK-toggles became the norm. But as the travails of Realogy, Freescale, and other distressed private equity portfolio companies show, these protections were there for a reason. In the future, investors will demand more protection and the restoration of the pre-2004 status quo. Debt is likely to become less complicated, and the slicing and dicing of capital structures that private equity specialized in will slow as investors seek simplicity and transparency.

The continued trend of tradable debt will continue making pricing easier and debt more utilizable. Moreover, the financial revolution will enable buyers and their bankers to structure and price new forms of capital and risk-allocation devices. Still, the terms of debt negotiated in this bubble time will put private equity in the catbird seat for companies apparently verging on the edge of insolvency, such as Harrah's and the like. Expect more debt-for-equity exchanges in the meantime and a continued struggle between distressed debt investors and private equity.

In this market, shareholders are likely to continue to flex their power. The good governance trend and shareholder activism of hedge funds were a start. The disruptions of the past two years will heighten the shareholder function, as boards remain particularly attuned to shareholder and public pressures and regulators attempt to increase shareholder say in the corporate enterprise. In the deal-making world, the failures of Yahoo and others adopting a just say no strategy will continue to encourage boards to be more open to hostile transactions. This should create a self-fulfilling loop, further spurring hostile transactions and creating opportunities for more acquisitions and consolidation.

The rise of the technology hostile and the mainlining of hostile transactions in the strategic sphere will further spur this activity. Buyers in these circumstances are more likely to be greeted rather than booed. Still, this is a prediction, and stronger responses by targets adopting 1980s-style defenses may result in changes in the Delaware law governing such responses. The gaps in Delaware's law in the short term will also probably result in further lockup creep and perhaps more novel transaction defenses, a trend Delaware courts should harshly scrutinize. The depressed market may spur new abuses that receive regulatory attention. I have highlighted the potential in the case of MBOs for this type of inappropriate activity.

Strategic transactions will remain the market mainstay, but the mega-deals of the past are unlikely as pricing continues to be difficult. Industries that are particularly suitable to consolidation and with vast cash reserves, such as the pharmaceutical sector, are particularly likely for further consolidation. Buyers and sellers will continue to struggle with consideration types and valuation gaps. Still, the lack of credit will spur the increased usage of stock consideration, and market volatility will lead to more unique types of contingent value arrangements or alternative consideration forms in transactions to close this gap. Strategic transactions will remain more opportunistic and confined to consolidating industries for the near future, as strategics eschew risk taking.

Private equity will also be lurking in the background with significant war chests, ready to return to deal-making, particularly in distressed acquisitions. In the process, though, like the banks, private equity will have to restore trust among targets for its actions of the past years. This will mean that private equity is apt to focus on smaller, easier-to-consummate transactions in stable, particularly cash-generative industries for the time being—at least to the extent such companies still exist. The private equity mega-deal is probably dead for a long time as private equity seeks forgiveness for its misdeeds.

The one growth area in strategic and private equity transactions is likely to be the distressed one. In March 2009, global bankruptcy takeover volume reached a four-year high at $698 million for the month.[4] This upward trend will continue, but the need for debtor-in-possession financing and the reforms from the Bankruptcy Abuse Prevention and Consumer Protection Act of 2005 will continue to hamper the ability of distressed companies in the United States to enter bankruptcy. Instead, lacking available credit and facing liquidation in the bankruptcy process, these companies are likely to turn to the acquisition process for salvation. The result will be buyers pushing the envelope in deal-protection devices to make these takeovers, mechanisms apt to be validated in the Delaware courts that may creep into normal, strategic deal-making. It may also spur reform to the bankruptcy process to assist companies in reorganizing rather than liquidating.

The government is now one of the largest shareholders in our financial system. Their continued deal-making and their need to eventually dispose of these stakes will drive yet more deal-making. As in distressed acquisitions, the creative structures the government has created to bail out the financial system are likely to seep into general deal-making. Again, it is likely for now that Delaware will tolerate this stretching. Eventually, though, if it reacts as it has in past crises, Delaware should react to curb these shareholder-unfriendly terms when the crisis diminishes.

Secretary Paulson and his crew showed their deal-junkie mettle, likely out of necessity adopting an investment banker mentality to the bailout. The financial crisis became a problem to be addressed through seriatim deal-making; dealmakers structured, negotiated, and then moved on. Deal-making, while more fun, can create rigid, inflexible structures and lacks a more comprehensive view, and the federal response was criticized for lacking just such coherency. Future reform is likely to give the government the flexibility it needs to deal with financial crises, or at least the one that just occurred since every crisis is different and regulation tends to be backward looking. Still, dealmakers would do well to take a step back during this downturn and rethink their own strategy based on the lessons of the government's actions and recent events. Forms should be rethought and redrafted, and dealmakers should rethink fundamental deal structures and financing arrangements. A deal should not just be done in the heat of the moment, but planned.

In the background, globalization will continue haphazardly, even during this crisis age. The near-term strength of the dollar will dampen inward investment, to be offset by the role of the United States as a safe-haven economy. But absent a new wave of protectionism, the deal-making world is too globalized at this point. The networks created and the attitudes of corporate leaders are too global to dampen the secular trend toward global deal-making. Mega-deals like BHP Billiton's failed $180 billion hostile takeover of Rio Tinto show that the potential of cross-border deals is immense and increasingly real. In fact, the sigh of relief that greeted Fiat's agreement to assist Chrysler ably illustrated this. But still, foreign acquisitions will continue to have political and public overtones that will need to be managed properly.

Finally, in all of this, the dealmakers will remain central. The ability to structure deals in this perilous environment means navigating all of these issues, as well as the new regulatory regime, and putting forth a deal that makes sense for a buyer and a target. Personality will continue to remain a key component of deals, as executives seek to manage their empires. It will be a less public ego, as the financial crisis has made the perils of a public CEO profile amply apparent. Nonetheless, the personality element of deals will continue to affect deal-making in a less public role.

The role of lawyers in the deal machine has become even more important. Over the course of the year, attorneys made a difference in a number of deals for the good and the bad. The lessons of the past years for lawyers and deal-makers generally were apparent.

- **No Deal Is a Deal Until It Is Complete.** In a number of private equity transaction deals in 2007 and 2008, prospective buyers were able to escape from their contractual obligations. In a pattern begun in 2007, either explicit language or ambiguities in agreements repeatedly allowed buyers to leverage their position and use litigation or the threat thereof to exit their commitments at a reduced cost. For example, in the failed acquisition of BCE, the transaction went through twist and turn, only to be felled at the last moment by an auditor's inability to issue a solvency opinion. Had the lawyers negotiated the condition so it wasn't to the benefit of BCE's buyers, BCE would at least have been entitled to the $C1.2 billion reverse termination fee. In these troubled times, lawyers should continue to take this lesson to heart by fighting for deal certainty and structuring transactions to close more quickly through, for example, the use of tender offers. It also leads to the next lesson.

- **The Details Matter.** Following the litigation between Cerberus and United Rentals, disputes again erupted over ambiguous contract language among ADS and Blackstone and Huntsman and Hexion. Moreover, in a number of transactions, including Jana's proxy contest with CNET, ambiguities in organizational documents allowed shareholders or bidders to circumvent staggered boards and nomination waiting periods. In other transactions, such as BCE and a number of other reverse termination private equity deals, like Reddy Ice–GSO, actual contract terms worked badly against targets. Once again, these failed deals represent the need for clear and simple drafting, as well as the importance of contract terms generally. Lawyers would do well to spend the extra hour to get the wording right in these documents, and clients would do equally well to realize the importance of such time.

- **An Optional Deal Structure Is an Option.** The private equity type of optional deal structure crept into the strategic model in 2008 and 2009. Wrigley–Mars, Pfizer–Wyeth, Foundry–Brocade, and Hercules–Ashland had optional-type structures, where the buyer could, in certain circumstances or any circumstance, terminate the deal for a reverse termination fee. Like private equity, some of these deals also foundered on their optionality. Foundry–Brocade was renegotiated, as Brocade leveraged an ostensible contractual right to walk to lower the purchase price, and i2 balked at a similar attempted maneuver by JDA Associates in i2's own deal. Similarly, management teams repeatedly took advantage of similar optionality in the Landry's, Zones, and the now-terminated CKX management buy-outs to attempt to renegotiate their deals. Optionality may be the only available option to achieve a bargain, but lawyers should attempt to negotiate for termination fees and other provisions that approximate the risk along the lines of the Pfizer model.

- **Complexity Can Kill.** Citigroup was burned ever so badly on the Wachovia deal. Unable to negotiate an asset purchase in the space of a day, Citigroup instead negotiated a letter of intent with no break fee. Wells Fargo used this time period to take advantage of the delay and take Wachovia, leaving Citigroup struggling and forced into a federal bail-out. The Citigroup case shows that complexity is sometimes necessary but in a distressed and volatile market is probably not worth the delay.

These are lessons that dealmakers and their attorneys have taken to heart. At conference rooms and internal team meetings, they now rehash the failed deals of the past years and the lessons learned, the more important of which have been highlighted here. The result will be a further shift in the details and structure of transactions, as attorneys respond to the cases of the past years, for example, the more explicit drafting and tightening of MAC clauses in light of the Huntsman–Hexion and Genesco–Finish Line cases. This is another reminder that deal-makers can add their own costs to transactions. Members of the deal-making community and those who train them (i.e., law and business schools) should be aware of this capacity and train future deal-makers to recognize and compensate for these costs allowing for lawyers and their clients to more efficiently bargain.

Finally, the coming regulatory reform will strongly affect deal-making. Hedge funds, derivatives, and the securitization process are likely to come under firmer regulatory supervision. Banks and other financial institutions will also be subject to stronger capital requirements and monitoring for systemic risk.

This will further shift capital flows for deal-making and give companies a clearer picture of shareholder activity with respect to their securities and derivatives thereupon. But in the short term, regulators will be addressing the systemic issues rather than the more particular areas of needed reform in deal-making highlighted in this book. This systemic regulation is likely to further reduce credit, as higher capital requirements are placed upon financial institutions. All of this will also further raise the importance of regulation and public relations for the course and success of deal-making. It will also take place in a world where capital more freely flows and the financial revolution allows market actors to structure around regulation. The question will be if this regulation responds appropriately or merely drives capital market activity abroad or to new, unregulated markets and securities. In this regard, we do not know what the next crisis will be. Congress would do well to respond by creating regulation that not just addresses past events but any future response and adjustment to any regulatory regime by the deal machine.

In this book, I have attempted to document the transforming deal machine. How recent event have irrevocably changed our capital markets and the way deals are structured and completed. These coming changes, the ones foreshadowed in this book and the unexpected events that will certainly occur, will make deal-making exciting both to watch and to participate in. It will result in more creativity in takeovers and a shift in deal-making profiles and structures, as lawyers and bankers struggle to accommodate this new regime.

It will also mean that the Ken Lewises of the world will be increasingly hampered in pushing through their big deals, as conservatism and shareholder pressure fight ego and the deal machine. The next few years are likely to see reduced deal-making activity and the massive deleveraging that has occurred in the past year will continue to further diminish deal-making activity. In the longer term, though, as the deal market revives and continues its sustained activity, takeovers are likely to enter a new stage of transformation, taking shape from the creative and disruptive trends of the past years described in this book. Our capital markets may have been irrevocably changed by recent events, but I believe the doom-sayers of the deal market are mistaken and that deals will continue to be a driving force in corporate America.

Notes

Prologue

1. For newspaper coverage of the party, see "Inside Stephen Schwarzman's Birthday Bash," *New York Times* DealBook, Feb. 14, 2007.

2. Blackstone Group LP, Registration Statement (Form S-1), at 1, filed on Mar. 22, 2007.

3. For less than glowing coverage of Schwarzman in the *Wall Street Journal* and *New York* magazine, see "How Blackstone's Chief Became $7 Billion Man: Schwarzman Says He's Worth Every Penny; $400 for Stone Crabs," *Wall Street Journal*, June 13, 2007; and Kurt Anderson, "Greed Is Good and Ugly," *New York* (July 23, 2007).

4. Dealogic Database.

5. Thomson/Reuters Database.

6. See Andrew Ross Sorkin and Terry Pristin, "Takeover Battle Ends in Sale of Big Landlord," *New York Times*, Feb. 8, 2008.

7. For accounts of these affairs, see Landon Thomas Jr., "Turning 60, and Doing So with 1,500," *New York Times*, Jan. 27, 2007; Andrew Ross Sorkin, "This Tyco Videotape Has Been Edited for Content," *New York Times*, Oct. 28, 2003. Dennis Kozlowski, in particular, suffered a humiliating downfall. In 2005, he was found guilty of stealing hundreds of millions of dollars from Tyco to pay for his lavish lifestyle. He was sentenced to serve a prison term of up to 25

years. Meanwhile, Saul Steinberg suffered a stroke, and his company, Reliance Group Holdings, went bankrupt in 2001. Steinberg was forced to sell off his art collection, including a $2 million antique bronze-plated commode. Ironically, Steinberg also sold his $35 million apartment in storied 740 Park Avenue to none other than Stephen Schwarzman.

Chapter 1: The Modern Deal

1. See John Steele Gordon, *An Empire of Wealth: The Epic History of American Economic Power* (2004), 214.

2. This account of the battle for the Erie Railroad is based on the histories set forth in Gordon, *An Empire of Wealth*, 213–18 and Jerry W. Markham, *A Financial History of The United States* (2002), 257–260.

3. See Owen Thomas, "Craig Newmark, Filthy Rich on eBay's Millions," *ValleyWag,* July 26, 2007.

4. Nick Wingfield, "eBay Buys Stake in craigslist," *Wall Street Journal*, Aug. 13, 2004.

5. This account of the craigslist–eBay dispute is taken from the facts alleged in the complaints filed by eBay in Delaware Chancery Court on April 29, 2008, and by craigslist in California Superior Court on May 13, 2008. Complaint, *eBay Domestic Holding, Inc. v. Newmark*, No. 3705-CC (Del. Ch. Apr. 29, 2008); Complaint, *craigslist, Inc. v. eBay, Inc.*, No. CGC-08-475276 (Cal. Super. Ct. May 13, 2008).

6. Connie Bruck has an account of this battle in *The Predators' Ball: The Inside Story of Drexel Burnham and the Rise of the Junk Bond Raiders* (1989).

7. See George Mair, *The Barry Diller Story: The Life and Times of America's Greatest Entertainment Mogul* (1998). See also "Indecent Proposals (Rival Bids for Paramount Studios)," *Economist*, September 1993; Ehud Kamar, "The Story of *Paramount Communications v. QVC Network*" in *Corporate Stories* (J. Mark Ramseyer, ed., 2009).

8. See Patrick A. Gaughan, *Mergers, Acquisitions, and Corporate Restructurings* (1996), 33. For a history of the conglomerateurs, see the classic financial history of the 1960s by John Brooks, *The Go-Go Years: The Drama and Crashing Finale of Wall Street's Bullish 60s* (1999), 150–181.

9. See Robert F. Bruner, *Deals from Hell* (2005), 265–280. See also Nina Munk, *Fools Rush In: Steve Case, Jerry Levin, and the Unmaking of AOL Time Warner* (2004).

10. See Bernard S. Black, *Bidder Overpayment in Takeovers*, 41 Stanford Law Review 597 (1989).

11. See Carol J. Loomis, "KKR: The Sequel," *Fortune,* June 13, 2005. See also Bryan Burrough and John Helyar, *Barbarians at the Gate: The Fall of RJR Nabisco* (1990), 133–136.

12. For a biography of Bruce Wasserstein, see Charles D. Ellis and James R. Vertin, *Wall Street People: True Stories of Today's Masters and Moguls* (2001), 149. Wasserstein's book is Bruce Wasserstein, *Big Deal: Mergers and Acquisitions in the Digital Age* (2001).

13. *Wall Street Journal* reporter Dennis Berman has written quite perceptively on the effect of the Deal Machine. See, e.g., Dennis K. Berman, "Kellner Thwarts the Voracious Deal Machine: Continental CEO Bucks Powerful Forces in an 11th-Hour Rejection of UAL Merger," *Wall Street Journal,* May 6, 2008.

14. *Smith v. Van Gorkom,* 488 A.2d 858 (Del. 1985).

15. See, e.g., *In re Netsmart Tech., Inc., Shareholders Litig.,* Del. Ch., C.A. No. 2563 (Del. Ch. Mar. 6, 2007).

16. For a discussion of Ken Lewis's misadventures, see Julie Creswell, "Price Paid for Merrill Is Rising," *New York Times,* Jan. 23, 2009.

17. The figure is as of 1904. See John Moody, *The Truth about the Trusts* (1904). These figures also appear in Lawrence E. Mitchell, *The Speculation Economy* (2007), 12–13.

18. See generally Naomi R. Lamoreaux, *The Great Merger Movement in American Business, 1895–1904* (2008).

19. See Mitchell, *The Speculation Economy,* 122. As Professor Lawrence Mitchell notes, this was perhaps the closest to date the country has come to enacting a federal incorporation act.

20. See inter alia Sherman Antitrust Act, ch. 647, 26 Stat. 209 (1890) (codified as amended at 15 U.S.C. §§ 1–7 (2000)); Clayton Act, ch. 323, 38 Stat. 730 (1914) (codified as amended at 15 U.S.C. §§ 12–27 (2000)); Federal Trade Commission Act, Pub. L. No. 63-203, 38 Stat. 717 (1914) (codified as amended at 15 U.S.C §§ 41–58 (2000)); Interstate Commerce Act, ch. 104, 24 Stat. 379 (1887) (codified as amended in scattered sections of 49 U.S.C.).

21. Act of June 18, 1898, ch. 466, 30 Stat. 476 (creating the Industrial Commission to investigate questions pertaining to immigration, labor, agriculture, manufacturing, and business); Act Establishing the Department of Commerce and Labor § 6, Pub. L. No. 57-87, ch. 552, 32 Stat. 825 (1903) (establishing therein the Bureau of Corporations to investigate "the organization, conduct, and management of the business of any corporation, joint stock company or corporate combination").

22. See Gaughan, *Mergers, Acquisitions, and Corporate Restructurings,* 18–26.

23. The primary source for the remainder of this subsection is my article, "The SEC and the Failure of Federal Takeover Law," 34 *Florida State University Law Review* 211 (2007).

24. See Malcolm Salter and Wolf Weinhold, *Merger Trends and Prospects for the 1980's* (1980), excerpted in Ronald J. Gilson and Bernard S. Black, *The Law and Finance of Corporate Acquisitions* (2d ed., 1995),12, 16–17.

25. The rise of the tender offer is evidenced numerically: in 1966, there were more than 107 tender offers on the New York Stock Exchange, contrasted with just 8 in 1960. See S. Comm. on Banking and Currency, Full Disclosure of Equity Ownership and in Corporate Takeover Bids, S. Rep. No. 90-550, at 2 (1967).

26. See, e.g., M. A. Weinberg, *Take-Overs and Amalgamations* § 2404 (2d ed., 1967), 270.

27. Williams Act, Pub. L. No. 90-439, 82 Stat. 454 (1968).

28. There was a profuse amount of academic commentary at the time on this issue. See, e.g., Arthur M. Borden, "Going Private—Old Tort, New Tort, or No Tort?" 49 *New York University Law Review* 987 (1974); Victor Brudney, "A Note on 'Going Private,'" 61 *Virginia Law Review* 1019 (1975); Victor Brudney and Marvin A. Chirelstein, "A Restatement of Corporate Freezeouts," 87 *Yale Law Journal* 1354 (1978); Edward F. Greene, "Corporate Freeze-Out Mergers: A Proposed Analysis," 28 *Stanford Law Review* 487 (1976); Edmund H. Kerr, "Going Private: Adopting a Corporate Purpose Standard," 3 *Securities Regulation Law Journal* 33 (1975); F. Hodge O'Neal and Ronald R. Janke, "Utilizing Rule 10b-5 for Remedying Squeeze-Outs or Oppression of Minority Shareholders," 16 *Boston College Industrial and Commercial Law Review* (1975); Anne Jentry, "Note, The Developing Law of Corporate Freeze-Outs and Going Private," 7 *Loyola University Chicago Law Journal* 431 (1976); "Note, Going Private," 84 *Yale Law Journal* 903 (1975).

29. Notice of Public Fact-Finding Investigation and Rulemaking Proceeding in the Matter of "Going Private" Transactions by Public Companies and Their Affiliates, Exchange Act Release No. 11231, [1974–1975 Transfer Binder] Fed. Sec. L. Rep. (CCH) 80,104, at 85,092 (Feb. 6, 1975).

30. See *Green v. Sante Fe Indus., Inc.*, 430 U.S. 462 (1977).

31. Going Private Transactions by Public Companies or Their Affiliates, Exchange Act Release No. 16075, [1979 Transfer Binder] Fed. Sec. L. Rep. (CCH) 82,166 (Aug. 2, 1979).

32. Salter and Weinhold, *Merger Trends and Prospects*, 32.

33. Gaughan, *Mergers, Acquisitions, and Corporate Restructurings*, 26. See also Laurence Zuckerman, "Shades of the Go-Go 80's: Takeovers in a Comeback," *New York Times*, Nov. 3, 1994, A1.

34. *Fortune* magazine, Dec. 26, 1983.

35. For a discussion of these developments, see John C. Coffee et al. (eds.), *Knights, Raiders, and Targets: The Impact of the Hostile Takeover* (1988).

36. See "Yahoo! Completes Acquisition," *Wall Street Journal*, June 1, 1999.

37. Jessica Hall, "Global M&A Falls in 2008, Ends 5 Years of Growth," Reuters, Dec. 22, 2008.

Chapter 2: KKR, SunGard, and the Private Equity Phenomenon

1. *Private equity* refers to the acquisition of both public and private companies by private investment funds utilizing a highly leveraged financing structure.

2. Dealogic Database.

3. This author was one of these people in another context, arguing that the financial revolution had made the private markets more important than the public ones. See "Paradigm Shift: Securities Regulation in the New Millennium," 2 *Brooklyn Journal of Corporate, Financial & Commercial Law* 339 (2008).

4. This history of KKR is generally drawn and based on the following sources: Brian Cheffins and John Armour, "The Eclipse of Private Equity," 33 *Delaware Journal of Corporate Law* 1 (2008); Allen Kaufman and Ernest J. Englander, "Kohlberg Kravis Roberts & Co. and the Restructuring of American Capitalism," 67 *Business History Review* 52 (1993).

5. See ibid. at 66 n. 37.

6. See Eric J. Weiner, *What Goes Up; The Uncensored History of Modern Wall Street as Told by the Bankers, Brokers, CEOs, and Scoundrels Who Made It Happen* (2005), 204.

7. Kaufman and Englander, "Kohlberg Kravis Roberts & Co.," 67.

8. See George Anders, *Merchants of Debt: KKR and the Mortgaging of American Business* (1992), 45.

9. See Weiner, *What Goes Up*, 208.

10. Bryan Burrough and John Heylar, *Barbarians at the Gate* (2003), 139.

11. For more background on the establishment of this fund, see Anders, *Merchants of Debt*, 46.

12. See Kaufman and Englander, "Kohlberg Kravis Roberts & Co.," 71.

13. See KKR Website, KKR Company: History, available at www.kkr.com/company/history.cfm.

14. Ibid.

15. See George P. Baker and George David Smith, "Leveraged Management Buy-outs at KKR: Historical Perspectives on Private Equity, Debt Disciplines, and LBO Governance," in *Private Equity and Venture Capital* (Rick Lake and Ronald Lake, eds., 2000).

16. Henry R. Kravis, keynote speech delivered at the Private Equity Analyst Conference (Sept. 22, 2004). See also Henny Sender, "Inside the Minds of Kravis, Roberts—Private-Equity Icons Opine on Their Craft; 'Any Fool Can Buy,'" *Wall Street Journal*, Jan. 3, 2007, C1.

17. Kaufman and Englander, "Kohlberg Kravis Roberts & Co.," 72.

18. See Sarah Bartlett, *The Money Machine: How KKR Manufactured Power and Profits*, (1992), 107.

19. Ibid., 118.

20. Ibid., 146.

21. Carol J. Loomis, "KKR: The Sequel, " *Fortune*, June 13, 2005, 64. See also George Baker and George David Smith, *The New Financial Capitalists* (1998), 207–208.

22. See Burrough and Heylar, *Barbarians at the Gate*, 140.

23. Ibid. See also Roy C. Smith, *The Money Wars* (2000), 180.

24. See Anders, *Merchants of Debt*, 125; Adam Lashinsky, "How Teddy Forstmann Lost His Groove," *Fortune* (July 26, 2004).

25. During this time, one of the key drivers was the growth in the high-yield market. See Glenn Yago, *Junk Bonds: How High Yield Securities Restructured Corporate America* (1991), 210. For a discussion of how the tax-deductibility of debt can provide private equity a financing advantage, see Robert P. Bartlett, *Taking Finance Seriously: How Debt-Financing Distorts Bidding Outcomes in Corporate Takeovers*, 76 Fordham Law Review 1975 (2008).

26. Michael C. Jensen first put forth this theory in his seminal article, "The Eclipse of the Public Corporation," *Harvard Business Review* (Sept.–Oct. 1989). For a summary of empirical research findings on the factors driving private equity performance, see Nicolaus Loos, *Value Creation in Leveraged Buy-outs* (2006).

27. See Jensen, "The Eclipse of the Public Corporation."

28. See Cheffins & Armour, "The Eclipse of Private Equity," 2–5. This would be a topic that would be revisited in the private equity boom of 2004–2007, with some proclaiming that it was driven in part by a desire by companies to go private to avoid the costs of the Sarbanes-Oxley Act. See generally Robert P. Bartlett, "Going Private but Staying Public: Reexamining the Effect of Sarbanes-Oxley on Firms' Going-Private Decisions," 76 *University of Chicago Law Review* 7 (2009).

29. Baker and Smith, *The New Financial Capitalists*.

30. For a somewhat negative history of Milken's creation of a high-yield market, see Connie Bruck, *Predator's Ball* (1988), 100. See also Anders, *Merchants of Debt*, 86.

31. See Bruck, *Predator's Ball*, 73, 119; Kaufman and Englander, "Kohlberg Kravis Roberts & Co.," 65–66.

32. See Anders, *Merchants of Debt*, 76.

33. *Mergers & Acquisitions*, May–June 1991, 52, and March–April 1990, 116.

34. See Maria Mallory, "The Burning Bed," *Business Week*, May 7, 1990, 127.

35. George W. Fenn et al., "The Private Equity Market: An Overview," 6 *Financial Market, Institutions and Instruments* 19 (1997).

36. "KKR's New Deal: A Kinder, Gentler Barbarian," *Economist*, Sept. 17, 1994, 83.

37. See Anise C. Wallace, "Capital Spending Cut by RJR," *New York Times*, July 2, 1991.

38. See Loomis, "KKR: The Sequel."

39. Dealogic Database.

40. See Federal Reserve Statistical Release, Flow of Funds Accounts of the United States (Dec. 6, 2007)

41. Thomson/Reuters Database (includes global buy-out, mezzanine, recap, and turnaround funds).

42. See Dennis Berman and Nicole Lee, "Blackstone Fund Sets a Record at $15.6 Billion," *Wall Street Journal*, July 12, 2006, C4.

43. See KKR & Co. LP Registration Statement (Form S-1), 133, filed on July 3, 2007 (hereinafter KKR Form S-1).

44. See Blackstone Group LP Registration Statement (Form S-1), 5, filed on Mar. 22, 2007 (hereinafter Blackstone Form S-1).

45. See Steven N. Kaplan and Antoinette Schoar, "Private Equity Performance: Returns, Persistence and Capital Flows," 60 *Journal of Finance* 1791, 1792, 1812 (2005). For other studies with similar findings, see Josh Lerner et al., "Smart Institutions, Foolish Choices? The Limited Partner Performance Puzzle," 62(2) *Journal of Finance* 731, 733 (2007); Alexander Ljungqvist and Matthew Richardson, "The Cash Flow, Return and Risk Characteristics of Private Equity" (draft dated Jan. 9, 2003); Ludovic Phalippou and Oliver Gottschalg, "Performance of Private Equity Funds" (draft dated Mar. 28, 2008).

46. See Christine Idzelis, "Blackstone Gains on Celanese," *Daily Deal* (May 11, 2006).

47. See David Carey and Vipal Monga, "KKR Quadruples PanAmSat Exit," *Daily Deal* (Aug. 30, 2005).

48. See Alexander Peter Groh and Oliver Gottschalg, *The Risk-Adjusted Performance of U.S. Buy-outs* (draft dated Nov. 14, 2006).

49. See Merissa Marr et al., "Sony Group to Buy MGM for $3 Billion," *Wall Street Journal*, Sept. 14, 2004, A3.

50. See Dow Jones, "KKR Leaves Rivals Standing with Record $104.5B Buy-out Volume" (Apr. 3, 2007).

51. This history of private equity financing arrangements is based on Steven M. Davidoff, "The Failure of Private Equity," 82 *Southern California Law Review* 481 (2009).

52. See Andrew Ross Sorkin, "Private Investment Firms to Pay $11.3 Billion for SunGard Data," *New York Times*, Mar. 28, 2005.

53. The structure of the SunGard deal is detailed in the SunGard Data Systems, Inc. Definitive Proxy Statement, (Schedule 14A), at 49–54, filed on June 27, 2005.

54. See Martin Sikora, "LBO Funds Offer Incentives to Drive High-Priced Deals: Groups Propose 'Reverse' Breakup Fees, Dropping the Financing Out While Angling for SunGard and Neiman Marcus Buys," *M&A: The Dealmakers' Journal*, Sept. 1, 2005.

55. This figure excludes transactions involving strategic buyers or families. Thomson/Reuters Database.

56. See Dennis K. Berman and Henny Sender, "Probe Brings 'Club Deals' to Fore," *Wall Street Journal*, Oct. 11, 2006, C1. One study found that target shareholders were paid approximately 10 percent less in deals involving multiple private equity firms than in private equity acquisitions involving only one firm. See Micah S. Officer et al., "Club Deals in Leveraged Buy-outs" (draft dated Oct. 28, 2008).

57. See Steven Davis et al., *Private Equity and Employment*, U.S. Census Bureau Center for Economic Studies Paper No. CES-WP-08-07 (2007), 6.

58. See Frank R. Lichtenberg and Donald Siegel, "The Effects of Leveraged Buy-outs on Productivity and Related Aspects of Firm Behavior," 27 *Journal of Financial Economics* (1990), 165–194. One later study sponsored by the Private Equity Council found that for companies with an acquisition value greater than $250 million, the average growth in capital spending was 14.6 percent versus a U.S. average of 3.5 percent. See Robert Shapiro and Nam Pham, *The Impact of Private Equity Acquisitions and Operations On Capital Spending, Sales, Productivity, and Employment* (draft dated Jan. 2009).

59. See Morten Sorensen et al., *Private Equity and Long-Run Investment: The Case of Innovation* (draft dated Feb. 1, 2008).

60. See Kurt Andersen, "Greed Is Good and Ugly," *New York* (July 23, 2007).

61. Ibid. See also " How Blackstone's Chief Became $7 Billion Man: Schwarzman Says He's Worth Every Penny; $400 for Stone Crabs," *Wall Street Journal*, June 13, 2007.

62. KKR had also resorted to hiring a public relations firm and congressional lobbyist back in the 1980s to combat accusations that it had "looted" targets it acquired. See Bartlett, *The Money Machine*, 257–270.

63. See Christine Idzelis, "Postponing the Inevitable?" *The Deal*, Oct. 31, 2008. For a review of companies acquired prior to 2008 with PIK toggles, see S&P Global Fixed Income Research, *Credit Comment: PIK-Tock, PIK-Tock, Delaying the Inevitable*, June 2008.

64. See Jason Kelly and Elizabeth Hester, "Blackstone Sells More Shares after IPO," Bloomberg News, June 27, 2007.

65. See Letter from Richard L. Trumka to Messr. John White & Andrew Donohue, re: The Blackstone Group L.P. Initial Public Offering, dated May 15, 2007.

66. Thomson/Reuters Database (includes global buyout, mezzanine, recap, and turnaround funds).

67. KKR Form S-1, iii (KKR figures are as of Mar. 31, 2007); Blackstone Form S-1, 1 (Blackstone figures are as of Mar. 1, 2007).

68. Dealogic Database.

69. See, e.g., Ronald Gilson and Charles Whitehead, "Deconstructing Equity: Public Ownership, Agency Costs, and Complete Capital Markets," 108 *Columbia Law Review* 231 (2008).

70. See Bartlett, *The Money Machine*.

71. Liz Moyer, "The Sunny Sides of the Street," *Forbes* (Jan. 4, 2008).

Chapter 3: Accredited Home Lenders and the Attack of the MAC

1. See Floyd Norris and Jeremy W. Peters, "Wall St. Tumble Adds to Worries about Economies," *New York Times*, Feb. 28, 2007, A6.

2. For a review of the subprime industry and its many failures during this period, see Gary Gorton, *The Panic of 2007*, at 3 (draft dated Aug. 4, 2008); Atif Mian and Amir Sufi, *The Consequences of Mortgage Credit Expansion: Evidence from the U.S. Mortgage Default Crisis* (draft dated Dec. 12, 2008).

3. Thomas K. Brown, *It's Time to Be Greedy*, bankstocks.com, Feb. 27, 2007. In hindsight, perhaps the fact that "greedy" was in the title of this article should have put investors on alert.

4. See Accredited Home Lenders Holding Co. Press Release, "Accredited Pursuing Strategic Options" (Mar. 13, 2007).

5. For a profile of Grayken, see Brendan M. Case and Eric Torbenson, "Lone Star Funds Chief John Grayken Is Value Spotter," *Dallas Morning News*, July 4, 2008.

6. For a full history of this auction and for further background to Accredited's sale, see Accredited Home Lenders Holding Co. Solicitation/ Recommendation Statement, (Schedule 14d-9) at 10, filed on June 19, 2007.

7. The terms of Lone Stars's original tender offer are set forth in the Offer to Purchase of LSF5 Accredited Merger Co., Inc. and LSF5 Accredited Investments, LLC (Schedule TO), Exhibit 99.(A)(1)(A), filed June 19, 2007.

8. Annual Report of Accredited Home Lenders Holding Co. (Form 10-K), 34, filed on Aug. 2, 2007.

9. See Gretchen Morgenson, "Bear Stearns Says Battered Hedge Funds Are Worth Little," *New York Times*, July 18, 2007.

10. Charley Blaine and Elizabeth Strott, "Stocks Storm Back from Steep Losses," MSNMoney.com, July 18, 2007.

11. See Defendant's Answer to Complaint and Counterclaims at 19, filed as an exhibit to the Schedule TO of LSF5 Accredited Merger Co., Inc., and LSF5 Accredited Investments, LLC, filed on Aug. 21, 2007.

12. The requirements are under the Hart–Scott–Rodino Antitrust Improvements Act of 1976, as amended. 15 U.S.C. § 18a(a)(2)(A). In addition, if the acquisition is between $65.2 million and $260.7 million, the acquisition is subject to a filing requirement and waiting period, depending upon whether certain size requirements are met. FTC Revised Jurisdictional Thresholds for Filings Made Pursuant to the Hart–Scott–Rodino Act, Jan. 6, 2009.

13. MAC clauses became an important focus point of negotiation only in the 1980s. See Ronald J. Gilson and Alan Schwartz, "Understanding MACs: Moral Hazard in Acquisitions," 21 *Journal of Law, Economics and Organization* 330, 331 (2005).

14. Agreement and Plan of Merger by and among Accredited Home Lenders Holding Co., LSF5 Accredited Investments, LLC, and LSF5 Accredited Merger Co., Inc., dated as of June 4, 2007, at § 1.01.

15. See Gilson and Schwartz, "Understanding MACs," 336–340. Two other professors have theorized that a MAC serves as a litigation screening device whereby the costs of litigation "enable the seller to better signal private information at the time of closing, in order to promote ex post efficiency in terminating or executing the acquisition." Albert H. Choi & George G. Triantis, *Vagueness in Contract Design: The Case of Corporate Acquisitions* (Apr. 3, 2009). See also Robert T. Miller. "The Economics of Deal Risk: Allocating Risk Through MAC Clauses in Business Combination Agreements" 50 *William & Mary Law Review* 2007 (2009) (arguing that MAC clauses are efficiently negotiated to take into account the risk of MAC claims by counter-parties).

16. Gilson & Schwartz, "Understanding MACs."

17. For further discussion of the scope and content of an MAC, see Kenneth A. Adams, "Understanding 'Material Adverse Change' Provisions," 10(6) *M & A Law* 3 (2006); Dennis J. Block and Jonathan M. Hoff, "Material Adverse Change Provisions in Acquisition Agreements," *New York Law Journal* 226(38), 5 (2001); Jonathon M. Grech, "'Opting Out': Defining the Material Adverse Change Clause in a Volatile Economy," 52 *Emory Law Journal* 1483 (2003); Kari K. Hall,

"How Big Is the MAC? Material Adverse Change Clauses in Today's Acquisition Environment," 71 *University of Cincinnati Law Review* 1061 (2003).

18. *In re IBP, Inc. S'holders Litig.*, 789 A.2d 14 (Del. Ch. 2001).

19. The history of this transaction is detailed in Tyson Food Inc. Information Statement (Schedule 14C), filed on Jan. 9, 2001.

20. *IBP*, 789 A.2d at 23. See generally Greg Winter, "IBP Inc. Sues Tyson Foods for Axing Sale," *New York Times*, Mar. 31, 2001.

21. *IBP*, 789 A.2d at 68.

22. Ibid.

23. Ibid. 82–84. See also Agreement and Plan of Merger, dated as of January 1, 2001, among IBP, Inc., Tyson Foods, Inc. and Lasso Acquisition Corp., filed as an Exhibit to Amendment 9 (Schedule TO), filed on Jan. 5, 2001.

24. *Frontier Oil Corp. v. Holly*, No. Civ.A. 20502, 2005 WL 1039027 (Del. Ch. April 29, 2005).

25. Ibid. at *34.

26. Ibid. at *36.

27. For example, the court in *Pan Am Corp. v. Delta Airlines, Inc.*, 175 B.R. 438, 493 (S.D.New York, 1994), held that a significant deterioration of business performance and business prospects—declines of 20 percent to 40 percent in advance bookings—constituted an MAC. However, the case highlighted the extreme deterioration necessary to show an MAC—the range of a 10 percent to 20 percent decline remains a gray area.

28. For a scholarly analysis of Vice Chancellor Strine's decision to award specific performance, see Yair Jason Listokin, "The Empirical Case for Specific Performance: Evidence from the Tyson-IBP Litigation," *Journal of Empirical Legal Studies* 469 (2005).

29. Antonio J. Macias, *Risk Pricing and Flexibility in Acquisitions: The Economic Impact of Material-Adverse-Change (MACs) Clauses* (draft dated Dec. 12, 2008).

30. Gilson and Schwartz, "Understanding MACs," 350–354. In their article, Gilson and Schwartz analyzed the prevalence of MAC carve-outs from 1993, 1995, and 2000. In 1993, nearly 81 percent of MAC clauses sampled did not contain a single carve-out. In 1995, approximately 68 percent of MAC clauses sampled did not contain any carve-outs.

31. Nixon Peabody, LLP, Sixth Annual MAC Survey (Oct. 19, 2007), available at www.nixonpeabody.com/linked_media/publications/MAC_survey_2007.pdf.

32. See Macias, *Risk Pricing and Flexibility in Acquisitions*, 1.

33. See Press Release to MGIC Investment Corp., Current Report (Form 8-K), ex. 99, filed on Aug. 7, 2007; Radian Group, Inc. Quarterly Report (Form 10-Q), filed on Aug. 9, 2007.

34. See Steven M. Davidoff, "MGIC/Radian Deal—MIA," M&A Law Prof Blog, Aug. 29, 2007, available at http://lawprofessors.typepad.com/mergers/2007/08/mgicradian-deal.html.

35. See Dennis K. Berman, "Buy-out Group Balks at Sallie Mae: J.C. Flowers Wants to Cut Bid amid Tighter Credit; Lender's Chief Fights Back," *Wall Street Journal*, Sept. 27, 2007, A3.

36. Agreement and Plan of Merger dated as of April 15, 2007, among SLM Corporation, Mustang Holding Company Inc. and Mustang Merger Sub, Inc., at § 1.01(a), filed as an exhibit to SLM Corporation Current Report (Form 8-K), filed on Apr. 18, 2007.

37. See *SLM Corporation v. J.C. Flowers II L.P., et al.*, C.A. No. 3279-VCS, Transcript of SLM Hearing, Oct. 22, 2007.

38. See Justin Baer and Jason Kelly, "Sallie Mae Rebuffs Reduced Offer from J.C. Flowers," Bloomberg.com, Oct. 2, 2007.

39. See Gregory Corcoran, "Sallie Mae Chief Comes Crawling Back," *Wall Street Journal* DealJournal, Dec. 13, 2007.

40. See Michael J. de la Merced, "Finish Line to Buy Genesco for $1.5 Billion," *New York Times*, June 19, 2007.

41. See Finish Line, Inc., Press Release, Sept. 28, 2007. For further analysis of the Genesco–Finish Line litigation, see Bradley C. Sagraves and Bobak Talebian, "Material Adverse Change Clauses in Tennessee: *Genesco v. Finish Line*," 9 *Transactions: Tennessee Journal of Business Law* 343 (Spring 2008).

42. See *Genesco, Inc. v. Finish Line, Inc. & Headwind, Inc.*, No. 07-2137-II(III) (12 D. Tenn., Davidson County, Dec. 27, 2007). For an analysis of the opinion, see Steven M. Davidoff, "*Genesco v. Finish Line:* The Opinion," M&A Law Prof Blog, Dec. 28, 2007, available at http://lawprofessors.typepad.com/mergers/2007/12/genesco-the-opi.html.

43. See Finish Line, Inc., Press Release, Mar. 4, 2008. See also Steven M. Davidoff, "Lessons from the Genesco Fight," *New York Times* DealBook, Mar. 4, 2008.

44. The facts are more particularly detailed in Judge Lamb's opinion in *Hexion Specialty Chemicals, Inc. v. Huntsman Corp.*, C.A. No. 3841-VCL, 2008 WL 4457544 (Del. Ch. Sept. 29, 2008).

45. See Press Release of Huntsman, Jul. 19, 2008.

46. Hexion, 2008 WL 4457544, at *16–20.

47. Ibid. at *15.

48. For further speculation on the scope and content of the future MAC, see Kenneth M. Wolff and Cason A. Moore, "In the Wake of the Crunch: Credit Market Turmoil and the Potential Effect on MAC Provisions," 11(10) *M & A Law* 7 (2007).

49. See also Eric Talley, On Uncertainty, Ambiguity and Contractual Conditions (Draft Dated Dec. 12, 2008).

Chapter 4: United Rentals, Cerberus, and the Private Equity Implosion

1. Jenny Andersen, "20/20 Hindsight through What Were Once Rose-Colored Glasses," *New York Times*, Aug. 31, 2007, C1.

2. See Andrew Ross Sorkin, "Can Private Equity Firms Get Out of Buy-outs?" *New York Times*, Aug. 21, 2007. In his article, Sorkin quoted from a piece I had written in August 2007, "Private Equity's Option to Buy," M&A Law Prof, Aug. 16, 2007, available at http://lawprofessors.typepad.com/mergers/2007/08/private-equitys.html.

3. See Dennis K. Berman, "Acxiom's Suitors May Drop Offer; ValueAct and Silver Lake Are Close to a Settlement That Will Cancel the Deal," *Wall Street Journal*, Oct. 1, 2007, A2.

4. See Acxiom Press Release, Oct. 10, 2007.

5. See Andrew Ross Sorkin, "Acxiom Shows Breaking Up Is Costly," *New York Times*, Oct. 10, 2007. Bank of America, the third financing bank, refused to pay part of the fee due to fears of legal exposure to a claim for tortious interference with Acxiom's contract with Silver Lake and ValueAct. Bank of America's fear would later be validated when targets subsequently began to bring just such claims against banks that balked at financing private equity acquisitions.

6. See Harman International Industries Press Release, Oct. 22, 2007. The discount the private equity firms received in the Harman settlement was probably greater, on account of allegations that Harman had breached the acquisition agreement by violating the limitations on capital expenditures therein. See Michael de la Merced, "Canceling Harman Deal, Suitors Buy Bonds Instead," *New York Times*, Oct. 23, 2007.

7. See United Rentals, Inc. Current Report (Form 8-K), filed on Nov. 14, 2007.

8. These shell subsidiaries were created by Cerberus and set up so that the acquisitions contract with United Rentals was only with them. The purpose of this was to ensure that Cerberus could limit its liability to either (1) payment of the reverse termination fee or (2) funding the acquisition. Cerberus accomplished this by not being party to the agreements, so only the shell subsidiaries were required to perform and otherwise be liable if there was breach of the agreement.

9. The details of the parties' arguments are discussed in Steven M. Davidoff, "Cerberus Sues in New York," M&A Law Prof, Nov. 23, 2007, available at http://lawprofessors.typepad.com/mergers/2007/11/cerberus-sues-i.html.

10. For a more thorough analysis of the two possible readings of this contract, see Steven M. Davidoff, "The Dog Bites," M&A Law Prof, Nov. 15, 2007, available at http://lawprofessors.typepad.com/mergers/2007/11/united-rentals-.html.

11. See Dennis K. Berman and Matthew Karnitschnig, "United Rentals, Cerberus Delay Start of Trial," *Wall Street Journal*, Dec. 17, 2007, A16.

12. See Gregory Corcoran, "Cerberus's Feinberg: The Money-Shot," *Wall Street Journal* Deal Journal, Dec. 18, 2007.

13. The negotiation history of the transaction is detailed in *United Rentals, Inc. v. RAM Holdings, Inc., et al.*, 937 A.2d 810, 834–43 (Del. Ch. 2007).

14. Ibid.

15. United Rentals Press Release, Dec. 24, 2007.

16. See Steven M. Davidoff, "The Four Buy-outs of the Apocalypse," *New York Times* DealBook, Apr. 9 2008.

17. See Steven M. Davidoff, "Who's Next for the Deal Dead Pool?" *New York Times* DealBook, Jan. 10, 2008.

18. See Michael J. de la Merced, "Deal to Buy Credit Card Processor Is in Peril," *New York Times*, Jan. 29, 2008.

19. See *Alliance Data Systems Corp. v. Aladdin Solutions, Inc., et al.*, Civil Action No. 3507-CVS (Jan. 29, 2008). For further commentary on the complaint, see Steven M. Davidoff, "Alliance Data's Complaint," *New York Times* DealBook, Jan. 31, 2008.

20. See Hearing Transcript, *Alliance Data Systems Corp. v. Aladdin Solutions, Inc. et al.*, Civil Action No. 3507-VCS, Feb. 4, 2008 (hereinafter ADS Hearing Transcript).

21. Heidi N. Moore, "Deal Journal Exclusive: Regulator Removes Major Block for Blackstone-ADS," *Wall Street Journal* Deal Journal, Mar. 20, 2008.

22. See ADS Hearing Transcript, 39–42.

23. See Alliance Data Systems Corp. Current Report (Form 8-K), dated Feb. 8, 2008.

24. See *Alliance Data Systems Corp. v. Blackstone Capital Partners V L.P., et al.*, Civil Action No. 3796-VCS (Del. Ch. Jan. 15, 2009).

25. Complaint in *BT Triple Crown Merger Co., Inc., et al. v. Citigroup Global Markets Inc.*, dated Mar. 25, 2008, at 4.

26. See Andrew Ross Sorkin and Michael J. de la Merced, "Bank's Suit May Hurt Deal for Clear Channel Unit," *New York Times*, Feb. 25, 2008.

27. See Asset Purchase Agreement dated April 20, 2007 by and among the company or companies set forth as Seller on the signature page thereto, Clear Channel Broadcasting, Inc., and the company or companies set forth as Buyer on the signature page thereto, at § 10.4, filed as an exhibit to the Clear Channel Communications, Inc. Current Report (Form 8-K), filed on Apr. 26, 2007.

28. See *Wachovia Bank, N.A., et al. v. Newport Television LLC, et al.*, Civil Action No 08-CVS-4056 (N.C. Gen Ct. Justice Feb. 22, 2007).

29. Hearing in *Clear Channel Broadcasting, Inc., et al. v. Newport Television LLC*, No. 3550-VCS, at 70-87, dated Feb. 26, 2008.

30. See Clear Channel Press Release, Mar. 14, 2008; Andrew Ross Sorkin and Michael de la Merced, "Lawsuit is Settled Over Sale of Clear Channel TV Unit," *New York Times*, March 15, 2008.

31. For a general review of these transactions and the role of the financing banks in these settlements, see Vipal Monga, "When Friends Fall Out," *The Deal*, Sept. 21, 2007.

32. The banks were Citigroup, Deutsche Bank AG, Credit Suisse Group, Morgan Stanley, Royal Bank of Scotland Group, and Wachovia Corp. See Complaint in *BT Triple Crown Merger Co., Inc., et al. v. Citigroup Global Markets Inc.*, No. 08-600899 (N.Y. Sup. Ct. Mar. 25, 2008).

33. Ibid., 16.

34. See Agreement and Plan of Merger, dated as of November 16, 2006, by and among BT Triple Crown Merger Co., Inc., B Triple Crown Finco, LLC, T Triple Crown Finco, LLC, BT Triple Crown Capital Holdings III, Inc., and Clear Channel Communications, Inc., a Texas corporation, § 8.02, filed as an exhibit to Clear Channel Communications, Inc. Current Report (Form 8-K), filed on Nov. 16, 2006.

35. See Memorandum of Law in Support of Defendants' Motion for Summary Judgment, *BT Triple Crown Merger Co., Inc., et al. v. Citigroup Global Markets Inc.*, No. 08-600899, dated Apr. 10, 2008.

36. Ibid., 16-24.

37. Heidi N. Moore, "Behind the Psychology of the Clear Channel Settlement," *Wall Street Journal* Deal Journal, May 14, 2008.

38. Ibid.

39. For a history of this transaction, see CC Media Holdings, Inc. Registration Statement (Form S-4), at 78-100, filed on June 2, 2008.

40. See Penn National Gaming, Inc. Definitive Proxy Statement (Schedule 14A), 90–91, filed on Nov. 7, 2007.

41. See Penn National Gaming, Inc. Press Release, exhibit 99.1 to Penn National Gaming, Inc. Current Report (Form 8-K), filed on July 9, 2008.

42. See Dale A. Oesterle, *The Law of Mergers and Acquisitions* (3d ed., 2005), 315 n. 8.

43. See Susan Pullman and Peter Lattman, "Buyout Bust Turns Bitter, A Major Deal Lands in Court," *Wall Street Journal*, Sept. 9, 2008.

44. *Hexion Specialty Chemicals, Inc. v. Huntsman Corp.*, C.A. No. 3841-VCL, 2008 WL 4457544 (Del. Ch. Sept. 29, 2008).

45. See Huntsman Press Release, dated Dec. 23, 2008.

46. See Peter Lattman, "Huntsman's Founder Got Fees for Work Settling Suit," *Wall Street Journal*, Mar. 30, 2009.

47. The decision was *BCE Inc. v. 1976 Debenture holders*, 2008 SCC 69 (Dec. 19, 2008).

48. See "Its Buyout Dead, BCE Starts a Fee Fight," *New York Times* DealBook, Dec. 11, 2008.

49. For a further discussion of the reasons for use of the reverse termination fee and its failings, see Steven M. Davidoff, "The Failure of Private Equity," 82 *Southern California Law Review* 481 (2009); Gregory V. Varallo and Blake Rohrbacher, "Lessons from the Meltdown: Reverse Termination Fees" (undated, unpublished manuscript). See Steven H. Goldberg, "Deals Gone Bad," Thedeal.com, Aug. 19, 2008.

50. Thomson Reuters Database.

51. Dealogic Database.

52. See *The Bank of New York Mellon v. Realogy Corp.*, C.A. No. 4200-VCL (Del. Ch., Dec. 18, 2008). See also Complaint, *ING Prime Rate Trust, et al. v. Freescale Semiconductor, Inc.* (N.Y. Sup. Ct. Mar. 24 2009).

53. Jason Kelly and Jonathan Keehner, "Blackstone Said to Cut About 70 Jobs as LBOs Falter," Bloomberg, Dec. 12, 2008.

54. See Julie Ziegler and Jason Kelly, "Harvard in Discussions to Sell Stakes in Private-Equity Funds," Bloomberg, Nov. 4, 2008.

55. Michael Wolff, "The Ultimate Bubble," *Vanity Fair* (Dec. 2008).

56. Kelly Holman, "PE Funds Amass More Than $1 Trillion," IDDMagazine. Com, Jan. 26, 2009.

57. Factset MergerMetrics Database (transactions greater than $100 million in value). See also Vijay Sekhon, "Valuation of Reverse Termination Fees in Mergers & Acquisitions," *New York University Journal of Law & Business* (forthcoming), 3.

58. For a discussion of the appropriate level for a reverse termination fee, see Vipal Monga, "Turning the Tide," *The Deal*, Aug. 29, 2008.

Chapter 5: Dubai Ports, Merrill Lynch, and the Sovereign Wealth Fund Problem

1. See Bob Davis and Dennis K. Berman, "Lobbyists Smoothed the Way for a Spate of Foreign Deals," *Wall Street Journal*, Jan. 25, 2008, A1.

2. Thomson Reuters; Dealogic Database.

3. Ibid.

4. CIC does not disclose its assets under management in a timely manner, so the current figure is unknown.

5. Press Release, Merrill Lynch & Co., "Merrill Lynch Economists Expect Sovereign Wealth Fund Assets to Quadruple by 2011" (Oct. 12, 2007); "Currencies: How Big Could Sovereign Wealth Funds Be by 2015?" Morgan Stanley Research Global (May 3, 2007).

6. The figure is accurate as of January 29, 2009. See web site of Alaska Permanent Fund Corporation, available at www.apfc.org/home/Content/home/index.cfm.

7. For details on the CIC Blackstone investment, see Blackstone Group LP Amendment No. 9 to Registration Statement (Form S-1), 4–5, filed on June 21, 2007. See also Chip Cummins, "The New Deal Diplomacy— Sovereign-Wealth Funds Buy Small Stakes and Keep Quiet, Winning Over Some Skeptics," *Wall Street Journal*, Nov. 28, 2007, C1; Rick Carew, "China's Sovereign Wealth Fund Forges Strategy, Hunts for Staff," *Wall Street Journal*, Nov. 20, 2007, A14.

8. See Ian Talley, "Politics & Economics: Gulf States Seen Raising Foreign-Asset Holdings," *Wall Street Journal*, Jan. 17, 2008, A10.

9. See Henry Sender et al., "As Oil Hits High, Mideast Buyers Go on a Spree— Dubai, Qatar Battle for Stakes in Bourses; Political Savvy Grows," *Wall Street Journal*, Sept. 21, 2007, A1.

10. United States Government Accountability Office, Report to the Committee on Banking, Housing, and Urban Affairs, U.S. Senate, Sovereign Wealth Funds: Publicly Available Data on Sizes and Investments for Some Funds Are Limited, at app. 3 (Sept. 2008).

11. Dealogic Database.

12. See Richard E. Caves, "Japanese Investment in the United States: Lessons for the Economic Analysis of Foreign Investment," 16(3) *World Economy* 279 (2007).

13. For details on the Kuwaiti and Norwegian funds, see Kuwait Investment Office in London, www.kia.gov.kw/En/KIO/About/Pages/default.aspx;

Government Pension Fund, Norges Bank, www.norges-bank.no/templates/article____69365.aspx.

14. The terms of the investment are set forth in the Merrill Lynch & Co. Amended Current Report (Form 8-K), filed on Dec. 28, 2007. See also Randall Smith and Jason Leow, "Merrill May Take More Steps to Fix Finances—Thain Doesn't Dicker as the Firm Sells Stake to a Singapore Fund," *Wall Street Journal*, Dec. 26, 2007, C1.

15. See Bank of America Corp. Quarterly Report (Form 10-Q), 25, filed on May 8, 2008.

16. See Heidi N. Moore, "Wall Street Banks: Will Sovereign Wealth Funds Speak Up?" *Wall Street Journal* Deal Journal, Jan. 8, 2009.

17. See Exhibit 99.1 to Merrill Lynch & Co. Amended Current Report (Form 8-K), filed on July 29, 2008.

18. See Saskia Scholtes and Greg Farrell, "Temasek Counts Cost of Paper Losses on Merrill Investment," *Financial Times*, Jan. 8, 2008, 13.

19. Bettina Wassener, "Temasek Holdings Loses 31 Percent of Portfolio," *New York Times*, Feb. 10, 2009.

20. The Blackstone Group L.P. Current Report (Form 8-K), filed on Oct. 16, 2008.

21. Mitsubishi purchased preferred stock yielding 10 percent per quarter and 117 million shares of common stock. See Morgan Stanley Current Report (Form 8-K), filed on Oct. 14, 2008. For coverage of the Mitsubishi investment, see Aaron Lucchetti, "Propped Up, Morgan Stanley Now Sets Forth to Right Itself," *Wall Street Journal*, Oct. 14, 2008, C1. The CIC investment was in equity units yielding a 9 percent dividend payable quarterly and mandatorily convertible to common stock on August 17, 2010. For further details on the CIC investment, see Morgan Stanley Current Report (Form 8-K), filed on Dec. 27, 2007.

22. Ibid.

23. See Andrew Edgecliffe-Johnson and Simeon Kerr, "Black Gold Meets Silver Screen as Abu Dhabi Goes to the Movies," *Financial Times*, Sept. 3, 2008, 1.

24. See Andrew Critchlow, "Big Mideast Funds Scale Back Investments: Last Year's Hot Investors at Davos Take Cautious Approach to West after Losses; Focus on Emerging Markets," *Wall Street Journal*, Jan. 27, 2009.

25. See Jason Dean et al., "China Jumps into Rio Tinto Saga—Chinalco, Alcoa Buy Stake, Complicating BHP Takeover Bid," *Wall Street Journal*, Feb. 28, 2008, A3.

26   Rio Tinto Press Release, Feb. 12, 2009.

27. Dealogic Database.

28. See Rick Care and Jason Leow, "Temasek Shakes Up Its Top Ranks," *Wall Street Journal*, Feb. 7, 2009.

29. See Jeffrey Ball and Chip Cummins, "Dow's Plan for Growth Threatened by Scuttled Kuwait Deal," *Wall Street Journal*, Dec. 29, 2008, A1.

30. See, e.g., Lester Thurow, *Head to Head: The Coming Economic Battle among Japan, Europe, and America* (1992), 113–151.

31. Although, to be fair, British enthusiasm for American railroad investment fluctuated, depending on returns and events. See A. W. Currie, "British Attitudes toward Investment in North American Railroads," 34 *Business History Review* (1960), 194, 199.

32. Interview by Michael Buchanan with Sultan Ahmed bin Sulayem, BBC Radio 4 (Feb. 29, 2008).

33. Sovereign Wealth Fund Institute, Linaburg-Maduell Transparency Index, as of Apr. 3, 2009.

34. See Bob Davis, "Wanted: SWF's Money Sans Politics," *Wall Street Journal*, Dec. 20, 2007, C1.

35. Press Release, International Working Group of Sovereign Wealth Funds, International Working Group of Sovereign Wealth Funds Reaches a Preliminary Agreement on Draft Set Generally Accepted Principles and Practices—"Santiago Principles" (Sept. 2, 2008).

36. International Working Group of Sovereign Wealth Funds, Sovereign Wealth Funds: Generally Accepted Principles And Practices—"Santiago Principles," app. I (2008).

37. Ibid., 7.

38. 50 U.S.C. § 2170(d) (2008).

39. Enforcement of United States Rights under Trade Agreements and Responses to Foreign Trade Practices, Pub. L. No. 100-418, 102 Stat. 1107 §§ 1305-07 (1988). For a history of the Exon-Florio Amendment and the Fairchild incident, see Jose E. Alvarez, "Political Protectionism and United States Investment Obligations in Conflict: The Hazards of Exon-Florio," 30 *Virginia Journal of International Law* 1, 56–86 (1989); Matthew R. Byrne, "Note, Protecting National Security and Promoting Foreign Investment: Maintaining the Exon-Florio Balance," 67 *Ohio State Law Journal* 849, 856–870 (2006).

40. Foreign Investment and National Security Act of 2007, Pub. L. No. 110-49, 121 Stat. 246 (2007).

41. Regulations Pertaining to Mergers, Acquisitions, and Takeovers by Foreign Persons, 31 C.F.R. 800 (2008).

42. The Bureau of Economic Analysis in the Department of Commerce administers a reporting requirement for all foreign acquisitions of 10 percent or greater interests in U.S. corporate entities.

43. See Chip Cummins, "World News: Nations Seek Aid from Gulf, but May Come Up Dry," *Wall Street Journal*, Oct. 29, 2008, A10.

44. Moreover, a status quo solution appears to be more appropriate at this point in time than other proposals to address sovereign wealth funds. One proposal by Professors Milhaupt and Gilson would require that sovereign wealth fund investments be deprived of any voting power while held by the fund. See Ronald J. Gilson and Curtis J. Milhaupt, "Sovereign Wealth Funds and Corporate Governance: A Minimalist Response to the New Merchantilism," 60 *Stanford Law Review* 1345 (2009). This proposal, however, does not deal with the monitoring function of any regulatory scheme, nor does it deal with the fact that most sovereign fund investment is currently nonvoting to begin with. A second proposal by Victor Fleischer would place a Pigouvian tax on these funds. Victor Fleischer, "A Theory of Taxing Sovereign Wealth," 63–66 (draft dated Aug. 12, 2008). This type of tax would be imposed because these funds have a lower hurdle rate for investment and can unduly compete and crowd out nonsovereign investment. The tax would restore a level playing field. Currently, sovereign wealth funds do not pay a dividend or any other tax in the United States because they are owned by a sovereign and are largely passive investments. Fleischer's proposal would repeal this tax exemption. This latter point appears to be a salient one, at least on a reciprocal basis. The United States should eliminate a tax benefit received by sovereigns who do not provide the same benefit to U.S. funds investing in their country. Nonetheless, a leveling tax at this point seems inappropriate, again because there has been no real harm shown yet, and secondarily because many U.S. government entities such as pension plans and endowments have similar cost of capital advantages over regular investors. See also Paul Rose, "Sovereigns as Shareholders," 87 *North Carolina Law Review* 83 (2008). Paul Rose agrees with my analysis that the current U.S. regulatory apparatus is sufficient but rightly notes that there is still a need to monitor sovereign wealth fund investment in other countries to the extent it affects U.S. interests.

45. Thomson Reuters Database.

46. Dealogic Database.

47. See David E. Sanger, "Under Pressure, Dubai Company Drops Port Deal," *New York Times*, Mar. 10, 2006, A1. For a history of the Dubai Ports saga, see Deborah M. Mostaghel, "Dubai Ports World under Exon-Florio: A Threat to National Security or a Tempest in a Seaport?" 70 *Albany Law Review* 583 (2007).

48. H.R. Res. 556, 110th Cong. (2007) (enacted).

49. Dealogic Database; Thomson Reuters Database.

50. See Mark E. Plotkin and David N. Fagan, *The Revised National Security Review Process for FDI in the US*, Columbia FDI Perspectives, No. 2, Jan. 7, 2009, 3.

51. See Russell Gold, "Chevron Purchase of Unocal Is Clinched in Shareholder Vote," *Wall Street Journal*, Aug. 11, 2005, A2.

52. See Eduardo Lachica, "Bush Orders Chinese Firm to Sell Stake in Mamco, a Seattle Maker of Plane Parts," *Wall Street Journal*, Feb. 5, 1990, A7.

53. See Hasan Jafri and Phillip Day, "Hutchison Whampoa Pulls Out of Bidding for Global Crossing—Security Concerns by U.S. Leaves Singapore Partner Alone in Purchase Attempt," *Wall Street Journal*, May 1, 2003, B4.

54. See "Buy-out of 3Com Is Up for Vote Despite Concerns," *Wall Street Journal*, Mar. 20, 2008, B4; Steven M. Davidoff, "3Com: A Failure to Communicate," *New York Times* DealBook, Feb. 20, 2008.

55. Agreement and Plan of Merger by and among Diamond II Holdings, Inc., Diamond II Acquisition Corp. and 3COM Corporation, dated as of September 28, 2007, at § 8.1(g), filed as an exhibit to 3COM Corporation Amended Current Report (Form 8-K), filed on Sept. 28, 2007.

56. See Stephanie Kirchgaessner, "'You Have to Figure How to Manage the Process,'" *Financial Times*, Apr. 25, 2008, 7.

57. See 3Com Press Release, Apr. 29, 2008.

58. See Paul Betts, "Danone Loses Its Taste for Economic Patriotism," *Financial Times*, July 4, 2007, 22.

59. Dealogic Database.

Chapter 6: Bear Stearns and the Moral Hazard Principle

1. The figure was obtained by searching the Capital IQ database for private or public offerings made by firms in the Financials (primary) sector between December 1, 2007, and March 1, 2008.

2. See Scott G. Alvarez, General Counsel, Federal Reserve Board, Sovereign Wealth Funds, Testimony before the Subcommittee on Domestic and International Monetary Policy, Trade, and Technology, and the Subcommittee on Capital Markets, Insurance, and Government Sponsored Enterprises, Committee on Financial Services, U.S. House of Representatives (Mar. 5, 2008).

3. For accounts of the collapse of these hedge funds and the state of Bear Stearns at the time, see Gretchen Morgenson, "Bear Stearns Says Battered Hedge Funds Are Worth Little," *New York Times*, July 18, 2007, C; Randall Smith, "Credit Crunch: Holders in Two Funds Want to Replace Bear," *Wall Street Journal*, Sept. 5, 2007, C2; Kate Kelly, "Cayne to Step Down as Bear Stearns CEO—Executive, under Fire, to Remain Chairman; 'Time to Pass the Baton,'" *Wall Street Journal*, Jan. 8, 2008, A1.

4. It was exactly 32.8:1. The Bear Stearns Companies, Inc., Annual Report (Form 10-K), ex. 13, filed Jan. 29, 2008. This was actually down from almost 44:1 back in August 2008. See William D. Cohan, *House of Cards: A Tale of Hubris and Wretched Excess on Wall Street* (2009), 382.

5. Kelly, "Cayne to Step Down."

6. See Roddy Boyd, "The Last Days of Bear Stearns," *Fortune*, Mar. 31, 2008.

7. See Boyd, "The Last Days of Bear Stearns."

8. See Brett Philbin and Rob Curran, "Boeing Rides Higher, But Bear Struggles—S&P Report Lifts Mood of Investors; Fannie, Freddie Up," *Wall Street Journal*, Mar. 14, 2008, C5. See also Kate Kelly, "Fear, Rumors Touched Off Fatal Run on Bear Stearns," *Wall Street Journal*, May 28, 2008, A1.

9. Press Release, Bear Stearns Companies Inc., dated Mar. 10, 2008.

10. See Boyd, "The Last Days of Bear Stearns."

11. Ibid.

12. Interview by David Faber with Alan Schwartz, CEO and president, Bear Stearns Co. Inc., CNBC (Mar. 12, 2008).

13. See Cohan, *House of Cards*, 41.

14. Ibid. at 52.

15. See Gregory Zuckerman, "Hedge Funds, Once a Windfall, Contribute to Bear's Downfall," *Wall Street Journal*, Mar. 17, 2008.

16. See The Bear Stearns Companies, Inc. Current Report (Form 8-K), filed on Mar. 19, 2008.

17. Cohan, *House of Cards*, 81.

18. See Kate Kelly, "Bear Stearns Neared Collapse Twice in Frenzied Last Days," *Wall Street Journal*, May 29, 2008, A1; Stephen Labaton, "Bear Stearns in the Committee Room," *New York Times*, Apr. 4, 2008, C1.

19. Two explanations have been proffered. First, that the guarantee had failed to convince lenders to again provide short-term repo financing and forestall Bear's clients from withdrawing funds and that Bear was going to default on the JPMorgan loan on Monday. By forcing Bear into a transaction, the Fed was protecting its guarantee and preventing any monetary loss. This is the story put forth by the New York Federal Reserve. See Timothy F. Geithner, President and Chief Executive Officer New York Fed, Actions by the New York Fed in Response to Liquidity Pressures in Financial Markets, Testimony before the U.S. Senate Committee on Banking, Housing and Urban Affairs, Washington, D.C. (Apr. 3, 2008). The second reason offered is a political one—the Treasury Department, particularly Secretary Paulson, did not want to be seen as bailing out Bear Stearns and facilitating future moral hazard. Given that the threat to the financial system remained if Bear

Stearns collapsed, it also remains unclear whether the government would have fulfilled its threat to cut off Bear Stearns if it did not find such a transaction. See Kelly, "Bear Stearn Neared Collapse."

20. Ibid. See also Cohan, *House of Cards*, 88.

21. See Robert Steel, Under Secretary for Domestic Finance of the Treasury, Actions by the New York Fed in Response to Liquidity Pressures in Financial Markets, Testimony before the U.S. Senate Committee on Banking, Housing and Urban Affairs, Washington, D.C. (Apr. 3, 2008).

22. See John Brooks, *The Go-Go Years* (1973), 329–333.

23. Agreement and Plan of Merger by and between The Bear Stearns Companies, Inc. and JP Morgan Chase & Co., dated Mar. 16, 2008, at § 5.1, filed as an exhibit to The Bear Stearns Companies, Inc. Current Report (Form 8-K), filed on Mar. 20, 2008 (hereinafter Bear Stearns Acquisition Agreement).

24. Ibid. at §§ 6.10 and 8.1.

25. Ibid. at § 6.11.

26. For details of the Dynegy option and the failed combination of Enron and Dynegy. See Bethany McLean and Peter Elkind, *Smartest Guys in the Room: The Amazing Rise and Scandalous Fall of Enron* (2003).

27. Bear Stearns Acquisition Agreement, § 6.11.

28. See Stock Option Agreement by and between The Bear Stearns Companies, Inc. and JP Morgan Chase & Co., dated Mar. 16, 2008, at 1, filed as an exhibit to The Bear Stearns Companies, Inc. Current Report (Form 8-K), filed on Mar. 20, 2008.

29. *QVC Network Inc. v. Paramount Commc'n Inc.*, 637 A.2d 34 (Del. 1993).

30. Del. Gen. Corp. Law § 262 (2009).

31. Bear Stearns Acquisition Agreement.

32. Landon Thomas Jr. and Eric Dash, "At Bear Stearns, Meet the New Boss," *New York Times*, Mar. 20, 2008.

33. See David A. Skeel Jr., "Governance in the Ruin," 122 *Harvard Law Review* 696, 737 n. 155 (2008). See also Cohan, *House of Cards*, 103–108.

34. Bear Stearns Acquisition Agreement, § 8.1.

35. Ibid. See also Guarantee from JP Morgan Chase & Co., dated Mar. 16, 2008, filed as an exhibit to The Bear Stearns Companies, Inc. Current Report (Form 8-K), at §§ 1,2, and 3, filed on Mar. 20, 2008.

36. See Andrew Ross Sorkin, "JPMorgan in Negotiations to Raise Bear Stearns Bid," *New York Times*, Mar. 24, 2008, A1.

37. See Kelly, "Bear Stearns Neared Collapse Twice," 18.

38. Share Exchange Agreement by and between The Bear Stearns Companies, Inc. and JP Morgan Chase & Co., dated Mar. 24, 2008, 1–2, filed as an exhibit to The Bear Stearns Companies, Inc. Current Report (Form 8-K), filed on Mar. 24, 2008.

39. New York Stock Exchange, Listed Company Manual, §§312.01, 312.05 (2009).

40. JP Morgan Chase & Co., et al. (Schedule 13D), The Bear Stearns Companies, Inc., filed on Apr. 3, 2008.

41. *Omnicare, Inc. v. NCS Healthcare, Inc.*, 818 A.2d 914 (Del. 2003).

42. Ibid., 936.

43. *Orman v. Cullman*, 2004 Del. Ch. LEXIS 150 (Del. Ch. 2004).

44. *Optima Int'l of Miami v. WCI Steel, Inc.*, C.A. No. 3833-VCL (Del. Ch. June 27, 2008).

45. See generally The Bear Stearns Companies Inc. Current Report (Form 8-K), filed on Mar. 24, 2008.

46. Kate Kelly, "Credit Crisis: Market Bounces: Bear Director Sells His Stock," *Wall Street Journal*, Apr. 2, 2008, C2.

47. See Motion for Temporary Restraining Order, *In re Bear Stearns Co. Inc. S'holder Litig.*, Civil Action 3643-VCP (Del. Ch. Mar. 25, 2008).

48. *Schnell v. Chris-Craft Indus., Inc.*, 285 A.2d 437 (Del. 1971).

49. Ibid., 439.

50. *Blasius Indus., Inc. v. Atlas Corp.*, 564 A.2d 651 (Del. Ch. 1988).

51. Ibid., 661–662.

52. *Commonwealth Assoc. v. Providence Health Care, Inc.*, 1993 WL 432779 (Del. Ch. 1993).

53. The case applying Blasius to a vote on a takeover was *State of Wisconsin Inv't Bd. v. Peerless Sys. Corp.*, No. 17637, 2000 Del. Ch. LEXIS 170 (Del. Ch. Dec. 4, 2000). In contrast, Vice Chancellor Strine in *Mercier et al. v. Inter-Tel, Inc.*, 929 A.2d 786, 808–809 (Del. Ch. 2007), only applied the *Blasius* doctrine as an alternative holding, while Vice Chancellor Lamb held in *In re Mony Group* that "when the matter to be voted on does not touch on issues of directorial control, courts will apply the exacting Blasius standard sparingly, and only in circumstances in which self-interested or faithless fiduciaries act to deprive stockholders of a full and fair opportunity to participate in the matter and to thwart what appears to be the will of a majority of the stockholders." *In re MONY Group, Inc.*, 853 A.2d 661, 674 (Del. Ch. 2004).

54. *Paramount Commc'n v. QVC Network*, 637 A.2d 34, at 48 (Del. 1994).

55. *Revlon, Inc. v. MacAndrews & Forbes Holdings, Inc.*, 506 A.2d 173 (Del. 1985).

56. *McWane Cast Iron Pipe Corp. v. McDowell-Wellman Eng'g Co.*, 263 A.2d 281 (Del. 1970).

57. *In re Bear Stearns Co. S'holder Litig.*, C.A. No. 3643-VCP, 2008 WL 959992, at *6 (Del.Ch., Apr. 9, 2008).

58. See Marcel Kahan and Edward B. Rock, "How to Prevent Hard Cases from-Making Bad Law: Bear Stearns, Delaware and the Strategic Use of Comity" 58 *Emory Law Journal* 714 (2009).

59. *In re Bear Stearns Litigation*, 600780/08 (N.Y. S. Ct. Dec. 4, 2008).

60. For a discussion of this variability, see Sean Griffith and Myron T. Steele, "On Corporate Federalism: Threatening the Thaumatrope," 61 *Business Law* 1 (2005).

61. See Kate Kelly, "Bear CEO's Handling of Crisis Raises Issues," *Wall Street Journal*, Nov. 1, 2007.

62. See Stephen Labaton, "S.E.C. Concedes Oversight Flaws Fueled Collapse," *New York Times*, Sept. 26, 2008. See also Securities and Exchange Commission, Chairman Cox Announces End of Consolidated Supervised Entities Program (Sept. 26, 2008).

Chapter 7: Jana Partners, Children's Investment Fund, and Hedge Fund Activist Investing

1. For one of the numerous optimistic views at the time, see, e.g., Gary E. Siegel, "In Brief: NABE: U.S. Will Come Close, but Avoid Recession," *Bond Buyer* (Feb. 26, 2008), 4.

2. Some activist shareholders also claim that the executive compensation problem was a driving cause of the financial crisis. See, e.g., Robert Kropp, "Executive Pay Comes under Fire from Activist Shareholders for Contributing to Financial Crisis," *Institutional Shareowner*, Oct. 28, 2008.

3. David Ellis, "Mortgage Mess CEOs Defend Pay," *CNN Money*, Mar. 7, 2008.

4. See "In Defence of the Indefensible, Is Showering the Boss with Perks Good for Shareholders?" *Economist*, Dec. 2, 2004. For an argument that perks encourage less employee saving and, therefore, decreased employee shirking due to a need to obtain later salary, see M. Todd Henderson and James C. Spindler, "Corporate Heroin: A Defense of Perks, Executive Loans, and Conspicuous Consumption," 93 *Georgetown Law Journal* 1885 (2005).

5. See Geraldine Fabrikant, "A Family Affair at Adelphia Communications," *New York Times*, Apr. 1, 2002.

6. Calculated using adjusted stock price from Jan. 1, 2007 to Dec. 31, 2008.

7. Salary information calculated from Ford Motor Co. Definitive Proxy Statement (Schedule 14A), for years 2001–2006.

8. See Bernard S. Black and John C. Coffee Jr., "Hail Britannia? Institutional Investor Behavior under Limited Regulation," 82 *Michigan Law Review* 1997 (1994).

9. See Marc Lifsher, "At CalPERS, Change in Style, Not Focus," *Los Angeles Times*, Jul. 25, 2005, C1.

10. See Joe Nocera, "From Raider to Activist, but Still Icahn," *New York Times*, Feb. 3, 2007, C1.

11. FactSet SharkWatch Database.

12. Ibid.

13. See Deepak Gopinath, "Hedge-Fund Rabble-Rouser," *Bloomberg Markets* (Oct. 2005). In another juicy letter, Loeb wrote in June 2006 upon Third Point taking a 9.5 percent position in Nabi Biopharmaceuticals, that "you [management] hide your heads in the nearest warm aperture in an apparent 'ostrich defense' and ignore your shareholders (the top three now owning over 28 percent of your shares in aggregate) in the hope that the Company's owners will go away before your next annual meeting." See Third Point LLC, Amendment No. 2, Letter Attached (Schedule 13D), Nabi Biopharmaceuticals, Inc., filed on June 15, 2006.

14. Alon Brav et al., "Hedge Fund Activism, Corporate Governance, and Firm Performance," 63 Journal of Finance 1729, 5 (forthcoming draft dated May 2008).

15. Ibid., 16.

16. FactSet SharkWatch Database.

17. Brav, "Hedge Fund Activism," 5.

18. Ibid., 3.

19. The results of these studies generally indicate that corporations that have been the target of activist hedge funds experienced higher stock returns and increases in firm operating performance than comparable control firms in the study. The studies identified several factors contributing to excess returns, including divestiture of unnecessary assets, reduction of excess cash, and changes in corporate governance. See inter alia Christopher Clifford, "Value Creation or Destruction? Hedge Funds as Shareholder Activists" (draft dated June 11, 2007); Nicole Boyson and Robert M. Moradian, "Hedge Funds as Shareholder Activists from 1994–2005" (draft dated July 31, 2007); April Klein and Emanual Zur, "Entrepreneurial Shareholder Activism: Hedge Funds and Other Private Investors" (draft dated June 24, 2008).

20. See Brav, "Hedge Fund Activism," 31.

21. Barclay Hedge, Event Driven Hedge Fund—Assets under Management.

22. Brav, "Hedge Fund Activism," 4.

23. See, e.g., Iman Anabtawi and Lynn A. Stout, "Fiduciary Duties for Activist Shareholders," 60 *Stanford Law Review* 1255 (2008). For a more skeptical view of these proposals, see Paul Rose, *Regulating Shareholder Influence* (draft dated March 2009).

24. *Portnoy v. Cryo-Cell Int'l, Inc.*, 940 A.2d 43 (Del. Ch. 2008).

25. Shareholders who are passive investors can elect to file a Schedule 13G instead of a Schedule 13D. The Schedule 13G requires disclosure of significantly less information and does not need to be as frequently updated as a 13D filing. However, the federal securities laws do not permit activist conduct until the shareholder converts to a Schedule 13D filing. Sometimes an activist investor will file a Schedule 13G but then still engages in activist activities. Rumors of an SEC crackdown on this practice have been circulating for years now, although no such thing has occurred.

26. If the buyer acquires more than 10 percent of the issuer, it will also be subject to the short-swing profit rules under Section 16 of the Exchange Act and required to report any sales or acquisitions of securities within two business days. Section 16(b) of the Securities Exchange Act of 1934 penalizes so-called short-swing profits made by insiders and others beneficially owning more than 10 percent of any company's stock. Under §16(b), short-swing profits are profits from any purchase and sale, or any sale and purchase occurring within a six-month period. An example would be a 10 percent owner purchasing Company X stock in month 1 and then selling in month 5. The penalty for such behavior is complete disgorgement of the profit from the transaction, payable to the issuer. This is an objective, strict liability scheme intended to prevent insiders from trading on and profiting from inside information. The requirements of Section 16 are probably one reason that hedge fund shareholder activists generally prefer to hold less than a 10 percent share interest in their targets.

27. Factset SharkWatch Database (as of Feb. 17, 2009).

28. See Richard Teitelbaum, "Icahn Ally Jana's Activism Loses Its Punch as Profit Run Ends," Bloomberg.com, Oct 24, 2009.

29. See Jana Partners, LLC (Schedule 13D), CNET Networks, Inc., filed on Jan. 7, 2008. The facts of Jana's investment set forth here are drawn from *Jana Master Fund, LTD v. CNET Networks, Inc.*, 954 A.2d 335 (Del. Ch. 2008).

30. Jana could obtain full control because there was a flaw in CNET's corporate documents. CNET's lawyers placed the requirements for a staggered board in CNET's bylaws, not in the company's certificate of incorporation. If, instead,

these provisions had been in the company's certificate of incorporation, Jana would not have been able to make this amendment proposal. Under Delaware law, only the board can propose amendments to the certificate, but shareholders can propose amendments to the bylaws. The bylaws provided that they could be amended by 66.67 percent of the shares entitled to vote at any shareholder meeting. Thus, by taking advantage of this failure, Jana could sidestep the requirements of the staggered board. Once again, the importance of getting the legal drafting right was emphasized to CNET's detriment.

31. *Jana Master Fund, LTD*, 954 A.2d 335, at 337-338.

32. Ibid., 346.

33. Henry Blodget, "How to Save CNET," *AlleyInsider*, Oct. 3, 2007, available at www.alleyinsider.com/2007/10/how-to-save-cne.html.

34. See Merissa Marr and Kevin J. Delaney, "CBS to Acquire CNET for $1.8 Billion," *Wall Street Journal*, May 16, 2008, B7.

35. See Morgan Stanley Current Report (Form 8-K), filed on Sept. 22, 2008; F. Mark Reuter, "Perils of Ambiguous Advance Notice Provisions," *Emerging Issues* 2581 (Jul. 19, 2008).

36. See Heather Timmons, "A Hedge Fund and Its Nonprofit Twin," *New York Times*, June 26, 2008, 3.

37. See Julia Werdigier, "Fight Seen for ABN; Stock Soars," *New York Times*, Apr. 17, 2007.

38. The facts of the Children's investment in CSX are drawn primarily from *CSX Corp. v. Children's Inv. Fund Mgmt.*, 562 F.Supp.2d 511, 523–535 (2008).

39. Alex Roth and Tamara Audi, "Historic Greenbrier under Cloud," *Wall Street Journal*, Jan 3, 2009.

40. See Michael J. de la Merced, "Hedge Funds Propose CSX Directors, Starting Proxy Battle," *New York Times*, Dec. 20, 2007, C2.

41. 17 C.F.R. § 240.13(d)-5(b)(1).

42. CSX Corp., 562 F.Supp. at 570.

43. Ibid. at 573–574.

44. For details on the meeting, see Michael de la Merced, "A Hedge Fund Struggle for CSX Is Left in Limbo," *New York Times*, June 26, 2008.

45. See "RiskMetrics Group–ISS Governance Services (ISS) Recommends CSX Shareholders Elect Four TCI/3G Board Nominees," *PR-Inside*, June 18, 2008.

46. CSX Press Release, "CSX Invites Two New Members to Join Immediately" (Sept. 16, 2008).

47. See *CSX Corp. v. Children's Inv. Fund Mgmt.*, No. 08-2899-cv (2nd Cir. 2008) (Summary Order).

48. See Michael de la Merced, "Economic Climate Hampers Activist Investors," *New York Times*, Mar. 26, 2009.

49. See "2008 Hedge Fund Performance Numbers: December & Year-End," *Market Folly*, Jan. 20, 2009. Available at www.marketfolly.com/2009/01/2008-hedge-fund-performance-numbers.html.

50. See Lauren Coleman-Lochner, "Ackman Says Investors Can Exit Target Fund in March," Bloomberg.com, Feb 9, 2009.

51. See "Hedge Fund Closures in 2008," *Market Folly*, Mar. 24, 2009. Available at www.marketfolly.com/search?q=jana+partners.

52. Factset SharkWatch Database.

53. See Robert Daines, et al., "Rating the Ratings: How Good Are Commercial Governance Ratings?" (Draft dated February 10, 2009).

54. See "FSA Proposes Greater Disclosure of 'Contracts for Difference,'" FSA/PN/114/2007, Nov. 12, 2007.

Chapter 8: Microsoft, InBev, and the Return of the Hostile Takeover

1. FactSet Mergermetrics Database.

2. Ibid.

3. Ibid.

4. Ibid. The numbers are 67 percent, 66 percent, and 68 percent, respectively.

5. Ibid. (Figures as of February 10, 2009).

6. See Lucian Bebchuk et al., "The Powerful Antitakeover Force of Staggered Boards: Theory, Evidence, and Policy," 54 *Stanford Law Review* 887 (2002).

7. See David Marcus, "Manifest Destiny," TheDeal.com, Nov. 7, 2008.

8. For a discussion of this new type of strategic hostile, see Peter D. Lyons, "Unsolicited, but Welcome," *Daily Deal*, July 25, 2006.

9. Microsoft Corporation, Press Release, "Microsoft Proposes Acquisition of Yahoo! for $31 per Share" (Feb. 1, 2008).

10. FactSet SharkWatch Database (figures as of February 7, 2009).

11. See Megan Davies, "Yahoo Has a Poison Pill at Disposal," Reuters, Feb. 2, 2008.

12. Ibid.

13. See Amended Bylaws of Registrant, Yahoo!, Inc. Current Report (Form 8-K), ex. 3.1, filed on July 27, 2007.

14. FactSet, SharkWatch Database (through 2008).

15. See Robert Guth et al., "Yahoo's Rejection Pressures Microsoft to Mull a New Bid," *Wall Street Journal*, Feb. 11, 2008, B1.

16. See Yahoo! Inc. Press Release, "Yahoo! Extends Deadline for Nominating Directors to Board" (Mar. 5, 2008).

17. Delaware law requires that a company hold its annual meeting within 13 months of the last one. See Del. Gen. Corp. Law § 211(c) (2008). So, Yahoo was required to hold its annual meeting by July 12, 2008. Microsoft chose not to sue for a violation of this law at the time. The reasons were probably twofold. First, it is unclear under the governing Delaware law about whether a shareholder could sue before that date. A target can thus typically obtain a few extra months advantaging themselves of this ambiguity in the statute. Second, the cost of suing on a one-month postponement probably wasn't worth the cost, given Microsoft's later hesitance about even proceeding with a proxy contest. Yahoo's lawyers leveraged this uncertainty to buy more time for Yahoo.

18. See Miguel Helft, "Yahoo Celebrates (for Now)," *New York Times*, May 5, 2008, 1.

19. See Eric Schonfeld, "Does Ballmer Need to Go," TechCrunch, May 4, 2008. Available at www.techcrunch.com/2008/05/04/does-ballmer-need-to-go/.

20. "Icahn Says Yahoo 'Completely Botched' Microsoft Talks," *New York Times* Dealbook, May 15, 2008.

21. See Joann Lublin and Jessica Vascellaro, "Yahoo Nears Clearing Biondi and Chapple to Join Board," *Wall Street Journal*, Aug. 13, 2008, B3.

22. Holden Frith et al., "Yahoo! Admits It Is Now Open to New Microsoft Bid," TimesOnline.co.uk, Nov. 6, 2008.

23. See Peter Whoriskey, "Yahoo Founder, CEO Yang Steps Down," *Washington Post*, Nov. 18, 2008, D1.

24. See "InBev's Offer for Anheuser-Busch: The Letter," *New York Times* Dealbook, June 11, 2008.

25. See Steven M. Davidoff, "A Budweiser Independence Plan," *New York Times* Dealbook, June 12, 2008.

26. Professor John C. Coates IV makes this argument in "Takeover Defenses in the Shadow of the Pill: A Critique of the Scientific Evidence," 79 *Texas Law Review* 271, 286 (2000).

27. Anheuser-Busch Companies, Inc., Press Release, "Anheuser-Busch Rejects InBev Proposal as Financially Inadequate, Not in Best Interests of Shareholders" (June 26, 2008).

28. See Andrew Ross Sorkin, "Chilling a Deal for Bud," *New York Times*, June 17, 2008; Patricia Sellers, "Bud-Weis-Heir August Busch IV Is Rebellious, Risk-Taking—and (Nearly) Ready to Rule the World's Largest Brewer," *Fortune*, Jan. 13, 1997.

29. See InBev S.A., Preliminary Consent Solicitation (Schedule 14A), filed on May 7, 2008.

30. Del. Gen. Corp. Law § 228(c) (2008).

31. Anheuser-Busch Companies, Inc. Definitive Proxy Statement (Schedule 14A), 20, filed on Oct. 6, 2008 (hereinafter Anheuser-Busch Proxy Statement).

32. "Bid May Spark Battle Royale for Anheuser-Busch," *New York Times* Dealbook, June 12, 2008.

33. See Complaint in *Anheuser-Busch Companies, Inc. v. InBev NV/SA*, July 7, 2008. See also David Kiley, "Anheuser Busch Fights for Time," businessweek.com, July 10, 2008.

34. Anheuser-Busch Companies, Inc. Current Report (Form 8-K), filed on June 26, 2008.

35. Del. Gen. Corp. Law §§ 213, 228 (2008).

36. Complaint in *InBev NV/SA v. Anheuser Busch Companies, Inc.*, June 26, 2008.

37. See David Kesmodel and David Luhnow, "Anheuser Courts an Ally in Mexico," *Wall Street Journal*, June 13, 2008, B1.

38. *Shamrock Holdings v. Polaroid Corp.*, 559 A.2d 278 (Del.Ch. 1989). In an earlier case in the battle between Shamrock and Polaroid, the Chancery Court upheld Polaroid's borrowing of $280 million to fund an employee stock ownership plan to which it issued 14 percent of its stock. The court upheld the action despite a pending tender offer by Shamrock and the antitakeover effect of the issuance under Delaware's business combination statute. See *Shamrock Holdings, Inc. v. Polaroid Corp.*, 559 A.2d 257 (Del. Ch. 1989).

39. See Michael J. de la Merced, "Anheuser-Busch Agrees to Be Sold to a Belgian Brewer for $52 Billion," *New York Times*, July 14, 2008.

40. Anheuser-Busch Proxy Statement, 45.

41. Lucian Arye Bebchuk et al., "The Powerful Antitakeover Force of Staggered Boards: Theory, Evidence, and Policy," 891.

42. Roche Holdings, A.G., Press Release, "Roche Says Offer for Ventana Medical Systems, Inc. Is Full and Fair" (July 11, 2007). See also Steven M. Davidoff, "It Only Takes One Flaw: Ventana and Kellwood," M&A Law Prof, Nov. 14, 2007, available at http://lawprofessors.typepad.com/mergers/2007/11/it-only-takes-o.html.

43. See, e.g., Charles M. Foster Jr. et al., "The Shareholder Wealth Effects of Pennsylvania Fourth Generation Antitakeover Law," 32 *American Business Law Journal* 399 (1995).

44. Factset Mergermetrics Database (excluding 2007 and as of February 7, 2009).

45. *Revlon, Inc. v. MacAndrews & Forbes Holdings, Inc.*, 506 A.2d 173 (Del. 1986).

46. Ibid., 184.

47. *City Capital Assocs. Ltd. P'ship v. Interco.*, 551 A.2d 787, 800 (Del. Ch. 1988).

48. For another 1988 case where the Chancery Court ordered that a target take no further steps to implement a poison pill, see *Grand Metro. Pub. Ltd. Co. v. Pillsbury Co.*, 558 A.2d 1049, 1061–1062 (Del. Ch. 1988).

49. See, e.g., *Weinberger v. UOP, Inc.*, 457 A.2d 701, 712 (Del. 1983).

50. *Unocal Corp. v. Mesa Petroleum Corp.*, 493 A.2d 946 (Del. 1985).

51. T. Boone Pickens, *The Luckiest Guy in the World*, (2000), 236.

52. *Unocal Corp.*, 493 A.2d at 949.

53. *Unitrin, Inc. v. American General Corp.*, 651 A.2d 1361 (Del. 1995)

54. Ibid., 1367.

55. Ibid., 1390.

56. Ibid., 1389.

57. See Robert B. Thompson and D. Gordon Smith, "Towards a New Theory of the Shareholder Role: 'Sacred Space' in Corporate Takeovers," 80 *Texas Law Review* 261, 284–286 (2001).

58. These cases are: *Omnicare v. NCS Healthcare, Inc.*, 818 A.2d 914 (Del. 2003); *Chesapeake Corp. v. Shore*, 771 A.2d 293 (Del. Ch. 2000); *Mentor Graphics Corp. v. Quickturn Design Systems, Inc.*, 728 A.2d 25 (Del. Ch. 1998); *Carmody v. Toll Bros., Inc.*, 723 A.2d 1180 (Del. Ch. 1998).

59. *Mentor Graphics*, 728 A.2d 25; *Carmody*, 723 A.2d 1180. A no-hand poison pill is one that contains "provisions…[which] suspend, limit or eliminate the board's power to redeem the poison pill after a majority of the board has been replaced." Peter V. Letsou, "Are Dead Hand (and No Hand) Poison Pills Really Dead?" 68 *University of Cincinnati Law Review* 1101, 1101 (2000). The effect of these limitations is to bar, for this measured period of time, a bidder's acquisition of corporate control after a successful proxy contest by the bidder to obtain control of the target board. The Delaware Chancery Court had also previously struck down a dead-hand poison pill mainly on statutory grounds, although it also found the provision disproportionate under *Unocal*. See *Carmody*, 723 A.2d 1180. Dead-hand poison pills are a more pernicious form of poison pill and "require redemptions of poison pills to be approved by 'continuing directors' (i.e., directors in office when the poison pill was adopted or directors who were elected with the support of such directors)." Letsou, "Are Dead Hand," 1101.

60. *Chesapeake Corp. v. Shore*, 771 A.2d 293 (Del. Ch. 2000).

61. See Thomson and Smith, "Towards a New Theory," 286.

62. *Blasius Indus., Inc. v. Atlas Corp.*, 564 A.2d 651, 659–661 (Del.Ch.1988).

63. *Williams v. Geier*, 671 A.2d 1368, 1376 (Del.1996) (quoting *Stroud v. Grace*, 606 A.2d 75, 92 (Del.1992)).

64. *MM Companies, Inc. v. Liquid Audio, Inc.*, 813 A.2d 1118 (Del. 2003).

65. Ibid., 1132.

66. *Mercier, et al. v. Inter-Tel*, 929 A.2d 786 (Del. Ch. 2007).

67. Ibid., 814.

68. The other is *Hollinger Int'l, Inc. v. Black*, 844 A.2d 1022, 1089 (Del. Ch. 2004).

69. One study of the proxy voting machinery has found that "[m]anagement is overwhelmingly more likely to win votes by a small margin than to lose by a small margin. The results indicate that, at some point in the voting process, management obtains highly accurate information about the likely voting outcome and, based on that information, acts to influence the vote." See Yair Listokin, "Management Always Wins the Close Ones," *American Law and Economics Review* (forthcoming).

70. See Edward B. Rock, "Saints and Sinners: How Does Delaware Corporate Law Work," 44 *U.C.L.A. Law Review* 1009 (1997)

71. Bebchuk et al., "The Powerful Antitakeover Force of Staggered Boards."

72. Ibid.; Lucian Bebchuk and Alma Cohen, "The Costs of Entrenched Boards," 78 *Journal of Financial Economics* 409 (2005). See also Thomas W. Bates et al., "Board Classification and Managerial Entrenchment: Evidence from the Market for Corporate Control," *Journal of Financial Economics* (forthcoming). This last paper finds that staggered boards can be beneficial and that the conventional wisdom that staggered boards facilitate management entrenchment may be misplaced.

73. Compare Bates et al., "Board Classification," 3 (finding target shareholders of companies with staggered boards receive a larger share of the proportional gains from a merger transaction than companies without a staggered board); Bebchuk et al., "The Powerful Antitakeover Force of Staggered Boards" (premiums are not different but shareholders of companies with staggered boards had a 10 percent difference in returns than companies without a staggered board). A board adoption of a staggered board has also been found to reduce share value. See James Mahoney and Joseph Mahoney, "An Empirical Investigation of the Effect of Corporate Charter Antitakeover Amendments on Stockholder Wealth," 14 *Strategic Management Journal* 17 (1993). Conversely, undoing the staggered board has been found to increase share value. See Re-Jin Gou, "Undoing the Powerful Anti-Takeover Force of Staggered Boards" (draft dated Oct. 10, 2006).

74. See generally "Response Symposium," 55 *Stanford Law Review* 791 (2002).

75. Factset MergerMetrics Database (through May 21 for each year). According to FactSet MergerMetrics, the volume of activity for this period was $18.46 billion in 2009 and $61.65 billion in 2008 for the same period of time.

76. Factset Mergermetrics Database.

77. Jeff Madrick, *How We Got from the First Hostile Takeover to Megamergers, Corporate Raiding, and Scandal* (1987).

78. See James Sterngold, "I.B.M.'s Big Move: The Corporate Culture; Suddenly, the Hostile Takeover Is a Benevolent Act," *New York Times*, June 7, 1995.

Chapter 9: Mars, Pfizer, and the Changing Face of Strategic Deals

1. Dealogic Database.

2. See Dennis K. Berman, "Apollo Makes Huntsman Bid—Equity Firm Tops Offer from Basell; A 'Strategic' Angle," *Wall Street Journal*, July 5, 2007, A10.

3. Andrew Ross Sorkin, "When a Bank Works Both Sides," *New York Times*, Apr. 8, 2007.

4. For a broad overview of these agreements and particular provisions negotiated therein, see Robert E. Spatt and Adam S. Booken, "Social Issues in Selected Recent Mergers and Acquisitions Transactions" (client memo dated Jan. 9, 2009).

5. See Policies for Management of the Feature Animation Businesses, filed as ex. 99.1.3 to the Pixar Current Report (Form 8-K), filed on Jan. 26, 2006.

6. See Dow Jones & Company, Inc. Preliminary Proxy Statement (Schedule 14A), 46–57, filed Sept. 7, 2007.

7. Dealogic Database.

8. See Peter Burrows, *Backfire: Carly Fiorina's High-Stakes Battle for the Soul of Hewlett-Packard* (2003).

9. Carly Fiorina, *Tough Choices: A Memoir* (2007).

10. *Consolidated Edison, Inc. v. Northeast Utilities*, 426 F.3d 524 (2d Cir. 2005).

11. See Agreement and Plan of Merger among Wm. Wrigley Jr. Company, Mars, Inc., New Uno Holdings Corp. and New Uno Acquisition Corp., dated April 28, 2008, exhibit 2.1 to Wm. Wrigley Jr. Co. Current Report (Form 8-K), 54–56, filed on Apr. 30, 2008.

12. See Wm. Wrigley Jr. Co. Current Report (Form 8-K), filed on Apr. 30, 2008. See also Colin Barr, "Buffett's Help Seems Over for Now," *Fortune*, Sept. 24, 2008.

13. These provisions were based on the private equity structure negotiated in the Alliance Data Systems, Inc. and Penn National Gaming, Inc. acquisitions discussed in Chapter 4.

14 See Agreement and Plan of Merger by and among Third Wave Technologies, Inc. Hologic, Inc. and Thunder Tech Corp., dated June 8, 2008, ex. 2.1 to

Hologic, Inc. Current Report (Form 8-K), filed on June 9, 2008; Agreement and Plan of Merger among Brocade Commc'ns Sys., Inc., Falcon Acquisition Sub, Inc., and Foundry Networks, Inc., dated July 21, 2008, ex. 2.1 to Foundry Networks, Inc. Current Report (Form 8-K), filed on July 23, 2008; Agreement and Plan of Merger, Dated as of July 10, 2008, among Ashland Inc., Ashland Sub One, Inc. and Hercules Incorporated, ex. 2.1 to Hercules Inc. Current Report (Form 8-K), filed on July 4, 2008.

15. See i2 press release, dated Dec. 4, 2008; Foundry Networks, Inc. Amendment No. 1 to Definitive Proxy Statement (Schedule 14A), 25–30, filed on Nov. 14, 2008.

16. See Agreement and Plan of Merger among Pfizer Inc., Wagner Acquisition Corp. and Wyeth, dated as of January 25, 2009, ex. 2.1 to Wyeth Current Report (Form 8-K), filed on Jan. 29, 2009.

17. See Agreement and Plan of Merger by and among Merck &Co., Inc., Schering-Plough Corporation, Blue, Inc. and Purple, Inc., dated as of March 8, 2009, ex 2.1 to Schering-Plough Corp. Current Report (Form 8-K), filed on Mar. 11, 2009.

18. See Joint Press Release Issued by Altria Group, Inc. and UST Inc., Oct. 3, 2008, ex. 2.1 to UST, Inc. Current Report (Form 8-K), filed on Oct. 3, 2008.

19. See Answer of Defendants, *Rohm and Haas Co. v. The Dow Chemical Co. and Ramses Acquisition Corp.*, C.A. No. 4309-CC (Del.Ch. Feb. 3, 2009).

20. See Steven M. Davidoff, "Lessons from the Dow-Rohm Battle," *New York Times* DealBook, Mar. 10, 2009.

21. Susanne Craig et al., "The Weekend That Wall Street Died," *Wall Street Journal*, Dec. 29, 2008.

22. The terms of the Constellation and MidAmerican transaction are taken from the Constellation Energy Group, Inc. Current Report (Form 8-K), filed on Sept. 22, 2008; Agreement & Plan of Merger by and among Constellation Energy Group, Inc., MidAmerican Energy Holdings Co., and MEHC Merger Sub Inc., dated Sept. 19, 2008, ex. 2.1 to Constellation Energy Group, Inc. Current Report (Form 8-K), filed on Sept. 22, 2008.

23. David Gauthier-Villars and Rebecca Smith, "EDF Beats Out Buffett in Energy Deal," *Wall Street Journal*, Dec. 18, 2008, B1.

24. Constellation was organized under the laws of Maryland. Maryland has statutorily rejected Delaware's heightened review of takeover transactions. See Maryland C. Corp. & Assoc. § 2.405.1 (2009). MidAmerican no doubt negotiated these extreme lockups aware that it was unlikely to be challenged by a Maryland court under this lower standard of review.

25. Stock Option Agreement by and between Merrill Lynch &Co., Inc. and Bank of America Corp., filed as an exhibit to the Bank of America Corp. Current Report (Form 8-K), §16(b), filed on Sept. 18, 2008.

26. Robin Sidel et al., "WaMu Is Seized, Sold Off to J.P. Morgan, in Largest Failure in U.S. Banking History," *Wall Street Journal*, Sept. 26, 2008.

27. See Peter Lattman, "WaMU Crushes TPG," *Wall Street Journal*, Sept. 27, 2008, B1. See also Investment Agreement between Washington Mutual, Inc. and the Investors Party Hereto, ex. 10.1 to Washington Mutual, Inc. Current Report (Form 8-K), filed on Apr. 11, 2008.

28. Share Exchange Agreement by and between Wachovia Corp. and Wells Fargo &Co., dated Oct. 3, 2008, ex. 2.2 to Wells Fargo &Co. Current Report (Form 8-K), filed on Oct. 9, 2008.

29. KPMG, *Unlocking Shareholder Value: The Keys to Success* (1999), 2.

30. McKinsey &Co., Inc., *Valuation: Measuring and Managing the Value of Companies*, (3rd ed., 2000), 114–115.

31. See Robert F. Bruner, "Does M&A Pay? A Survey of Evidence for the Decision-Maker," 12 *Journal of Applied Finance* 48 (2002).

32. Although Bruner in his study "Does M&A Pay? A Survey of Evidence for the Decision-Maker" finds that takeovers can pay, there are real issues with these studies that make them only partly reliable. The bulk of these studies use time series analysis to measure gains and losses. Essentially, time series analysis analyzes the buyer and target stock prices during a period around the announcement of the transaction. The decline or gain from the acquisition transaction is measured by comparing the decline or gain in the stock prices at the time with a market measure. But this assumes that the market is strongly efficient and publicly reflects all of the public and private information available concerning the transaction. As we know, much of the company information given to the buyer by the target is confidential; the market does not know this information. And despite rules set by the SEC, much of this information is not disclosed at or after the time of the acquisition. Moreover, the public typically does not know the buyer's specific plans for the target at this time. The result is that these studies are based on a fundamental assumption—the market is calculating perfectly the gain or loss from the acquisition—that is almost surely not true.

Longer-term studies attempt to get around this problem by looking at accounting metrics or comparing returns with comparable companies. But the problem with these studies is that too much noise enters into the picture—events happen that change the comparison and distort it. Ultimately, these studies fail because they don't look to how the buyer would have done without the acquisition. The buyer may fare poorly in these studies but would have done worse had it not made the acquisition. Think where AOL would be without having bought Time Warner. From that perspective, AOL's acquisition was brilliant. It didn't work out as well for Time Warner.

33. See KKR &Co. LP Registration Statement (Form S-1), 133, filed on July 3, 2007; Blackstone Group LP Registration Statement (Form S-1), 5, filed on Mar. 22, 2007.

34. *Paramount Comm., Inc. v. Time Inc.*, 571 A.2d 1140 (Del. 1989).

35. *Paramount Comm., Inc. v. QVC Network Inc.*, 637 A.2d 34 (Del. 1994).

36. John C. Coates IV and Guhan Subramanian, "A Buy-Side Model of M & A Lockups: Theory and Evidence," 53 *Stanford Law Review* 307, 310 (2000).

37. Ibid., 391–392.

38. Ibid., 324.

39. *Brazen v. Bell Atlantic*, 695 A.2d 43 (Del. 1997).

40. *In re IXC Comm. Inc. S'holder Litig.*, 1999 WL 1009174, at *10 (Del. Ch. Oct. 27, 1999).

41. But see *Energy Partners v. Stone Energy*, CA No. 2402-N (Del. Ch. Oct. 11, 2006).

42. *Omnicare v. NCS Healthcare, Inc.*, 818 A.2d 914, 930–931 (Del. 2003).

43. *In re Toys "R" Us, Inc. S'holder Litig*, 877 A.2d 975, 1016 n. 66 (Del. Ch. 2005). For a further fleshing out of Vice Chancellor Strine's approach, see Leo E. Strine Jr., "Categorical Confusion: Deal Protection Measures in Stock for Stock Merger Agreements," 56 *Business Law* 919, 939 (2001).

44. Coates and Subramanian, "A Buy-Side Model," 310.

45. Ibid., 389.

46. Thomas W. Bates and Michael L. Lemmon, "Breaking Up Is Hard to Do? An Analysis of Termination Fee Provisions and Merger Outcomes," 69 *Journal of Financial Economics* 469, 470 (2003); Micah S. Officer, "Termination Fees in Mergers and Acquisitions," 69 *Journal of Financial Economics* 431, 442 (2003). Coates and Subramanian ("A Buy-Side Model," 331) have argued that this increase was the result of the Delaware courts rulings in *QVC* and *Brazen*.

47. *Omnicare v. NCS Healthcare, Inc.*, 818 A.2d 914 (Del. 2003).

48. *Orman v. Cullman*, 2004 WL 2348395 (Del. Ch. Oct 20, 2004).

49. Transcript of Oral Argument on Plaintiffs' Motion for Preliminary Injunction and Ruling of the Court at 117–144, *Optima Int'l of Miami, Inc. v. WCI Steel, Inc.*, C.A. No. 3833-VCL (Del. Ch. June 27, 2008).

50. Ibid., 127.

51. Factset Mergermetrics Database (all friendly public acquisitions with a transaction value greater than $100 million for which an agreement was available).

52. Coates and Subramanian, "A Buy-Side Model," 335.

53. Factset Mergermetrics Database.

54. The Delaware Supreme Court recently confirmed that Revlon duties only come into effect once the company decides to engage in a change of control transaction. See *Ryan v. Lyondell Chemical Co.*, No. 401, 2008 (Del. Mar. 25, 2009).

55. *In re Pennaco Energy, Inc. S'holders Litig.*, 787 A.2d 691, 702–707 (Del. Ch. 2001).

56. *In re MONY Group S'holder Litig.*, 852 A.2d 9, 18–24 (Del. Ch. 2004).

57. *In re Toys "R" Us, Inc. S'holder Litig.*, 877 A.2d 975 (Del. Ch. 2005).

58. Ibid., 1014–1015.

59. See Guhan Subramanian, "Go-Shops vs. No-Shops in Private Equity Deals: Evidence and Implications," 63 *Business Law* 729, 730–731 (2008). See also Christina M. Sautter, "Shopping during Extended Store Hours: From No Shops to Go-Shops—the Development, Effectiveness, and Implications of Go-Shop Provisions in Change of Control Transactions," 73 *Brooklyn Law Review* 525 (2008).

60. *In re Netsmart Tech. Inc. S'holders Litig.*, 924 A.2d 171 (Del. Ch. 2007).

61. See Louise Story and Julie Creswell, "Love Was Blind," *New York Times*, Feb. 8, 2009; Dan Fitzpatrick et al., "In Merrill Deal, U.S. Played Hardball," *Wall Street Journal*, Feb. 5, 2009.

62. Factset Mergermetrics Database.

63. Ibid.

64. See Adam H. Golden, "The CVR Alternative," *The Deal*, Oct. 17, 2008.

Chapter 10: AIG, Citigroup, Fannie Mae, Freddie Mac, Lehman, and Government by Deal

1. This is aptly illustrated by Robert F. Bruner and Sean D. Carr in their book *The Panic of 1907: Lessons Learned from the Market's Perfect Storm* (2007).

2. See Louise Story, "Regulators Seize Mortgage Lender," *New York Times*, July 12, 2008; E. Scott Reckard and Andrea Chang, "Banks Hit by Fallout from the Crisis at IndyMac," *Los Angeles Times*, July 15, 2008.

3. See James R. Hagerty and Serena Ng, "Banks Hit as Fannie Mae, Freddie Mac Get Downgrade," *Wall Street Journal*, Aug. 23, 2008, A1.

4. Ibid.

5. See Gretchen Morgenson and Charles Duhigg, "Mortgage Giant Overstated the Size of Its Capital Base," *New York Times*, Sept. 6, 2008, A1; Charles Duhigg et al., "As Crisis Grew, a Few Options Shrank to One," *New York Times*, Sept. 8, 2008, A1.

6. See James R. Hagerty, "Regulator Plans to Bar Big Severance," *Wall Street Journal*, Sept. 15, 2008, A19.

7. See Federal National Mortgage Association, Current Report (Form 8-K), filed on Sept. 11, 2008 (hereinafter FNMA Form 8-K); Federal Home Loan Mortgage Corp., Current Report (Form 8-K), filed on Sept. 11, 2008 (hereinafter FHLM Form 8-K). These would later be increased to $200 billion each. See Statement by Secretary Tim Geithner on Treasury's Commitment to Fannie Mae and Freddie Mac, Feb. 18, 2009.

8. The terms of this investment are set forth on the Treasury Preferred Stock Purchase Agreement Fact Sheet (Sept. 7, 2008) (hereinafter Preferred Stock Purchase Agreement Fact Sheet).

9. See FNMA Form 8-K; FHLM Form 8-K.

10. Fannie Mae's total mortgage portfolio in the consolidated balance sheets as of December 31, 2007, was $2,832 billion with an additional $206.5 billion for other guaranties not recorded in the consolidated balance sheets. Federal National Mortgage Association Annual Report (Form 10-K), filed on Feb. 27, 2008. Freddie Mac's total mortgage portfolio as of December 31, 2007, was $2,102,676 million. Federal Home Loan Mortgage Association Annual Report, dated Feb. 28, 2008. The combined mortgage portfolios and guarantees of both GSEs amounted to $5,141,969 million. See also James R. Hagerty et al., "U.S. Seizes Mortgage Giants, Government Ousts CEOs of Fannie Mae, Freddie Mac; Promises Up to $200 Billion in Capital," *Wall Street Journal*, Sept. 8, 2008, A1.

11. See David M. Dickson and David R. Sands, "Overseas Debt Drives Bail-out of Fannie Mae, Freddie Mac; Some U.S. Banks Take Big Loss," *Washington Times*, Sept. 9, 2008, A1.

12. For a more detailed look at the possible reasons for the government's failure to fully nationalize the two GSEs, see Steven M. Davidoff and David Zaring, "Regulation by Deal: The Government's Response to the Financial Crisis" *Administrative Law Review* (Forthcoming).

13. See Federal National Mortgage Association Quarterly Report (Form 10-Q), filed on August 8, 2008; Federal Home Loan Mortgage Corp Quarterly Report (Form 10-Q), filed on August 6, 2008.

14. The figure is as of September 20, 2008. See Federal National Mortgage Association Quarterly Report (Form 10-Q), filed on Nov. 10, 2008; Federal Home Loan Mortgage Corp. Quarterly Report (Form 10-Q), filed on Nov. 14, 2008.

15. See Preferred Stock Purchase Agreement Fact Sheet.

16. See Press Release, Henry M. Paulson Jr., "Treasury and Federal Housing Finance Agency Action to Protect Financial Markets and Taxpayers" (Sept. 7, 2008).

17. See Press Release, Federal Reserve Bank (Sept. 16, 2008).

18. Lehman Brothers intended to spin off $25 billion to $30 billion of its commercial real estate portfolio into a separate publicly traded company, Real Estate Investments Global, in the first quarter of 2009. See Lehman Brothers Holdings, Inc. Current Report (Form 8-K), filed on Sept. 10, 2008.

19. See Randall Smith, "Lehman's Revamp Plan Draws Doubters; Analysts Wonder If Fixes Can Occur in Time to Be of Help," *Wall Street Journal*, Sept. 11, 2008, C1.

20. See Carrick Mollenkamp et al., "The Two Faces of Lehman's Fall; Private Talks of Raising Capital Belied Firm's Public Optimism," *Wall Street Journal*, Oct. 6, 2008, A1. On September 11, JPMorgan demanded from Lehman Brothers $5 billion in additional collateral to cover lending positions that JPMorgan's clients had with Lehman Brothers.

21. See Merrill Lynch &Co., Inc. Definitive Proxy Statement (Schedule Form 14A), 49–50, filed on Nov. 3, 2008. See also Jonathan Keehner and Bradley Keoun, "Bank of America Said to Reach $44 Billion Deal to Buy Merrill," Bloomberg, Sept. 14, 2008.

22. See Merrill Lynch & Co., Inc. Current Report (Form 8-K), filed on Sept. 15, 2008.

23. See Carrick Mollenkamp et al., "Crisis on Wall Street as Lehman Totters, Merrill Is Sold, AIG Seeks to Raise Cash; Federal Reserve Will Expand Its Lending Arsenal in a Bid to Calm Markets; Moves Cap a Momentous Weekend for American Finance," *Wall Street Journal*, Sept. 15, 2008, A1; "Lehman Brothers Files for Chapter 11 Bankruptcy Protection," Associated Press, Sept. 15, 2008; Ben White et al., "The Street after Lehman Brothers," *New York Times*, Sept. 16, 2008, 1.

24. See Jeffrey McCracken et al., "Lehman in New Talks to Sell Assets to Barclays," *Wall Street Journal*, Sept. 16, 2008, C1.

25. See Jeffrey McCracken, "Lehman's Chaotic Bankruptcy Filing Destroyed Billions in Value," *Wall Street Journal*, Dec. 29, 2008.

26. McCracken et al., "Lehman in New Talks."

27. See Michael J. de la Merced et al., "As Goldman and Morgan Shift, a Wall St. Era Ends," *New York Times*, Sept. 21, 2008, A1.

28. As of September 30, 2008, the net unrealized market valuation loss of AIG's London Subsidiary, AIG Financial Products Corp., from super senior credit default swap portfolio amounted to $21.726 billion. American International Group, Quarterly Report (Form 10-Q), filed on Nov. 10, 2008 (hereinafter AIG Third Quarter Form 10-Q). See also Jeffrey McCracken et al., "Lehman in New Talks."

29. For a more detailed discussion of the AIG bailout, see William K. Sjostrom, "The AIG Bailout" (draft dated Feb. 23, 2009).

30. See Hugh Son, "AIG Rating Cuts Threaten Funding Quest, Shares Plunge," *Bloomberg*, Sept. 16, 2008.

31. See Matthew Karnitschnig, et al., "AIG Faces Cash Crisis as Stock Dives 61 percent," *Wall Street Journal*, Sept. 16, 2008, A1; Mark Pittman, "Goldman, Merrill Collect Billions after Federal Reserve's AIG Bailout Loans," *Bloomberg*, Sept. 29, 2008

32. See AIG Third Quarter Form 10-Q.

33. See Karnitschnig, "AIG Faces Cash Crisis as Stock Dives 61 Percent."

34. See American International Group, Inc. Quarterly Report (Form 10-Q), filed on Aug. 6, 2008.

35. American International Group, Inc. Current Report (Form 8-K), filed on Sept. 18, 2008. Initially, AIG stated that the government would only take up to a 79.9 percent interest. This led to speculation that a market loan could be arranged. Rumors were that former AIG CEO Hank Greenberg would arrange an alternative that would prevent shareholders from being wiped out. He never did.

36. See American International Group, Inc. Current Report (Form 8-K), filed on Sept. 26, 2008.

37. The details of this loan are set forth in the Credit Agreement by and between American International Group, Inc. and the Federal Reserve Bank of New York, dated Sept. 22, 2008 (hereinafter AIG Credit Agreement), filed as an exhibit to the American International Group, Inc. Current Report (Form 8-K), filed on Sept. 26, 2008.

38. See AIG Credit Trust Facility Agreement, dated Jan. 16, 2009 (released Jan. 22, 2009).

39. See AIG Credit Agreement.

40. NYSE Listed Company Manual §§312.01, 312.05 (2009).

41. See American International Group, Inc., Notice to Shareholders; JPMorgan Chase & Co. Current Report (Form 8-K), filed on Mar. 24, 2008.

42. See AIG Transcript of Court Proceedings in Delaware Chancery Court, dated Nov. 7, 2008. See also Steven M. Davidoff, "Notes from the Maelstrom," *New York Times* DealBook, Sept. 26, 2008.

43. See Joanna Chung, "Former AIG Chief's Alternative Rescue Plan," *Financial Times*, Oct. 13, 2008.

44. See American International Group, Inc. Current Report (Form 8-K), filed on Oct. 30, 2008.

45. See Federal Reserve Bank, Press Release, Nov. 10, 2008.

46. See generally Edmund L. Andrews and Peter Baker, "AIG Planning Huge Bonuses after $170 Billion Bailout," *New York Times*, Mar. 14, 2009; Steven

M. Davidoff, "Seven Sad Truths about AIG," *New York Times* Dealbook, Mar. 17, 2009; Steven M. Davidoff, "Dissecting the AIG Bonus Contract," *New York Times* Dealbook, Mar. 18, 2009.

47. See Wachovia Corporation Current Report (Form 8-K), filed on Sept. 29, 2008.

48. See Wachovia Corporation Current Report (Form 8-K), filed on Oct. 3, 2008 (hereinafter Wachovia Form 8-K).

49. Ibid.

50. See Share Exchange Agreement by and between Wachovia Corporation and Wells Fargo & Co, dated Oct. 3, 2008, filed as an exhibit to the Wachovia Corporation Current Report (Form 8-K), filed on Oct. 9, 2008.

51. See Ibid.

52. For an account of this litigation, see Steven M. Davidoff, "The Mad Legal Dash for Wachovia," *New York Times* DealBook, Oct. 5, 2008.

53. See Francesco Guerrera and James Politi, "Citigroup Pulls Out of Battle for Wachovia," *Financial Times*, Oct. 9, 2008.

54. Wachovia was organized under the laws of North Carolina and so the agreement of Wachovia's board to be acquired was governed by North Carolina law, not Delaware law. A North Carolina court would later deny a motion by Wachovia's stockholders to preliminary enjoin the Wachovia shareholder vote on the acquisition by Wells Fargo. See *Ehrenhaus v. Baker*, 2008 NCBC 20 (N.C. Super. Ct. Dec. 5, 2008). Again showing the preference of courts to stay out of the government's sponsored deal-making, the court stated: "This case does not fit neatly into conventional business judgment rule jurisprudence, which assumes the presence of a free and competitive market to assess the value and merits of a transaction. But other than insisting that he would have stood firm in the eye of what can only be described as a cataclysmic financial storm, Plaintiff offers nothing to suggest that the Board's response to the Hobson's choice before it was unreasonable" (Op. at 124–125).

55. See Morgan Stanley Press Release, Oct. 13, 2008.

56. See Louise Story and Andrew Ross Sorkin, "Morgan Agrees to Revise Terms of Mitsubishi Deal," *New York Times*, Oct. 12, 2008, A1.

57. See Securities Purchase Agreement by and between the Company and Mitsubishi UFJ Financial Group, Inc., dated as of September 29, 2008, and the amendment thereto entered into on October 3, 2008, filed as an exhibit to the Morgan Stanley Current Report (Form 8-K), filed on Oct. 3, 2008.

58. *Bear Stearns Co. v. Jardine Strategic Holdings*, No. 31371187, slip. op. (N.Y. Sup. Ct. June 17, 1988).

59. See Morgan Stanley Press Release, Oct. 13, 2008. See also Story and Sorkin, "Morgan Agrees to Revise Terms."

60. See Jon Hilsenrath, "Paulson, Bernanke Strained for Consensus in Bailout," *Wall Street Journal*, Nov. 10, 2008.

61. Emergency Economic Stabilization Act of 2008, Pub.L. 110-343, Div. A at §3 (Oct. 3, 2008).

62. Ibid.

63. See Mark Landler, "U.S. Investing $250 Billion in Banks," *New York Times*, Oct. 13, 2008.

64. For a history of this phase of the bailout, see Davidoff and Zaring, "Regulation by Deal."

65. See "White House Consulted with Obama Team on Auto Rescue Plans," CNN.com, Dec. 19, 2008.

66. The Fed agreed only to charge an interest rate at the Overnight Index Swap, plus 300 basis points. As of February 3, 2009, the one-month OIS rate was 2.3 percent.

67. The terms of the Citigroup bailout are set forth in Citigroup, Inc. Current Report (Form 8-K), filed on Nov. 26, 2008.

68. See U.S. Treasury press release, "Treasury Releases Guidelines for Targeted Investment Program" (Jan. 2, 2009).

69. See Bank of America, Inc. Current Report (Form 8-K), filed on Jan. 16, 2009; Bank of America, Inc., Current Report (Form 8-K), filed on Jan. 22, 2009. See also Dan Fitzpatrick et al., "In Merrill Deal, U.S. Played Hardball," *Wall Street Journal*, Feb. 6, 2009, A1.

70. See Edmund L. Andrews and Stephen Labaton, "Bailout Plan: $2.5 Trillion and a Strong U.S. Hand," *New York Times*, Feb. 10, 2009.

Chapter 11: Restructuring Takeovers

1. See 17 C.F.R. §240.14e-1 (Rule 14e-1(a)).

2. The all-holders best price rule is embodied in 17 C.F.R. §240.14d-10 (Rule 14d-10).

3. See, e.g., Del. Gen. Corp. L. § 262 (2009).

4. Factset Mergermetrics Database. See also Jim Mallea, "M&A Year-End Review," Factset Mergers, Jan. 23, 2009.

5. Amendments to the Tender Offer Best-Price Rule, Exchange Act Release No. 34-54684 (Dec. 8, 2006). For a discussion of these rulings and this bias, see David Marcus, "Tender Returns," *Daily Deal*, Jan. 30, 2006; Jason K. Zachary, "Love Me Tender, Love Me True: Compensating Management and Shareholders under the 'All-Holders/Best-Price Rule,' 31 *Securities Regulation Law Journal* 81 (2003).

6. Regulation of Takeovers and Security Holder Communications, Exchange Act Release No. 42055, [1999–2000 Transfer Binder] Fed. Sec. L. Rep. (CCH) 86,215 (Oct. 22, 1999) (hereinafter M&A Release).

7. Factset Mergermetrics Database.

8. Mallea, "M&A Year-End Review."

9. See Peter D. Lyons, "Unsolicited, but Welcome," *Daily Deal*, July 25, 2006; Steve Lohr and Laurie J. Flynn, "Oracle to Acquire PeopleSoft for $10.3 Billion, Ending Bitter Fight," *New York Times*, Dec. 14, 2004, C1.

10. A significant example is in the case of fairness opinions. Federal securities law mandates disclosure of the analyses underlying a fairness opinion in a merger transaction but not a cash tender offer. There is no compelling reason for this disparity. See Steven M. Davidoff, "Fairness Opinions," 55 *American University Law Review* 1557, 1590–1594 (2006). There are also significant unwarranted timing distinctions in the delivery of information. In a cash tender offer transaction, information is typically published in the tender offer document within 5 to 10 business days. In a merger, however, there is no public disclosure until the definitive proxy statement is mailed to stockholders one to two months later.

11. 17 C.F.R. § 230.14d-10 (2009).

12. 17 C.F.R. § 230.14e-5 (2009). See generally M&A Release, 82,608-12.

13. Adoption of Rule 10b-13 under the Securities Exchange Act of 1934, Exchange Act Release No. 8712, [1969–1970 Transfer Binder] Fed. Sec. L. Rep. (CCH) 77,745, at 83,708 (Oct. 8, 1969) (hereinafter 10b-13 Release).

14. 17 C.F.R. § 230.14d-7 (2009).

15. See Rule 10b-13 Release, 83,708.

16. See 17 C.F.R. § 230.14e-5 (2009).

17. Sandra Betton et al., "The Toehold Puzzle," CEPR Discussion Paper (May 2005), 1.

18. See Jeremy Bulow et al., "Toeholds and Takeovers," 107 *Journal of Political Economy* 427 (1999); Sanford J. Grossman and Oliver D. Hart, "Takeover Bids, the Free-Rider Problem and the Theory of the Corporation," 11 *Bell Journal of Economics* 42–64 (1980).

19. The Panel on Takeovers and Mergers, the City Code on Takeovers and Mergers, at Rule 28 (2006).

20. Guidant Corp. Definitive Proxy Statement (Schedule 14A), 70, filed on Mar. 1, 2006.

21. Gillette Co. Definitive Proxy Statement (Schedule 14A), 41, filed on May 25, 2005.

22. The panel's recommendations were set forth in SEC Advisory Committee on Tender Offers, *Report of Recommendations and Commission Positions* (July 8,

1983), and reprinted in *Tender Offers* (Marc I. Steinberg, ed., 1985), 303–434. In March 1984, the SEC commissioners considered the recommendations; the SEC rejected the sweeping ones, including a prohibition on charter and bylaw amendments that erected "high barriers to change of control." See Statement of John S. R. Shad, Chairman of the Securities and Exchange Commission, before hearings of the House Subcommittee on Telecommunications, Consumer Protection, and Finance Concerning the Recommendation of the SEC Advisory Committee on Tender Offers, reprinted in Exchange Act Tender Offers Advisory Committee Recommendations—SEC Response [1983–1984 Transfer Binder] Fed. Sec. L. Rep. (CCH) 83,511, at 86,681 (March 28, 1984).

23. Del. Gen. Corp. L. § 211(c) (2009).

24. See Steven M. Davidoff, "BEA Systems: Icahn Goes to Delaware," M&A Law Prof, Oct. 29, 2007, available at http://lawprofessors.typepad.com/mergers/2007/10/beas-icahn-goes.html.

25. See web site of Delaware Division of Corporations, http://corp.delaware.gov/. See also Robert Daines, "The Incorporation Choices of IPO Firms," 77 *New York University Law Review* 1559, 1601 (2002).

26. For a recent study finding this preference, see Matthew Cain & Steven M. Davidoff, "Deleware's Competitive Reach: An Empirical analysis of Public Company Merger Agreements" (Draft dated June 11, 2009). See also Theodore Eisenberg and Geoffrey Miller, "Ex Ante Choices of Law and Forum: An Empirical Analysis of Corporate Merger Agreements," 59 *Vanderbilt Law Review* 1975 (2006).

27. See Marcel Kahan and Edward B. Rock, "How to Prevent Hard Cases from Making Bad Law: Bear Stearns, Delaware and the Strategic Use of Comity," 58 *Emory Law Journal* 714 (2009).

28. For a summary of these positions, see Roberta Romano, "The State-Competition Debate in Corporate Law," 8 *Cardozo Law Review* 709, 710–717, 720–725 (1987). See also Frank H. Easterbrook and Daniel R. Fischel, *The Economic Structure of Corporate Law* (1991), 4–8; Lucian A. Bebchuk and Allen Ferrell, "Federalism and Corporate Law: The Race to Protect Managers from Takeovers," 99 *Columbia Law Review* 1168, 1172, 1190–1191 (1999). For an argument that Delaware has won the state competition for public charters and its main competitor is now the federal government, see Mark J. Roe, "Delaware's Competition," 117 *Harvard Law Review* 588 (2003).

29. See Press Release, "North Dakota Governance Council, North Dakota Enacts First Shareholder Friendly Corporation Law" (Apr. 11, 2007).

30. See Faith Stevelman, "Regulatory Competition, Choice of Forum and Delaware's Stake in Corporate Law," 34 *Delaware Journal of Corporate Law* 57 (2009).

31. See *In re Netsmart Tech., Inc., S'holders Litig.*, Del. Ch., C.A. No. 2563 (Del. Ch. Mar. 6, 2007).

32. See Roe, "Delaware's Competition."

33. Ibid. See also Mark J. Roe, "Delaware's Politics," 118 *Harvard Law Review* 2491 (2005).

34. Chancellor Chandler's recent opinion in *In Re Citigroup Inc. Shareholder Derivative Litigation*, C.A. 3338-CC (Del. Ch., Feb. 24, 2009), shows this potential. There Chandler refused to dismiss as a matter of law claims that payments to Charles O. Prince in connection with his termination from Citigroup were not corporate waste.

35. See *Weinberger v. UOP, Inc.*, 457 A. 2d 701 (Del. 1983).

36. *In re Wheelabrator Tech., Inc. S'holders Litig.*, 663 A.2d 1194 (Del. Ch. 1995).

37. The facts about the Landry's buy-out are set forth in Landry's Restaurants, Inc. Amendment No. 7 to Preliminary Proxy Statement (Schedule 14A), filed Jan. 5, 2009, 19–57 (hereinafter Landry's Proxy Statement).

38. Exhibit 99.1 to Landry's Restaurants, Inc. Current Report (Form 8-K), filed Jan. 12, 2009.

39. See Landry's Proxy Statement, 152.

40. See James Politi and Aline van Duyn, "Investors Reject $22bn Move for Cablevision," *Financial Times*, Oct. 24, 2007.

41. See Victor Brudney and Marvin A. Chirelstein, "A Restatement of Corporate Freezeouts," 87 *Yale Law Journal* 1354, 1367 (1978).

42. Guhan Subramanian, "Go-Shops vs. No-Shops in Private Equity Deals: Evidence and Implications," 63 *Business Law* 729, 730–731 (2008).

43. This idea was put forth by Louis Lowenstein in "Management Buyouts," 85 *Columbia Law Review* 730 (1985).

Chapter 12: Deal-Making Beyond a Crisis Age

1. See Ronald J. Gilson, "Value Creation by Business Lawyers: Legal Skills and Asset Pricing," 94 *Yale Law Journal* 239 (1984). For another view on the role of transactional lawyers see George W. Dent, Jr., "Business Lawyers as Enterprise Architects," 64 *Business Lawyer* 279 (2009)

2. The most developed theory of investment banking highlighting the importance of the partnership model is in Alan D. Morrison and William J. Wilhelm, *Investment Banking: Institutions, Politics, and Law* (2007).

3. For a narrative history of the decline of this model, see Jonathan A. Knee, *The Accidental Investment Banker* (2006).

4. Thomson Reuters Deals Intelligence.

About the Author

Steven M. Davidoff is a nationally known authority on takeovers and corporate law. He writes as "The Deal Professor" for the *New York Times* "DealBook." Davidoff also writes in trade journals, such as the *Deal*, lectures, has testified before the United States Senate, and is frequently quoted in the national media on issues related to our capital markets. He is a professor of law at the University of Connecticut School of Law and a graduate of the Columbia Law School, where he was a Harlan Fiske Stone scholar. Davidoff practiced for almost a decade as a corporate attorney, primarily at Shearman & Sterling in their New York and London offices. Davidoff also has a BA from the University of Pennsylvania and an MS in finance from the London Business School.

Acknowledgments

This book could not have been written without the help of my research assistants, Austin Anderson, William Carl Means Jr., Nik Ristev, Stephen M. Salley, and Nicole Small. If their hard work is any sign, they will all make excellent lawyers. I am also indebted to both Dean Jeremy Paul of the University of Connecticut School of Law and Dean Alan C. Michaels of the Michael E. Moritz College of Law at The Ohio State University for research support and assistance.

I would also like to thank the editors and staff at John Wiley and Sons: Skyler Balbus, Bill Falloon, Meg Freeborn, and Stacey Fischkelta for their patience and helpful comments and suggestions. Thanks also go to my agent, Pilar Queen. I hope that one day she can represent me in all of my life dealings.

Everything that we do is due to our own efforts but even more so to the help we receive from others. I would particularly like to thank my mother and father and all of the rest of my family (yes, Bob, Ila, Josh, Nikki, and Tony, you too). And of course, my grandmother whom I dearly love.

I cannot thank everyone else, both colleagues and dear friends, who have helped in this and my other endeavors, but I would be remiss if I did not thank Professor Peter Henning. It was he who got me my first writing gig as the M&A Law Prof. Without him, this book would not exist. Final thanks go to those who reviewed earlier drafts of this manuscript or provided their thoughts and suggestions: Adam Davis, Alan Fishbein, Stephen Haas, Dale Oesterle, Paul Rose, Michael Weisbach and David Zaring. All errors are my own.

My last love goes to Idit. Her soul and wisdom in things of this world and beyond are my delight and fortune. She is my own personal merger. I thank her for everything. :דתנומת ץיקהב העבשא ךינפ הזחא קדצ

Steven M. Davidoff
Bexley, Ohio
June, 2009

Index